THE MYTHS OF AUGUST

ALSO BY STEWART L. UDALL

To the Inland Empire
The Energy Balloon
Agenda for Tomorrow
The Quiet Crisis

THE MYTHS OF AUGUST

*A Personal
Exploration of Our
Tragic Cold War
Affair with the
Atom*

STEWART L. UDALL

A Cornelia & Michael Bessie Book

Pantheon Books, New York

Copyright © 1994 by Stewart L. Udall

All rights reserved under International and Pan-American Copyright Conventions.
Published in the United States by Pantheon Books, a division of Random House, Inc.,
New York, and simultaneously in Canada by Random House of Canada Limited,
Toronto.

Library of Congress Cataloging-in-Publication Data

Udall, Stewart L.
The myths of August : a personal exploration of our tragic Cold
War affair with the atom / Stewart L. Udall.
p. cm.
"A Cornelia & Michael Bessie book."
Includes bibliographical references and index.
ISBN 0-679-43364-3
1. United States—Foreign relations—1945–1989. 2. United States—
Military policy. 3. Nuclear weapons—United States—History.
4. Cold War. 5. Udall, Stewart L. I. Title.
E840.U33 1994
327.73—dc20 93-32777
CIP

Book design by JoAnne Metsch

Manufactured in the United States of America

First Edition

9 8 7 6 5 4 3 2 1

To
OUR CHILDREN AND GRANDCHILDREN
AND THEIR GENERATIONS
WITH THE HOPE THEY CAN
BUILD A BETTER WORLD

S.L.U.

AUGUSTANA UNIVERSITY COLLEGE
LIBRARY

Contents

CONTENTS

Acknowledgments

My wife, Lee, has been more than a companion on the odyssey that encompassed the prolonged legal battles I have depicted in Section III as our nation's "radiation tragedies at home" and in the writing of this book. The struggle to obtain justice for the Navajo uranium miners and their widows would have faltered without her steadfast support. Every page of this book has benefited from her understanding of sentence sounds, the elements of literary style, and her sense of the human frailties that mark events of contemporary history. At every step she tempered my intemperate judgments and toned down my preachments. Quite simply, this book would not have come to fruition without her love and wisdom and patience.

I also owe a primary debt to a stalwart friend, Dr. Ernest Partridge, now the Hulings Professor of Humanities at Northland College in Wisconsin. Partridge is a philosopher whose work over the past two decades has focused on environmental ethics and the responsibilities we owe to future generations in formulating and executing public policies. As a moral mentor who is also an accomplished writer, Ernest perused the entire manuscript; his insights and judgments are imprinted on the pages of this volume.

I am also indebted on two counts to my Santa Fe neighbor, author Roger Morris. As a onetime defense intellectual who worked for Dean Acheson and Henry Kissinger, Roger contributed invaluable criticisms and suggestions on two crucial chapters. He also did me a great favor by introducing me to Michael Bessie, a veteran of the New York literary scene who became a cherished friend and proved to be the perfect editor for this book.

I am grateful to four historians—Barton Bernstein, John Dower, Robert Divine, and Richard Rhodes—and five scientists—Drs. David Hawkins, Murray Gell-Mann, Frank von Hippel, John Gofman, and Victor Weisskopf—for vital counsel on evidence and interpretation. I likewise owe profound thanks to Sterling Black, Herbert Brown, Victor Gilinsky, Father Ted Hesbergh, Clifford Honicker, Alexander Leighton, Chalmers Roberts, James Reston, Jr., Keith Schneider, Peter Steers, George Taylor, James R. Udall, Kathleen Taylor, and Jay Udall for important insights, criticisms, and assistance.

Preface

Fifteen years of labor as a lawyer groping for truths in the dark woods of the Cold War—preceded by six years as a congressman in the 1950s and eight years of service in the cabinets of Presidents Kennedy and Johnson—made me a student of atomic age excesses and produced the insights and anxieties that convinced me to write this book.

During my long search for facts, I was constantly reminded that the America I had known as a young man in the 1930s had been drastically disfigured by abnormal political and cultural changes which were outgrowths of the Cold War. It was one of my personal articles of faith that the strength and character of my country was intertwined with its moral values, and the trends that jarred me most were those that had altered American ethical attitudes and corrupted core institutions of our government.

My experiences and observations told me that the cold warriors' contempt for restraint had poisoned our politics. In the 1980s, I cringed as Mikhail Gorbachev and Andrei Sakharov emerged as the world's most effective partisans for peace at the same time that two U.S. presidents, imbued with military machismo, were saddling future generations with trillions of dollars of debt by amassing an unprecedented array of superexpensive weapons of mass destruction.

I was dismayed when, although the contest with Communism

ended without violence, Cold War attitudes and values continued to dominate American policies and policy making. At times the harm done to the fabric of our national life dominated the news. Leslie H. Gelb, the veteran diplomatic correspondent of the *New York Times,* summarized some of the damage in an essay he wrote just before the 1992 election. "Lies about national security affairs have become so routine, so inevitable," Gelb wrote, "that Americans no longer seem interested in the truth." And he continued, "As practiced by Presidents and their minions for over two decades, foreign policy seems to have produced endless trouble: scandals from Watergate to Iraqgate, fodder for political trashing, smoke screens for domestic failures, enervating hypocrisy, billions of wasted dollars, lies, and dead Americans."

The prime challenges facing the world in the coming decades will encompass concern about international law and international institutions and global issues like the environment and the promotion of sustainable development in third-world countries. If the United States wants to be faithful to its ideals, it will decide to champion such causes and diminish its role as the world's martial Big Brother.

What follows is a report to the next generations by one who believes that America should try to return to the aims and moral principles that emboldened President Lincoln to characterize his country as "the last, best hope on earth." I am convinced that one way to begin such a reorientation is through a dialogue featuring the honesty and candor which, in the first decades of our republic, made American democracy the envy of other nations.

To do that, we must face the facts surrounding our tragic affair with the atom, from Hiroshima through the Cold War to today's sense of global unease. Here is that story as I have seen it and lived it.

Stewart L. Udall
Santa Fe
October 1993

I

THE DAWN TIME OF
THE ATOMIC AGE

1

Notes on a

Journey

My notion is to try to live life—live life now . . . and bear an
honest witness to my time.

—ROBERT PENN WARREN (1977)

There are times when, in the course of life's journey, a new landscape
alters lines of sight and invites reflection that changes the horizon.
Such a turning point came for me in 1979 when, after a quarter of
century in Washington, Lee and I decided to go home to Arizona,
whereupon I decided to become involved, as a private investigator
and lawyer, in the task of making the federal government face up to
the radiation tragedies it had inflicted on innocent people in my
native region.

In retrospect, I realized that I would never have written this
book if we had stayed in Washington. Social and cultural environments subtly constrict critical thought, and in the long half century
of the Cold War the nation's capital acquired all of the attributes of
a big club. Human experience tells us that aging members of clubs
usually succumb to certain predispositions: they are inclined to bask
in the glow of their past achievements, and they tend to cast a lenient
eye on the failures and misdeeds of their generation. The late Joe

Alsop had these frailties in mind when, in his final memoir, he wondered whether his judgments were marred by the "frozen attitudes of the past."

What melted my frozen attitudes was not Arizona's sunshine, but facts our legal team uncovered as we pierced the veil of secrecy surrounding the radiation tragedies of the 1950s. This research not only opened my eyes to gross abuses of power by top-echelon federal officials, but also led me to question the assumptions, values, and practices that had guided U.S. policy making during the Cold War years.

Our initial research focused on clandestine decisions made by the leaders of the Atomic Energy Commission. The AEC had been one of my generation's sacred cows, and once-secret documents we obtained (with help from two teams of congressional investigators) contained shocking information about what I had always presumed was a science-oriented organization. As incriminating documents piled up on my desk, I became preoccupied with one insistent question: How did the officials who ran the AEC, some of whom I had known and admired, become so intoxicated by their national security responsibilities that they recklessly—indeed needlessly—sacrificed the lives of other Americans?

By forcing me to confront the dark side of the Cold War, and the damage it had done to American institutions and to our nation's moral authority, this question and the revelations about the AEC's duplicity animated the research that led to this book. Criticisms and questions I had long suppressed agitated my thoughts as I sought to understand the past and to offer honest testimony about the achievements and failures of my generation.

To provide a focus for what became a decade of research, in 1980 I drew up a list of the big issues. Some were recast; others fell by the wayside. Here are some that survived to shape the form of this work:

• How did the atom, the brilliant star that appeared on the horizon one summer morning in 1945, scintillate in the 1950s and 1960s with promises that it would "change the world," and then sputter out in the following decades?

- What were the influences that allowed a Cold War mentality to cow critical thought in this country and to gain such a powerful grip on the minds of our nation's leaders?

- Why were members of Congress and the American people intimidated for so long by claims of insiders that only they should have access to information needed to make rational decisions about our country's security?

- What were the influences that pushed America's once-prized moral principles into the background and encouraged our leaders to approve Cold War modes of conduct here and abroad that diminished our claim to moral leadership?

- As members of the only nation in the world that used nuclear bombs as weapons of war, why have U.S. citizens and their leaders refused to view the destruction of Hiroshima and Nagasaki as a grievous lapse of American morality, and as an American tragedy?

- And what factors have combined to encourage our elected leaders to consciously mislead the American people and to hide behind classified information rather than admit mistakes?

As I began groping for answers to these and other questions, it was clear to me that the search had to start with the dramatic unveiling of what my generation would call "the atomic age," and also encompass the disturbing alterations imposed on the culture and the government of our country by the Cold War. Moreover, a personal element crept into the equation as I realized that the overlap between my adult years and the era of the atomic age meant that I would be making an effort to trace the journey of my generation. I saw, too, that if I was unsparing in depicting the mistakes and misjudgments of my contemporaries, I would of necessity offend some of my friends and former associates.

There is nothing in the history of this century that rivals the awe created by the sudden announcement in August 1945 that a group of eminent scientists, working in hidden laboratories, had discovered "the secrets of the universe" and had invented bombs that could destroy whole cities. Under the influence of the wonder we felt, my generation never doubted that we would live to see the atomic utopias sketched in the months after Hiroshima by scientists who had worked on the glittering Manhattan Project. Wonder usually begets faith, and although it seemed sensible that it would take time for the wizards of this new science to "harness" the atom, there was a universal expectation that our world would be transformed.

The first big change of the atomic age, however, did not involve a technological advance, but a move to alter the American system of government so that officials in the executive branch of government could protect our nuclear secrets and combat the inroads of Communism. Stalin's unrelenting opposition to East-West cooperation, and the emergence of passionate, doctrinaire anti-Communism as a staple of U.S. politics ushered in the Cold War and lent support to President Truman's argument that government had to be reorganized so the country could marshal its power to meet future crises. Congress responded by passing laws that created a separate national security state within the executive branch of the federal government. The names given to the entities constituting this state were National Security Council (NSC), Central Intelligence Agency (CIA), and Atomic Energy Commission (AEC).

There was no peacetime precedent for the powers conferred on the CIA and the AEC. In the past, presidents had suspended parts of the Constitution during wars. Now, only two years after the end of the Second World War, these two agencies were given authority to operate under a cloak of secrecy and were advised they had discretion to function above the laws that constrained the conduct of other officials of the federal government.

Such charters encouraged the leaders of these organizations to see themselves as the paramount guardians of their nation's security. They soon realized that they had been provided with tools they could use to build walls that would minimize intrusions into their sanctuaries. The handiest of these tools, the power to "classify" the material generated by their work as "SECRET," gave them near-absolute control over who could have access to their data and the decisions they had made. This power monopoly also gave the heads of these organizations authority to decide who in the government "needed to know" about the action that was to be taken. It was sometimes possible, they would later learn, to use this open-sesame to keep even presidents and secretaries of state in the dark concerning mistakes and failures.

Another development that magnified their authority was that although a tiny corps of senior congressmen was designated as the "watchdog" of these agencies, little real oversight was actually performed. In 1955, not long after I arrived in Washington as a freshman congressman, I learned this supposed surveillance was a sham. In the political climate created by the rampages of Wisconsin's senator Joe McCarthy, it was rare if a member of Congress dared to request access to classified information.

My mentor in the capitol was Arizona's Carl Hayden, the chairman of the Senate's powerful Appropriations Committee. Senator Hayden had served for many years as a leading overseer of the CIA and other national security organizations. The senator summarized the conventional wisdom on this subject one morning, just after a CIA briefer had left his office, when he told me, with a wink, "I don't want to know what they're doing. If I did know, then I would be responsible."

The end result of this know-nothing charade was a gross diminution of government-by-the-people in the name of national security. There was little a freshman congressman could do to correct the situation, but it was obvious that republican self-government was losing out as citizens and their elected representatives were kept in the dark concerning crucial facts. How could any democracy properly function, I remember asking myself, if a "cleared" elite was given power to frame the action options, and members of Congress were not allowed to debate policy options or to participate in the making of decisions that affected the nation's security?

As I looked back in the 1980s, it was painfully evident that the United States of America had paid a heavy moral and political price by ignoring the open-government commands of our Constitution. To me, it was no accident that most of the blunders that have marred the history of our nation over the past half-century were the outgrowth of secret decisions made by presidents and by unelected national security wizards. To recite the names of these blunders—Hiroshima, Nagasaki, the Bay of Pigs, Vietnam, Watergate, and Iran-Contra—is to underscore lessons of history the next generations of Americans should never forget.

In 1956, when the Khrushchev thaw was the talk of Washington, I learned more about the peripheral role of members of Congress in national security affairs when I attended a seminar convened by the Carnegie Council to discuss options to relax global tensions. About ten new members of Congress (including FDR's son Jimmy Roosevelt) were present, along with a special guest, former Secretary of State Dean Acheson.

There was talk about the benefits of U.S.–USSR cultural exchange programs, but most of the discussion that afternoon focused on the feasibility of proposals to gradually "winnow down" the size of the conventional armies confronting each other in central Europe. This idea was viable, of course, only if the Soviet Union found it attractive, but it seemed so sensible that most of the congressional participants felt that the Eisenhower administration should be urged to support it.

At the end of the meeting, Dean Acheson, who had silently observed the proceedings with a querulous mien, was invited to make a summation. With a magisterial manner, Acheson scolded us by indicating that we were engaging in a futile exercise. Like a headmaster rebuking his pupils, he stated that since we lacked access to the latest intelligence about Khrushchev's intentions, we were engaging in "puerile speculation." Didn't we realize, he inquired, that the Soviet Union was a rigid society and the only thing the rulers of the USSR would ever respond to was military force?

All of us were deflated, but I left that meeting with a feeling that Acheson (who was later described by one of his biographers as "a giant who regarded his successors as pygmies") was one of the most arrogant men I had ever met. It was hard to swallow the idea that members of Congress were prevented from making meaningful contributions to a dialogue about possible pathways to peace. Although I esteemed Acheson as one of the architects of the postwar world, it was difficult to accept his assumption that events and changes in the world scene (including initiatives by the new post-Stalin leaders in the USSR)) might not, in the long run, produce a peaceful resolution of the Cold War contest.

Later, as I watched the two presidents I served take the country into the swamp that became the Vietnam War, I concluded that Dean Acheson, more than any other American, was the person whose advice set the stage for that tragedy. Acheson was the most formidable and fierce of the elderly cold warriors (dubbed "the wise men") whom John Kennedy and Lyndon Johnson consulted from time to time, and knowing the dogmatic force of his arguments, I will always believe that he exerted inordinate influence on the go-to-war and stay-the-course decisions of those presidents.

Evan Thomas, a student of the Kennedy years, has written that "JFK quailed before what he called Acheson's 'intimidating seniority.' " Lyndon Johnson, judging by statements I heard him make, was similarly intimidated by Acheson's unswerving advice that the United States had no choice but to take a stand and provide whatever force was needed for "an all-out victory" over Communist aggression in Vietnam. The options available to Kennedy and Johnson were further restricted when no one in their inner circle had the audacity to challenge Acheson's pronouncements and assumptions.

If Dean Acheson gave bad advice in his later years, it was because the Cold War blinders he wore prevented him from recognizing changes that were altering the world of the Truman years he had described in his immodest memoir, *Present at the Creation.* Did his life, I wondered, exemplify the maxim "Yesteryear's wise men, with mind's closed, are candidates to be tomorrow's fools"?

My first term in Congress was a civics lesson in the decline of congressional government. The blinds drawn around the national security sectors of the government meant, for example, that the main function of members of Congress in this area of policy making was not to make policy, but to rubberstamp the laws and appropriations recommended by senior colleagues and other watchdogs who, we presumed, had been given access to rudimentary facts about secret decisions made by officials in the executive branch of government.

One of my vivid memories of that period relates to a simplistic appeal Joe Martin, the aging minority leader, made one afternoon at the request of the White House in support of an increase in the appropriation for the development of guided missiles. Martin didn't marshal facts to bolster his argument, but amid the titters of his colleagues, repeated again and again the theme, "If President Eisenhower says we need more gilded *[sic]* missiles, I say we have no choice but to vote more money for gilded missiles." With the most important facts hidden from view, nearly all discussions of national security issues were stultified. The only real foreign policy debates in the 1950s related to whether the United States should continue to appropriate funds for specific "foreign aid" programs.

Congressional leadership was further crippled by the circumstance that most of the information about the technological miracles that were supposed to transform our lives (such as rockets, atomic airplanes, and nuclear power) was also classified. By restricting the reach of members of Congress, this veil of secrecy deprived the nation of critical insights it sorely needed. This was evident in 1957 when the Russians lofted their sputnik into outer space and Congress made spectacular miscalculations concerning what this feat said about the prowess of Soviet scientists and engineers.

This deprivation was manifest, too, in 1955 when the AEC commissioner, John von Neumann, gave a special briefing for members of Congress on the prospect for atomic electricity at which he announced that in the foreseeable future atomic energy would be produced so inexpensively that it wouldn't be necessary to meter it. I was one of the group that listened to this presentation, and our knowledge was so meager that no one asked von Neumann a single probing question about his expansive prophecy.

Congressional ignorance born of secrecy was likewise on display at a 1955 hearing when Senator Estes Kefauver, a prospective candidate for president, sought to extract rudimentary facts about Nevada fallout from Commissioner Willard F. Libby. Kefauver held the first public hearing on this subject because scientists who had tracked the paths of radioactive debris across the continent were alarmed and members of Congress wanted information about the health risks associated with bomb fallout. The dialogue between Commissioner Libby, a Nobel laureate, and the senator went like this:

KEFAUVER: Is the fallout problem the same with atomic bombs as it is with hydrogen bombs, the only difference being the strength of the detonation?

LIBBY: I am unable to answer that question, sir.

KEFAUVER: Is there any instrument that will warn of A-bombs or H-bombs, or is there any method by which they can be discovered?

LIBBY: I am afraid I should not answer that question.

KEFAUVER: The Civilian Defense Program contemplates among other things an evacuation. Under some circumstances that might be the wrong thing to do, wouldn't you think so?

LIBBY: It is a very complicated problem. You speak of fallout particularly?

KEFAUVER: Yes, I am speaking of fallout.

LIBBY: It is a very complicated problem.

The Kennedy government, like its immediate predecessors, was divided into airtight compartments. Cold War decision making was the exclusive province of the National Security Council members, who, with their staffs, had access to the daily flow of classified information about the global contest with the Communists. The members of the president's cabinet who were not "cleared" to see these secrets got their facts from newspapers and kept their opinions about security issues to themselves.

In the summer of 1962, a trip to the Soviet Union lifted me out of this rut and gave me an opportunity to form independent judgments about the Cold War. This trip was the fruit of a friendship Lee and I had formed with Ambassador Anatoly Dobrynin and his wife after they were posted to Washington in 1961. At a dinner in our home, I told Dobrynin that I would like to visit the Soviet Union to see their huge hydroelectric dams and to inspect the advanced technologies their engineers had devised to transmit large blocks of electricity from eastern Siberia to western industrial centers. He subsequently made arrangements that enabled me, accompanied by a team of U.S. experts, to be the first member of President Kennedy's cabinet to visit the USSR.

After we introduced the Dobrynins to Robert Frost, the scope of this exchange was enlarged when Frost (with President Kennedy's encouragement) agreed to join my party and exchange views with Russian poets and literary figures. I learned en route, to my dismay, that the main reason Robert, then an ailing eighty-eight, had decided to undertake such a strenuous mission was that he had a message he wanted to deliver to Chairman Nikita Khrushchev and that he would be sorely disappointed if he didn't get to see "the Russian ruler."

During my eleven-day tour I spent most of the time far from Moscow in the countryside in the company of engineers who were busy developing their nation's resources. My host was Ignaty Novikov, a Ukrainian engineer who later built a huge stadium in Moscow and was in charge of his country's Olympic Games in 1980. On our tour we saw some of the enormous rivers in eastern Siberia, the dam under construction at Bratsk downstream from Lake Baikal, hydrodams on the Volga River, and the scene of the great battle at Stalingrad.

Having gone with an open mind, I was startled that so many of my impressions varied from the prevalent Cold War clichés in the West. I encountered no overt animosity. I sensed that Khrushchev had started a process of liberalization that, in time, could alter Soviet aims and change the outlook of his people. I saw many indications that Soviet scientists and technicians were aware that their ability to compete was being inhibited by the secrecy and suspicion inherited from Stalin's regime. And I included this observation in the report I filed with President Kennedy: "There is an unmistakable and deep-seated respect for American power and American prowess. This means that at all levels the Soviet people are inordinately curious about the American way of getting things done."

These and other impressions were confirmed when, to my surprise, I was invited to fly to the Black Sea for a visit with Chairman Khrushchev. Khrushchev, as I realized later, had an urgent ulterior motive in extending invitations to me and, the next day, to Robert Frost, to come to Gagra: any day the United States would discover that Soviet missiles were being installed in Cuba, and his talks with us served Khrushchev's purpose by sending Kennedy a message that he was sane and still had his hands on the levers of power.

The Khrushchev I conversed with that afternoon came across as a dedicated Communist who, behind his blustering talk about Berlin, was a cautious leader who believed time was on his country's side in the struggle for economic supremacy. As Khrushchev related "I-was-there" details about the battles of Stalingrad and Kursk, it was clear to me that he knew far more about the horrors of war than the world's other postwar leaders. How, I wondered, could a leader steeped in the gore of war—and a nation that had been devastated by as many as twenty million deaths—not look on new military conflicts with caution?

None of Robert's friends later suggested that his hour-long private conversation with Nikita Khrushchev influenced the course of history, but after three decades it still stands as one of this century's cultural milestones. To me, it is breathtaking that a great poet—on the eve of what would become the Cold War's moment of maximum danger—would have an opportunity to present an extraordinary appeal for peace to a leader who, in a few weeks, would have to make fateful decisions about the world's first nuclear showdown.

Robert Frost had rehearsed what he wanted to say, and he surely sensed that the argument he made would be his farewell to "the big world." During our talks en route, I could see that he planned to speak, not as an American, but as an ambassador for humanity. He knew that he could not compose a common rallying cry that would appeal to Khrushchev unless his words conveyed esteem for the Soviet leader's performance and for the potential of Soviet society. This was the reasoning behind his references to a competition of "two democracies" that would subsequently set some teeth on edge in Washington.

Frost told Khrushchev that he saw the United States and the USSR as contending nations "laid out for rivalry in sports, science, art, and democracy." The chairman interrupted to add "peaceful economic competition" to this list. Then Robert elaborated about a slogan of "mutual magnanimity" as a code of conduct for the contestants. Frost abhorred Khrushchev's word "coexistence," so he capped his argument with a prediction that a hundred years of peaceful rivalry would lead to a convergence of the two nations' political systems.

I never had any doubt that cold warriors on both sides of the Iron Curtain regarded Robert Frost's appeal to Nikita Khrushchev as a naive cry in the wilderness. But I believe Frost would have been gratified had he lived another decade and watched President Nixon and Khrushchev's successor, Leonid Brezhnev, implement a policy of mutual respect which they described as "détente."

In his talk with Khrushchev, the old poet intended to strike a blow against chauvinism and the impatient ideologues on both sides who wanted to resolve Gordian issues by military victories. He surely would have gloried in the circumstance that his basic concepts were vindicated by the outcome of the Cold War. Both good policies and good poems, he might have observed, quoting himself, contain truths that are "hard to get rid of."

For me, two epilogues were evoked by Robert Frost's mission to Moscow. The first related to an article I finished in November as an anxious world drew back from the Cuban abyss. In my piece, I provided details of Frost's conversation with Chairman Khrushchev and described his plan for a *modus vivendi* that might point the nuclear superpowers in a direction that could lead to constructive rivalry.

As statesmen were admiring the mutual restraint of Kennedy and Khrushchev, I thought the story would have value as a positive footnote to the Cuban showdown. I nevertheless decided it would be advisable to obtain clearance from the White House before I submitted it to the *New York Times Magazine*. The response was a brusque rebuke from the president's national security advisor, McGeorge Bundy. Bundy returned my draft with a note suggesting that we talk before I proceeded further. The conversation that followed was curt. Bundy, a Harvard friend of Frost's, had a negative reaction both to Robert's message and to the tenor of my story. "I thought the old man had more steel in him," he said as he hung up the phone.

Robert Frost died a month later, but the following summer I recalled his concept of coexistence when Kennedy and Khrushchev, wiser for their encounter at the brink of a nuclear Armageddon, made peaceful overtures that produced a treaty banning atmospheric tests of atomic weapons. In September, when the Senate ratified that landmark treaty, I was at President Kennedy's side during a five-day Western conservation trip. His speeches describing the hope implicit in this achievement evoked such enthusiasm that his entourage sensed that he had found a major theme for his reelection campaign.

We have no way of knowing whether, had Kennedy lived and been reelected, the spirit of accommodation embodied in the Nuclear Test Ban Treaty would have influenced him to alter the course of the Cold War or to pursue a different policy toward Vietnam. The ifs associated with these questions will long haunt our history as part of the legacy of President Kennedy's assassination.

Mac Bundy's metaphor came to mind in the last two years of the Johnson administration, as an angry dispute over the Vietnam War divided the country and large numbers of Americans rejected the steely axioms of the Cold War the president and his national security advisors were using to justify the expansion of that conflict. As citizens challenged decisions made by their leaders and began questioning the sacrosanct assumptions of Washington's cold warriors, a democratic groundswell indicated that millions of ordinary Americans wanted their voices and values heard where issues of war and peace were concerned.

By the fall of 1967, I was in the throes of a personal dilemma. My moral qualms grew each time the level of destruction in Vietnam was escalated, but I thought I had the best job in the government and wanted to complete work under way that would give the nascent environmental movement a chance to flourish.

At a cabinet meeting one September morning, President Johnson sharpened my dilemma when he angrily asserted that he and Secretaries Rusk and McNamara were "bloodied every day" by the war protests, while the rest of us were standing on the sidelines doing nothing. "When Roosevelt was under attack," he said, with a glance in my direction, "Harold Ickes always fired back and others in his cabinet defended their president."

When a cabinet colleague made the sheepish comment that we didn't know enough to present convincing arguments, the president ordered rump cabinet meetings where Rusk and McNamara could provide the facts we needed to give effective war speeches. To find out what the others were thinking, I spoke with several colleagues and had intense evening discussions with Averell Harriman and Bob McNamara.

I gleaned from oblique comments that Bob McNamara was harboring doubts about the course of the war, and that the president's domestic cabinet's private opinions about the Vietnam War mirrored the split in the country. Most of us, I learned, were troubled by what the war was doing to our programs and to the fabric of our political party and the nation as a whole. The special cabinet dinner we had in Secretary Rusk's dining room ended in a malaise: one of the vivid memories I have of that event is the sharp exchange between Dean Rusk and HEW Secretary John Gardner about academic freedom and the role universities were playing as "hotbeds" of the antiwar movement.

Vietnam was in my face again a few days later when my younger brother, Morris, who had my old seat in Congress, dropped by to tell me that he was going home to announce the withdrawal of his support of the Vietnam War. Mo's decision was no surprise. We had discussed the issue several times and I shared many of his conclusions. Concerned that if he learned what was afoot, President Johnson would demand that I dissuade Mo, I requested that he withhold publicity until he delivered his speech in Tucson.

My brother had many unusual talents, and two of them were on display when he decided to question the policies surrounding the Vietnam War. He had an uncommon ability to analyze the pros and cons of public issues; and once he concluded that President Johnson was taking the nation in the wrong direction, he had the courage to disagree and set forth the reasons for his dissent.

Mo was not daunted by the circumstance that he was a lowly member of the House who lacked access to the national security secrets that supposedly dictated the Vietnam War policy. He based his analysis on common sense and on his own beliefs about his country's ideals and the appropriate use of U.S. power. He set forth his basic conclusion foursquare: the president and his advisors had made a tragic misjudgment in investing the lives of U.S. soldiers and the nation's resources in a conflict against a peasant society that was trying to find its own path to nationhood.

Mo used this language to cut through the national security cant of our war leaders: "In the long run a nation's prestige and greatness and 'face' depend on doing what is right for its own people and taking the consequences. There is no dignity greater than that of a strong man, or a strong nation, admitting a mistake, correcting it, and taking the consequences. There is no course more likely in the long run to destroy one's dignity or 'face' than to become a prisoner of past mistakes."

My brother was vindicated a few months later when events influenced the president to announce his retirement and to change his war policy. That experience altered my attitude toward our national security apparatus and caused me to look with skepticism at the men who, we had been led to believe, had distilled a special wisdom from secret sources and were uniquely qualified to help presidents formulate their foreign policy.

It had been a spectacular mistake, I saw, to confine decision making to the president and a tiny coterie of "wise men." A national security apparatus that minimized the participation of members of Congress inevitably diminished government by the people and for the people. When one cast a critical eye on this inner circle of policy makers it was clear that some advisors were prisoners of their own dogmas, others considered deception a tool of their trade, and still others were busy grinding special axes behind the curtains that shielded them from public scrutiny. In the days ahead this insight colored my attitude toward Walt Rostow, Henry Kissinger, Zbigniew Brzezinski, and the godfather of them all, Paul Nitze.

THE 1970S: REALITY TIME

My life underwent a reorientation after I left government service. The anguish of the Vietnam War impacted our family in the fall of 1969 when Scott, our second son, deserted the army and sought refuge in Canada; and a few weeks later we marched from the National Cathedral to the White House to protest the Christmas bombing of Vietnam cities ordered by President Nixon.

The turbulence of the 1970s presented so many conflicting visions about the future—and mocked so many of the cherished assumptions of my generation about the "new world" we supposed we were creating—that my perspective was steadily changing. The first years of that decade marked both the zenith of technological optimism and the emergence of the environmental movement as a counterforce to the conquest-of-nature plans of atomic age prophets.

Our euphoria about our nation's technological prowess peaked when the Apollo astronauts walked on the moon in the summer of 1969. That achievement unleashed a spree of second-coming rhetoric. Adolf Hitler's onetime rocketeer, Wernher von Braun, pontificated that the exploration of space was "the salvation of the human race." President Nixon exulted that the moonwalk was a consummation that constituted "the greatest week since the creation of the earth." A NASA spokesman said this feat demonstrated that Americans were now "masters of the universe," and the cliché-of-the-week bandied about by TV commentators was "This proves that our country can do whatever it decides to do."

A very different message about mastery was presented a few months later when the environmental movement came of age during the first Earth Day celebrations in the spring of 1970. Those of us who spoke at these events reminded our audiences that our planet was a fragile spaceship and that the whole human enterprise would be imperiled if our species did not learn the arts of earthkeeping and nourish an ever-widening concept of land stewardship.

In my postcabinet years, my work as a lawyer, a lecturer, and an environmental planner became intertwined with America's illusions about resources. Unlike the two preceding decades, the 1970s proved to be a time when energy shocks dominated the news and cracks developed in the golden promises of atomic-age abundance.

The nation's faith in our nuclear establishment was jarred as grassroots groups in all parts of the country began opposing the Atomic Energy Commission's sacrosanct projects. It was a shock to the high priests of atomic science when ordinary citizens began appearing at public hearings and asking penetrating questions about the radiation risks associated with the "clean, safe" projects the AEC planned to site near their communities.

While writing a nationally syndicated column on environmental issues, I became acquainted with some of these activists and soon realized that these indigenous campaigns marked a turning point of the atomic age. Nuclear scientists and engineers whose statements had been treated as facts were angered by what they regarded as "intrusive interventions," but the controversies which followed meant that thereafter issues relating to the future of the "friendly atom" would be thrashed out in the everyday crucible of American democracy.

These antinuclear campaigns—subsequently described by the editor of the *Bulletin of the Atomic Scientists* as "a crusade unprecedented in the history of technology"—which were usually led by local conservationists and concerned scientists, began in out-of-the-way places and soon reached across the continent from San Luis Obispo, California, to Long Island. One effort I watched with special interest involved a tenacious group in Wyoming County, Pennsylvania, which ultimately blocked the siting of a plutonium-fueled Liquid Metal Fast Breeder Reactor in their valley when AEC experts could not fully answer the health and safety issues they raised.

These efforts were not coordinated by a national organization. Each campaign had its own spontaneous beginnings, and by 1971 *ad hoc* coalitions had formed in Minnesota, Michigan, and Maryland and were raising environmental issues concerning the siting of nuclear power plants on their shorelines and rivers. The questions being posed by concerned citizens were thrust into the mainstream of American politics when Maine's Senator Edmund Muskie held hearings on radiation pollution, and "heretic" scientists, like Dr. John Gofman, who had been cast out of the AEC's sanctuaries were given forums in Washington where they could present testimony about the health risks associated with radiation exposures.

The second resource shock of the 1970s came when the OPEC nations crippled the U.S. economy with an oil embargo in the fall of 1973. This development did not surprise me, as I had been responsible for our nation's oil policy in the 1960s and had predicted such a crunch two years earlier in an *Atlantic* magazine article.

Few were ready to listen, but the warning delivered by the OPEC nations sent an urgent message about petroleum to the American people. OPEC's embargo made the term "energy crisis" part of our common vocabulary. It told us that it was unreasonable for a nation whose oil output was declining to assume that it could indefinitely continue to consume over 40 percent of the world's gasoline, and, for energy experts, it made the point that cheap petroleum had made the whole postwar "miracle of technology" possible.

The response of our last four presidents to the energy crisis dramatizes the way illusions about technological prowess distorted American thinking. Seeing no need to curb the gargantuan energy appetites of his constituents, President Nixon whipped up a crash dig-and-drill program he called Project Independence in order "to make America self-sufficient in energy by 1980." Needing a magic wand to assure his countrymen that his plan was achievable, Nixon, a true apostle of the atomic age, issued his call for action ". . . in the spirit of Apollo [and] with the determination of the Manhattan Project."

Three years later, President Jimmy Carter wisely proposed a

pioneering plan to conserve energy. However, the centerpiece of his energy program—a grandiose, costly effort to develop a domestic synthetic fuels industry by tapping our supplies of coal and oil shale—was based on a flawed assumption that big technology could produce economical substitutes for petroleum.

President Reagan was also a believer in big technology (witness his devout commitment to his Star Wars military program), but his vaulting faith in free markets encouraged him to belittle the need for conservation, and to assume that Saudi Arabia, Kuwait, and our other Arab friends could be counted on to preserve our oil lifeline to the Persian Gulf. Reagan's hands-off policy set the stage for Saddam Hussein's 1990 power grab, and for George Bush's bombastic campaign to organize a high-tech $35 billion war to assure the West's access to cheap Arab oil and, in President Bush's own words, "to preserve the American way of life."

THE 1980S: CONFRONTING THE MYTHS

Facts uncovered by the 1979 congressional hearings, and a subsequent review of over 30,000 previously classified documents relating to our radiation lawsuits, aroused my indignation and encouraged me to pursue a program of wide-ranging research that ultimately laid the groundwork for this book.

During the years we were preparing the cases for trial, I thought that when the lawsuits were finished I might write a critical, "adventure-in-the-law" book describing the crude cover-ups of the AEC and what I had learned about flaws in the U.S. system of justice, while working with other lawyers to pioneer a new field of law. One theme emerged when the House investigations subcommittee entitled its report on the Nevada fallout "*The Forgotten Guinea Pigs*," a figure of speech that conjured up images of the inhumane experiments some Nazi physicians had performed during World War II.

A second theme pivoted around a troublesome moral issue: How did our country's policy makers justify dealing with their fellow citizens in ways which violate common standards of decency? It was clear that for three decades our nuclear weapons establishment had acted on the assumption that they occupied a special, Olympian niche in the nation's government. The documents told me that they had conducted their activities as though they were authorized to ignore the laws that governed the lives of other Americans; and, like the apparatchiks in Communist countries, they made and executed their decisions on the assumption that they were the guardians of their nation's security and therefore accountable only to themselves.

As our quest for justice in the courts turned into a ten-year marathon, my research encompassed the whole panorama of the nuclear age from Hiroshima to Star Wars, and a more comprehensive book formed in my mind. This larger effort would trace the adverse impacts that secrecy policies and the operations of our national security apparatus have had on American morality and on the functioning of our free system of government.

In the first two decades of its existence, the Atomic Energy Commission was considered the most high-minded, best-organized entity in the U.S. government. Yet the classified documents I had studied revealed an apparatus of Big Brothers who systematically masked their mistakes with deceit. Although many disclosures did not surprise me, I concluded that the Cold War had been an incubator of deceitful practices and harmful illusions, and that if one was to gain a clear picture of this period of our history, it was essential to distinguish myths from truths.

This conviction led me to focus my research on the myths and mythmakers of the Cold War. One of the first subjects I turned to was the Manhattan Project and the wartime decision to use atomic bombs to destroy two Japanese cities. Although I had never questioned the official explanations of these events, I was troubled by the ethical questions posed in John Hersey's 1946 book, *Hiroshima*.

Yet it was painful for me to raise doubts about deeds of war carried out by Franklin Roosevelt, Harry Truman, and Henry L. Stimson, political leaders I had always revered. I was daunted, too, by the reality that a story of the making of the atomic bomb and the use of this weapon to force the Japanese warlords to capitulate had been transformed into a legend inscribed in our histories and in the minds of millions of Americans. The men and women of my generation had, for a half-century, nurtured the belief that

- the U.S. had won a race with Hitler's scientists;
- the bomb was an American breakthrough in physics;
- the bombing of Hiroshima and Nagasaki ended the war; and
- these two bombs saved the lives of hundreds of thousands of American soldiers and Japanese civilians.

But were these beliefs rooted in realities, or were they manifestations of myths? This book describes an effort to ascertain the truth about these issues.

As I studied the Cold War's baleful influence on our national life, other beliefs that had blurred our nation's vision and distorted its purpose came into view. Among these was the dangerous illusion (shared by the two superpowers) that the country which had the largest number of nuclear bombs and missiles was more secure than its adversary. There was the illusion that our democracy would be more secure if important decisions about our national security were made by a tiny, "cleared" elite; and, on a different level, there was the illusion fostered by the high priests of the atomic age that our energy problem had been solved and perpetual sources of cheap resources were at hand.

As the 1980s drew to a close, a startling new era was ushered in when a remarkable Russian leader, Mikhail Gorbachev, astonished the world with bold statesmanship that ended the Cold War without violence. This breathtaking development made the superpowers' ponderous military superstructure obsolete. It deprived the ideologists and war planners of their reason for existence. It offered humankind a potential turning point toward peace; and it afforded Americans an opportunity to honestly evaluate our Cold War triumphs and mistakes.

This cascade of events took me back to August 6, 1945, when, at an air base in Albuquerque, I first heard the news about Hiroshima. No one realized it at the time, but President Truman's announcement signaled not one, but two beginnings that would put the twentieth century on a course of unparalleled peril. Hiroshima heralded the advent of what would be called the atomic age. It also served as the starter's gun for a weapons race between the United States of America and the Union of Soviet Socialist Republics that would carry the world to the edge of a nuclear abyss.

2

The Myths of August

It is an atomic bomb. It is a harnessing of the basic power of the universe. . . . It is the greatest thing in history.
—President Harry S Truman
(August 6, 1945)

It is well to recall the temper of those early days of the Atom. No predictions seemed too fantastic, whether of the doom of civilization through nuclear holocaust or of a world beneficently transformed through the peaceful use of this great new source of energy.
—David E. Lilienthal (1963)

In the first weeks after Hiroshima, extravagant statements by President Truman and other official spokesmen for the U.S. government transformed the inception of the atomic age into the most mythologized event in American history. These exhilarating, excessive utterances depicted a profoundly altered universe and produced a reorientation of thought that influenced the behavior of nations and changed the outlook and the expectations of the inhabitants of this planet.

Hard facts about the event that generated this historical drama were meager. The president of the United States revealed that, working in secret, a team of U.S. scientists had made "cosmic" discoveries and built atomic bombs that could destroy entire cities. The War Department released eyewitness reports of the atomic explosions and official descriptions of the secret installations where the bomb materials were produced and fashioned into the most destructive war weapons ever devised by human minds.

Had our government's spokesmen simply provided facts about the atomic bombs—and the awesome power they bestowed on the U.S. military machine—the implications for humanity would have been defined with some degree of clarity and restraint. But the Pentagon's announcements that summer soared beyond bombs to prophecies of atomic miracles-to-come and prospects of a brighter and better new world. August 1945 saw more than explosions of nuclear bombs. It witnessed an unprecedented explosion of dreams and images of a new world in which hunger would be eliminated, diseases would be conquered, and humankind would enjoy the benefits of superabundant sources of inexpensive energy.

A few days after Hiroshima, I heard an excited radio commentator utter the cliché that became a hallmark of the atomic age, exemplifying the general optimism that the atomic scientists could achieve unending technical breakthroughs (a new word just added to our vocabularies). This pithy slogan—"Today's science fiction is tomorrow's reality"—expressed the national mood so well that it enjoyed a semantic half-life of over three decades.

As historians have long noted with fascination, myths can sometimes envelop events and obliterate essential truths about actual happenings. The history of the atomic age confirms the force of this axiom. In the weeks after Hiroshima, the histrionic half-truths and fictions promulgated by the government's official spokesmen transformed the atomic age into something larger than life. President Harry S Truman was, of course, the nation's first and foremost spokesman. The second was William L. Laurence, a senior science writer for the *New York Times,* who had been given a secret, exclusive assignment by General Leslie R. Groves to write for the general public an account of the making of the atomic bomb.

Bill Laurence was at the pinnacle of his profession in the spring of 1945 when General Groves asked him to take a leave of absence from his job as a newspaper reporter and undertake a mission for the War Department's top-secret Manhattan Project (MED). Laurence was not surprised when the general approached him. He had written many stories for the *Times* about advances in atomic physics, and in 1940 he had authored an article for the *Saturday Evening Post* about the possibility that uranium fission might be converted into a superexplosive.

W. L. Laurence played two distinct roles in the history of the atomic age. As the journalist who wrote the only official press releases describing the first atomic explosions, he was, for a season, the authority on the research and the industrial development that produced that epoch. But the other Laurence was a frustrated dramatist who believed science had a sacred mission to "save" civilization, and who saw an opportunity to embellish his eyewitness stories with millennial phrases that would make him the messiah of the new age. This Laurence became the mythmaker-in-chief of the atomic age, described by one historian as "the world's foremost prophet of atomic miracles."

William L. Laurence came to the United States as part of the last large wave of eastern European immigrants who entered this country prior to World War I. His life itself was a drama. Born in 1888 in a Lithuanian Jewish village, he participated as a student protester in the 1905 Russian Revolution, was smuggled out of Russia in a barrel, and at age seventeen arrived penniless at Ellis Island. Unprepossessing in appearance but endlessly inquisitive, Bill Laurence made the American dream come true by mastering English and making an academic record that won him a scholarship to Harvard, where he studied law and dabbled in drama.

A professed atheist, Laurence nevertheless nurtured a mystical attitude toward science: his belief in the paramount role of science made that enterprise his religion. He yearned to know the "secret" of life, and on one occasion he exhorted his fellow science writers to "take fire from the scientific Olympus, the laboratories and universities, and bring it down to the people."

There is ample evidence that Bill Laurence, a longtime member of the Dramatists Guild of Authors, had a flair for drama and never totally abandoned his ambition to be a playwright. One of his plays was staged by a Harvard theatrical group, and his adaptation of Maxim Gorky's work *The Lower Depths* was produced in New York in 1930.

One cannot read the "histories" Laurence wrote in the summer of 1945 without realizing that although a journalist was hired by General Groves, a dual personality reported for duty at the Pentagon. Bill Laurence the science writer (who was already personally acquainted with several of the scientists he encountered as he made his rounds) crammed notebooks full of facts as he interrogated the leaders of the Manhattan Project and inspected its secret factories and laboratories at the University of Chicago, at Oak Ridge in Tennessee, at Hanford in the state of Washington, and at Los Alamos in New Mexico.

The other Bill Laurence, the frustrated dramatist, jumped to the conclusion that he was in the presence of an apocalyptic pageant that would change the world and resorted to the Bible and to Greek mythology for analogies and creation symbols to depict the wonderland, the "Atomland-on-Mars," he was observing. One can surmise that this latter Laurence was emboldened to describe what he was seeing as something cosmic, something comparable to a second Creation. His assigned story, he hinted to a friend at the *Times*, had a framework that made it "a sort of Second-Coming-of-Christ yarn."

Bill Laurence must have experienced ambivalent impulses as he wrestled with the competing interpretations of the situation he was encountering. Should he stick to the facts, like a good reporter? Or, having luckily drawn what appeared to him the news story of the millennium, should he draw on the writing techniques and images the Old Testament writers had used to describe the first Creation?

There is no evidence that Laurence ever discussed his dilemma with anyone. But events moved swiftly that summer, and once it was clear that he would be the only outsider to witness and describe the first atomic explosion in the New Mexico desert and the only journalist to fly on an escort B-29 and write a story about the incineration of Nagasaki, Bill Laurence's instincts as a dramatist took over and he racked his brain for ideas and images that would help him interpret to the world what he perceived as a turning point in human history.

The outcome—the victory of Laurence the dramatist over Laurence the reporter of facts—had a powerful influence on postwar thought. His histrionic dispatches provided the tinted glasses through which people everywhere peered to gain insights into the shiny utopias envisioned by many atomic scientists.

Laurence, of course, did not have the field of official news all to himself that summer. Stodgy, authentic science reporting had an inning a few days after the Hiroshima explosion with the publication of a report summarizing the technological achievements of the Manhattan Project. President Roosevelt's top science advisors, Drs. Vannevar Bush and James Bryant Conant, had advocated the postwar release of a technical treatise that would explain the obvious to the scientific community without revealing the essential military secrets. This report, written by a Princeton physicist, Dr. Henry DeWolf Smyth, was a model of circumspect science writing, but it was written for the scientific elite and only 1,000 copies were released by the Pentagon.

As a consequence, the writer who brought the "news" of the atom "down to the people" was W. L. Laurence. The Smyth Report was pondered by a few thousand specialists, while Bill Laurence's neo-Biblical metaphors captured the imaginations of opinion-molders and, through the popular press, resonated in the minds of tens of millions of readers around the globe. His eyewitness reports won him the Pulitzer Prize. And his flamboyant book *Dawn Over Zero*, an international bestseller, described the many ways this new force would alter the lives of earth's inhabitants.

Although he was a prophet for a long interval after Hiroshima, history has not been kind to William L. Laurence. In the 1990s we are aware that his theatrical depiction of the atom-splitters as "masters of the universe" who would turn the world into a utopia of ease and affluence was a work of monumental mischief. Laurence's Eden has faded, for we now recognize that most of his scenarios were based on fantasies, not facts. We know now that the atom has not changed the world, either as a source of energy or as a technology catalyst that would transform the way we live.

A modest writer in search of a lyrical theme might have been attracted to the famous lines William Butler Yeats wrote after the Easter Uprising of the Irish in 1916:

All is changed, changed utterly.
A terrible beauty is born.

But such a theme would have been too mundane for Bill Laurence. His playwright's eye was trained on the cosmos, on a concept that would equate the achievements of the atomic scientists with the work of the Almighty and on a scenario that would transmute the control of fission into the most portentous event in the history of human civilization. Thus, the metaphors of antiquity danced in his mind as he traveled in mid-July to the Trinity test site in southern New Mexico in the company of General Groves and the bombmakers. The drama at Trinity was, plainly, the catalyst that broke any remaining barriers in Bill Laurence's mind between fact and myth. Now he was certain he was witnessing an earth-changing event, and words that invoked millennial wonder flowed into the press releases he wrote for the Pentagon.

His "historic eyewitness" description of the Trinity explosion might be called "The Myth of the Second Creation":

On that moment [July 16, 1945] hung eternity. Time stood still. . . . One felt as though he had been privileged to witness the birth of the world— to be present at the moment of creation when the Lord said: "Let there be light."

At that great moment in history, ranking with the moment in the long ago when man first put fire to work for him and started on his march to civilization, the vast energy locked within the hearts of the atoms of matter was released for the first time in a burst of flame such as never before seen on this planet, illuminating earth and sky for a brief span that seemed eternal with the light of many super-suns.

The paean he composed to the atom after he surveyed the Manhattan Engineering District's ugly, gargantuan plutonium-manufacturing plants near Pasco, Washington, might be described as "The Myth of the Creation of Matter":

The feeling one gets on visiting these plants is something akin to a strange awareness of the supernatural. . . . In these Promethean structures, that may well stand as eternal monuments to American genius and enterprise heralding the new Age of Atomic Power, as well as the Spirit of Man Challenging Nature, mighty cosmic forces are at work such as had never been let loose on this planet in the million years of man's existence on its surface. . . .

Here, for the first time in history, man stands in the presence of the very act of elemental creation of matter. Here in the great silences . . . new elements are being born, a phenomenon that, as far as man knows, has not happened since Genesis.

One stands before it as though beholding the realization of a vision such as Michelangelo might have had of a world yet to be, as indescribable as the Grand Canyon of Arizona, Beethoven's Ninth Symphony or the "Presence that dwells in the light of setting suns."

And the hosannas he wrote to introduce the secret laboratory at Los Alamos and the atomic scientists who designed the "gadgets" that made atomic bombs feasible deserves to be alluded to as "The Myth of the Supermen":

Here the unbelievable meets one everywhere. Here a new species of man, Mesa Man, is laying the foundation of the civilization of tomorrow, if there is to be a tomorrow.

For the power not utilized in a weapon for destruction could also, with the same application, be developed for bringing man much mastery of his material universe. Man has it in his power at last to realize the dream of the ages, for he has found the veritable "Philosopher's Stone" sought in vain by the alchemists, a key to the very power that keeps the universe going.

Most spectacular of all, our scientists and engineers have contrived, by the greatest miracle of modern alchemy, to create two entirely new elements, neptunium and plutonium. . . . When the full details of the development of the atomic bomb can finally be told, the story of the creation, production and purification of Element 94, named plutonium, will stand out as one of the great epics of history and as a distinct turning point in the life of man on earth.

In the exciting days of August, the primary source of information available to journalists and commentators appeared in these and other similar press releases written by W. L. Laurence. The real facts, of course, were shrouded in secrecy, and this circumstance not only made Laurence's word pictures authoritative, but invited imaginative writers and editors to embrace his vision of a new age and to fashion their own futuristic scenarios.

The editors of *Time*, for example, pontificated that the atomic scientists had "tossed" man into "the vestibule of another millennium." *Life* magazine, borrowing images from Laurence, advised its 6 million readers that "limits to our Promethean ingenuity" had been eliminated, and proclaimed that "one of the great revolutions in human society" had been achieved by absentminded professors who had "donned the tunic of Supermen."

And the University of Chicago's omnipresent chancellor, Robert Maynard Hutchins (who, many presumed, had obtained inside information from scientists who had spent the war years working for the MED at his institution), slipped into a seer's mantle on his national radio *Roundtable* and offered his audience a vivid forecast of upcoming utopias. "A very few individuals working a few hours a day at very easy tasks in the central atomic power plant," the chancellor intoned, "will provide all the heat, light, and power required by the community, and these utilities will be so cheap that their cost can hardly be reckoned."

The men and women of my generation accepted the "facts" and blueprints Laurence and his imitators laid before us. We had no questions because we had no information that would have enabled us to formulate serious inquiries. We bought into their new Edens—and in the thesis that the atomic scientists were wizards who would transform life on earth—because the "Mesa Men" confirmed the veracity of these visions by remaining silent. This, after all, was a moment of glory. Spencer Weart, a historian who has given particular attention to the postwar milieu, observed, "The scientists tended to agree that almost nothing lay beyond their cosmic powers."

Nevertheless, there is evidence that some of the leading scientists were distressed by Laurence's grandiose distortions. In May, Dr. Conant was agitated when he read the statement Laurence had drafted for President Truman to use when he revealed the existence of atomic weapons to the world. To Conant, the reporter's word pictures were "highly exaggerated and essentially phoney," and his objections resulted in an editing committee that revised Laurence's language. But when the August climax came, Dr. Conant apparently suppressed his reservations, and Laurence's equally phoney, myth-ridden dispatches were released as the official interpretation of the atomic scientists' achievements.

In the months after the war ended, Laurence expanded his interpretations. In his book *Dawn over Zero*, published in January 1946, he offered the magisterial judgment that the "basis of human existence" had been changed and prophesied that atomic science held the key to such "dreams of the ages as postponing old age" and solving "the mysteries of living processes." Post-atomic man, he affirmed, could be compared to "Moses on Mt. Pisgah gazing on a land of promise." Moreover, he pontificated that human beings were poised at a gateway that would "set man on the road to the millennium."

These additions to a growing body of atomic folklore attained fresh resonance that winter when a few of the supermen began to offer variations on Laurence's tune. One of them, Dr. Arthur Holly Compton, averred that "atomic energy may vastly enrich human life if given a chance." And Dr. Alvin Weinberg, an Oak Ridge physicist, wrote an article forecasting that radioactive isotopes "could provide mankind's fuel and food as long as the sun continues to shine."

Time did not dampen William Laurence's enthusiasm for nuclear nostrums or his optimism about the imminent conquest of nature. In 1948 he told a national radio audience that in its lifetime atomic energy would turn deserts and jungles into "new lands flowing with milk and honey." All limits could be overcome: "We can," he avowed, "air condition the jungles . . . make the Arctic wastes livable . . . and lick disease."

Bill Laurence was not the only exaggerator in the dawn days of the atomic age. From President Truman to Fred Kirby (the most popular country-western songwriter of the war years) to Arthur Compton, we were bombarded with declarations that depicted the bomb as God's gift to the American people. Harry Truman launched this ecclesiastical barrage in the aftermath of the Nagasaki holocaust by rendering thanks to God that the bomb had "come to us and not to our enemies" and expressed the wish that "He may guide us to use it in His ways and for His purposes." A freshman U.S. senator from Connecticut, Brien McMahon, eclipsed Truman's ecstasy by declaiming, "This is the most important thing in history since the birth of Jesus Christ." Kirby's lyrics for his hit tune "Atomic Power" saturated the airwaves in the fall of 1945 with the apocalyptic message "They're sending up to heaven to get the brimstone fire," and comforted his countrymen with assurances that the bombings were a divine act of retribution ("Hiroshima, Nagasaki paid a big price for their sins"). And Dr. Compton, a leading Protestant layman, told a gathering of churchmen, "Atomic power is ours, and who can deny that it was God's will that we should have it."

Inevitably the nation's outlook gradually shifted under the impact of pronouncements by people who "knew the facts" about the emerging new age. If the "basis of existence" had been altered and if (as one writer pontificated in a famous essay) modern man was rendered "obsolete" by changes implicit in the atomic revolution, it was urgent that individuals adjust their thinking to the new realities of life. The postwar scene was accurately described in 1946 by historian Allan Nevins when he observed that his countrymen were "beholding a new heaven and a new earth, to which they somewhat dazedly tried to adjust themselves."

These adjustments had a profound impact on the consciousness of the American people. They generated support for the creation of an elitist, military-civilian atomic establishment that would, in secret, make the nation's crucial nuclear decisions. They also forged attitudes, concepts, and values that exerted a powerful influence on our culture and our politics.

In large measure, these attitudes were begotten by the myths of August. To enumerate them today is to make a list of ideas and presuppositions that guided American politics and policy making during the postwar period.

Among these assumptions were:

• Given adequate financial support, scientists and engineers could reach any goal the American people set out to achieve. (In the 1950s, this axiom would be called "technological optimism" and it would be encapsulated in the catchy slogan of the "soaring '60s," "There are no problems, only solutions").

- The potential of scientific invention was inexhaustible, and the same kinds of minds that had unlocked the secrets of the atom could solve any physical problem.

- Science could, and should, "conquer" all barriers imposed by the natural world and its complex ecological systems. Conservation was no longer important, because when the world began to run out of petroleum or any other vital resource, technology would promptly come forth with better, cheaper substitutes.

- In due course, "free" atomic energy would eliminate resource shortages everywhere and open a door to global industrialization.

- If the environment was disrupted by technological mistakes, resilient scientists and engineers would "handle" such problems by developing appropriate solutions.

- And, finally, the atomic establishment could be trusted to protect the public's health from the radiation released into the environment by its bombmaking activities and by programs to develop the peaceful uses of atomic energy.

Inevitably, the mind-set produced by these concepts had a pervasive influence on our culture and on the outlook of individuals. Politically, it circumscribed normal democratic processes by creating a separate, secret sector of our national life, where a few of Laurence's supermen and a tiny group of elected leaders would make decisions about the future of the atom. Where citizens were concerned, the new mood had two impacts: it intimidated critical thought; and it persuaded men and women to repose blind trust in the programs and projects of the atomic establishment. At the end of 1945, the editors of *Time* used these extravagant figures of speech to explain the import of the year's atomic revelations, ". . . all men were pygmies . . . Even Presidents . . . [were] mere foam flecks on the tide."

The myths of August and the concepts of national prowess they generated left a long-lasting legacy. The conviction that Americans can accomplish the impossible has been an article of faith in this country for the past four decades. When they have proposed projects that were out of the ordinary, presidents have invariably invoked the spirit of the Manhattan Project. John Kennedy used the MED as a talisman when he launched his Apollo program. In 1973, Richard

Nixon conjured up the same image when he laid out his crash program for the nation to achieve "energy independence" by 1980. And Ronald Reagan used the same incantation in 1983 when he announced his grandiose "Star Wars" plan.

In the last half of this century, the American people have learned the hard way that myths—and the illusions they spawn—can indeed overpower judgment grounded in facts.

3

The Manhattan Project Plain

The Manhattan Project was a feat of technology and scientific administration. . . . The essential science had been done earlier. This was application on a gigantic scale.
—C. P. SNOW (1980)

As an image of American genius and scientific derring-do, the Manhattan Project has been an enduring symbol of our national life. But as the Cold War winds down and new relationships between nations evolve, it is vital for U.S. citizens to conduct an unflinching examination of the work of the Manhattan Engineering District (MED) and put the realities of atomic-age science in perspective. As we have seen, this project has always been a strange mixture of myth and fact, of formidable feats of technology magnified by interpretations that transformed them into superhuman deeds. As the chastened superpowers struggle to foster peace-promoting institutions, it is important to sweep away the illusions that have long blurred our view of crucial facts surrounding the birth of the atomic age and its bombs.

THE MYTH OF THE RACE WITH HITLER

For nearly a half-century, the concept that W. L. Laurence's Mesa Men were locked with Adolf Hitler's scientists in a "desperate race" for the atomic bomb has enveloped the Manhattan Project in an aura of high drama. This "verity" was the backdrop of the official history that appeared in 1962 and acquired added credence as a result of "authoritative" assertions in the memoirs of General Groves and Dr. Vannevar Bush, the wartime leaders of the MED.

With the declassification of key documents, two books have recently appeared that present unassailable proof that the race with the Nazis was a fiction. McGeorge Bundy concludes in his 1988 work, *Danger and Survival,* that the Germans "never even tried" to initiate work on an atomic bomb. To Bundy, this failure was a "consequence of deep-seated realities" rooted in Hitler's obsessions, in the anti-Semitic policies that led to the flight of Jewish physicists, in German physics, in Nazi politics, and in the circumstance that the Führer expected to end the war on the European continent in 1942 by concentrating the bulk of his nation's resources on crushing the Soviet Union's armies.

In his 1993 work, *Heisenberg's War,* Thomas Powers presents exhaustive evidence that Germany's wartime nuclear research was negligible. Powers, moreover, moves beyond Bundy to present a highly controversial argument that the Nazi effort was stillborn because Werner Heisenberg, the Nobel laureate physicist who would have been the logical leader of any German effort to produce a weapon, consciously obstructed the development of an atomic bomb.

It is painful in the 1990s for Manhattan Project veterans to accept the fact that their legendary race was a myth. Indeed, it reflects profoundly on American leadership that certainly by the fall of 1943 when the MED's crash program was ready for its takeoff, there was not a single scrap of solid evidence from any source that Germany was mounting a campaign to build an atomic bomb.

The United Kingdom was our partner in the bomb project and from the onset of the war, British agents were giving close scrutiny to the possibility that Hitler might mount a campaign to build atomic bombs. According to the official history of the British Secret Intelligence Service (SIS), those agents maintained "contacts with scientists in neutral countries and, through them, with well disposed scientists in Germany." By the summer of 1943, the information SIS agents had gathered convinced them that there was no German bomb project.

Even in wartime, it was not difficult to garner information about the status of Germany's scientific community. Hitler's anti-Semitism had propelled him to drive many of his country's finest physicists into exile, and those outcasts had a thorough knowledge of the structure of Germany's scientific institutions and the professional qualifications and idiosyncrasies of the senior scientists who remained in the Third Reich.

It is plain that if the Führer had made a decision to initiate an atomic-bomb program, he would have begun by ordering his nation's leading physicists out of their laboratories and classrooms and into a cadre supervised by military men he trusted. Such an action would have been an unmistakable sign (as it was in the United States at the end of 1942) that leading physicists were being enlisted in an unusual undertaking of far-reaching importance.

In Britain an émigré German physicist, Rudolph Peierls, was asked by the SIS to evaluate whether scientists were being mobilized to develop an atomic weapon. In 1942, Peierls analyzed German science journals obtained from neutral countries by a unit of the U.K.'s Intelligence Service, and he concluded that Germany had no "crash . . . large-scale" project under way that required a "major participation by scientists." Peierls's search convinced him that nearly all of Germany's physicists "were in their normal places and teaching their normal subjects."

Even more compelling evidence of German indifference was gleaned in Occupied France by Frédéric Joliot-Curie, a French scientist of international renown who had performed experiments involving chain-reaction neutrons in January 1939. The Germans had no cyclotron, but at the time France fell, in the summer of 1940, Joliot-Curie, a winner of the Nobel Prize in physics, was putting the finishing touches on such a machine in the basement of his Paris laboratory.

A few months later, prominent German physicists put Joliot-Curie's cyclotron into operation and used it to conduct experiments in his laboratory. The French scientist secretly inspected their notes at night. Insights from these notes and information he gleaned from discussions with his visitors furnished what, to him, was overwhelming proof that Germany was not exploring the potential of atomic explosions.

Where nuclear espionage was concerned, Frédéric Joliot-Curie was equipped to be a superspy. Even as he was conversing with German physicists at his laboratory, Joliot-Curie was living a double life as a leader of the French Resistance. Information he relayed to London through the French underground should have carried great weight as evidence that the Germans were not working on atomic weapons.

It was another negative piece of evidence, however, which cried out that there was no German Manhattan Project. As the man in charge of the MED, Leslie Groves knew with certainty that if Hitler were bent on making an A-bomb, he would begin by authorizing a crash construction program to build one or more gargantuan factories to produce the fissionable materials needed for an atomic explosion.

General Groves excelled as a supervisor of huge construction projects, and the paramount activity of the Manhattan Project in the first two years of its existence involved the building of atomic-extraction plants in Oak Ridge, Tennessee, and Hanford, Washington. When these two factories were completed, as General Groves well knew, they would be the largest industrial plants in the world under one roof. As a large-continent country isolated by oceans from all combat zones and from aerial reconnaissance, the United States could conceal such plants and the traffic of over 70,000 workers, housed in nearby barrack-cities, who toiled around the clock in these mammoth structures. But it was patently impossible to conceal or camouflage such a facility anywhere in western Europe.

It would not have been difficult in the fall of 1943 for the U.S. Army Air Force to ascertain whether the Germans were building a Manhattan Project. U.S. airpower was a formidable, expanding presence in Europe. In preparation for its upcoming campaign to choke off Hitler's petroleum supplies and cripple factories that sustained the German war machine, air force intelligence officers were photographing all important industrial enterprises in Germany.

In his prize-winning book *The Making of the Atomic Bomb*, Richard Rhodes expressed puzzlement that General Groves and other U.S.

officials did "so little" in 1942 and 1943 to determine whether Hitler was mounting a Manhattan Project of his own. Rhodes characterized this failure as one of the "mysteries of the Second World War."

In truth, there was no mystery. This lapse can be explained by analyzing the motives and the mind-set of the soldier who directed the day-to-day work of the Manhattan Project.

GENERAL GROVES'S MISGUIDED GUILE

The son of an army chaplain, Leslie Groves spent all of his years in military environments until he retired after World War II. Endowed with vaulting determination and an incisive mind, Groves graduated with honors from West Point, and in the two decades prior to Pearl Harbor he performed so well for the Army Corps of Engineers that by age forty-three he had achieved the rank of brigadier general. His reputation as a human bulldozer was enhanced when he oversaw the on-time, on-budget construction of the Pentagon. In the summer of 1942, just before the chief of the corps chose him to take charge of the nascent Manhattan Project, Groves was supervising crash construction projects in all parts of the country.

Although he was initially disgruntled by what he regarded as a dead-end assignment that would frustrate his dream of becoming an overseas combat commander, the general's imagination quickened once he realized the breathtaking potential of the Manhattan Project. The novel challenges appealed to the sensibilities of this bright, abrasive, egocentric man. The opportunity to run a secret show with very little oversight from other military men, the prospect of working directly under President Roosevelt and his secretary of war, Henry L. Stimson, and the circumstance that he would be matching wits with—and guiding the work of—some of the world's greatest scientists soon convinced him he had lucked into World War II's most exciting assignment.

From a managerial standpoint, Groves's strengths were made to order for the Manhattan Project. It needed a freewheeling military leader who was not intimidated by those who outranked him and who was adept at cutting red tape and breaking bureaucratic bottlenecks. It needed a lone-wolf executive who was unafraid of high-risk gambles and knew how to identify and delegate authority to a diverse crew of problem-solving industrialists, engineers, and scientists. And it needed a supervisor who could get to the heart of intricate techno- logical issues and make crisp decisions about promising solutions. This brand of leadership was Leslie Groves's forte, and the dyna- mism he generated was a major factor in the success of the Manhattan Project.

General Groves was also a cunning political operator who saw that the cloak of secrecy draped over his project gave him the opportunity, as the director of "the President's secret project," to create a secluded empire of personal power. The general had the instincts of a Napoléon and at every turn he used the authority given to him by his supervisors to tighten his control over the domain he governed. After his death, his streak of megalomania was vividly described by his deputy, Colonel Kenneth D. Nichols. Nichols re- membered his burly, intimidating boss as ". . . the biggest sonovabitch I've ever met in my life, but also one of the most capable individuals. He had an ego second to none . . . and absolute confidence in his decisions. . . . You never had to worry about the decisions being made or what it meant."

No mystery hovers over Leslie Groves's seeming lack of con- cern, in 1943 and 1944, about Hitler's supposed bomb project. He had an urgent ulterior motive in ignoring the findings and conclusions of Britain's SIS and in not asking Secretary Stimson to order the air force to conduct reconnaissance missions to determine whether Ger- many was building an Oak Ridge–type facility.

The general was wary of any hard facts that might reveal that the "desperate race" with Hitler's scientists was a fantasy. He rightly feared that negative news from credible sources that the Germans posed no nuclear threat would sound the death knell for a program that had one of the highest priorities when war budgets were pre- pared. Groves was always acutely aware that the race with the Nazis was the *raison d'être* of the Manhattan Project, the moral glue that held the whole effort together and kept the Mesa Men on the mesa.

THE ALSOS CAPER

As part of his strategy to keep Hitler's bomb hovering ominously over the Manhattan Project, in the fall of 1943 General Groves got authority from Secretary Stimson to create, under his command, a secret espionage operation named ALSOS. The mission Groves assigned his ALSOS group was that of following the Allies' ground armies into Europe to "capture" the German scientists who were leading Germany's effort to manufacture atomic weapons.

British intelligence officials, who were almost certain that there was no German bomb project, were baffled when an eager cadre of ALSOS agents descended on London. They had forwarded this summary of their findings to General Groves in early January 1944:

> All the evidence available to us leads us to the conclusion that the Germans are not in fact carrying out large-scale work on any aspect of [atomic-bomb building]. We believe that after an initial serious examination of the project, the German work is now confined to academic and small-scale research, much of which is being published in current issues of their scientific journals.

In his reply, General Groves did not quarrel with this conclusion. Determined to keep the race-with-Hitler myth alive, the general was not interested in facts that did not fit the egocentric script he had formulated in his own mind for the outcome of his project. As a result, since it became a drama based on a fantasy, ALSOS deserves to be described as a caper. The James Bond (or, better, Maxwell Smart) figure who led this charade was Colonel Boris T. Pash, a former high school teacher who had won his spurs as Groves's principal security aide.

When the Allied armies liberated Strasbourg in the fall of 1944, the ALSOS team confirmed (in dramatic cables to General Groves) what their British colleagues had tried to tell them a year earlier: the Germans did not have any semblance of a bomb project. This "discovery," combined with a revelation that a bureaucrat in Germany's Postal Department was the individual in charge of his country's atomic research, gave ALSOS all the trappings of a comic opera. But Pash pushed ahead and later sent exciting bulletins to Groves describing the daring exploits of his agents. There were many bold "triumphs" to report during the collapse of the Third Reich in the spring of 1945.

Among the dispatches Pash forwarded to Groves was the revelation that he and his ALSOS underlings had found "the secret hiding place" of Hitler's top scientist, the Nobel laureate Werner Heisenberg, and had "rounded up" Germany's leading physicists and placed them "under guard" to await interrogation. They also seized and destroyed the "secret laboratories" of scientists who had been working on possible peaceful uses of atomic energy. And, in a cloak-and-dagger feat that fed Leslie Groves's obsession that he could give the United States atomic supremacy by cornering the world's supply of uranium, Pash's men captured several tons of raw uranium ore that had been sitting, unused, in a German shed for many years and shipped it by air to London.

In Washington, General Groves took steps to make certain America's war leaders understood that by forcing Hitler's scientists to "surrender their secrets," his forces had scored a tremendous victory. Even though he knew full well that Heisenberg and other German physicists had not learned how to generate a chain reaction in a uranium pile or how to produce plutonium, Groves sought to convert Heisenberg's incarceration into one of the war's great milestones. The detention of Heisenberg, Groves boasted, was "worth more to us than ten divisions of Germans." After the seizure of the German uranium, Groves fired a showboating memo to General George C. Marshall to inform him that "the capture of this material removes any possibility of Germany making any use of an atomic bomb in this war."

To Groves, ALSOS was a shining chapter in the history of the Manhattan Project. In 1962 he devoted one-fifth of his book, *Now It Can Be Told*, to descriptions of the dashing accomplishments of Pash and his men. Trained historians, however, had reservations about his efforts to prepackage the history of the MED. The two historians who wrote the Atomic Energy Commission's official history of the Manhattan Project, also published in 1962, made no mention of the heroics of ALSOS.

History tells us that General Groves's decision to ignore the facts and to use the race-with-Hitler to keep the Manhattan Project on its fateful track led the United States to Hiroshima and into a sensationalized unveiling ceremony in the month of August 1945. History would have followed a different path had Secretary of War Stimson and General Groves allowed visible, valid evidence about the German failure to guide American decision making. The exaggerations and fantasies that have swirled around the atomic age for nearly a half-century were an outgrowth of their decision to keep the scientists in the dark and continue crash bombmaking as the be-all of the Manhattan Project.

The atomic age would have had a more modest and balanced beginning if Japan had surrendered before the bombs were ready, or if an objective assessment of Germany's plans had influenced our leaders to slow the pace of the Manhattan Project and convert it into a clandestine, postwar-oriented program of research and development. The surprise announcement of the success of this venture in 1946 or 1947 would have added to America's military and moral strength and encouraged a thoughtful global dialogue about the role of the atom in the modern world. With more facts and less emotion, there would have been no wild-eyed Bill Laurence, no Godlike men standing "in the light of 1,000 super-suns," no claims that an explosive that could wipe out cities was "the greatest moment for science in history," and no extravagant promises that humankind was poised at the "gateway of a better world."

But concealing the truth about the Nazis' decision not to pursue bomb research sustained the momentum of the MED and swept it, following Germany's defeat, onto a path that led to Hiroshima and to the creation of misinformation that has obscured essential truths concerning the Manhattan Project and the epoch it initiated.

THE FEATS OF THE MAESTROS OF TECHNOLOGY

A persistent question that hovers over the MED is why the efforts of the physicists were exalted while the equally remarkable work of the project's engineers was disparaged by faint praise. An unending stream of books about the bomb and the feats of the bombmakers has appeared, while only one volume of any distinction, Stéphane Groueff's *Manhattan Project: The Untold Story of the Making of the Atomic*

Bomb, has been devoted to the unsung achievements of our first nuclear engineers.

In 1939, when certain scientists convinced themselves that it might be feasible to make an atomic bomb, they were aware that such a project would involve a two-step process. They assumed that the first and perhaps most daunting task would involve assembling a team of inventors and industrial engineers who, in two or three years, could design, build, and operate atom-processing plants to produce fissionable materials that might be fashioned into bombs. The second step would entail efforts by physicists and chemists to configure those materials into a detonatable "critical mass" that could be transformed into a weapon of mass destruction. But atomic explosions were mere conjecture unless sufficient quantities of fissionable materials could be manufactured.

Experiments in European laboratories—by James Chadwick in England, by Fermi in Italy, by Bohr in Denmark, by Frédéric Joliot-Curie and his wife, Irene Curie, in France, and by Otto Hahn and Otto Frisch and Lise Meitner in Germany—encouraged optimistic scientists to believe in the feasibility of atomic explosives. The British physicist C. P. Snow later used these words to describe the scene, as war clouds gathered at the end of the 1930s:

> Pure science had produced the possibility [of bombs]. By the summer of 1939 it was known all over the world. . . . It was now feasible at least in principle that explosives could be produced of a different order from any so far in human hands. Was this practicable? Could quantities of these fissile elements ever be made? If so, could it happen in the realistic future, that is within the duration of any foreseeable war?

Snow underscored the predominant role of the industrial engineers through the answers he supplied to his rhetorical questions:

> That wasn't a scientific problem. Science had done its job. All the scientific knowledge was there and ready. If it could be applied, that would be a matter of engineering, in particular of abnormally difficult chemical engineering. The only way to separate the uranium isotopes from one another on an industrial scale would be to apply techniques similar to those that the chemical industry already used to separate and purify chemical compounds.

"As it was," Snow concluded, "the ultimate production of the atomic bomb ... was not a scientific triumph, but an engineering one."

Working in his Berkeley laboratory to improve his electromagnetic method of separating atoms, the Nobel laureate Ernest O. Lawrence advocated an engineering-first policy for the nascent Manhattan Project. He frequently reminded his associates that all efforts would be frustrated unless they could find ways to produce seventy pounds of weapons-grade uranium before the war ended. In 1943, Lawrence told General Groves it was unwise to create a laboratory to design bombs before there was solid evidence that sufficient quantities of fissionable material could be manufactured. "It's wrong to start this now," Lawrence asserted, "because we'll be taking men from the *biggest job of all,* which is getting the fissionable material, and putting them on work that is premature. In three months," he advised Groves, "thirty scientists could design this bomb if we had the fissionable material."

E. O. Lawrence practiced what he preached. Unlike most physicists, he was comfortable tackling complex industrial-engineering problems, and he gave this work such a high priority that he spent little time at Los Alamos. Indeed, Lawrence's conduct demonstrates that he probably agreed with his colleague, Caltech president Robert Millikan, that it was a mistake "to concentrate fifty prima donnas of physics in any one place."

It was a daunting task to develop designs for atom-processing factories, which would dwarf anything built previously. Creating technologies to separate radioactive isotopes entailed the invention of novel machines and devices that thrust engineers into pioneering work with new metals and new tools. One historian described the total effort as "tantamount to replicating the U.S. auto industry" in two years. At Oak Ridge, for example, it required construction of the first fully automated factory, the first plant operated by remote control, and the first sterile industrial environment featuring a vacuum-tight system geared to leak-proof joints and valves.

The engineer who ramrodded through the construction of the Oak Ridge bomb factory was Percival Cleveland ("Dobie") Keith, a Texan who had studied at MIT and become an expert in the chemistry of coal and petroleum. As an engineer's engineer, Dobie Keith was ideally equipped to manage a hurry-up project where crucial decisions had to be made on the run. A forty-two-year-old leader who set an example of commitment his associates emulated, Keith had a mind driven by enormous energy and curiosity. Once he had evaluated his options, he made high-risk decisions with never a backward look.

Keith relished tackling tasks others deemed impossible. He was not intimidated, for example, when it emerged that his gaseous-diffusion plant would have to be enlarged by adding a "cascade" requiring thousands of stages to enrich U-235 to bomb-grade material. Arthur Squires, a chemical engineer who labored alongside Keith for three years, admired his boss's resourcefulness and remembered how, "often long after his associates had given up a problem as hopeless—Keith would come in one morning with a fresh idea that at least encouraged us to attack the problem along a new line."

Had Japan surrendered before the atomic bombs were available, Dobie Keith and the atomic engineers would undoubtedly have been front and center when U.S. officials unveiled the Manhattan Project and its new weapons. But the use of the bombs as weapons of war on two Japanese cities produced a different, far more dramatic unveiling that heaped so much glory on the physicists that the critical contributions of the atomic engineers were obscured.

Although facts have overtaken many myths in the intervening years, it is still uncertain whether the Dobie Keiths of the MED—ingenious men such as Manson Benedict, Clarence Johnson, George Watts, Judson Swearingen, Ludwig Skog, J. S. Hobbs, and Albert Nier—will ultimately stand as full partners alongside the bombmakers. There is ample evidence that new insights are helping historians balance the Manhattan Project's books. The encomium Arthur Squires has written to explain the achievements of his colleagues will surely accelerate this process. He attributes the success of their war work to the panache of a "network of maestros of technology" who directed the atom-splitting at Oak Ridge and Hanford. These industrial impresarios, Squires recounts, accomplished seemingly impossible feats because they were able to "locate superb managers" and knew how to "discover inventors who found timely solutions for critical problems."

SEEING, AT LAST, THE BOMBMAKERS PLAIN

The demythologizing of the Manhattan Project has put the dawn years of the atomic age in a different perspective. The New Mexico mesa of this revised environment emerges not as a "Magic Mountain" where physicists concocted miracles, but instead as a laboratory where scientists studied the behavior of conventional explosives in order to devise techniques to compress the new materials extracted at Oak Ridge and Hanford into usable bombs. This mesa, contrary to myth, was not peopled by supermen, but by chemists and ordnance experts and physicists who were designing "gadgets" that might fit in airplanes and could detonate "critical" quantities of purified uranium and plutonium over selected military targets.

Seen plainly, the Manhattan Project yields many fresh insights that correct our perceptions of this seminal episode of world history. Liberated from its folklore, it is clear that

- Los Alamos was, first and last, a bomb factory.
- The work of the maestros of technology was as important as, if not more important than, the accomplishments of the physicists.
- The MED's achievements were not (as the mythmakers asserted) attributable to a "stroke of American genius," but exemplified a logical extension of two generations of work in physics by the world's scientists.
- Three historical advantages put the United States in a position where it could mount a massive effort during World War II to make atomic explosives:
  — Adolf Hitler's racial bias made it feasible in 1942 for the United States to assemble an international team that included some of central Europe's most gifted scientists.
  — Atomic factories on the American continent lay beyond the reach of enemy aircraft.
  — There was a sufficient surplus of economic resources and manpower within the United States to sustain such a project.

- Scientists in several countries discovered the fissioning of atoms before the United States launched its Manhattan Project.

- The "high moral purpose" that brought the project's scientists together and drove their endeavors was the presupposition that Hitler's scientists were making strenuous efforts to develop atomic bombs.
- Much of the design of the Hiroshima bomb involved a straightforward application of existing military ordnance engineering.
- The technical obstacles confronting the scientists and engineers who made the first nuclear weapons (as China, a semi-industrial nation, demonstrated in 1964) were greatly exaggerated.
- The risks and hazards attending the making of the first atomic bombs were also greatly exaggerated.

In an era when nations with stockpiles of nuclear weapons are agreeing to reduce their arsenals, the Earth's inhabitants need a clear view of the bombmakers and of the cataclysms that would occur if their bombs are ever used. It is urgent in the 1990s both to understand the illusions that confused the early years of the atomic age and the assumptions that led the Soviet Union and the United States to base their systems of military "defense" on a belief that the nation that had the greatest number of deliverable nuclear weapons enjoyed more "security" than its adversary. In fact, and paradoxically, as we and our Soviet rivals discovered, the more we invested in "defense" and "security," the less secure we were and the less well we were able to defend ourselves.

Not surprisingly, some of the severest critics of this mindless, yet paradoxical, pursuit of security have been distinguished alumni of the Manhattan Project. In 1983, Isador I. Rabi and Victor Weisskopf, two atomic elders, expressed their dismay about strategies that had turned atomic scientists into pliant accessories of an unending drive for "better" nuclear weapons. Speaking at a program to commemorate the fortieth anniversary of the establishment of the Los Alamos laboratory, Dr. Rabi used the lament "We meant so well" to convey his unease that the latter-day laboratories had become a driving force behind the nuclear arms race. Weisskopf, responding in part to the impact of Edward Teller's Star Wars escalation, defended the demonstrators who had marred the "celebration" and issued an urgent call for efforts to end a "senseless, deadly arms race" that threatened to "destroy everything on Earth that we consider worth living for."

4

Hiroshima: The American Tragedy

THE MORALITY
OF THE OLD ORDER

> For nearly two hundred years a model of war had developed
> in the West which held that, if at all possible, inhabitants of
> "civilized" nations should be spared from attack, great cities
> preserved, and the artifacts of high culture left unharmed.
> —RONALD SCHAFFER
> *Wings of Judgment* (1985)

In the immediate aftermath of World War II, few Americans questioned the decision of their war leaders to incinerate the Japanese cities
of Hiroshima and Nagasaki with atomic weapons. The conclusion of a
long and bloody conflict produces a mood of thanksgiving that encour-
ages the survivors to contemplate ways to create a world that might
give meaning to the horrors and sacrifices that have dominated their
lives. This was the outlook that encouraged my generation—the
generation that fought the war—to accept the explanations of our
leaders that the atomic bombs shortened the war and saved the lives of
hundreds of thousands of American and Japanese soldiers and civilians.

But in the 1990s, the world regards these bombings in a light that
casts dark shadows on the decision the leaders of the United States
made in 1945 to drop atomic bombs on two Japanese cities. Ours is

the only nation that has ever used atomic weapons in a war, and as the twentieth century nears its close many thoughtful men and women around the globe view the holocausts of Hiroshima and Nagasaki as examples of mindless destruction. This is a legacy of our atomic age that should force us, at long last, to confront Hiroshima as also an *American* tragedy.

As war clouds gathered in the 1930s, the United States of America stood on moral high ground. Our nation had not been associated with war atrocities in World War I; American idealism was exemplified by President Woodrow Wilson's optimistic peace aims; and our goodwill toward other peoples was embodied by the humanitarian relief and reconstruction work carried out in Europe during and after World War I under the leadership of Herbert Hoover.

Thus, as the first battles of what would become World War II were fought, it was foreseeable that Americans would be among the first to decry atrocities against civilians. Ernest Hemingway expressed the moral outlook of his countrymen when he wrote angry dispatches from Spain about the bombing and shelling of the civilian populations during the Spanish Civil War. Hemingway, a veteran of the First World War, admired brave soldiers who were killed on battlefields in an "honest" war, but he was outraged by military thrusts directed "against the people of a country instead of a war between armies."

Hemingway's indignation boiled over as he watched Nazi aviators bomb Spanish towns and cities. In an effort to "raise the world" against such crimes, in the summer of 1938 the novelist wrote an accusatory article, "Humanity Will Not Forgive This." This was his message to the world:

> During the last 15 months I saw murder done in Spain by fascist invaders. Murder is different from war. . . . You have anger and hatred when you see them do murder. And you see them do it almost every day.
>
> You see them do it in Barcelona where they bomb the workers' quarters from a height so great it is impossible for them to have any objective other than the blocks of apartments where the people live. You see the murdered children with their twisted legs, their arms that bend in wrong directions, and their plaster powdered faces. . . . And you hate the Italian and German murderers who do this as you hate no other people. . . .

When they shell the city indiscriminately in the middle of the night to try to kill civilians in their beds it is murder. When they shell the cinema crowds, concentrating on the squares where the people will be coming out at 8 o'clock, it is murder.

Stating he felt that he was "speaking for the whole American people," Secretary of State Cordell Hull also denounced the bombing of Barcelona. "No theory of war," Hull said, "can justify such conduct." And Herbert Hoover simultaneously sought to solidify world opinion by proposing an outright international ban on the bombing of cities.

During the century that preceded the onset of World War II, statesmen had made sustained efforts to place curbs on the most inhumane excesses of war. Beginning with the Geneva conventions of 1864 that adopted rules concerning the treatment of sick and wounded soldiers and brought the International Red Cross into existence, the leading nations of the world entered into a series of treaties establishing rules of war to govern the treatment of prisoners, to protect noncombatants and hospitals, and to define the legal rights of neutral nations. The capstone of this effort to enlarge the conscience of humankind came in a burst of idealism with the signing of the Kellogg-Briand Pact in 1928 through which forty-two nations renounced war "as an instrument of national policy" and affirmed that "the settlement or solution of all disputes or conflicts . . . shall never be sought except by peaceful means."

From the beginning, the United States was a stalwart advocate of these reforms. Over the decades, the "laws of war" embodied in these pacts were incorporated into our army field manuals, taught in our military academies, and enforced by courts-martial and military commissions. The moral imperatives in these manuals were written in stern, crisp prose. They included such commands as these:

It is especially forbidden . . . to kill or wound an enemy who . . . has surrendered at discretion. . . . It is especially forbidden . . . to employ arms, projectiles or materials calculated to cause unnecessary suffering.

Many of the admirals and generals who commanded our armed forces during World War II were indoctrinated in these rules of war.

And, as we shall see, when moral dilemmas arose over the use of airpower, some of these old soldiers were more sensitive to humanitarian concerns than were their civilian superiors.

President Franklin Roosevelt articulated the ethical values of the old order in a somber message he addressed to the nations drawn into belligerent status by Hitler's invasion of Poland on the first day of September, 1939:

> The ruthless bombing from the air of civilians in unfortified centers of population during the course of the hostilities which have raged in various quarters of the earth during the past few years, which has resulted in the maiming and the death of thousands of defenseless men, women and children, has sickened the hearts of every civilized man and woman, and has profoundly shocked the conscience of humanity.
>
> If resort is had to this form of inhuman barbarism during the period of the tragic conflagration with which the world is now confronted, hundreds of thousands of innocent human beings who have no responsibility for, and who are not even remotely participating in, the hostilities which have now broken out, will lose their lives. I am therefore addressing this urgent appeal to every government which may be engaged in hostilities publicly to affirm its determination that its armed forces shall in no event, and under no circumstances, undertake the bombardment from the air of civilian populations or of unfortunate cities, upon the understanding that these same rules of warfare will be scrupulously observed by all of their opponents.

In response to FDR's request for an "immediate reply," the government of Great Britain issued a positive rejoinder the same day, but there was a foreshadowing of tragedies to come when Adolf Hitler waited until his bombers had terrorized Warsaw before he responded to the American president with a hypocritical pledge not to bomb cities.

In 1939, President Roosevelt could speak with conviction on this subject, for a decision his country had made earlier about bombers and bombing policies conformed to the moral standards he espoused in his appeal. The United States had made a clear statement concerning its concept of acceptable air warfare in 1935 when it ordered its first B-17 bombers, machines designed and equipped to fly at high altitudes and use an unusually accurate bombsight to attack strategic military targets.

EUROPEAN BOMBING AND THE DESCENT TO BARBARISM

These new and terrible instruments of uncivilized warfare represent a modern type of barbarism not worthy of Christian man.

—ADMIRAL WILLIAM D. LEAHY (1949)
Chief of Staff to Presidents
Roosevelt and Truman

As a champion of civilized warfare, it would have been unthinkable for President Roosevelt to launch city-destroying attacks against Japan, if first Germany, and then England in retaliation, had not bombed each other's cities. No American city was touched by an enemy bomb in World War II: Pearl Harbor was a naval base, not an urban area.

For Germany's noncombatant population, Hitler's most fateful wartime mistake was his decision in August 1940 to strike at England's cities in an effort to knock that nation out of the war. Intoxicated by the awesome power his armies had demonstrated in their blitzkrieg through France, the Nazi leader was convinced that the British people's will to fight could be crushed by terror bombing. Now Hitler could flaunt the contempt he had always felt for the world's "rules of warfare," for the victories of his war machine had confirmed his long-held belief that his countrymen were a master race entitled to make their own rules of war and to proclaim their own "purer" code of moral conduct.

The best historian of Hitlerism, William L. Shirer, informs us that one of the reasons the Führer scorned the hard-won gains of international law and the ethical principles of "bourgeois morality" was that he subscribed to Nietzsche's dark doctrine that "When a man is a master . . . he has the pure conscience of a beast of prey . . . [and] of what importance are treaties to him?" Now Hitler was free to cast off the restraints of pacts and treaties erected by decadent nations and to fulfill his dream of making a "spiritual break" with the West. Hitler's concept of total war evolved out of his malevolent conviction that the members of his master race could do no wrong. And it was, of course, this amoral dogma that led the Nazis, unerringly, to bombings of innocent civilians, to the ovens of Auschwitz, and to the killing grounds of Babi Yar.

It was Winston Churchill's retaliatory response to Hitler's attacks on the cities of England that eventually put all European cities on the target lists of the German Luftwaffe and the Royal Air Force's Bomber Command and sealed the doom of Germany's principal cities. At the outbreak of the war in 1939, Prime Minister Neville Chamberlain was the first European leader to accept President Roosevelt's appeal to renounce the bombing of civilian targets, and until France fell and Churchill replaced Chamberlain, British bomber crews flew under orders to bring their bombs home if they could not visually identify their assigned targets. The prospect was favorable that, had Hitler not made his ineffective attacks on Britain's urban areas in the fall of 1940, the war leaders of the United Kingdom probably would not have considered a bombing campaign directed at Germany's cities as either a morally permissible war aim or a wise allocation of scarce war resources.

But Hitler's blitz turned events in a different direction, and by the time the United States entered the war, a year later, Great Britain had embraced the total-war concept by making the production of a formidable fleet of heavy bombers the centerpiece of its war strategy. Winston Churchill was the architect of this program, and in the first weeks of 1942 he was ready to put into effect his "area-bombing" program aimed at the centers of Germany's principal cities. This strategy, like Hitler's in 1940, was based on the assumption that the fighting spirit of the German people could be shattered if their cities were demolished. Churchill's program was not an attack on the industrial sinews of the German war machine. He was forthright about his goal. His bombing campaign was conceived as an "attack on German morale," an attempt to win the war outright by forcing Hitler to capitulate after millions of German women, children, and factory workers were killed or terrorized or "dehoused" by city-leveling air raids.

Developed by England's air marshals, this victory-through-airpower became the linchpin of Churchill's grand strategy. It fit the limited resources of the United Kingdom; it dangled the prospect of a cheap victory before his Allies; and, most important, it provided Winston Churchill with a cogent argument to delay an invasion of the European continent until the land armies of the Soviet Union had decimated German troops and consumed the critical resources that nation needed to prosecute its war.

Winston Churchill knew what he was doing when he picked Air Marshal Arthur Harris to direct the operations of England's Bomber Command. Harris, like other airmen of his generation, was obsessed with the idea that bombers could win wars. A stubborn, single-minded man, Bert Harris eagerly embraced the concept of total war. From the day the Americans arrived with their concept of daylight precision bombing keyed to the destruction of critical resources like oil refineries and aircraft factories, Harris exhibited contempt for their technique. In Bert Harris's view, such "panacea bombing" was a wasteful, peripheral use of airpower. The way to force Hitler to surrender was to pulverize the centers of his cities with night bombing. After the war, historian Max Hastings described the plan Churchill and Harris pursued for three long years as an effort to concentrate "all available forces for the progressive, systematic destruction of the urban areas of the Reich, city block by city block, factory by factory, until the enemy became a nation of troglodytes, scratching in the ruins."

"Bomber Harris," as he became known, relentlessly executed his country's terror-bombing strategy guided by an assumption that the best way to shorten the war was to accelerate the casualties in his urban killing grounds. His pitiless outlook toward life and human suffering was exhibited one night when a motorcycle policeman stopped him while he was racing his auto at high speed en route to the Air Ministry and reproached him with the accusation "You might have killed somebody, sir." The brisk response of Bomber Harris, "Young man, I kill thousands of people every night," expressed the prevailing attitude at his headquarters during his years of directing the Bomber Command.

By the end of 1944, Harris's aerial campaign had achieved levels of death and destruction that exceeded the hopes and forecasts of his most bullish bomber men. Harris had concentrated his attacks on

Germany's most densely populated urban areas, and his statisticians were reporting that nearly a half-million civilians had been killed and that his bombs had "virtually destroyed" forty-five of Germany's sixty largest cities.

But in the winter of 1945 two facts were obvious. It was clear that Hitler's days were numbered—and it was plain that Bomber Command's urban infernos hadn't knocked Germany out of the war. It was equally obvious that Winston Churchill and the advocates of morale-bombing had made a gruesome miscalculation in assuming that millions of terror-stricken civilians could force a paranoid dictator to end a war. And it was equally clear, since the campaigns of the great ground armies were positioned to play the decisive role in ending the war, that further raids on German cities not only would not shorten the war, but would create ruins that would make the task of postwar rebuilding more difficult.

However, it was apparently unthinkable for the bomber men not to flaunt the power they had amassed, and destruction that was essentially mindless predominated in the last weeks of the war. The program devised that winter by Bomber Harris became a Götterdämmerung of the total-war concept. It featured a campaign that saw thirty-six major operations against Dortmund, Chemnitz, Kassell, Munich, Nuremberg, Weisbaden, Worms, Mainz, Mannheim, and Bonn. And it came to a grisly climax with a fearful "double-blow" by the RAF at Dresden on the night of February 13.

Dresden contained no targets of military significance that winter. Like the monuments of Paris and Florence, its art and architecture and culture exemplified the cultural history of its country. It lay undefended on the night of February 13, jammed with refugees (mainly women, children, and older men) who were streaming westward ahead of the oncoming Russian armies. The attack on Dresden created a firestorm with such flawless precision that the official historians of Britain's air war later described it as Bomber Command's "crowning achievement." This attack gutted this handsome city and probably killed over 100,000 human beings. Because it was the most pointless air expedition of the war in Europe, this murder mission is a blot on English honor—and on Winston Churchill's war leadership—that, in the words of one British historian, "will be remembered a thousand years hence."

Although the Dresden firestorm was a British operation, the United States and its air force were caught in an international cross-fire of moral indignation when a war dispatch that declared: "Allied air bosses have made the long-awaited decision to adopt deliberate terror bombing of the great German population centers as a ruthless expedient to hasten Hitler's doom" slipped by the censors at General Eisenhower's headquarters. This furor forced high-level U.S. officials to issue disclaimers. General Marshall informed reporters there had been no departure from "the historic American policy of avoiding terror bombing." And on February 22, Secretary of War Stimson told a press conference that "our policy never has been to inflict terror bombing on civilian populations."

Fifteen days later, on March 9, USAAF bombers loaded with incendiary bombs attacked the center of Tokyo in the most terrifying—and destructive—terror-bombing attack of World War II. This attack, and similar terror-bombing operations in the days and weeks that followed, left a legacy of searing questions that no U.S. official has answered to this day:

- Why did the United States abruptly abandon the bombing policy that embodied "U.S. ideals" when it came time to bomb targets in Japan?
- Why did U.S. strategic bombers avoid attacking German cities, but target the very centers of Japanese cities with unmerciful ferocity?
- How did uses of airpower that were deemed morally abhorrent in Europe become ethically acceptable in the Pacific?

And, finally, who ordered the drastic policy change that brought death to nearly 400,000 civilians—and that made the decision to devastate Hiroshima and Nagasaki with atomic bombs morally tolerable?

THE PATH TO HIROSHIMA

A Hidden Hand Paves the Way

The precise moment is concealed in the mists of history, but sometime in the fall of 1944 or the winter of 1945 a fateful decision was made in Washington: the strategic, precision-bombing policy the United States had adopted at the beginning of World War II—and had followed with considerable diligence in Europe—would be altered for the air war against Japan. In Europe, U.S. bombers concentrated on strategic targets and (unlike England's Bomber Command) did not conduct raids directed at the heart of German cities. There were a few notable instances in the last months of the war when departures from this policy violated what General George Marshall called "the historic American policy of avoiding terror bombing," but these exceptions underscored a general adherence to precision attacks on discrete military and industrial targets.

The destruction of cities by terror bombing became the centerpiece of the new policy adopted for the air war against Japan. The objective of the air raids that began in February 1945 was to attack the hearts of Japan's largest cities with incendiary bombs in an attempt to incinerate the homes and extinguish the lives of as many Japanese civilians as possible. This extermination program was so successful that it set records for wartime destruction that have never been surpassed in conventional warfare.

The origin of the macabre decision that altered America's "historic" bombing policy has confronted historians with a blank wall. We know how General Curtis LeMay executed that decision, but the concealment of the facts concerning its author, or authors, qualifies as the most masterful cover-up of that war. The questions that surround this decision relate to the circumstance that this was, first and last, a decision that could have been made only by the commander in chief, that is, the president of the United States, or someone to whom he might have delegated his decision-making authority. Any inquiry must focus on Franklin Roosevelt. Did he give an oral order to Stimson? Or to Robert Lovett, his assistant secretary for air? Or, did he issue the order in a cryptic statement to General Marshall or General Henry H. ("Hap") Arnold? Or did the top generals of the army air force usurp the president's authority?

There are no concrete answers to this riddle, but we do know that General Arnold chose General Curtis LeMay to execute the new policy. Curtis LeMay had been the most innovative pioneer of high-altitude precision bombing in the European theater. In August 1943, he had led a high-risk, high-loss mission that penetrated deep into the heartland of Germany to bomb aircraft plants at Regensburg. LeMay knew all there was to know about the marked differences between British and American bombing techniques—and the blunt account of his leadership he presented in his 1967 book, *Mission with LeMay,* reveals that he was aware that General Arnold wanted him to employ British-style city-bombing in an effort to create firestorms in the centers of the big cities of Japan.

LeMay was not only the most daring, resourceful bomber man in the USAAF, he was, like Bomber Harris, a firm believer that the quickest way to end the war was to maximize the destruction of enemy civilians and soldiers and enemy real estate. Curtis LeMay knew what his boss wanted and he set to work to perfect a fiery solution. The sleek B-29 had been designed as America's super-bomber for daylight, high-altitude precision bombing, but in the Pacific's powerful jet streams, precision bombing from 30,000 feet had proved to be a daunting task. LeMay's ingenuity was inspired by an intelligence report that Japan lacked adequate antiaircraft weapons to fend off attacks by low-level aircraft, and soon he was considering the feasibility of converting his B-29s into low-level nighttime bombers. Stripping and converting the B-29s and cramming them with incendiary bombs would allow him to make night drops on the most flammable sections of Japan's highly flammable cities.

Overboard went more than two tons of guns, ammunition, bombsights, and gunners. Out, too, went the bomb-bay tanks and their tons of extra fuel. And in went a mix of the latest and best napalm and thermite incendiary bombs, to be dropped from 5,000 feet in patterns of spreading clusters on the huge urban expanse targeted for destruction by fire.

LeMay's first experiment with his new machine involved a raid on Tokyo on the night of March 9, 1945, that took rank in history as the most destructive single air raid ever carried out by any nation. The

AUGUSTANA UNIVERSITY COLLEGE
LIBRARY

well-aimed incendiaries of LeMay's 334 B-29s fell, by luck, into a heavy wind that whipped the initial fires into a conflagration that swept as a superheated tidal wave of flame across the city. Sixteen square miles of that immense city were incinerated, and a quarter of a million structures were destroyed. An accurate death toll was never compiled, as it was impossible to count the cremated children in the inferno the bombers created. The estimates range from 34,000 to 100,000.

For General Arnold, this was the climactic day of the war, for his bombers had demonstrated once and for all—particularly to skeptical admirals and army generals—that airpower would be the decisive weapon of the future. General LeMay, elated with his masterpiece, pocketed Arnold's telegram congratulating him on his "guts" and swiftly laid out a plan of action to end the war in ten days by a fire blitz that would wipe out all of Japan's major industrial cities. This scheme, as it turned out, was unrealistic. The element of surprise and the high winds that made the attack on Tokyo an airman's dream could not be replicated. Nature did not provide winds, and LeMay's men flew so many missions so fast that in a few days all their supplies of incendiary bombs were depleted and it took several weeks to replenish them.

Guided by a special team of targeters Arnold had trained, LeMay's men soon turned city-burning into a science. Zone maps with designated "urban areas" (UAs) were prepared for each targeted city, and when the desired number of these UAs had been obliterated, that particular city was removed from the list of target cities. As there was no way to tally body counts, LeMay's scorekeepers decided to use square-miles-destroyed as the yardstick to measure their progress. By the middle of June, when the navy supplied enough firebombs to complete the first phase of their "urban area program," the incineration list included 56.3 square miles of Tokyo, 12.4 in Nagoya, 8.8 in Kobe, 15.6 in Osaka, 8.9 in Yokohama, and 3.6 in Kawasaki.

These man-made infernos were war's high-water mark of death and destruction. In ninety days, the Americans had destroyed more homes and killed almost as many civilians as had Bomber Harris in three years. This "achievement" is a monument to area-bombing that may be eclipsed only if, one day, there is an Armageddon between nations armed with nuclear weapons.

For nearly a half-century, a profound military question has

hovered over the destruction caused by LeMay's area-bombing. Did the incineration of these cities—and the creation of a civilian death toll that exceeded the number of Japanese soldiers killed in all of World War II—contribute anything essential to the defeat of Japan?

There is overwhelming evidence that the decisive battle in the Pacific war occurred at Leyte Gulf in the Philippines during four days in late October 1944, when ships of the U.S. Navy's seventh fleet annihilated a great Nipponese armada and cut Japan's lifelines to the oil and other resources this island empire needed to sustain its war-making power. It took time for this stranglehold to take effect, but by the time General LeMay's B-29s began their campaign against Japan's civilians and cities, the entire military machine of that nation was grinding to a halt. This is the reality that has cast clouds of doubt over the U.S. Army Air Force's claim that its urban-area raids cut "the industrial heart" out of Japan's war machine.

The fact that few Japanese fighters appeared to defend their homeland against the lethal onslaught of the B-29s was, by itself, an indication that Japan was prostrate, because the U.S. Navy had severed Japan's access to the overseas oil it needed to operate its war machine. It took a heavy dose of self-deception in the spring of 1945 for the chiefs of the U.S. Army Air Force to pretend that they were going to "win" the war by gutting Japan's industrial cities. They knew everything there was to know about the impact of an oil cutoff on the ability of an enemy nation to wage war. The interdiction of petroleum supplies had been the paramount achievement of their precision bombing in Europe, and Arnold's generals knew that war production is meaningless if a nation has no oil.

This awareness raises grave doubts about the motives and goals of the USAAF's leaders as they launched their city-burning campaign on the night of March 9, 1945. If their urban conflagration incidentally consumed some aircraft, for example, were they justified in asserting that they were striking "decisive" blows at the enemy, when fuel was not available to keep significant numbers of Japanese planes airborne? How much did it cripple Nipponese power that spring to pound cities that sustained steelworks or tank factories or harbors, when the Japanese had insufficient fuel to operate their mechanized ground forces and ships? And how were Arnold and his aides able to rationalize that their urban-area bombing was choking vital piecework manufacturing in millions of Japanese homes, when Japan's capacity to wage mechanized war was sputtering to a halt?

But the results of these raids reveal nothing about who ordered a policy change that certainly qualifies as the most far-reaching moral decision made by any U.S. leader during World War II. The appearance that the decision makers used verbal commands, but conspired to conceal what actually occurred, has forced latter-day historians to engage in speculation that focuses on the personal qualities of our leaders and their reactions to crucial episodes and events.

Students of Franklin Roosevelt's twelve-year presidency have given us important insights into his habits as the nation's chief executive: FDR, we are told, had a passion for secrecy that caused him to hold his cards close to his vest; he was a constitutional commander-in-chief who insisted that he and his civilian advisors exert control over important military decisions; he was not averse to delegating authority to strong-minded associates whom he trusted; and, as demonstrated by the humanitarian appeal he made in 1939 at the outset of the war, he believed his country should play a strong role as a guardian of international morality.

These presidential behavior patterns, and Roosevelt's long experience as an administrator, suggest that he made the fateful decision. Both Secretary Stimson and General Marshall would have recognized instinctively that a drastic change in the nation's bombing policy was a decision for their commander-in-chief. One battlefield question that was presented to, and decided by, FDR in the last days of February, six weeks before his death, was whether the marines should be allowed to save the lives of U.S. soldiers by using poison gas to force Japanese soldiers from their bunkers on the island of Iwo Jima. Roosevelt vetoed this plan, and as his record shows again and again, if Roosevelt decided to exercise his power secretly, he did not hesitate to act in this fashion.

Roosevelt's exquisitely sensitive political antennae surely cautioned him that damaging moral issues would be raised if the United States were perceived as being a violator of the treaties designed to humanize warfare. An overt decision by FDR to authorize terror bombing and the leveling of Japan's cities would have put him in an untenable moral posture. It was equally obvious that if the United States were caught in a moral crossfire, he would imperil his ambitious postwar plans to lay the foundations of peace through the creation of a world organization of nations—and to convene new international tribunals to set pioneering legal standards by punishing war crimes and atrocities directed at innocent civilians.

If one assumes that FDR orally approved the air force's city-burning plan, it is also logical to presume that he qualified his decision with critical caveats. He would have first insisted that the bombings in Japan be presented to the world as merely a continuation of the precision-bombing strategy used by the United States in Europe. And he would have demanded strict secrecy to prevent his name from being associated with any change in the historic American bombing policy.

If Franklin Roosevelt did make such a hidden-hand decision, it is obvious that there was one of his assistants who had to know about, and to concur with, such a profound policy change. This, of course, would have been Secretary of War Stimson, the executive who supervised the activities of the air force. And Stimson, in turn, would have had to take one individual into his confidence, his veteran assistant secretary for air, Robert Lovett. Lovett would have been the crucial partner. He knew all of the air chiefs, and his office was next door to General Arnold's. And as the day-to-day overseer of the air war, Bob Lovett had been heavily involved in the disputes about bombing policies in the European theater, and had refereed many of the controversies about target priorities between the commanders of the Royal Air Force and the USAAF.

It is the eerie conduct of FDR, Stimson, and Lovett in the weeks and months after the firebombing of Tokyo that offers solid circumstantial evidence that a hidden-hand decision had been made at the highest echelons of government. A study of the record of that period produces reverberations that can only be described as uncanny, for all available facts suggest that in March 1945 these three war leaders inexplicably closed their eyes and ears to the crescendo around them and made extra efforts not to know what their bombers were doing over Japan. One of President Roosevelt's biographers would have us believe, for example, that in the last month of his life he was so feeble that "it is doubtful that Roosevelt understood the enormity of the civilian losses" resulting from the bombing of Japan's cities. And admirers of Henry Stimson, who meticulously traced many of the main trends of the war in his diary, want us to accept the premise that the secretary did not know that his bombers were engaged in a systematic, relentless campaign directed at Japan's cities and the civilians who inhabited them.

Stimson made a studied effort in his journal to portray himself as a leader who assumed his subordinates were keeping restraints in the air force, and who therefore didn't know that a new bombing policy had been adopted for the war in the Pacific. In one entry he said that he had extracted a promise from Lovett that "there would only be precision bombing in Japan," and told President Truman on May 16—after the fire raids that had gutted the main Japanese cities—that he was holding the air force "so far as possible to the precision bombing which has done so well in Europe."

However, these assertions are inherently unbelievable when one realizes that the secretary or his aides had access not only to the exciting stories in the newspapers about the Tokyo firestorm, but to vivid photographs and detailed reports from General LeMay's headquarters about the carnage wreaked by what appeared to be the most destructive attack on any city in the history of warfare. In his thoughtful book, *Wings of Judgment: American Bombing in World War II,* Dr. Ronald Schaffer has questioned Secretary Stimson's credibility with these incisive questions.

> Was it possible that the Secretary of War knew less about the March 10 bombing of Tokyo than a reader of the *New York Times?* Why did he accept [General] Arnold's statement about attempting to limit the impact of bombing on Japanese civilians? Was he signaling that he really did not wish to be told what the AAF was doing to enemy civilians? Or did the Secretary, seventy-seven years old . . . often unable to put in a full day's work, find it too difficult . . . to inquire into all the actions of the AAF which seemed to raise disturbing moral questions?

A change in the tenor of the bombing stories emanating from Tinian gave evidence that high-placed civilians in the Pentagon were disturbed by the implication that the United States was engaging in terror bombing. One communiqué sought to create the impression that Japan's cities were being damaged inadvertently from flames leaping beyond the discrete targets of the bombardiers. It read:

"Commanders insisted that it was not 'area bombing' of the sort practiced by the British in Europe, but rather 'precision area bombing' on target area outlines that were 'carefully drawn' so every effort could be made to hit the targets."

This bombing-as-usual cover-up was a triumph of military public relations. It quieted concerns that the United States had abandoned its opposition to "morale bombing," and the absence of any mention of the probable civilian casualties helped to divert attention from the prospect that tens of thousands of civilians might have been cremated in the firestorms created by the B-29s. And this deft maneuver also served General Arnold's purposes by leaving the USAAF free to demonstrate that airpower, by itself, could win a war.

All of these facts and circumstances lead inexorably to the conclusions that a hidden decision by President Roosevelt (a) cleared the way for the program area-bombing of Japan's cities; and (b) enabled America's war leaders to put a mantle of moral acceptability over the atomic bombings of Hiroshima and Nagasaki.

The days immediately after the Tokyo raid were surely the most exhilarating of the war at General Arnold's headquarters. The capital of the enemy had been smashed by the most destructive air bombardment in history, and aerial photographs were soon available that told, with stunning power, the story of this triumph of airpower. This was the great fulfillment Arnold and his colleagues had been waiting for, and it defies belief that they did not exuberantly rush to the offices of General Marshall and Secretary Stimson to share the dramatic details of this history-making event.

WHO CHANGED THE U.S. BOMBING POLICY IN THE PACIFIC?

A Report of a Personal Search by the Author

In no field has the pursuit of truth been more difficult than that of military history.

—B. H. Liddell-Hart
Military Historian

As a gunner on B-24 bombers, I flew over thirty missions with the 454th Bombardment Group of the Fifteenth Air Force in the spring and summer of 1944. The oil-interdiction campaign of the USAAF commenced just as we arrived in southern Italy, and the mission that introduced my crew to the world of strategic bombing was a strike at installations in Europe's largest oil field, at Ploesti, Rumania.

The crews of our heavy bombers were trained to bomb strategic, military-industrial targets with high-explosive bombs from altitudes above 20,000 feet. Precision bombing was our assigned task, and before each mission we were briefed about the geography and the military significance of that day's target. During my five-month tour of duty with the Fifteenth Air Force, its primary targets across a wide arc in southern Europe were oil refineries, synthetic oil plants, and aircraft factories. Some of our assigned targets were located on the outskirts of large cities such as Vienna and Munich, but we were never dispatched to bomb the cities themselves. There were, for example, missions to bomb an aircraft factory near Friedrichshafen, an oil-refinery complex near Vienna, an airfield close to Munich, and I have a vivid memory of bombs aimed with pinpoint accuracy at harbor facilities in Italy's La Spezia naval base.

It was inevitable that ill-aimed bombs from some of these raids would demolish homes and kill some civilians, but efforts were made to minimize such damage by the approach angle of the bomb runs. A careful review of the targets bombed by the Fifteenth Air Force in its sixteen months of operations in Italy from January 1944 until April 1945 reveals no instance when the primary target was a large city.

My combat experiences convinced me that the air force generals in Europe were making a conscientious effort to minimize impacts on cities and civilians, and I was surprised during the final months by the war communiqués from the Pacific that the air force was waging a campaign to incinerate Japan's cities by unprecedented low-level attacks by B-29 bombers loaded with incendiary bombs. By then I was an instructor at a training school for B-29 gunners, and the word that gunners were superfluous on these missions told me that a decision had been made to abandon the bombing plan the United States had used in Europe in favor of a different strategy in the Pacific.

When I commenced my research on this subject in 1987, I assumed that details about the making of this decision would be available. President Roosevelt, after all, had proclaimed his nation's abhorrence of city bombing when the war began, and Secretary Stimson had assured the American people that U.S. bombers were targeting their bombs on strategic targets. It was obvious that a decision to abandon the long-established bombing policy could not have been made without the concurrence of the president and his secretary of war. The blank wall I encountered in my effort to learn the truth about this decision soon told me that the facts I was searching for had been deliberately concealed. Almost against my will, I finally concluded that Roosevelt and Stimson, two of my political heroes, had covered up their participation in this decision. I learned that war leaders who are given complete power to manage war "news" usually try to control how the histories of wars—and their roles in those wars—are written. I learned to be wary of interpretations advanced by historians hired by generals to write official histories in the aftermath of wars. I also learned to be skeptical about self-serving statements in memoirs written by war leaders. And I finally learned that even after pertinent documents have been declassified there are instances when hidden decisions must be deduced from circumstantial evidence.

In my effort to determine who made the decision to adopt terror bombing as the policy for the final phase of the war with Japan, the first source I consulted was the five-volume official history entitled *The Army Air Forces in World War II* (1948), prepared under the editorship of Princeton's Lesley F. Craven and the University of Chicago's James L. Cate. Other than an offhand reference to the "nonchalance with which area bombing was introduced in Japan," Craven and Cate do not pursue this mystery. Similarly, the memoirs and official papers of the bomber chiefs (Generals Arnold, Carl Spaatz, Ira Eaker, Haywood Hansell, and LeMay) who oversaw the execution of the war plans of the USAAF provide few clues.

After discovering that the papers of President Roosevelt, Secretary Stimson, and Stimson's air deputy, Robert Lovett, were not helpful, I turned next to two recent books that are required reading for anyone who wants to understand the moral, military, and political crosscurrents that swirled around the bombing decisions our war leaders made during World War II. Each of these overlapping volumes grew out of years of research in libraries that contain once-classified documents, and each was written by a tough-minded historian who sought to trace the history of American strategic bombing in World War II. The first work is Ronald Schaffer's *Wings of Judgment: American Bombing in World War II* (1985). The second, a more wide-ranging study, is Michael S. Sherry's *The Rise of American Air Power: The Creation of Armageddon* (1987).

Schaffer and Sherry provide the first comprehensive look at the origins of our bombing policy and at the competing claims of morality and military necessity that made decisions about the use of American airpower difficult for some generals and statesmen. Their studies also enlighten us about the dilemma that hovered over the air force and led General Arnold and some of his deputies to engage in shameless exhibitions of playacting and hypocrisy. From the outset of the war, the leaders of the USAAF were driven by irreconcilable aims that added a Jekyll-Hyde overlay to their lives. Arnold was a better publicist than strategist, and one of his consuming concerns was the image of his service. He wanted the American people to perceive the air force as a futuristic, white-hat service that was carrying out its missions with due regard for humanitarian concerns. But this was a mask, and Schaffer and Sherry present, in vivid detail, the beliefs and aims of the Hyde behind the smiling "Jekyll-mask." General Arnold and most of his chiefs were convinced that wars could be won by the sheer destruction of cities, and soon after the attack on Pearl Harbor he initiated work on a plan to end the Pacific war by firebombing the "paper cities" of Japan.

Schaffer and Sherry reconstruct the political, cultural, and military matrices of the war years, tracing the developments that led the United States to cast aside the rules and values that had restrained bombing in Europe, to launch a campaign of terror bombing against Japan, and to use nuclear weapons to destroy two Japanese cities. They outline the influences of racism and a desire for vengeance that made techniques of mass destruction, which were unthinkable in Europe, acceptable in Japan. And they document how General Arnold recruited an elite group of civilians (lawyers, businessmen, educators, and one future justice of the U.S. Supreme Court) who spent over two years formulating a master plan for the incineration of Japan's cities without ever addressing the chilling moral issues that hovered over their work.

Schaffer and Sherry also analyze the ethical predicament that confronted our civilian and military leaders in the aftermath of the history-making cataclysm of death and destruction wreaked on Tokyo on the night of March 9, 1945. This feat of American airpower, they inform us, put our nation's war leaders on tenterhooks. Our civilian leaders could not openly hail this accomplishment, for it constituted a betrayal of President Roosevelt's appeals for the observance of civilized rules of warfare. And General Arnold and his ecstatic chiefs had to momentarily mute their exuberance and present their skillfully executed holocaust to the world as a freakish, wind-whipped continuation of their European precision bombing.

It is almost impossible not to conclude that there was a hidden-hand decision that changed the bombing policy of the United States in the Pacific. Yet the absence of direct evidence of such a covert decision apparently influenced Drs. Sherry and Schaffer to see American airpower policy making more as a bureaucratic process than as a moment of truth when leaders made a far-reaching decision. Dr. Sherry, for example, advances the thesis that our war leaders were in the grip of a mind-set of "technological fanaticism," and that a new policy "came about [in the winter of 1945] through a slow erosion of the distinction between precision and area bombing." He resists "the understandable temptation to simplify the decision-making process" and concludes that there was no "moment of supreme moral choice." In his view, "The sin of atomic bombing, like the sin of the whole war's bombing, certainly resulted from choices but not from a moment of choice. Both were products of a slow accretion of large fears, thoughtless assumptions, and incremental decisions."

Dr. Schaffer also subscribes to a "slow erosion" thesis, and he puts as much, or more, blame on the air chiefs than on Roosevelt and Stimson. Schaffer rejects the idea that there was a "moment of choice" when the bombing policy in the Pacific was altered, because he is convinced that America's precision-bombing policy in Europe was "substantially fictitious and misleading." "There was a policy," he states, "on paper. Sometimes it was adhered to; often it was not, or it was so broadly interpreted as to become meaningless."

Dr. Schaffer's indictment is overdrawn. There were serious lapses in Europe in the final months of the war when the air force ran out of meaningful targets, but I believe an objective study will reveal that over 90 percent of the bombs from our heavy bombers fell on or near the strategic targets at which they were aimed. Some of the attacks on railroad marshaling yards in the winter of 1945 are hard to distinguish from the city-center bombings of Britain's Bomber Command, but the contention that the overall three-year campaign of the USAAF was based on a duplicitous policy will not stand close scrutiny. Even the justly criticized bombing of Berlin that killed 25,000 civilians on February 3, and the Operation Clarion "morale" bombings of small German cities that same month, rebut the charge that the policy itself was meaningless. Generals Jimmy Doolittle and Nathan Twining, the commanders of the Eighth and Fifteenth air forces, which carried out these unusual missions, lodged strenuous objections about the nature of the targets—and the orders to go ahead came not from Washington civilians but from General Eisenhower's headquarters.

My conviction that this fateful decision was made by our civilian war leaders rests on a familiarity with the manner in which executive power is exercised in Washington. There is a grave moment of choice any time a decision about the use of American airpower must be made. The decisions U.S. presidents made in the postwar years underscore this point. President Truman's decision not to use atomic weapons during the Berlin crisis in 1948 or during the Korean War, President Eisenhower's veto of a scheme advanced by Admiral Radford in 1954 to "nuke" the Vietnamese troops that had a French army besieged at Dien Bien Phu, the restraint President Kennedy displayed in his two Cuban crises, and President Johnson's weekly lunches, at which he personally picked the targets for conventional bombing during the Vietnam War, remind us of the gravity with which U.S. presidents discharge their commander-in-chief responsibilities. No modern president demonstrated a greater commitment to civilian control of the armed forces than Franklin D. Roosevelt. All of his aides and all of the generals who served under him were aware of his convictions on this subject, and the high-ranking officials to whom FDR had delegated authority took care not to make decisions that belonged on the desk of their commander-in-chief. This reality is the backdrop against which the role of President Roosevelt—and the involvement of Secretary Stimson and Robert

Lovett—in the mystery decision that changed the nation's long-established bombing policy must be assessed.

History has left Stimson and Lovett in a particularly awkward posture, for they were the supervisors of the day-to-day activities of the air force and had to know about any important changes in the bombing policy. Yet they escaped censure for decades by participating in a know-nothing charade and by taking steps to obliterate all evidence relating to the bombing-policy change in the last months of the war. Stimson went further, and made entries in his diary designed to exculpate him from any responsibility for the incineration of Japan's cities. These cover-ups were successful until it was revealed that the air force's Office of Statistical Control (operated by the famous "whiz kids" who ran the Ford Motor Company after the war) gave the same daily briefings about the Japanese terror bombings to Stimson and Lovett that they gave to General Arnold and his aides.

Today, knowing the truth about American bombing is far more important than any concern for the reputations of the leaders who ran a great war a half-century ago. As a consequence, searchers for that truth must attempt to answer these questions:

- Would not a decision to adopt a different bombing policy for Japan be, ipso facto, a moral and tactical decision that would have to be made by the commander-in-chief? Having destroyed much of the capital city of the enemy through an unprecedented display of airpower, is it rational to believe that General Arnold and his ecstatic deputies would not have shown their cables and photographs to all of the war leaders in Washington?

- Since he followed the firebombing of Japan's cities step by step, is it not absurd to suggest that Air Secretary Robert Lovett did not know about the policy change that opened the door to these bombings?

- And is it not equally absurd *not* to assume that Secretary Stimson knew everything Lovett knew?

HIROSHIMA: HENRY STIMSON DISHONORS HIS IDEALS

With a career of public service spanning four decades, Henry L. Stimson at his death in 1950 was regarded here and abroad as the most impressive American statesman of the twentieth century. His record of service as secretary of war under Presidents Taft and Franklin Roosevelt, and as Herbert Hoover's secretary of state, was considered exemplary. But the laurel that distinguished Stimson from his peers was the honor he conferred on his country by his performance as a self-appointed guardian of America's moral ideals.

Stimson's admirers and biographers all emphasize that probity was the hallmark of his character, and he became the patron saint of the foreign policy establishment because he was an exponent of high-minded internationalism and held a Lincolnlike conviction that the United States had a duty to humanity to exert moral leadership in world affairs.

During the first, long phase of my Hiroshima research, Henry Stimson's omnipresent shadow as an icon of American morality colored my evaluations and led to two glaring misjudgments. I was duped by the boastful "I-was-the-hero-of-Hiroshima" claims advanced by General Leslie Groves in his 1967 book, *Now It Can Be Told*. And, bent on giving Secretary Stimson the benefit of every doubt, I composed a first draft of this chapter in which I concluded that his role as a Hiroshima decision maker was a passive one and that he had allowed the general to aggregate power that enabled him to make commander-in-chief decisions that were not his to make.

Two developments forced me to forswear my pro-Stimson bias and to reorient my research. Critiques by two perceptive historians who perused my manuscript (Stanford's Barton Bernstein and John Dower, the Naiman Professor of History and Japanese Studies at the University of California, San Diego) shredded my thesis and suggested that I study Stimson's war diary and other documents that, they averred, would give me a better understanding of the dynamics of the Hiroshima decision. Stimson's journal not only opened my eyes to new facts, but, more important, encouraged me to study the process by which Presidents Roosevelt and Truman and their war advisors formulated crucial decisions during the final, climactic months of the Second World War.

Henry Stimson's diary is a fascinating, if elliptical, document. For me, every rereading provided fresh insights about the actions and inactions that led to the Hiroshima tragedy. Secretary Stimson craftily concealed more than he revealed about the terror bombing of Japan's cities. Moreover, entries in his journal provide a tortuous map that demonstrates that General Groves was Stimson's faithful aide and that the hand that kept our atomic weapons on a track to Hiroshima and Nagasaki was the hand of Henry L. Stimson.

Available facts do not allow us to fix the precise date when Secretary Stimson decided to act as a de facto commander-in-chief and to execute his plan to use the atomic bombs as a "MasterCard" to end the war. Stimson would have been the last person in Washington to encroach on the prerogatives of a president, so we know with certainty that his "command decision" was made sometime between the death of President Roosevelt on April 12, 1945, and the meeting he had with Harry Truman on April 25 to tell the new president the secrets about the success of the Manhattan Project.

Many entries in his diary help us to understand Stimson's acts and thought processes after Roosevelt's death. With FDR gone and a new president in the White House who knew absolutely nothing about this supersecret project, Stimson's authority as the surviving supervisor was paramount, and he apparently decided it was his duty to make the final decisions about the deployment and use of the new weapon.

The upshot of this fateful decision was an obsession that influenced Secretary Stimson to personalize atomic issues and to dishonor ethical principles he had long championed. Soon thereafter, he made a reference in his diary to "my secret," and it seems clear that, in his mind, the atomic weapons became "my bombs" and the plan to use the two bombs to destroy Japanese cities became the Stimson plan.

By following the steps he took—and by reading between the lines of his diary—one can trace the strategies and stratagems the secretary used to implement his plan:

April 25: The day he briefed President Truman about the astonishing secrets of the Manhattan Project, Henry Stimson did not present a decision document to the new president. Instead, he apparently intimated that since President Roosevelt had approved the operational plan it was not necessary for Truman to decide anything. This maneuver left the war secretary in the driver's seat, for Truman was wisely wary during his first weeks of on-the-job training to alter any of the war plans of his revered predecessor.

May 8: For many statesmen and millions of soldiers, Victory in Europe Day quickened hopes that Japan's leaders would recognize their perilous plight and soon sue for peace. It is peculiar that Henry L. Stimson, then one of the world's most respected diplomats, was in a frame of mind that caused him to oppose any peace negotiations in the aftermath of Germany's surrender.

May 16: By mid-May, the moral incongruities implicit in Stimson's strategy to prolong the war and end it with the explosion of his A-bombs, were compelling him to dissemble and to lace his diary with deceptive accounts of his stewardship. One example involved his former chief, ex-President Herbert Hoover. Instead of carefully analyzing Hoover's challenging let-them-keep-the-emperor peace plan, the secretary dismissed it as "rather dramatic and radical." And although he knew the lurid facts about the firebombing of Japan's biggest cities, on May 16 Stimson informed Truman that he was holding the air force, "so far as possible, to the precision bombing [of Japan] which it has done so well in Europe" because "the reputation of the United States for fair play and humanitarianism is the world's biggest asset for peace in the coming decades."

Late May: In an effort to fend off developments that might have sidetracked his Hiroshima plan, Secretary Stimson spent considerable time putting a damper on advocates of serious peace negotiations. Acting Secretary of State Joseph Grew knew more about the predicament of Japan's war leaders than any official in the government. On May 29, Grew presented the secretary of war with a plan to activate peace negotiations by sending a signal that the United States was willing to consider the retention of the imperial institution as part of a peace settlement. Although Stimson felt that FDR's unconditional-surrender ultimatum should be modified, he brusquely ended their exchange with the comment "The timing is wrong, and this is not the time to do it."

A similar scene took place the same week when Stimson met with George E. Taylor and Clyde Kluckhohn, two high-level officials of the Office of War Information (OWI), to discuss a propaganda campaign prepared by that agency to persuade Japan's leaders to surrender. This plan, prepared by a prestigious team of social scientists, was the outgrowth of an innovative yearlong study of war documents and Japanese culture. The OWI experts' report concluded that the prospect of surrender would be enhanced if the United States made it clear that Japan could retain its imperial institution. When I interviewed Dr. George Taylor forty-five years later, he had a vivid memory of Secretary Stimson's response to the OWI's proposal:

> He more or less suggested that our analysis of Japanese morale was not worth the paper it was written on. Stimson accepted the view that the Japanese would fight to the end. I quote him: "I have seen the island of Kyushu which we are to invade, and it is full of rocks and trees. They will fight behind every rock and tree." We failed to shake him from this stupid non-sequitur.

(When one studies Stimson's conduct in the spring of 1945, the overarching question that recurs again and again is: What influenced this magnanimous man to be so stubborn in his opposition to peace negotiations? The explanation, I am convinced, can be found in his obsession with his secret weapon as a war-ending *deus ex machina*. To understand Stimson's behavior, one must understand that his behavior was guided by the premise that the way to end the war was to "lay the atomic bomb on Japan" and then negotiate.)

June 6: The secretary's diary description of his long conversation with President Truman has an Alice-in-Wonderland overlay that underscores the extent to which self-deception was crowding out reality in Henry Stimson's mind. Japan is prostrate, her major cities and industries have now been gutted by firebombings, and Curtis LeMay, the general in charge of this devastation, is complaining that there is nothing left for his bombers but "garbage can targets." But Stimson, wanting to convince Truman that his bomb would be used on important military targets, substituted fantasies for facts and interspersed his presentation with homilies on American morality. He again reassured his chief that he was holding the air force to the precision bombing of strategic targets, adding that he was "anxious" about this issue because "he did not want the United States to get a reputation for outdoing Hitler in atrocities." This posturing was followed by Stimson's self-contradictory statement that he was "fearful" that before the A-bombs were ready to be delivered, the air force would have Japan so "bombed out" that the new weapon "would not have a fair background to show its strength." Stimson concluded this diary note with the observation that "Truman laughed and said he understood."

June 19: At a luncheon, Henry Stimson's war-cabinet colleagues (Navy Secretary Forrestal and Acting Secretary Grew) argued that the time had come for a peace initiative and a change in the unconditional-surrender policy. However, this discussion reached a dead end when Stimson (who had not shared his secret with them) intimated the president would probably want to wait and take such an initiative after the Potsdam conference in late July.

In large measure due to Henry L. Stimson's covert opposition, the Truman administration made no effort in May or June to explore the possibilities of reaching a surrender agreement with the Japanese. This window of opportunity was slammed shut the first week in July, and the final preparations for the delivery of the A-bombs moved forward when James Byrnes, an unconditional-surrender hard-liner, who became Truman's predominant war advisor, was sworn in as the new secretary of state.

Stimson's final act as the overall commander of the project involved a decision to remove Kyoto from the target list prepared by the military machine. On August 6 and August 9, 1945, atomic bombs were dropped on Hiroshima and Nagasaki by two B-29 crews whose special training Secretary Stimson had approved a year earlier, but the master bombardier who laid the projectiles on these targets was Secretary of War Henry L. Stimson.

In his autobiography written after the war, *On Active Service in Peace and War,* Stimson offered explanations of his atomic-bomb decisions that amounted to a series of non sequiturs.

All his life Stimson had been renowned as a champion of the Rules of War formulated by the world community, but now, in the twilight of an illustrious career, he presided over one of the century's most heinous violations of those rules.

Both as a lawyer and as a moralist Henry Stimson had always viewed the bombing of cities as a crime against humanity, yet in the aftermath of the atomic bombings he dissembled when he informed his countrymen that the Hiroshima bomb was dropped on a "military base" and the Nagasaki bomb was exploded over a "seaport . . . of great wartime importance."

Secretary Stimson was one of the world's most respected diplomats, but even though he knew many Japanese leaders and considered them "susceptible to reason," he stubbornly refused to support efforts of the acting secretary of state to initiate negotiations that might have emboldened Emperor Hirohito to order a surrender in the spring of 1945.

Stimson recognized that it "would substantially add to the chances" that Japan's leaders would surrender if assurances were given that the nation could retain the vestiges of its imperial system, but he opposed making this concession until after the atomic bombs were "laid on" two of Japan's cities.

Although Stimson knew that Japan's warmaking power had been crippled and her access to food and fuel had been severed, he nevertheless argued that the atomic bombs shortened the war by over a year and avoided a million U.S. casualties.

Stimson surely sensed that none of these explanations squared with the moral principles he had long espoused. But although he never pronounced an outright *mea culpa* in his last years, there was both agony and regret in an admission relating to the firebombings which appeared in the third-person autobiography he wrote with his protégé, McGeorge Bundy, in 1947:

> For 30 years Stimson had been a champion of international law and morality. As a soldier and a cabinet member he had repeatedly argued that war itself must be restrained within the bounds of humanity. . . . Now in the conflagration bombings by massed B-29's he was permitting the kind of war he had always hated.

Once I realized that Henry Stimson played *the* crucial role in the decision to incinerate Hiroshima, I saw him as a great public servant who, at the climax of his career, lost his ethical moorings and abandoned the moral convictions that had always guided him in dealing with momentous issues of war and peace. His tragedy was that he became so engrossed in the potential of the secret weapon he supervised that he forgot that forbearance is an indispensable element of civilized life.

Hiroshima will always hover over the legacy of Henry L. Stimson. He may have unwittingly written an apt epitaph for the lives of Japanese citizens snuffed out by "his bombs" when he confided to his diary that the destruction of Dresden was "terrible and probably unnecessary."

THE BOMBS OF AUGUST

Wars without [political] objectives end as senseless slaughters.

—HANSON W. BALDWIN
Military Analyst, New York Times
Great Mistakes of the War *(1950)*

Secretary Stimson's military machinery was on a war track in the month of July, and only two adverse developments could have derailed it: the failure of the midmonth test of the plutonium implosion bomb in the New Mexico desert, or an outbreak of armistice talks with the rulers of Japan. The Trinity explosion on July 16 in the New Mexico desert removed the first roadblock. And the let-negotiations-wait-until-after-the-bombs-are-dropped stance of Secretary Byrnes guaranteed that there would be no peace talks with Japanese leaders before the exterminating power of the new miracle weapon was tested on two ill-fated Japanese cities.

One of the most puzzling and heart-rending lapses of twentieth-century American diplomacy was the failure of our political leaders, in the days after the defeat of Nazi Germany, to define, for Emperor Hirohito and the war leaders of his hopelessly defeated country, the peace terms that would be acceptable to the United States. This was a time for diplomacy, a time to stop the killing, and three days after our victory in Europe, Joseph W. Grew, the acting secretary of state, inaugurated a month-long effort to initiate serious discussions of our political aims and of satisfactory surrender terms. Our last peacetime ambassador to Tokyo, Grew had intimate insights into the power structure of the Japanese state, and he was certain that the way to stop the slaughter and get peace talks started was to offer assurances that the emperor could remain as the symbolic leader of his nation.

His caretaker status at the State Department hampered Joe Grew's efforts, but history tells us that in the aftermath of Germany's surrender, one of the main reasons Grew failed was that Henry Stimson was so obsessed with the atomic bomb that he had little interest in diplomacy. Although he was then the secretary of war, Henry L. Stimson had served earlier as secretary of state and his record as an advocate of international morality would have inevitably turned his mind in the direction of negotiations. But as one of the "fathers" of the atomic bomb, he was entranced by the prospect that its use as a dramatic new force might be the catalyst that would compel the Japanese to surrender.

James F. Byrnes, who was one of President Truman's trusted advisors even before he became secretary of state in July, gave Grew and his concept of a war-ending diplomatic initiative the brush-off for similar reasons. Byrnes, a politician who had had no background in diplomacy, saw the new superweapon as an expression of his country's emerging martial supremacy. He wanted a demonstration of its city-destroying power to put the United States in a position "to dictate our own terms at the end of the war."

Henry Stimson was weary and troubled that summer. He expressed his personal anguish in his diary when he wrote of his fear that the American war machine was running out of control and he and his countrymen appeared to be "outdoing Hitler in atrocities." A recognition that the political leaders of a nation bore the responsibility to define and expound surrender terms caused Henry Stimson, Undersecretary Grew, and Navy Secretary James Forrestal to confer and agree in late June that Roosevelt's unconditional-surrender formula was unrealistic and had to be altered to help Japan's leaders "escape from their desperate dilemma."

This led to a meeting on July 2 at which Stimson attempted to persuade President Truman that the ultimatum being prepared for release at the Postdam conference should indicate that the United States was willing to consider allowing Japan to retain its "constitutional monarchy." But Byrnes, bent on excluding other voices from Truman's innermost circle at Potsdam, felt that Stimson's draft smacked of appeasement, and he kept the Hiroshima express rolling by excluding any language from the July 26 Potsdam declaration that might have encouraged immediate armistice negotiations. Byrnes's bombs-before-diplomacy policy set the stage for the final acts that unleashed the fateful bombs of August. Although Secretary Stimson had emphatically vetoed Kyoto, Japan's cultural capital, as a target in May, General Groves had always considered it the ideal target, and he risked a charge of insubordination when he surreptitiously placed it back on the list while Stimson was at the Potsdam conference. But Stimson was adamant and Kyoto was spared.

General Groves made no bones about his preference for Kyoto. His long work with his scientists had taught him a lot about the value of experiments, and to him Kyoto was ideal because it was a city of the right size, with an urban configuration that would allow him to "gain complete knowledge of the effects of an atomic bomb." As an untouched, living city of over one million human guinea pigs, it was a laboratory where military experts could later gather important data about the "kill radius" and the "arc of destruction" of these new weapons. By not budging—and forcing Groves to bomb much smaller cities—Stimson probably reduced Japan's civilian death list by as many as 200,000 lives. However, Leslie Groves later had the audacity to make the claim in his memoir that he "saved" Kyoto by keeping it on the air force's list of proscribed targets.

With the Kyoto issue resolved, the air force's targeteers substituted the port city of Nagasaki for Kyoto, and the atomic attacks were officially scheduled. The military order to carry out the bombings was then delivered to General Marshall's office for a signature. Marshall cabled his approval from Potsdam, and on July 25 his deputy, General Thomas T. Handy, signed the order authorizing the dropping of the bombs on two of the four cities on the target list "as soon as made ready by the project staff."

Through an egregious omission, the plan embodied in this order left no room for diplomatic action if the first atomic bomb produced immediate truce overtures from the Japanese. Did Secretary Stimson, one wonders, contemplate whether it would violate international standards of morality to drop a second bomb (and snuff out the lives of tens of thousands of additional civilians) without giving the leaders of Japan a decent interval to react to the news of the first bomb?

But alas, the action plan developed by Stimson and Groves was grounded in a concept that the enemy would have to know that the United States had "more than one" bomb before it would capitulate. This stark and somber sequence of events then followed, generating a fateful tragedy for Japan and the United States:

July 26: Ultimatum to Japan demands unconditional surrender.

August 2: Potsdam conference ends; President Truman heads homeward on the cruiser *Augusta*.

August 6: The first atomic bomb is dropped on Hiroshima, a city located 500 miles from Tokyo; U.S. announcement describes the new weapon; Japan sends soldiers to determine damage done to Hiroshima.

August 7: With communications cut, no report on Hiroshima.

August 8: News of Hiroshima holocaust arrives in Tokyo; Emperor Hirohito instructs his prime minister to "make every effort to end hostilities at once"; in Moscow, Japan's ambassador is advised that the Soviet Union will declare war on Japan on August 9.

August 9: The Japanese war cabinet (the Big Six) holds inconclusive conferences in response to a second request by the emperor to "end the war at once"; second atomic bomb is dropped on Nagasaki while these deliberations are under way; the Big Six are deadlocked, leaders ask the emperor to call an imperial conference to resolve the peace issue.

August 10: Emperor convenes meeting at 2:30 A.M., decides to accept the Potsdam ultimatum with the proviso that the imperial house be maintained; Japan's acceptance is delivered to U.S. officials.

August 11: Secretary of State Byrnes responds ambiguously by neither accepting nor rejecting the Japanese proviso.

August 12–13: Plots and maneuvers in Tokyo by Big Six hawks and doves.

August 14: Emperor convenes another imperial conference and reads statement accepting the U.S. response; Washington advised of emperor's acceptance.

August 15: Emperor Hirohito reads his surrender message to the Japanese people on the radio. War officially ends when President Truman accepts Japan's unconditional surrender.

5

Hiroshima in Retrospect:
The Questions That Linger

For nearly a half-century, few Americans have viewed Hiroshima as a moral issue. Long wars end with a great sigh of relief, and my generation saw no reason to question President Truman's war-end pronouncement that the use of atomic bombs to decimate two Japanese cities served a humanitarian purpose by shortening the war and saving the lives of "a half-million boys on our side."

Yet later generations cannot come to grips with the moral issues that hover over the American tragedy of Hiroshima—or understand how our nation lost its moral compass in the final phase of the war—unless they are willing to confront the myths that have distorted our nation's view of that fateful landscape of history.

American thinking about the end of the Second World War and the role of nuclear weapons in that ordeal has been colored by two myths that became embedded in our folklore. One myth states that the atomic bomb was decisive in winning that war. A second myth holds that if Hitler had acquired this weapon first he would have used it to conquer the world.

DID THE ATOMIC BOMBS SHORTEN OR
LENGTHEN THE WAR?

Americans have long felt comfortable with President Truman's oft-repeated avowal that the atomic explosions in Japan were justified because they shortened the war and saved the lives of "a half-million boys on our side." The long view provided by history not only undermines the factual foundations of this contention, but offers powerful evidence that the existence of the bombs may have prolonged the war by influencing Secretary Stimson and President Truman to ignore an opportunity to negotiate a surrender that would have ended the killing in the Pacific in May or June.

By May 10, the stage had been set for serious surrender negotiations. Germany's defeat, the crushing impact of America's military actions against Japan's home islands, and the prospect that Stalin would soon enter the Pacific war and unleash the victorious armies of the Soviet Union against Japanese forces on the Asian mainland sounded the death knell for Japan's military ambitions. By any logic of war, Japan was a defeated nation: her German ally had fallen; nearly all of the capital ships of her once-proud navy lay at the bottom of the Pacific Ocean; U.S. bombers had devastated all of her great industrial centers; and the American navy had severed the island empire's lifeline to the oil and other resources it needed to wage war. U.S. war leaders knew these facts, and more. Recently declassified documents reveal that in the first days of May Secretary Stimson and his staff had access to information that many high-ranking Japanese war leaders were willing to surrender. This information was supplied by codebreakers who were recording messages transmitted by Axis ambassadors stationed in Tokyo. Using "Magic Intercepts," these agents decoded the following cable sent to Berlin three days before Germany surrendered:

> Since the situation is clearly recognized to be hopeless, large sections of the Japanese armed forces would not regard with disfavor an American request for capitulation even if the terms were hard.

This intelligence confirmed earlier signs that Japan wanted to end the war. The Japanese war cabinet had been forced to resign in

April, and Kantaro Suzuki, a frail, aged admiral who had served previously as the grand chamberlain to the emperor, became prime minister. Suzuki was a navy man who knew the war was lost, and peace feelers soon began emanating from his government.

No one in Washington was better prepared to assess Japan's predicament than Joseph Grew, the acting secretary of state. Having served as America's ambassador to Japan for nearly a decade before Pearl Harbor, Grew knew Suzuki and had every reason to believe that he had the ear of the emperor and that he distrusted the hardliners who wanted to continue the war. Moreover, Secretary Grew's insight into Japanese culture told him that a promise that Japan could retain the emperor and maintain its established constitutional structure would provide a framework that would give negotiators an opportunity to formulate surrender terms that would end the war.

Grew first outlined his formula at a private conference with President Truman on May 28. The president responded by suggesting that Grew explore the subject with his Big Three cabinet colleagues, Stimson and Navy Secretary James Forrestal. These men agreed that the unconditional-surrender doctrine should be modified, but Stimson (who had kept Grew in the dark about the bomb) opposed any immediate action. Forrestal renewed the discussion of this issue at a subsequent meeting of the Big Three when he asserted that he considered it "one of the most important questions confronting the nation." Grew, encouraged, advised his associates that his department was working on a definition of war aims that would afford the Japanese "an escape from the desperate dilemma."

Ambassador Grew then submitted a proposed statement by the president that would have altered the nation's demand for unconditional surrender. This document offered two concessions to Japan: it affirmed that once Japan was demilitarized, the Japanese people would be permitted to determine for themselves the nature of their future political structure; and it offered assurances that Japan would be allowed to develop a peacetime economy and work its way "back into the family of nations." When Grew and Truman met on June 18 to discuss this proposal, the president (having already informally delegated power on diplomatic issues to Secretary-designate James Byrnes) told Grew that he liked the idea but had decided to reserve judgment until after his summit meeting with Stalin and Churchill in late July.

Joseph Grew was unable, in his final days as acting secretary of state, to sway Truman or Byrnes or Stimson, but there were signs that war-weary Americans would have supported the kind of peace negotiations he was proposing. Public opinion polls in May found that most Americans preferred to "take time and save lives" rather than to "end the war quickly despite casualties." President Truman might have garnered unexpected support from many quarters if he had encouraged a neutral nation like Sweden or Switzerland to discuss surrender terms with Japanese diplomats.

One eminent American who was ready to endorse Grew's plan was Herbert Hoover, then the only living ex-president. Hoover was the world's leading expert on the problems of war relief and postwar reconstruction, and in May, President Truman, who had a high regard for Hoover, sought his counsel about these emerging issues. This was Herbert Hoover's first visit to the White House in twelve years, and he relished the opportunity to confer with the new president. As their meeting ended, Hoover impulsively raised the subject of Japan and urged Harry Truman to make a shortwave radio broadcast to the people of Japan and "Tell them they can have their emperor if they surrender, that it will not mean unconditional surrender except for the militarists." The ex-president proffered his advice in a bipartisan spirit: "You'll get a peace in Japan," he told Truman, "you'll have both wars over."

The same week in May, President Truman also received some Machiavellian advice from Joseph Stalin that, had he been open-minded, might have encouraged him to let Ambassador Grew explore surrender terms through diplomatic channels. The Soviet Union was not at war with Japan, but Truman had sent Harry Hopkins to Moscow as his special envoy to explore the postwar issues on the agenda at the upcoming Potsdam conference. Stalin and Hopkins had developed mutual trust during the war years, and blunt talk usually characterized their conversations. Harry Hopkins reported to Truman that when the subject of Japan arose, the Soviet leader suggested that the United States might want "to agree to milder peace terms but once we get into Japan to give them the works."

But an obsession with the atomic bomb as a *deus ex machina* that would end the war had apparently caused Stimson's mind to snap shut, and neither Grew nor Hoover could pry it open. In early July, Stimson made a halfhearted effort to persuade Truman to modify the terms of surrender in the ultimatum that was scheduled to be issued at the conclusion of the Potsdam conference, but James F. Byrnes quietly smothered this initiative. Byrnes, now fully empowered as secretary of state, was calling the shots for Truman and regarded any concession to Japan as "appeasement." It was President Truman's acquiescence in this hard-line approach that barred the door to surrender talks that summer and kept Secretary Stimson's atomic operation on its track to Hiroshima.

Like all historical questions involving roads not taken, there is no way to know whether a well-orchestrated peace effort in June—involving perhaps a bombing pause and a standstill cease-fire on Okinawa—might have shortened the war and saved hundreds of thousands of American and Japanese lives. We do know that our experts on Japanese politics (including General Douglas MacArthur) believed that Emperor Hirohito was the one person who could intervene and bring about a surrender. And we know, too, that Hirohito was involved in an effort that began in June to get the Soviet Union to mediate surrender terms. U.S. leaders in Washington had a clear picture of the mood that guided these efforts, for its code-breakers had intercepted this message cabled by Foreign Minister Togo on July 17 to his ambassador in Moscow: "If only the United States and Great Britain would recognize Japan's honor and existence we would terminate the war."

Would the emperor have exerted decisive leadership if the United States had indicated in June or July that it might modify its unconditional-surrender formula? This is one of the nagging Hiroshima questions that will not go away. The American moral philosopher Michael Walzer capsulized the lingering agony attached to this inquiry in his book *Just and Unjust Wars*.

> In the summer of 1945, the victorious Americans owed the Japanese people an experiment in negotiation. To use the atomic bomb, to kill and terrorize civilians, without attempting such an experiment, was a double crime.

Did America's war leaders take the rational course or did they make a historic blunder? Did the atomic bomb shorten or prolong the war? The shadow cast by these profound questions is part of the American tragedy of Hiroshima, for the history of this epoch tells us unerringly that our civilian policy makers were so close-minded, so intent on experimenting with atomic power as a decisive weapon of war, that they were unwilling to give diplomacy a chance to end the war on a note of magnanimity.

It is interesting to speculate what might have happened if, during the month of May, Henry Stimson had been true to himself and made a vigorous, statesmanlike effort to persuade President Truman to pursue a peace settlement. Stimson had the stature and moral authority to persuade his inexperienced chief on this issue. When Cordell Hull resigned as secretary of state the previous December, Harry Hopkins told Stimson that he had to stay on because he was "the only man of commanding stature in the cabinet."

Secretary Stimson was not only the towering figure in the cabinet Truman had inherited from Franklin Roosevelt, but as a former secretary of state he had dealt with Japanese leaders and had a realistic, judicious understanding of their culture. As he demonstrated in a memo he submitted that summer to Truman, Stimson was not infected with the racism that permeated the thinking of many U.S. war leaders. He said Japan was "not a nation of fanatics," made a favorable reference to her "liberal leaders," and asserted that these leaders would "be more susceptible to reason than most assume."

Had he been inclined to lead a serious effort to explore the potential of peace negotiations in May or June, it is clear that Secretary Stimson would have had the strong support of Joseph Grew and Navy Secretary Forrestal, his war cabinet colleagues. Also, to lend a bipartisan aura to such an effort, Stimson could have enlisted the support of Herbert Hoover. And, had Henry Stimson put his prestige on the line and sought to muster their support, it is also likely that the key military leaders—General Marshall, Admiral Leahy, and the field commanders in the Pacific, General MacArthur and Admiral Nimitz—would have backed his initiative.

It is part of the American tragedy of Hiroshima that when the opportunity to explore chances for a negotiated peace appeared after V-E Day, Henry L. Stimson, the one leader who probably could have persuaded President Truman to try this alternative, rejected the mantle of leadership because his mind was locked into a strategy of delaying negotiations until after his bombs had delivered a "spectacular shock" to Japan's leaders.

MIGHT A DEMONSTRATION BLAST HAVE DELIVERED AN ATOMIC SHOCK WITHOUT SACRIFICING THE LIVES OF TENS OF THOUSANDS OF CIVILIANS?

One of the myths that, like a barnacle, has attached itself to the saga of Hiroshima is that some of the atomic scientists were afforded an opportunity to propose a nonmilitary demonstration but were unable to devise such an option. This is not a valid interpretation of what happened. The atomic scientists were never given sufficient facts— or sufficient time—to explore alternatives to Secretary Stimson's plan to use the atomic bomb to incinerate two cities and send a psychological shock to end the war.

By the end of April, Stimson's plan had matured into a churning piece of military machinery under his personal command, and all the secretary needed to put the finishing touches on his scheme was to ask air force experts to select the logical targets. But a nonlethal demonstration was never seriously studied, because Stimson's single-minded scheme contemplated the use of the first bombs to destroy two cities. This in turn explains why the subject of demonstrations was not an item on the agenda of the Interim Committee appointed by Secretary Stimson.

The creation of an "interim" committee to study the portentous future impacts of atomic weapons and nuclear science on international affairs—and to begin the work of preparing recommendations to Congress about the postwar development and control of nuclear weapons and atomic energy—had been proposed in September 1944 by President Roosevelt's science advisor, Dr. Vannevar Bush. When Stimson belatedly convened such a committee in early May, President Truman endorsed his suggestion that James F. Byrnes serve as the president's personal representative on this committee. The members selected by Stimson were Navy Undersecretary Ralph Bard, Assistant Secretary of State Will Clayton, and the three scientists, Dr.

Bush, James B. Conant, and Karl T. Compton, who had helped Secretary Stimson make his decisions about the Manhattan Project. Secretary Stimson also created two panels of experts to give technical advice to the Interim Committee: a four-man panel of industrialists representing the companies that had built the great atomic factories, and a panel of four front-line Manhattan Project scientists, Robert Oppenheimer, Enrico Fermi, Arthur H. Compton, and Ernest O. Lawrence.

Accounts of a luncheon hosted by Stimson at the Pentagon on May 31 for these scientists and the members of the Interim Committee indicate that both Lawrence and Arthur Compton, at separate tables, spontaneously put forward the idea of conducting a "striking but harmless" demonstration before the bomb was used "in a manner that would not cause great loss of life." The official account of this meeting informs us that the demonstration concept was discussed in the general session "for perhaps ten minutes" only and was inundated by objections. General Groves was present to explain and defend the Stimson plan, and Arthur Compton later recalled in his memoir that a military operation was already under way, and that "throughout the morning's discussions it seemed a foregone conclusion that the bomb would be used."

Stimson later informally requested that the scientific panel submit reports on postwar issues they deemed significant and prepare a memorandum regarding possible demonstrations. When the four scientists conferred two weeks later in Los Alamos, their discussion of possible demonstrations was carried out in a factual vacuum. As Oppenheimer testified later, he and his colleagues "didn't know beans about the military situation in Japan," and indicated that their conversation took place within the framework of the daunting assumption that the execution of Secretary Stimson's bombing plan might save as many as a million American casualties. This straitjacket deprived them of the opportunity to evaluate other options and forced them to conclude their written report by observing that they were unable to propose a technical demonstration likely to end the war and therefore "saw no acceptable alternative to direct military use." These words became the gossamer enveloping one of the enduring and outlandish myths of the atomic age—the thesis that the leaders of the atomic scientists "recommended" the bombings of Hiroshima and Nagasaki.

There is no evidence that Secretary Stimson gave serious thought to a demonstration or wanted other officials to second-guess his assumption that the destruction of two Japanese cities would end the war. General Groves later explained that, for him, the "governing factor" was to choose targets that "would most adversely affect the will of the Japanese people to continue the war." Stimson said the same thing with different words: "We should seek to make a profound psychological impression on as many of the Japanese as possible."

Did such a strategy make sense when Japan, like Adolf Hitler's Germany, was ruled by an authoritarian government that was not responsive to the will of the people? Henry L. Stimson surely knew in May of 1945 that the rulers of Japan were in Tokyo—and that any offer of surrender had to originate with the emperor and his six-man war cabinet. If the United States wanted to deliver a profound shock that would make an immediate impact on the thinking of Japan's decision makers, wasn't it obvious that the first atomic bomb should be detonated where most of these leaders would be eyewitnesses? And wouldn't such an imperative dictate that the first bomb be dropped from a higher altitude than the Hiroshima bomb above the center of the fifty-six-square-mile area of rubble created by the firebombings of General LeMay's B-29's?

It is beyond argument that a night bomb on the rubble of Tokyo would have had a dramatic impact on Japan's war leaders, and, more important, would have probably galvanized action by an emperor who was desperately searching for a way to achieve a surrender. Such a bombing mission could have been executed with the same precision that was used at Hiroshima, for General LeMay had marker squadrons on Tinian that could have illuminated the midpoint of the rubble for the bombardier on the B-29 carrying the first atomic weapon.

The essence of the American tragedy of Hiroshima is that our civilian leaders did not perceive in the summer of 1945 that there was a better way for the United States of America to unveil one of the century's great scientific achievements. It was the obsessive power of

Stimson's end-the-war-plan that prevented the president's advisors from recognizing that the wise and humane course was not to use the atomic bombs to destroy two cities, but to give a peace-promoting demonstration that would at once hasten the termination of a brutal war and warn humankind of the power and the peril that accompanied this breakthrough of science. There was a better, more American, way to conclude a great war. Had not Abraham Lincoln taught his countrymen that a bloody, prolonged conflict should be ended on a note of magnanimity?

In detonating the first atomic bombs, America was sending a message to the world, not just to the leaders of a defeated adversary. A Tokyo demonstration could have been accompanied with a statement that would have been a challenge to the globe's statesmen. Our leaders might have said: "The new weapon we have demonstrated today in Tokyo was developed by an international team of scientists. It can wipe out whole cities, but our respect for the humanity of others has caused us to demonstrate its power before we use it as a military weapon. We will give the leaders of Japan ten days to sue for peace, and we will not use this bomb again if a surrender can be arranged."

By using atomic weapons to destroy cities, our leaders made two tragic miscalculations. They ignored the world community, and they failed to send a clear signal to those in Tokyo who were desperately trying to develop a surrender strategy. Hiroshima was five hundred miles from Japan's capital city, and it took two full days for Japanese military investigators to confirm the extent of the holocaust caused by the first atomic bomb. And on the third day, with insufficient time in Tokyo for assessment, decision, and a reply to Washington, the second atomic bomb exploded over Nagasaki.

This delay casts a macabre shadow over the claim of Stimson and President Truman that their A-bombs "ended" the war. By the time the emperor's advisors verified the scope of what had happened in Hiroshima, and Hirohito took action to convene a meeting of the Supreme Council to discuss surrender terms at 2 A.M. on August 9, the Soviet Union had altered the calculus of the decision-making process by declaring war on Japan.

Steps approved by Hirohito in the weeks before Hiroshima inform us that the emperor was awaiting a development that would put him in a position where he could assert his imperial prerogative and order surrender negotiations. But the quick cascade of events has made it impossible for students of history to ascertain whether it was the atomic bomb, or the Soviet declaration of war—or other considerations uppermost in Emperor Hirohito's mind—that motivated the unprecedented action he took to order a surrender in the early-morning hours of the ninth of August.

DID ATTITUDES OF RACISM AND VENGEANCE INFLUENCE DECISIONS?

> . . . stereotyped and often blatantly racist thinking contributed to poor military intelligence and planning, atrocious behavior, and the adoption of exterminationist policies.
> —JOHN W. DOWER (1986)
> War without Mercy: Race and
> Power in the Pacific War

The merciless conclusion of the war against Japan—and the relentless refusal of Stimson, Byrnes, and Groves to weigh cherished American moral values in their deliberations about the use of our atomic weapons—has puzzled sensitive men and women of the post-war generations. Present-day Americans who respect Japanese culture and view Japan as a peaceful nation have wondered, for example, why Stimson and Byrnes were so cavalier in rejecting suggestions that a well-conceived demonstration might be more effective than the destruction of a city? And why, they ask, did the nation's policy makers mindlessly order the dropping of the second bomb on the first day the weather allowed visual targeting?

There is cogent evidence that some of our leaders behaved atrociously because they were influenced by racial hatred whipped up by war propaganda, and that others were motivated by a desire for revenge that crested in the final savage months of the war against Japan. There are several ways to assess the influence these biases had on the thinking of President Truman and his associates. The intensity of anti-Japanese attitudes can be gauged, for example, by comparing the only-bomb-strategic-targets policy the United

States usually followed in Germany with the single-minded city-incineration plan pursued as soon as Japan's home islands came within the range of U.S. bombers.

That policy change had a cataclysmic impact on the civilian population of Japan, for U.S. bombers killed four or five times as many noncombatants in the final five months of the Pacific war as were killed in three years of Allied bombing in Europe. Perhaps it was his awareness of this startling contrast that influenced Secretary Stimson to make an entry in his diary in early June that the United States was now "outdoing Hitler" in atrocities.

The sources and reach of America's wartime racism—and an evenhanded analysis of the racist ideas and attitudes that were contemporaneously inculcated in her citizenry by Japan's rulers—was summarized in an unsparing 1986 book, *War without Mercy,* by a California historian, John W. Dower. Professor Dower traces the stream of racism that added an extra dimension of death and destruction to the war in the Pacific and culminated in what he describes as the "exterminationist policies" adopted by both antagonists.

Dower's analysis reveals that concepts of genocide were being openly expressed in 1945, not just by embattled soldiers in the Pacific, but by prominent Americans. President Roosevelt's son Elliott privately told Henry Wallace that the United States should continue bombing Japan "until we have destroyed about half of the civilian population." And the chairman of the War Manpower Commission, Paul V. McNutt, declared in a public address that he "favored the extermination of the Japanese *in toto.*"

Dower's work is a powerful warning for humankind. It helps us understand how racism can generate emotions and attitudes that warp the judgment of leaders and cause a nation's ethical values to become deranged. He shows us, too, how animosity for an allegedly subhuman enemy can lead an otherwise civilized people to decide that mercy is unjustified and that the extermination of any enemy is an acceptable war aim. Dower believes that racism combined with wartime fervor can foster impulses that allow a civilized nation to contemplate the destruction of whole cities as a legitimate goal of warfare.

Evidence that racism or a desire for revenge motivated some of our leaders is exhibited by spontaneous public and private statements made by prominent Americans after Hiroshima. General Marshall was in a somber mood when Leslie Groves brought the initial bombing report to his office, and Groves remembered later that Marshall

> ... expressed his feeling that we should guard against too much gratification because it undoubtedly involved a large number of Japanese casualties. I replied that I was not thinking so much of those casualties as I was about the men who had made the Bataan death march.

This was a typical military reaction, but President Truman's statements will always be interpreted as the official American reaction to the Hiroshima tragedy. Truman exhibited no restraint whatsoever, and the manner in which he displayed his joy on the cruiser *Augusta* brought this rebuke from Robert Donovan, an otherwise admiring biographer:

> When a captain handed him the message about Hiroshima, Truman ... exclaimed, "This is the greatest thing in history." It was the most ominous day in history. While sailors cheered ... mindlessly, he said he had never been happier about any announcement he had ever made.

One truth about the "greatest thing in history" the president did not mention was that the new bombs were incredibly efficient cremation machines. Each atomic bomb vaporized the bodies of tens of thousands of human beings in a split second.

Apparently racism and revenge were intertwined in Harry Truman's mind. At Potsdam, ten days before Hiroshima, he recorded in his diary that the bomb had to be used because the Japanese were "savages, ruthless, merciless, and fanatic." And in a subsequent radio address to the nation, he used retribution as the main theme of his report to the American people: "Having found the bomb we have used it. We have used it against those who attacked us without warning at Pearl Harbor, against those who have starved and beaten and executed American prisoners of war, against those who have abandoned all pretense of obeying international laws of warfare."

What President Truman failed to acknowledge was that those it had been used against were, overwhelmingly, ordinary men, women, and children who were living far from the seats of Japanese power.

PRESIDENT TRUMAN'S TORTUOUS RIDE

> I wanted to save a half million boys on our side. . . . I never
> lost any sleep over my decision.
>
> —HARRY S TRUMAN (1959)

There is a logical political explanation of Harry S Truman's tortuous atomic ride during the first four months of his presidency. He was never in a position to be decisive about atomic issues because Franklin Roosevelt did absolutely nothing to help him prepare to be president.

President Roosevelt knew in the winter of 1945 that his executive energy was waning and his grip on life was slipping. It would have been logical for him to lay out a sensible training program for his new vice-president. He could have enhanced Harry Truman's experience and stature by inviting him to participate in the summit conference at Yalta with Churchill and Stalin. He could have directed that he preside jointly with Admiral William D. Leahy over the regular meetings of the army and navy chiefs of staff. Or FDR could have delegated responsibility to Truman to oversee the progress of the Manhattan Project, as he did with Vice-President Henry Wallace in 1943.

But Franklin Roosevelt had a bad habit of compartmentalizing military and political decision making, and apparently he was too self-absorbed to realize that it would be wise to provide on-the-job training for the modest man from Missouri who might suddenly assume his responsibilities.

Thus it was inevitable that Harry S Truman would have overwhelming feelings of inadequacy when FDR died and he found himself one April morning pitchforked onto the world stage, working alongside the generals and civilian cabinet officers (all hand-picked by his departed commander-in-chief) who were guiding a global war machine surging toward long-awaited victories in Europe and the Pacific. Later, when experience had heightened his self-confidence, Truman would become one of the decisive presidents of this century, but when Secretary Stimson gave him his first detailed briefing about the existence of the atomic bomb, he could see that the new president was laboring under a "terrific handicap."

It took months to overcome this handicap, and in the beginning Truman relied on his down-to-earth, Missouri pragmatism to deal with the issues that came to his desk. His political instincts told him the best way to deal with the climactic events that were crashing around him was to be a good listener, to go with the flow of events, and not to question the decisions President Roosevelt and his team of war leaders had made.

It was this passive approach, and his insecurity in the presence of men like Secretary Stimson, General Marshall, and Jimmy Byrnes, that caused him to be passive all summer and not interfere in any way with Stimson's plan to level two Japanese cities in order "to end the war." This was a shrewd strategy on Truman's part. If the plan misfired, or the atom bomb was a dud, the Congress and the American people would not blame the new president.

What is bewildering about President Truman's strident, I-made-the-decision claims in the aftermath of Hiroshima is the absence of any hard evidence that he made any real-world judgments about the atomic attacks prior to August 6, 1945. Truman insisted until the day of his death that he personally made the decision to drop the atomic bombs, but he gave so many conflicting accounts about when and where and how he "made" it that dispassionate historians now treat his assertions with skepticism.

It is indisputable that Truman had the power to stop or to alter General Groves's original plan. It is also irrefutable that no decision document has been found attesting that President Truman ordered the dropping of the atomic bombs. Indeed, the memoirs of the participants support a conclusion that the president and his advisors had discussions at the late July Potsdam conference and simply decided, in the words of one historian, to allow "the machinery already in motion to continue in the direction and on the schedule that had been set long before."

But this was a moment of high drama, and although Truman knew that he had rubber-stamped the most historic decision of the war, it is apparent that he was tempted to stretch the truth and claim it as his own. After all, he was the president, all of the pertinent records were labeled "top secret," and he realized no one would have the effrontery to challenge his account while he was alive.

Over the years, Harry Truman undermined his pretense by

relating four different versions about where and when he personally made the decision to drop the bombs on Hiroshima and Nagasaki. He wrote that it took place on July 21 during a meeting of his advisors at the Potsdam conference. In the memoir of his presidency he composed in 1955, he fixed the date as on or just after July 25. He once recalled that he made the decision after the Potsdam ultimatum to Japan on July 28. Then, during his last week in the White House he sent a letter to Professor James Cate, one of the air force's official historians, which contained this categorical assertion:

> I asked Secretary Stimson which cities in Japan were devoted exclusively to war production. He promptly named Hiroshima and Nagasaki among others. . . . I ordered atomic bombs dropped on the two cities named on the way back from Potsdam when we were in the middle of the Atlantic Ocean.

President Truman sailed from England on the cruiser *Augusta* on the morning of August 2, 1945, exactly one week after the written military directive that flashed a green light for the actual military operation was signed in Washington by Marshall's deputy, General Thomas T. Handy.

The order Handy signed was the original directive Stimson and Groves had prepared in May and revised on July 23 to add Nagasaki to the list of approved targets. Dated July 25, it was addressed to General Carl Spaatz as "Commanding General, United States Air Force." It read:

1. the 500th Composite group, Twentieth Air Force, will deliver its first special bomb as soon as weather will permit visual bombing after about 3 August 1945, on one of the targets: Hiroshima, Kokura, Niigata, and Nagasaki. . . .

2. Additional bombs will be delivered on the above targets as soon as made ready by the project staff. Further instructions will be issued concerning targets other than those listed above. . . .

. . . .

4. The foregoing directive is issued to you by direction and with the approval of the Secretary of War and the Chief of Staff. . . .

The hyperbole he used in dealing with other aspects of the Hiroshima holocaust cast additional shadows on President Truman's credibility on this issue. Once he decided to shoulder the responsibility for crushing the two cities, Truman sought to justify the carnage by emphasizing that he decided to drop the bombs for a patriotic reason. He wanted, in short, to save the lives of the U.S. soldiers who would have died in the planned invasion of Japan's home islands. This explanation is an integral part of the popular myth that the atomic bombs saved a half-million American lives.

The diligent digging of Stanford historian Barton Bernstein has made him the authority on the shifting numbers that Truman and others used to justify the atomic bombings. Professor Bernstein informs us that while Harry Truman was president he usually placed the number of lives he had saved at about a quarter of a million, but that in his postpresidential years he began increasing the number to a half-million "except on those rare occasions when he doubled it to a million."

This episode illustrates how an oft-repeated myth can be transformed into a historical fact. The simplicity and patriotic power of President Truman's myth has distracted attention from military realities that undermine the assumptions he used to support his thesis that he saved hundreds of thousands of lives. The most realistic pre-Hiroshima estimates of the military planners who were assessing probable invasion casualties ranged from 20,000 to 46,000. Truman's myth is undercut further by the circumstance that even before the atomic bombs were dropped, the two on-the-ground field commanders in the Pacific, Generals Douglas MacArthur and Curtis LeMay, were confident no invasion would be necessary. Two weeks before Hiroshima, MacArthur told Air Force General George C. Kenney that he was convinced the Japanese would surrender "by September 1 at the latest and perhaps sooner." It is amazing that the opinions of the men who were running the war in the Pacific were not solicited by Washington's decision makers in the summer of 1945.

President Truman again undermined his credibility when he asserted that the atomic bomb was "just another weapon"—and by erroneously reiterating that Hiroshima was targeted because it was a "military base" (a myth enshrined as a fact in the *Encyclopaedia Britannica* to this day) and a city "devoted almost exclusively to war production." Yet by July the navy's blockade and LeMay's successful incineration attacks on the nation's industrial centers had so impaired Japan's war production that U.S. analysts knew that the bombing of Hiroshima had little military meaning. This was the paramount fact of the Pacific war that summer, and both sides were living with this truth. Indeed, a delegation of Japanese industrialists had informed their top military officials in May that "our production was finished. It could produce war materials for only a few days more . . . But worst of all, we had no raw materials."

Apparently the use of the atomic bomb never troubled President Truman's conscience. When asked in 1958 if his approval had come after considerable soul-searching, he snapped his fingers and said, "Hell, no, I made it like that." And he characterized the bomb itself as "nothing else but an artillery weapon."

Many world citizens felt otherwise, and their views found expression in the dissenting opinion filed by one of the judges who served on the Tokyo War Crimes Court at the trial of some of Japan's war leaders. Justice Radhabinad Pal of India declared: "If any indiscriminate destruction of civilian life and property is still illegitimate in warfare, then, in the Pacific War, the decision to use the atomic bomb is the only near approach to the directives of the German Emperor during the first World War and of the Nazi leaders during the Second World War. Nothing like this could be traced to the credit of the present accused."

An irony that has long hovered over Harry Truman and Hiroshima is the circumstance that he assumed the glory, and the blame, for a decision he passively ratified. On paper, he had the power to stop, or alter, the use of the atomic bombs. But in the summer of 1945 he did not have a firm grip on the reins of that power. One historian, Michael Sherry, has astutely adjudged that even if Truman had had ideas of his own, it would have required "exceptional intellectual and political courage" for him to have stopped Stimson's plan to use the bombs.

THE ROOSEVELT CONUNDRUM

Had he lived, would President Roosevelt have dispatched the bombers to Hiroshima and Nagasaki? Any search for a definitive answer to this question leads to a blank wall, but things we know about FDR's outlook and about the secretive, guarded approach he used to exercise his presidential prerogatives raise some tantalizing questions.

During their Hyde Park conference in September 1944, Roosevelt and Churchill agreed that "when a bomb is finally available, it might perhaps, after mature consideration, be used against the Japanese...." Four days later, FDR and his science advisor, Dr. Vannevar Bush, discussed whether, if an atomic weapon was produced, it should be used against the Japanese or tested and held as a threat. Bush recorded that their conclusion was that any decision could be "postponed for quite a time." This postponement continued until Roosevelt's death, so the best evidence we have about his attitude is that he felt that if a usable bomb became available, alternatives should be given "mature consideration."

One of President Roosevelt's shortcomings as an administrator was his habit of holding important policy issues so close to his vest that he often failed to ask high-level advisors to develop options. The atomic bomb is a case in point. When Secretary Stimson informed him at the end of December that the bomb would probably be ready in August, it was a signal that the time had come to widen the circle of secrecy and authorize a small coterie of trusted advisors to develop policy choices for the president.

Franklin Roosevelt's failure to take such action probably set the stage for the Hiroshima tragedy. It is hard to fathom why, soon after his January inaugural, FDR did not act on this front. Bedridden much of the time, he was aware that his vitality was ebbing and surely had intimations that his days might be numbered.

It is part of wisdom for any busy official whose health is failing to delegate authority and turn to trusted friends for help. Some of the decisions that loomed ahead were momentous. FDR needed help to assess how he wanted the war to end and to determine what kind of peace with Japan would serve the vital interests of the United States.

The logical leader to provide the kind of analysis that was needed was the newly elected vice-president, and it is a measure of

Franklin Roosevelt's self-centeredness that he apparently never considered asking Harry Truman to serve him in such a capacity. It would have been immensely valuable for the nation if Truman had known about the bomb and had been invited to help assess whether—and how—the unconditional-surrender formula should be altered, and to explore with Roosevelt's top advisors the prospect of a quick negotiated peace with Japan once Germany was defeated.

One of the sad legacies of Franklin Roosevelt's shortsightedness was that when Truman became president the only atomic bomb option presented to him, in haste, was a military option.

THE INTERIM COMMITTEE: A BLACK COMEDY?

> The whole thing was engineered by Stimson and Groves . . .
> For quite a while I couldn't tell what the hell was going on.
> —RALPH BARD
> *Navy Undersecretary*

The sessions on May 31 and June 1, 1945, where the now-famous Interim Committee (IC) supposedly made crucial "decisions" about the wartime use of the atomic bomb surely qualify as a black comedy of the atomic age. This committee was convened by Secretary Stimson to "make recommendations on temporary controls, to approve the public announcements that would be made when the first bomb was exploded, and to ponder future legislation and the postwar organization of atomic affairs." He termed it "interim" because he knew Congress would create its own policy-making committees once the facts about the atomic revolution were revealed to the world.

In fact, the IC was not formed to decide how the atomic bombs should be used during the war, and all of its supposed deliberations on this topic amounted to a charade. There was no briefing about diplomatic and military realities that would have enabled the members of the committee to make well-reasoned judgments concerning alternative courses of action. Furthermore, the target decision the committee discussed in a rambling fashion had already been made three weeks earlier by Secretary Stimson's military target committee.

The myth that administrators such as Ralph Bard and Dr.

Vannevar Bush and scientists such as Oppenheimer, Compton, Fermi, and Lawrence were decision makers who helped guide the bombers to Hiroshima and Nagasaki is not only inaccurate, it places an unfair moral burden on these men. Henry L. Stimson was the author of this fable. He was the first member of the committee to publish a memoir about the climactic events that launched the unveiling of the atomic age, and since all of the pertinent documents were official secrets, Stimson's account of what happened established a baseline of "facts" that historians and journalists could not question.

Stimson had an ulterior motive for implicating the Interim Committee as a moving force behind the Hiroshima decision. By the time his book, *On Active Service,* appeared in 1947, the world's reaction to the horror of Hiroshima and Nagasaki had put Henry Stimson, the self-appointed guardian of American morality, on the defensive. He needed an explanation for the bombs of August that would assure his critics that the "best minds" in government and science had endorsed his bombing plan. Thus, it was Stimson himself who wrote a script that elevated the role of the Interim Committee and saddled it with some of the moral responsibility for the bombings of Hiroshima and Nagasaki.

The contention that the Interim Committee's perfunctory discussion of the bomb was a black comedy is buttressed by evidence that even before the IC was created, Henry Stimson was the architect of the plan he had presented to the president on April 25. It is patent that there was conscious playacting by Stimson during the charade that followed. The secretary of war knew that his military operation was moving on a fast track at the very moment he was carrying on a masquerade of "consulting" with the Interim Committee about this very subject. Stimson knew in April, for example, that the special air force unit he had created was on its way to its new base on Tinian— and he also knew that this unit was making final decisions about the bombing techniques to be employed and the cities to be destroyed.

To fully understand the truth about this masquerade, one must compare the chronology of the actions taken by Stimson's military machine with the schedule of the Interim Committee. (Note that this chronology begins two weeks after the death of FDR on April 12.)

Such an analysis punctures the myth that the Interim Committee made a "decision" about dropping the atomic bombs. And this

Track One	*Dates*	*Track Two*
The Military Machine		The Interim Committee
The prime target given to the target committee is Hiroshima.	April 27	
	May 8	Stimson presides over a meeting to fix the agenda of the Interim Committee.
	May 9	Briefings by Stimson and General Groves at first meeting of the Interim Committee.
The target committee completes its work. Hiroshima still the prime target. A military *directive* to put the operation into effect is signed by General Marshall.	May 10–11	
	May 14	IC considers global implications at the second meeting.
Target committee finishes work. Decides aiming point shall be the "center" of the cities targeted.	May 28	
Stimson looks at target list; orders the deletion of Kyoto.	May 30	
	May 31–	IC has final sessions.
	June 1	Bombing policy injected into talks; Byrnes pushes through recommendation that bombs be used but "not concentrate on civilian areas."

Track One	Dates	Track Two
The Military Machine		The Interim Committee
With one change (Nagasaki substituted for Kyoto) General Marshall's May *directive* is signed by the acting army chief-of-staff.	July 25	
Hiroshima is bombed	August 6	
Nagasaki is bombed	August 9	

conclusion is strengthened further by recollections of two members of the committee. Writing of his work on the IC in his book, *Atomic Quest,* Dr. Arthur Compton noted that "the strategy for military use had already been worked out . . . [and] for the shaping of this strategy General Groves was primarily responsible." And Navy Undersecretary Ralph Bard came away with the conviction that "the Committee approved a decision that had already been made." The final, irrefutable evidence came from General Groves himself. Unlike Stimson, Leslie Groves did not want a shield to protect his reputation from the moralists. When he wrote his book after Stimson's death, he arrogated for himself credit for being the commander who won the war by making the crucial decisions to destroy the two Japanese cities.

The general used 70,000 words to present his version of the making of the atomic bomb and the events that led to its use as a weapon of war. Groves went out of his way to underscore his profound difference with Stimson over the role of the Interim Committee by making only one reference—in a footnote—to the work of that committee. It reads:

The Interim Committee was composed of nine civilians appointed by President Truman on Secretary Stimson's recommendation in the spring of 1945. They were to draft essential postwar legislation, prepare the White House release of news, and advise generally on the steps needed to prepare the future handling of atomic energy in the United States.

THE PEACEMAKERS THEY IGNORED:
RALPH BARD AND JOHN MCCLOY

Ralph Bard, the undersecretary of the U.S. Navy, and John McCloy, the assistant who had the closest personal relationship with Secretary Stimson, have the distinction of being the only civilians who lodged moral protests against the Hiroshima plan and proposed that peaceful alternatives be explored.

Ralph Bard

The veteran navy undersecretary Ralph Bard knew nothing about the atomic bomb when Secretary Stimson assigned him to the Interim Committee in early May. Bard and Navy Secretary James Forrestal shared the opinion that Japan was already defeated, and they were agitating in Washington for surrender concessions that would induce Japan to capitulate before the Soviet Union entered the war. Although he was upset by the plan outlined by General Groves, at the first meeting Bard expressed no disagreement because, as noted earlier, he had the impression that the committee was being asked to "approve a decision that had already been made" by Secretary Stimson and General Groves.

The undersecretary's misgivings were heightened by a conviction he shared with Forrestal that Japan's plight was desperate and it was "quite logical to hope and expect that with the proper kind of warning the Japanese would then be in a position to make peace, which would [make] it unnecessary for us to drop the bomb." He subsequently prepared a statement of conscience that he framed as an appeal to Stimson, the chairman of the Interim Committee, for reconsideration of the Hiroshima decision. That paper contained both pragmatic and moralistic arguments of the sort that Henry Stimson would undoubtedly have used if he had adhered to the moral principles that had animated his life.

As a prominent Chicago industrialist and civic leader, Ralph Bard was in a good position to exercise independent judgment. At sixty-one, he was a man of strong ethical convictions who had devoted three and one-half years to service in the office of the secretary of the navy and wanted the war to end on a note of magnanimity. It was clear to Bard that using the bomb "over a city with women and children and noncombatants as the probable victims was incompatible with either our war aims or with the necessity of demonstrating the power of the weapon."

Though a bewildered Bard did not dissent during the first two meetings of the Interim Committee, after analyzing the plight of the Japanese and the plan to drop the bomb on a city without any warning, his reaction was sharp and critical:

> The Pacific war was a Navy war. The Army didn't know what the hell was going on there. The Navy had sewed up those islands so that nothing was coming in or going out. The Navy knew the Japanese were licked. The Army wanted to be in on the kill. The Japanese approached Russia and Switzerland for peace. The elements of peace were there. I thought we should give them a warning and approach them on terms of peace.

Hoping to score a point with Secretary Stimson, Bard began his dissent by paraphrasing one of Stimson's oft-repeated clichés about America's moral responsibilities: his conclusions, he wrote, were animated by "the position of the United States as a great humanitarian nation and the fair-play attitude of our people generally." He then sketched a rough outline of an approach that might get surrender talks started and commented that he didn't see that the United States had "anything in particular to lose in following such a [warning] program." He ended his memo with the challenge "The only way to find out is to try it out."

When Ralph Bard's beliefs fused into a decision to resign, Secretary Forrestal arranged an appointment so he could present his views to the president. Harry Truman was courteous and complimented the undersecretary on his interesting ideas. But Bard had the impression that no one was really listening to his arguments, and he ended his one-man crusade with a feeling he was "hammering on locked doors."

John McCloy

In his memoir, *Deadline*, John McCloy's old friend James Reston of the *New York Times* remembered him as a "plain, spunky, cheerful

THE DAWN TIME OF THE ATOMIC AGE

man . . . who never saw a problem he didn't think he could solve." During the war years McCloy served as a special assistant to Secretary Stimson, and they developed what amounted to a father-son relationship.

It was an accident that McCloy became involved in the decision to release the atom bomb on Hiroshima and Nagasaki. The president scheduled a meeting in the White House on June 18 to discuss the army's plan for the invasion of Japan. The night before this meeting, Secretary Stimson was not feeling well and asked McCloy to attend in his place. On his own initiative, Jack McCloy had been holding long talks with Joseph Grew about the possibility that Japan's leaders might surrender if the United States offered acceptable peace terms. As a result of his exchanges with Grew, McCloy became convinced that the United States had "nothing to lose" by initiating negotiations and warning the Japanese that we possessed a cataclysmic new weapon which had the power to destroy a city with a single blow.

McCloy remembered that he did most of the talking that evening and that he went home with the strong impression that they had "reached full agreement" and he "had Mr. Stimson's authority to develop with the President and the Joint Chiefs of Staff the conclusions we had reached." John McCloy was startled the next morning when his secretary appeared for the meeting, and he was even more startled when Stimson played a passive role and went along with the consensus that the only rational alternative was to implement the army's plan to attack Kyushu.

As the meeting was ending, President Truman impulsively turned to Stimson's aide and said, "McCloy, you didn't express yourself and nobody gets out of this room without standing up and being counted. Do you think I have any reasonable alternative to the decision that has just been made?" McCloy, nobody's yes-man, responded with a hard-hitting presentation that surely startled Truman and his advisors. He said, "We ought to have our heads examined if we don't seek a political solution in preference to an invasion." He said such a search should begin with an assurance on the future of the emperor. And he stunned his august audience and produced a gasp (and violated Stimson's cherished code of secrecy) when he spoke of the atomic bomb as a powerful bargaining chip and concluded by expressing the view that the "moral position" of the United States would be better if Japan was given a specific warning about the potential of this new weapon.

There was no discussion of McCloy's audacious proposals, but Harry Truman took him aside, thanked him for his "interesting ideas" and told him to "take the matter up" with James Byrnes, the secretary of state–designate, who was not present at this meeting. By now Byrnes had replaced Stimson as the engineer of the Hiroshima Express, and he curtly informed McCloy that he was opposed to his proposal "because it appeared to him that it might be considered a weakness on our part." Byrnes likewise avowed that he was also opposed to "any 'deal' as a concomitant of a demand for surrender."

Here, sadly, were all of the elements of a modern morality play. Two peacemakers appear and present to the warmakers a challenge that they should "have their heads examined" if they do not explore the prospects of a negotiated peace. There is a long silence. Then mutterings make it clear that the minds of the warmakers are closed and they don't want to be bothered by facts about alternatives that might produce a peace.

The appeals of Bard and McCloy threw a harsh light on Henry L. Stimson, the self-appointed guardian of America's moral principles. By any standard, Stimson's performance must be adjudged a masterpiece of hypocrisy. He listened to the powerful ethical arguments of both men (and appeared to share the views of McCloy, his closest friend in Washington). However, he brushed aside their entreaties and lent unswerving support to a history-making spasm of violence that U.S. military lawyers at Nuremberg would soon define and denounce as "a crime against humanity."

An appalled John McCloy was haunted the rest of his life by the "gruesome results" of the Japanese bombings and by the opportunity that was missed to achieve a surrender "completely satisfactory to us, without the necessity of dropping the bombs." As a loyal friend, he studiously avoided criticizing Henry Stimson, but on the twentieth anniversary of the bombings he told a reporter, "I am absolutely convinced that had we said they could keep the emperor, together with the threat of the atomic bomb, they would have accepted, and we would never have had to drop the bomb."

THE OLD SOLDIERS

> The soldier, be he friend of foe, is charged with the protection of the weak and unarmed. . . . When he violates this sacred trust, he not only profanes his entire cult but threatens the fabric of international society.
> —GENERAL DOUGLAS MACARTHUR (1943)

In an irony that challenges conventional assumptions, the most prominent Americans who had humanitarian reservations about crushing the civilian populations of cities with atomic bombs were soldiers—whereas the leaders who elected to end the war with a bloodcurdling flourish were civilians. If Truman, Stimson, and Byrnes had listened to their two great field commanders, generals MacArthur and Eisenhower, and to Admiral William Leahy, the president's chief of staff, a different atomic strategy might have evolved.

When he first learned of the bomb's existence at the Potsdam conference, Dwight Eisenhower's spontaneous reaction reflected the commitment to honor and to the moral methods of waging war that had been imprinted on the minds of some old soldiers in their military academies. Eisenhower's vehement moral and strategic objections to the use of the atomic bomb infuriated Secretary Stimson. Eisenhower asserted that Japan was "already defeated," and he argued that the United States should "avoid shocking world opinion" by using "something as horrible and destructive as this new weapon." The general also displayed a prescience lacking in Washington when he told Stimson that he "hated to see [the United States] be first to use such a weapon" because such a military move would start a nuclear arms race.

When General Douglas MacArthur in Manila first learned about the bomb's existence three days before Hiroshima, his instinctive reactions were similar to Eisenhower's. MacArthur was already contemplating the coming peace in the Pacific, and his biographer William Manchester tells us that despite all the fearsome talk about Japanese fanaticism, MacArthur sensed "there was another [peace-oriented] Japan, and [he] was one of the few Americans who suspected its existence." Two weeks before Hiroshima, MacArthur had predicted to George Kenney, his air force aide, that Japan would surrender "by September 1 at the latest and perhaps even sooner." Using atomic bombs on urban targets was, to General MacArthur, "completely unnecessary from a military point of view."

Moreover, General MacArthur had been "appalled" by the Potsdam ultimatum with its demand that Japan unconditionally surrender or face "prompt and utter destruction," for he was convinced that the retention of the emperor was the key to an orderly transition to peace. With Japan floundering in the ashes of defeat, it was MacArthur's view that the paramount war aim of the United States should not be punishment and an escalation of the killing, but to pursue a course of action that would bind a demilitarized Japan to the United States and lay the foundation for a lasting peace.

Admiral William D. Leahy, the blunt chief of staff President Truman inherited from FDR, was an old sailor who was adamantly against using the atomic bomb for moral and strategic reasons. Leahy had a habit of speaking his mind to presidents. In the summer of 1944 when some advisors were urging Franklin Roosevelt to approve a biological warfare project, Leahy denounced it, saying: "Mr. President, this would violate every Christian ethic I have ever heard of and all of the known laws of war. It would be an attack on the noncombatant population of the enemy."

Now, in the summer of 1945, Leahy found the lethal possibilities of atomic warfare "frightening" and he used even stronger words in conferences with Truman and Byrnes to condemn the use of this "barbarous" new weapon against Japanese cities. One can sense the moral outrage that motivated the old admiral in the memoir he wrote after the war:

> My own feeling was that in being the first to use it, we had adopted an ethical standard common to the barbarians of the Dark Ages. I was taught not to make war in that fashion, and wars cannot be won by destroying women and children.

But our civilian war leaders, bent on testing the destructive potential of their new weapon, were so obsessed with the scenario they had crafted that they were not interested in advice from old soldiers. This odd twist led to the irony that it was the engineer

General Groves, and the nation's top civilian war leaders—not the field commanders—who wrote the script for the American tragedy of Hiroshima.

WAS THE BOMBING OF NAGASAKI DEFENSIBLE?

For the American people, Nagasaki is the Banquo's ghost of World War II. The poignant moral issue it poses to civilized men and women will not go away. One English scientist used these words to characterize this act of war, "If ever the dark view of human nature had a profound source, the destruction of Nagasaki touched that source."

What has made it impossible for Americans to defend Nagasaki is that General Groves's account—the official, and only, explanation this country has ever offered to the world—is so stark and simplistic, and so totally out of touch with any military realities. The general first said the Nagasaki bomb was exploded to "show them we had more than one," and later announced, in *Now It Can Be Told,* that "the importance of having the second blow follow the first one quickly, was so that the Japanese would not have the time to recover their balance."

These statements by General Groves amount to an admission that the bombing of Nagasaki had no military significance whatsoever. General Curtis LeMay, who was running the daily bombings of the Twenty-first Air Force from Tinian, considered both atomic explosions a superfluous use of airpower.

Nor can a case be made that the leveling of Nagasaki put added pressure on Japan's leaders to surrender, for the emperor had ordered the issuance of a surrender offer before the Nagasaki bomb was dropped. Even those who profess that the Hiroshima bomb forced the emperor to surrender are hard-pressed to explain why we did not allow a decent interval for Japan's leaders to react before the second bomb was dropped. Nagasaki represents an utter abdication of responsible diplomacy by our civilian leaders. "It was," as one historian has written, "destroyed with hardly a pause for a measured Japanese response" to the bombing of Hiroshima.

The official record of that fateful summer makes us uneasy

because neither Truman nor Byrnes nor Stimson ever considered that plain common sense (apart from the obvious humanitarian concerns) required that Japan's leaders be given a reasonable interval to respond to the initial atomic attack. Stimson was surely aware that proud nations invariably need time to debate and formulate terms of surrender. As anxious soldiers in France at the end of World War I, both he and Harry Truman must have recalled that thirty-nine days elapsed between Germany's first peace offer to President Woodrow Wilson and the armistice agreement that was finally concluded on November 11, 1918.

The moral issue raised by Nagasaki lies at the heart of the American tragedy of Hiroshima. It is a recurring nightmare, because straightforward reasoning has led the world to perceive Nagasaki as an experiment by Americans to ascertain the killing power of its implosion bomb. The persistent question that has hovered over this episode of war for nearly half a century is this: if this bombing was not a means designed to serve a military or diplomatic end, were not the lives of the inhabitants of Nagasaki wasted?

THE OPPENHEIMER RIDDLE

Robert Oppenheimer left Los Alamos in the fall of 1945, first to teach at Cal Tech and then in 1947 to become director of the prestigious Institute for Advanced Study at Princeton, where Albert Einstein was the leading luminary. But urgent invitations from cabinet secretaries and members of Congress soon made him the lead-off witness at every important hearing and a seemingly indispensable member of every vital advisory committee. These were intoxicating days for the forty-one-year-old scientist. To have leaders at the highest levels of government listening with awe to every word one uttered was an experience bound to create intimations of omniscience in any expert.

In the first four years after Hiroshima, Oppenheimer wrote the Acheson-Lilienthal report, which became the blueprint for the Atomic Energy Commission. He was the star witness at hearings held by congressional committees that were trying to understand the policy implications of the atom. He sat at the side of Bernard Baruch as Baruch presented the United States plan for international control to the United Nations and, since he was the chairman and guiding light of the General Advisory Committee (GAC) of the AEC, Oppenheimer's opinions were sought and pondered by policy makers in the Pentagon and by the secretaries of state and defense.

Robert Oppenheimer's most remarkable gift—the talent that made him such a superb, inspiring administrator at Los Alamos—was a lucid, computerlike mind that enabled him to distill a consensus (including, when necessary, subtle shadings of dissent) out of prolonged, abstruse discussions and summarize the conclusions in incisive, eloquent prose. Cyril Smith, the top metallurgist at Los Alamos, described Oppenheimer's genius at summarizing group discussions with the statement, "Robert would put things so that after he had spoken no one else felt there was any need to do any thinking."

Dr. Oppenheimer's zest for exercising this skill drove him to accept invitations to serve on, and usually dominate, most of the crucial advisory committees that sprouted in Washington in the first years of the atomic age. But his zest also inflated Oppenheimer's ego and narrowed his sense of himself and his future. It was, in the end, a fatal infatuation with his ubiquitous status as the premier Washington insider that estranged him from friends and caused him to overlook opportunities to turn away from his nation's atomic apparatus and to think and speak for humankind.

The reaction of Philip Morrison, one of his closest friends at Los Alamos, is a measure of the alienation produced by Oppenheimer's ascension into Washington's corridors of power. Morrison, a onetime favorite pupil, made these observations about his teacher's new role as an indispensable prince of the Washington establishment: "When Oppie started talking about Dean Acheson as simply 'Dean' and General Marshall as merely 'George,' I knew that we did not move in the same circles anymore and that we had come to a parting of the ways. I think that his sudden fame and the new position he now occupied had gone to his head so much that he began to consider himself God Almighty, able to put the whole world to rights."

Sometimes the dazzle of fame distorts an individual's view of his or her environment, and there are many indications that this happened to Robert Oppenheimer. There are no signs, for example, that he grasped that his own situation—and the relationship that had evolved in the postwar period between science advisors and Washington's policy makers—was altered irrevocably when Stalin's scientists and engineers detonated an atomic bomb in September 1949. The Soviet bomb had many reverberations. It generated immediate demands in Congress for a crash program to arm U.S. planes and ships with thousands of atomic weapons. It whipped up a national security crisis four months later when a British physicist, Klaus Fuchs, confessed that during the war he had transmitted bomb secrets from Los Alamos to Soviet intelligence agents. And it escalated the atomic-arms race to a frightening new level when, on the last day of January 1950, President Truman rejected the unanimous advice of Oppenheimer's General Advisory Committee and approved a crash program to produce hydrogen bombs capable of destroying a region as large as western Europe.

Scientists who were close to Oppenheimer saw Truman's decision as a moral watershed for the human race and issued warnings about the global impacts of this potential new weapon. His great friend Hans Bethe said, "We believe that no nation has the right to use such a bomb, no matter how righteous its cause. This bomb is no longer a weapon of war but a means of extermination of whole populations." And Albert Einstein, whose words always reached an international audience, issued this statement from his office in Princeton: "If [the H-bomb] is successful, radioactive poisoning of the atmosphere and hence annihilation of any life on earth has been brought within the range of technical possibilities.... In the end there beckons more and more clearly general annihilation."

These developments cried out that Robert Oppenheimer's career had come to a crossroad where fateful decisions had to be made. Enrico Fermi read the handwriting on the wall and resigned from the GAC. Fermi realized that under the new order of things the strategic-planning role of the atomic scientists would shrink, and that their paramount task would involve decisions about the design and production of a new generation of atomic weapons. Oppenheimer briefly considered resigning, but his conduct suggests that he had few second thoughts when he elected to resume consulting. This decision is hard to understand, because an assiduous hunt for atomic spies had begun two years before Klaus Fuchs's confession. Robert Oppenheimer had been singed by this search when his physicist brother, Frank, had been driven from academic life and the FBI had put a brand of disloyalty on two of Frank's Berkeley students.

The Oppenheimer riddle encompasses other, more baffling, inconsistencies and contradictions. Dr. Bethe states that while they were at Los Alamos none of the scientists envisioned that any nation would ever want to possess more than twenty or thirty atomic weapons. And Oppenheimer himself had delivered this resounding warning in his farewell speech to his Los Alamos associates in October 1945: "If atomic bombs are to be added to the arsenals of a warring world or to arsenals of nations preparing for war, then the time will come when mankind will curse the names of Los Alamos and Hiroshima."

Yet in 1950, Oppenheimer was busy leading study teams that were formulating plans to dramatically expand the nation's arsenal of atomic weapons and to guide an emergency effort to build "tactical" nuclear bombs for deployment in Korea and western Europe. But when the arms race he supposedly dreaded was in full swing, and the United States had a competent corps of bombmakers, why, one is forced to ask, did Oppenheimer feel impelled to be involved in such activities? And when his friends Bethe and Einstein were outside the government's tent issuing warnings about atomic annihilation similar to his Los Alamos statement, why did he remain inside? And why did he continue working for an organization that was becoming increasingly paranoid about its "secrets" when he knew his phones were being tapped and the leaders of the atomic establishment were still harboring doubts about his loyalty?

Oppenheimer was apparently not troubled by such questions. He made a fateful election to continue on the old road, and all that remains of his story is an ignominious trial—and a lament.

Robert Oppenheimer's spirit was broken by the Atomic Energy Commission's star chamber trial (described by his Los Alamos friend John Manley as a "treason disgrace" proceeding) that stripped him of his security clearance in 1953. His Princeton intimate George Kennan observed at his memorial service in 1967 that he spent his last years "eating out his heart in frustration over the consciousness that the talents . . . once welcomed and used by the official establishment of his country to develop the destructive possibilities of nuclear science, were rejected when it came to the development of the great positive ones he believed that science to possess."

The authentic lament—Robert Oppenheimer's "it-might-have-been" Greek chorus—is more complex and profound than Kennan implied. Oppenheimer had a charisma and a renown that might have made him a memorable peacemaker had he elected to emulate Einstein. During the prime years of Robert Oppenheimer's life the world desperately needed a moral leader who could speak with scientific authority about the folly of the nuclear arms race, the importance of curbing atmospheric testing to protect the health of earth's inhabitants, the urgency of effective arms control, and the need for a brand of mutual magnanimity that would enable the United States and the USSR to quiet and contain the hatreds and fears that could have ignited a nuclear exchange. But Robert Oppenheimer did not see, or did not take, this path.

Indeed, on closer analysis, the Oppenheimer riddle is not a riddle after all. Robert Oppenheimer, in truth, was a scientific genius who had very ordinary moral convictions and very little moral courage. His public record is unmistakable. He never took a stand where he used moral arguments as part of a campaign for a cause—not at the time of the Hiroshima decision, not when he voted against the creation of the H-bomb, not when the safety of inland bomb testing in the United States arose, not when some of his fellow scientists mounted a campaign to stop open-air testing of nuclear weapons, and not when the professional career of his younger brother was crushed.

Robert was a virtuoso who cherished harmony, not dissonance, and he performed all his solos with one orchestra. Once, in 1960, long after his public service had ended, Oppenheimer aroused a seminar with the outcry, "I find myself profoundly in anguish over the fact that no ethical discussion of any weight or nobility has been addressed to the problem of atomic weapons." But he failed to mention that he had had many opportunities from day one to lead such dialogues, but had never engaged in public or private dissent on this issue.

With an irony that still resonates, one year after Oppenheimer's death another brilliant physicist who had been a bombmaker struck the overarching themes his American counterpart neglected. His first manifesto, an analysis of the predicament of humankind, was a call for a global dialogue in an environment free of false national pride and militarism. It read:

> The division of mankind threatens it with destruction. Civilization is imperiled by: a universal thermonuclear war, catastrophic hunger for most of mankind, stupefaction from "mass culture" and bureaucratic dogmatism, a spreading of mass myths that put entire peoples and continents under the power of cruel and treacherous demagogues, and destruction or degeneration from the unforeseeable consequences of swift changes in the conditions of life on our planet.
>
> In the face of these perils, any action increasing the division of mankind, any preaching of the incompatibility of world ideologies and nations is madness and a crime.

This bold scientist dared to print his declaration in a totalitarian state, and he was denigrated and sent into exile for his effrontery. But he persisted, and his words of hope reached into the far corners of the world and became a rallying cry for his own people.

His name, of course, was Andrei Sakharov. And his efforts to start a fresh dialogue based on moral principles and the free exchange of ideas won him the Nobel Peace Prize.

GENERAL GROVES: THE SELF-ANOINTED "HERO OF HIROSHIMA"

Leslie Richard Groves deserved the medals and the praise bestowed on him at the end of the Second World War for his exceptional performance as the manager of the most daunting war-related research and development project in history. But the general, saddled with a massive ego, felt he deserved a greater glory and sought recognition after the war as the overall combat commander who won the war in the Pacific by dropping bombs on Hiroshima and Nagasaki.

Groves presented his claim to this martial laurel in his memoir, *Now It Can Be Told*. This is a self-centered and boastful book which might have been subtitled: "How I Produced and Dropped the Atomic Bombs and Won the War." In it, Groves presents himself as a freewheeling commander who made all of the crucial decisions, and whose plans were merely "ratified" by Secretary Stimson and General Marshall.

Although when he came aboard in the fall of 1942, the Manhattan Project was a gamble surrounded by awesome scientific and engineering problems, Groves makes the grandiose assertion in his book that some unidentified official ordained him with a personal "mission" to "develop an atomic bomb of such power that it would bring the war to an end at the earliest possible date." Modesty was not one of the general's attributes: he implies throughout his memoir that he made all of the "original decisions" about using the bombs as war weapons; and informs us that he selected the targets and was the author of the plan to drop the first bombs on two Japanese cities.

A canny operator described by one Los Alamos executive as a "tremendous lone wolf," Leslie Groves realized that it would be extremely difficult for anyone to contradict his expansive claims. The key officials who had supervised his work (Roosevelt, Stimson, Marshall) were dead. He was aware, too, that many truths would be concealed for decades in top-secret documents. He also knew that no one could controvert his self-promoting accounts of conversations with Roosevelt and Stimson.

General Groves's affinity for gloating colors his memoir. He takes credit (which belonged to Stimson) for excluding Admiral Leahy and the Joint Chiefs of Staff from participating in the city-bombing decision. He chortles about the daring feats of the security agents and counterspies who functioned under his command. And with ill-concealed glee, he compares President Truman's involvement in the decision-making process to the participation of "a boy on a toboggan rushing downhill."

The general habitually bullied those who worked under him, and in his book he reveals the deceit he used to cow the leading scientists at Los Alamos and prevent them from offering opinions about the city-bombing issue. He informed Robert Oppenheimer that the use of the bombs was a military decision that lay in the domain of "the responsible authorities." This message undoubtedly had a chilling effect, for Dr. David Hawkins, one of the official Los Alamos historians, told me during an interview that everyone who worked directly with Groves in the spring and summer of 1945 sensed that he would regard opposition to the bombing plan he was pushing as "something approaching treason."

In his zeal to portray himself as the grand captain in all atomic matters, General Groves minimizes the constraints on his power. The leader President Roosevelt put in charge of the Manhattan Project was Secretary Stimson, and any recommendations Groves put forward went nowhere unless Henry Stimson approved them. The confidence the president had in Stimson—and the quality of the supervision provided by the secretary and his excellent staff—is indicated by the circumstance that during the three-year life of this costly, complex venture President Roosevelt apparently never questioned any of his decisions.

The war secretary's status as a senior statesman and his reputation for integrity made him the Iron Man of the bomb project. Stimson's prestige, for example, enabled him to get the appropriations needed for his mystery program without revealing its secret aims to key members of Congress. And when suspicious congressmen (including Senator Harry Truman) wanted to investigate what was going on at the vast factories built from scratch in Tennessee and Washington, a cautionary word from Henry Stimson was enough to allay their concerns.

In his memoir, General Groves intimates that his unique "command system" put him in a situation where he could usurp the prerogatives of his superiors and make momentous "original decisions" on his own. This was a fantasy, and Henry Stimson would have been startled had the general made this claim while he was alive. When the secretary and the general saw eye to eye, it was Stimson, not Groves, who made the big decisions and had orders issued to implement them.

Two examples from the history of the Manhattan Project underscore this point. When the secretary was persuaded that Groves needed security and counterintelligence forces to investigate the loyalty of the atomic scientists and to track the progress of Germany's purported bomb program, such entities were created. And when Stimson concluded in the spring of 1944 that a secret air force unit should be trained to give the president the option to use A-bombs as war weapons (in the event the atomic scientists completed their work before the war ended), General Marshall, under

Stimson's aegis, issued appropriate orders and activated such a special squadron.

Leslie Groves envisioned that his egocentric memoir would enshrine him as a great military hero, but it actually revealed that his mind was a moral wasteland and that his humanity was shriveled. In contrast to the perfunctory praise General Groves extended to his Manhattan Project associates, General Eisenhower was motivated by magnanimity when he composed his war memoir, *Crusade in Europe.* Ike's book is a model of military modesty, for his aim was to give an honest account of his stewardship and to share the glory with the officers and soldiers of the Allied armies that made victory in Europe possible.

Although he was the son of an army chaplain, there is no hint in *Now It Can Be Told* that mercy was part of Leslie Groves's makeup. In contrast, a few months after Hiroshima, commenting on an article he had written for *Harper's* magazine, Stimson confessed to a critical friend, Supreme Court Justice Felix Frankfurter, "I have rarely been connected with a paper about which I have so much doubt at the last moment." And one of General Marshall's biographers informs us that dropping atomic bombs on Japanese cities "disturbed" Marshall and that he told John McCloy, "Don't ask me to make *that* decision."

But vengeance is the mortal enemy of mercy, and Groves made it plain that his animating impulse in August 1945 was revenge.

WHAT DID THE HIROSHIMA EXPLOSION ACCOMPLISH?

The principal argument Secretary Stimson and General Groves used in their memoirs to justify destroying "a whole city" with an atomic bomb was that such a demonstration would compel Japan's leaders to sue for peace. Stimson reasoned that if a "tremendous shock" were administered it would "extract a surrender from the Emperor and his military advisors." Groves asserted that the incineration of a city "would most adversely affect the will of the Japanese people to continue the war."

Two largely unexamined questions still hover over the carnage created at Hiroshima by the detonation of the first atomic bomb:

1. Was the Stimson-Groves shock strategy well conceived?

2. Did the Hiroshima explosion alter the mind-set or change the outlook of the emperor of Japan, the one person who had the power that August to order a surrender?

In light of the fact that during the war years Japan was ruled by a military dictatorship, it seems mindless that any American could have believed that the "will of the people" could somehow influence the decisions of a nation's war leaders. It also seems strange that a man with Henry Stimson's political acumen would have thought that bombing a city five hundred miles from Tokyo would have a powerful, immediate impact on "the Emperor and his military advisors." And finally, one wonders how Stimson could have thought that the incineration of a relatively unimportant city would produce a "tremendous shock" in Japan's capital when all of that nation's big industrial centers had already been devastated by incineration bombings.

Almost a half-century after the event, there is still no consensus concerning whether, in the fateful hours while Emperor Hirohito was making his decision to intervene and order a surrender, the explosion of the first atomic bomb influenced his thinking or the outlook of his personal advisors. In 1990, new rays of light were thrown on this issue with the release of 100 pages of verbatim notes taken during a series of conversations between Hirohito and a small group of his close aides in 1946. When this oral-history inquiry came to the subject of the emperor's motive when he decided to break the deadlock in his war cabinet, Hirohito did not identify Hiroshima as a catalyst. Here are his words: "I was told that even Tokyo cannot be defended. I thought that the Japanese race would be destroyed if the war continued."

One cannot contemplate the moral issues surrounding Secretary Stimson's shock strategy without recalling General Eisenhower's response at Potsdam when Stimson informed him of his plan to use the atomic bomb as a city-destroying weapon. Ike used these words in his memoirs to describe his reaction and the very different shock uppermost in his mind:

I had been conscious of a feeling of depression and so I voiced to him my grave misgivings, first on the basis of my belief that Japan was already defeated and that dropping the bomb was completely unnecessary, and secondly because I thought that our country should avoid shocking world opinion by the use of a weapon whose employment was, I thought, no longer mandatory as a measure to save American lives.

If Dwight Eisenhower's misgivings were apposite, what purpose was served on August 6 and 9 in 1945 by extinguishing the lives of over 150,000 Japanese civilians and soldiers?

THE AMERICAN TRAGEDY: A SUMMATION

Leon V. Sigal's 1988 book, *Fighting to the Finish: The Politics of War Termination in the United States and Japan*, is a study which challenges the main assertions and assumptions that have supported the conventional conclusions about the war-ending events and nonevents in the Pacific theater in the spring and summer of 1945.

The evidence Dr. Sigal has assembled refutes the Truman-Stimson-Byrnes thesis that the shock effect of the atomic bombs altered the outlook of Japan's leaders and forced them to surrender. It also lends support to these conclusions about U.S. statesmanship—and the lack thereof—in the climactic months of the Second World War:

1. As Japan's military and economic power crumbled, our civilian leaders failed to develop a peace strategy that would probably have hastened the war's end.

2. President Truman's military and civilian advisors never presented to him the war-ending options he should have had an opportunity to evaluate.

3. In May, these same advisors knew, or should have known, from cable intercepts that a signal that the emperor system might be spared could have tipped the scales in favor of surrender, but these officials refused to take any initiative to explore this avenue to peace.

4. Evidence that the Hiroshima bomb induced any member of Japan's six-man war cabinet to shift his position on the surrender issue is inconclusive—and the subsequent arguments of American leaders that the atomic bombs produced the surrender offer by Japan is not supported by demonstrable facts.

5. There is little evidence that the Hiroshima explosion induced Emperor Hirohito to assert himself and issue the order that produced the surrender.

As a consequence, the claim that the Hiroshima bomb shortened the war and saved the lives of hundreds of thousands of U.S. soldiers and Japanese soldiers and civilians is a myth.

It has been nearly a half-century since Hiroshima. Although several nations have manufactured nuclear weapons—and there have been many major military conflicts during this interval—the United States stands alone as the only country to have used atomic bombs as instruments of war. The history of the world's restraint since Hiroshima offers real hope, for it proffers evidence that the moral opinion of mankind is real and exerts a powerful influence on the leaders of modern nations.

The weight and rigor of this opinion has made it either unthinkable, or unacceptable, for the United States and Russia, or any of the other nations with atomic arms, to use nuclear weapons to resolve conflicts that have produced conventional wars. But Americans must recognize that this forbearance throws a special moral light on the bombings of Hiroshima and Nagasaki. It says that this was an American as well as a Japanese tragedy, and it puts special moral burdens and responsibilities on the citizens of the United States of America.

And now that scientists tell us that the outcome of a nuclear war might be a genocidal "nuclear winter," the great lesson for humankind is that the surest way for nations to extend and deepen this tradition of restraint is to cherish all policies and values that foster life and peace on this planet.

Once we Americans decide, with unblinking honesty, to come to terms with our Hiroshima legacy, we may want to memorize the ecumenical judgment expressed by a French war correspondent who surveyed the wasteland where that city once stood. "Our feeling," Robert Guillain wrote, "was one of stunned consternation, mixed for me with a heavy feeling of shame—and I think my companion shared my remorse. 'I am ashamed for the West,' I thought. 'I am ashamed for science. I am ashamed for mankind.'"

II

THE COLD WAR AND THE
SUBVERSION OF DEMOCRACY

6

The Crazy Race for
Nuclear Supremacy

... ever since World War II the military power of the United
States has been steadily increasing, while at the same time
our national security has been rapidly and inexorably de-
creasing. The same thing is happening to the Soviet Union.
—HERBERT YORK
Race to Oblivion (1970)

These fears . . . have brought us into the craziest arms race
in history, where each side has more than a hundred times
what is needed to destroy all of us, knowing all full well
. . . that any actual use of those weapons means the annihilation of both sides.
—VICTOR F. WEISSKOPF (1983)

The detonation of the Soviet Union's first atomic bomb in August
1949, four years and twenty-three days after Hiroshima, changed
American thinking about the role of atomic weapons in warfare and
launched what Victor Weisskopf later described as "the craziest arms
race in history." Dr. Hans Bethe, one of the division captains at Los
Alamos, has stated that at the end of World War II most atomic

scientists assumed that the United States would never need, or want to have, more than twenty or thirty atomic bombs. These scientists envisioned that the new force they had created would never be used as conventional weapons of war, but would be held in reserve, under tight control, as a trump card to be used in dire emergencies by the president himself.

In a rational world dominated by nations whose political leaders shared common convictions, these assumptions might have been valid. However, history did not provide such a setting for the launching of the atomic age. The outcome of World War II conferred military superpower status on two nations whose political ideologies aroused visceral disagreements about the future. It was inevitable that Joseph Stalin, the suspicious, iron-fisted dictator of a totalitarian society, would order a crash effort to secure his own trump card and make the race for nuclear weapons a central reality.

Although many Manhattan Project veterans had predicted that the Soviet Union could duplicate their feat in four or five years, the brisk performance of Stalin's scientists and engineers sent shock waves through the corridors of power in Washington. These tremors, magnified by military triumphs that gave Mao Tse-tung's armies control of China earlier that year, stirred intense reactions in military and scientific circles. The Soviet bomb exploded the myth that the United States had a long lead in nuclear technologies. ("Maybe," the physicist Eugene Wigner commented, "we will stop glorifying our past.") It intensified the debate among the nation's atomic scientists about whether the United States should explore the feasibility of creating a hydrogen bomb. As well, it aroused demands for more atomic weapons, and evoked proposals in some quarters for preventive war strikes.

David Lilienthal, the civilian chairman of the Atomic Energy Commission, was appalled by the impassioned arguments of drop-the-bomb-now advocates. He believed that such an action would leave a "terrible ethical stain on the American people." On November 1, 1949, he wrote this account of an outburst by Connecticut's Senator Brien McMahon, the chairman of the special committee Congress had created to oversee the commission's work:

> Last evening a couple of hours in my office with Senator McMahon. Pretty discouraging. What he is talking is the inevitability of war with the

Russians, and what he says adds up to one thing: blow them off the face of the earth, quick, before they do the same to us—and we haven't much time. He uses all sorts of words to justify this, and part of the time he is practicing speeches on the floor of the Senate at us. The whole world revolves around the exploding Atom, as he sees it—that's the whole of it, and there is no hope.

Fortunately for earth's inhabitants, President Harry S Truman, now the surefooted leader of the non-Communist world, exhibited no interest in such doomsday counsels. By the end of 1949, Truman had spent four eventful years building structures to resist an expansion of Soviet power in Europe, and he was confident that his country and its allies had the economic strength and technological resilience to contain efforts by the Communists to expand their empire. This mature leader had been a staunch supporter of the United Nations, and had presented a plan for international control of the atom to that new institution. A steady president who presided over the creation of NATO, Truman had also persuaded his countrymen to give billions in foreign aid to support the reconstruction of western Europe through the Marshall Plan. And, as a level-headed commander-in-chief, without brandishing his nation's tiny arsenal of atomic bombs, he had used American airpower to call Stalin's bluff during the 1948 blockade of Berlin.

The news that Soviet scientists had detonated an atomic bomb did not produce panic in Harry Truman's White House. There were no crisis meetings, and no alarms were sounded at the United Nations. The Atomic Energy Commission, by his decision, had retained custody of all nuclear weapons during his presidency—and now he took the view that the United States should make a calm assessment of steps it could take to respond to the Soviet challenge. In a private conversation one week after Senator McMahon's prediction of an impending Armageddon, the president told David Lilienthal, ". . . we're going to use this for peace and never use it for war—I've always said this and you'll see. It'll be like poison gas [never used again]."

THE 1950 WATERSHED

President Truman kept his word and did not use atomic weapons, even during the darkest days of the Korean War. But the distrust and the ideological enmities that fueled the engines of the Cold War forced the leaders of the two superpowers to make decisions that plunged them into a forty-year race of nuclear one-upmanship and put the whole human enterprise in peril. In haste, and with a paucity of long-range planning, U.S. leaders discarded the trump-card strategy and, in response to a clamor from the three military services for atomic weapons, made two overarching decisions in 1950 that guided policy making during the ensuing technological arms race. The first involved the approval of a program to arm our conventional military forces with "tactical" nuclear weapons. The second decision involved the approval by President Truman of a crash research program to develop superbombs capable of destroying immense cities and demolishing the industrial might of an adversary.

As we look back and try to understand the dynamics of the Cold War, those decisions are fascinating, for they illuminate a seminal turning point of the atomic age. It astonishes us, for example, to realize that they were made in secret by fewer than twenty men, without a word of public debate. And we are startled as we contemplate how little thought this tiny elite gave to the impact their initiatives would have on their nation's security—and on the safety of humankind—when the United States armed itself to the teeth with weapons of mass destruction.

In the winter of 1950 there was a great debate concerning whether to proceed with all-out superbomb research, pitting diplomats against military men. President Truman's advisors unanimously supported an emergency effort to develop a panoply of nuclear weapons for the nation's armed forces. Historically, it was this decision to arm our army, navy, and air force with tactical weapons, rather than the acceleration of research on a superbomb, that launched the race for atomic supremacy with the Soviet Union.

Now that time's alchemies have transformed secrets into facts, the revelation that startles us most is how little thought was given by the president's advisors to the absurdities of the arms race they were creating. They must have hoped that the green light they flashed would generate a great leap forward in the design and deployment of nuclear weapons. But did they contemplate that within a decade the United States would have an atomic arsenal of nearly 20,000 bombs, including 10-megaton monsters that could level all of the cities in western Europe? Did they envision that in addition to megaton-size bombs for long-range bombers, U.S. bombmakers would be able to produce warheads for tactical missiles and torpedoes, shells designed for artillery pieces, and various kinds of bombs for land-based and carrier-based aircraft? And did the president and his cohort of advisors reflect that competition among our three military services would create enormous pressures for overkill?

The historical records of that watershed year inform us that there was little reflection, and that none of the participants foresaw the potential of the excesses their decisions would unleash. One dissenter who favored reflection was George F. Kennan, then a counselor to the State Department and a former ambassador to the USSR. Long afterward, Kennan wrote this lamentation about the outcome: "We have gone on piling weapon upon weapon, missile upon missile, new levels of destruction upon old ones. We have done this helplessly, almost involuntarily, like the victims of some sort of hypnotism, like men in a dream, like lemmings headed for the sea."

An analysis of the hypnotic undertow Kennan described leads to a study of the interacting influences that produced the paranoias of the Cold War and sustained it for so many decades. One reason weapons were piled upon murderous weapons was that, from 1945 until President Eisenhower and Chairman Khrushchev talked face-to-face at Camp David in 1959, there were no summit conferences and little direct, meaningful communication between the superpowers. In most instances, balanced decision making was foreclosed by the fears and emotions generated by the Cold War. For example, the day he approved accelerating work on the superbomb, President Truman told David Lilienthal that he had no alternative "because of the way the Russians were behaving" and because political pressure for action had reached a fever pitch in this country.

Thus, it was inevitable that the upward spiral produced by this psychology would spawn other influences that would give the nuclear arms race a mad momentum. Leaders of the superpowers invariably used the all-purpose cliché "The only thing they respect is power" to demolish the arguments of those who opposed a new weapon or who favored restraint. And there was the momentum provided by the ever-present, "worst-case analysis" method developed by war planners. Herbert York, a front-line scientist who was the first head of the Livermore bomb factory, once observed that this Cold War invention made it "utterly impossible for both superpowers simultaneously to recognize any given strategic situation as being safe for each of them."

Dr. York subsequently composed the classic account of the technique a tiny elite of Cold War planners used to attain inordinate power over events. "Scientists and technologists," he wrote in *Race to Oblivion,*

> had acquired the reputation of being magicians who were privy to some special source of wisdom out of the reach of the rest of mankind. . . . But it was not only the general public that believed the technologists understood something the rest of the world could not. Many of the technologists themselves believed that only they understood the problem. As a consequence, many of them believed it was their patriotic duty to save the rest of us whether or not we wanted them to. They looked at what the Soviets had done. They used their own narrow way of viewing things to figure out what the Russians ought to have done next. They decided then that since the Russians were rational (about these things anyway) what they ought to have done next was what they must now be doing, and they determined to save us from the consequences of this next Russian technological threat.

But the "influence" that did the most to clear the track for an unimpeded, no-questions-asked arms race was exerted by Senator Joseph McCarthy. McCarthy grabbed headlines and made a name for himself in the spring of 1950 by sensational charges that the federal government had been infiltrated by Communist spies who were delivering our atomic secrets to the Soviet Union. His subsequent stream of accusations created a climate of fear that made dissent appear to be the work of Communists or their sympathizers, chilled rational discussion of nuclear alternatives, and, in due course, branded Robert Oppenheimer as a disloyal "security risk." In short,

McCarthyism helped paralyze debate about the wisdom of amassing an arsenal of nuclear weapons that were, as Congress began demanding, "second to none." In the 1990s, this episode exemplifies the Cold War lesson that superpatriots who peddle horror stories about impending military threats usually generate excesses that paradoxically decrease that country's national security.

CONGRESS UNBOUND

The authors of the official history of the Atomic Energy Commission make the point that until Soviet scientists shattered the myth of American supremacy by exploding their first atomic bomb, the joint committee (JCAE) established by Congress to oversee atomic issues refused to "accept classified information" and did not "exert any effective influence [on the] central policy decisions" made by the commission. But this passive posture was altered dramatically when President Truman approved a crash program to produce tactical atomic weapons. With the opening of this door, members of the JCAE saw an opportunity to be players in the exciting new game of atomic preparedness. Senator McMahon, a politician who nursed presidential ambitions and consequently craved recognition as the "atomic senator," was the first and the most flamboyant of the congressional actors who mounted the new stage created by Mr. Truman. Exploiting his access to secrets as the chairman of the JCAE, McMahon began his crusade by expounding a conviction that strategic bombing with atomic weapons should be "the keystone of our military policy and a foundation of our foreign policy as well."

Then, two days after the president announced his new program, McMahon seized the national spotlight with a battle-cry address in which he used apocalyptic language to describe the crisis facing the American people. After predicting that the United States confronted "certain catastrophe" if the Russians got a superbomb first, McMahon warned that "a failure to press ahead with the hydrogen bomb might well mean unconditional surrendering in advance by the United States to alien forces of evil." He subsequently expanded his concept of nuclear preparedness by stressing that our national security should be measured by the number of war-fighting nuclear weapons in the hands of our soldiers—and by a salvo that included a declaration that the nation "could never have enough" atomic bombs.

As a member of Congress in the 1950s, I can testify that there was never a nuclear weapon waved before our eyes we didn't like. The awesome atom fostered a politics that can only be described as knee-jerk jingoism. The psychology of self-preservation it embodied was outlined with stark simplicity in 1951 by Congressman Henry M. Jackson, another JCAE insider, when he urged his colleagues to support a tenfold increase in the AEC's budget:

> How can we conceivably not want to make every possible atomic weapon we can? I cannot imagine any member of this House going before his constituency and saying he is not in favor of making every single weapon it is within our power to produce.

Patriotism in those days meant that members of Congress who were not privy to atomic secrets did not ask questions about the wisdom or feasibility of proposed new weapons. Our role was not to reason why, but to give blind, unswerving support to the projects pushed by the Pentagon and the weaponeers in the AEC's laboratories. Such passivity inevitably encouraged a race among the nation's three military services that generated dubious schemes for new weapons and weapons systems. I do not recall a single serious floor debate in my six years in the House of Representatives about such expensive, ill-conceived programs as Skybolt, Dyna-soar, Navaho, Snark, the Manned Orbiting Laboratory, and the harebrained Nuclear Energy Powered Aircraft effort (NEPA) to supposedly add a new chapter to the saga of the Wright brothers.

NEPA, an expansive research effort supported with exceptional vigor by Henry Jackson and the JCAE, deserves special attention, for it illustrates how technological optimism and inflated Cold War fears about the prowess of Soviet scientists could interact to produce a spectacular fiasco of nuclear engineering. When the atomic airplane was first proposed in 1945, it was obvious that the concept was impracticable unless a lightweight metal shield could be built that would protect pilots from the intense radiation produced by a reactor. This was the primary reason a review committee led by Robert

Oppenheimer and Harvard's president James Conant flatly recommended to the Pentagon in 1947 that NEPA research be "terminated promptly."

Because of the unquenchable support it enjoyed from a churning military-industrial-congressional combine, NEPA had nine lives and persisted for fourteen years. It acquired one of its new lives in the first dark winter of the Korean War, when, in the final months of 1950, the Defense Department approved a "crash" effort to put an atomic airplane in the air by 1957. A peak level of 14,000 employees in seven states ultimately worked on this ill-managed atomic Kittyhawk program (described afterward by one U.S. manager as "a pretty good monument of how not to run a technical program"), but there was no real progress to report when the 1957 deadline arrived.

But the project was born again through the midwifery of a pseudo-event that historians now rank as one of the classic Red scares of the 1950s. This rebirth came about as a result of a sensational "news" story in the December 1, 1958, issue of *Aviation Week,* the booster trade journal of the thriving aerospace industry. In an account that featured renderings of this fantastic machine, the magazine announced that "A nuclear-powered bomber is being flight tested in the Soviet Union." That story, an utter fabrication "leaked" to *Aviation Week* by a Pentagon "source," caused an uproar in Washington that inspired Senator Richard Russell of Georgia (the home of Lockheed's ANP laboratory) to deplore this "ominous threat to world peace and yet another blow to the prestige and security of our nation and the free world."

This "resurrection" of NEPA provided an injection of fear and enthusiasm that kept this nuclear boondoggle going for another two years until President John F. Kennedy canceled it outright. In the end, this absurd program cost American taxpayers over half the cost of the Manhattan Project itself. The long quest for this elusive master weapon set many Cold War records. It offered proof that some atomic-age technologies had limits. It inspired the JCAE to hold an unprecedented thirty-six secret hearings on a single project. It provided the prime contractor, General Electric, with $457 million worth of business. And it won distinction in U.S. industrial history as an endeavor where, to borrow John Tierney's phrase, "never have so many worked so long for so little."

Worse yet, when the Cold War ended and the truth trickled out, Soviet scientists revealed that their country never participated in the race for the A-plane!

It is lamentable that in the first phase of the atomic age, an unbound, hyperactive Congress failed the American people. Democracy withers when dissent is suppressed and it was symbolic of the time that any member of Congress who voted against a Defense Department appropriation bill was putting his or her political future at risk. Most members of Congress failed by being passive, some by promoting extravagant projects which poured precious resources into black-hole projects, and still others by lobbying incessantly for exotic and bizarre weapons programs that quickened the momentum of an arms race already running out of control.

THE MILITARY UNBOUND

President Truman's decisions produced a great leap in war technology that dwarfed all previous breakthroughs in arms and military machines. His directive had a major thrust at Los Alamos by accelerating ongoing work of the atomic scientists, but it had a revolutionary impact on the U.S. military establishment by handing generals and admirals opportunities to create a new generation of weapons and weapons systems that would extend the reach—and destructive force—of American power.

Prior to the president's decisions, atomic policy making had been held in abeyance at the Pentagon. Shortages of fissionable materials had initially restricted expansion of the nation's atomic arsenal, and the Atomic Energy Commission, by law, had retained physical custody of a stockpile of fewer than 100 atomic bombs. These inhibitions had combined to prevent strategic planners at the Pentagon from acquiring sufficient information "to make sound recommendations to the Joint Chiefs of Staff" regarding potential uses of atomic weapons.

As 1950 began, devices designed to be dropped from long-range bombers were the only atomic weapons at hand. However, Truman's announcement—and the frenetic demands it evoked from Senator McMahon for thousands of atomic weapons and for the use of atomic energy "as fire power in the hands of troops, sailors and airmen"—drastically altered the martial ground rules of the atomic age and propelled our military establishment into a race for nuclear security that became the centerpiece of the Cold War.

Two momentous developments in 1950 returned military men to the forefront of American life. With numbers and varieties of atomic arms as an emerging new symbol of U.S. prowess, the first transforming event was the president's call for accelerated production of nuclear weapons. The second was a war on the Korean peninsula which evoked the condemnation of the United Nations and plunged the United States into a brutal, prolonged police action that some feared might ignite a hot war with the Soviet Union.

Unbound and embattled, our military establishment lost little time expanding its influence over decisions about tomorrow's nuclear weapons. Each of the three services began pushing pet projects to augment its role in the atomic wars of the future. As a consequence, by the time the United States detonated its first H-bomb almost three years later, the Pentagon (with timely assists from hawkish members of Congress) was calling the shots on strategies. Meanwhile, the attitudes and aims that would dictate the course of the race for nuclear weapons were hardening into dogmas that would, for the duration of the Cold War, dominate American thinking about nuclear war and efforts to achieve arms control agreements with Soviet leaders.

The first competing power center to be diminished by Pentagon pressures was the AEC. By 1953 the interface between the atomic scientists and the military services had been utterly altered. In the first weeks of his presidency, Dwight Eisenhower, subject only to his powers as commander-in-chief, had transferred custody of all combat-ready nuclear weapons to military officials. Shorn of its authority to influence weapons-oriented policy making, the AEC's paramount task was to meet the ever-growing "requirements" of the military services by designing "better" bombs and manufacturing new lines of battlefield weapons.

One Manhattan Project veteran who observed these changes with misgivings was J. Carson Mark, a mathematician who for many years headed the theoretical division at the Los Alamos laboratory. He and his associates responded as good soldiers to the incessant demands of the three services. However, misgivings turned to dismay as orders for additional weapons piled up. These involved numbers, types, end uses, and deployments of weapons which far exceeded anything envisioned by the original atomic scientists, and sent a signal that Pentagon planners were contemplating monstrous levels of overkill.

When he saw the race for weapons of mass destruction running out of control, Dr. Mark scrutinized the justifications presented by the advocates of incessant expansion and realized that the atomic scientists and the American people were being flimflammed by "a great deal of meretricious lobbying to the effect that we are danger-ously 'behind,' that our 'security' depends on being 'ahead,' and that a nuclear war might be 'winnable' if we only had enough firepower, and so on." In a postretirement memoir, Mark, a wry man who often understated his opinions, observed: "An assumption that there [was] something incoherent and mindless in these developments might well be correct."

Carson Mark's observations also told him that the dynamo driving the overproduction of nuclear weapons was the assumption that the United States could not be "secure" unless each military service had enough deliverable warheads to "destroy" the Soviet Union. The atomic triad (a Cold War construct sustained over the years by the parochial loyalties of members of Congress who served on the military committees) dominated U.S. war planning for four decades and generated bloated appropriations for the defense estab-lishment and the arms industry. An ever-changing array of lavish army, navy, and air force weapons systems bearing names such as Polaris, Trident, B-52, Stealth, Minuteman, and MX have been the progeny of the mindless "security" logic spawned by the triad con-cept.

THE TRIAD AND GAP GAMESMANSHIP

At intervals, when a service wanted to whip up support for a particu-lar weapons system, a Machiavellian maneuver was perfected by the military-congressional-industrial complex to convince the country that a perilous "gap" had emerged in a vulnerable area of the triad.

Normally (as in the case of the atomic airplane), the service in trouble would initiate action by leaking critical "facts" to the press. A congressional committee would then conduct a hearing at which military and industrial witnesses trumpeted revelations that the Soviet Union had stolen a march and was about to gain a war-winning advantage in strategic weaponry. Demands for catch-up action would come next, followed by a crash program to close the gap.

One of these exercises involved the "bomber gap." Using flimsy evidence, in 1955 the air force warned a committee headed by Senator Stuart Symington, secretary of the air force during the Truman administration, that Moscow was planning to deploy 600 to 800 Bison jet bombers and turboprop Bears by the end of 1959. The upshot was a huge buildup of bombers that wasted billions on aircraft such as the never-deployed B-70. (The Pentagon subsequently admitted that by 1962 the Russians had built fewer than 200 Bisons and Bears.)

Another, more sensational "gap" surfaced in the fall of 1957, when the Soviets surprised the West by using a large rocket to loft the first earth-circling satellite into space. Although a calm President Eisenhower put the Sputnik launch in perspective with the observation "We never considered ourselves to be in a race," the launching of this 184-pound sphere was interpreted by many journalists and by Democrats who were eyeing the 1960 presidential campaign as a humiliating defeat for the United States. The media hype that made this spectacle in outer space seem Olympian created confusion and a sense of national failure by magnifying this "first" into a stunning technological victory for the Soviet Union. The truth, as the actual deployment of ballistic missiles in the next four years would soon demonstrate, was that where military applications of this art were concerned, army rocket experts at the Redstone Arsenal in Alabama enjoyed a substantial lead over their Russian counterparts. Yet the furor created a "crisis in American confidence" that dominated and dampened the national mood for many months.

In his trenchant 1985 book, *The Heavens and the Earth: A Political History of the Space Age,* the historian Walter McDougall has illuminated the truths and illusions that were hovering over the rocketry race between the United States and the USSR at the time of America's highly publicized Sputnik "defeat." Several subtle truths, McDougall informs us, were hidden in the folds of this episode.

President Eisenhower had vigorously supported a secret effort to develop rockets and missiles that, experts believed, would have the potential to deliver nuclear bombs on targets thousands of miles away. If Ike had considered it vital for the United States to put a small satellite in outer space in 1956, a year ahead of Sputnik, the army's Redstone rocket was ready to fly and could have been used to achieve this objective.

It was Eisenhower's view that until tests were completed and ICBMs were in hand, "first and foremost, space was about spying," and his experts had been working overtime developing a top-secret spy satellite that would use advanced photographic techniques to provide intelligence about the Soviet Union's military preparedness. However, the lack of any legal precedent for such overflights, as Professor McDougall explains, confronted Ike's advisors with this quandary:

> There were two ways the legal path might be cleared for spy satellites—the real priority of U.S. policy. One was if the United States could launch an innocent little scientific grapefruit under international auspices . . . thus establishing by common consent the right to orbit satellites over the territory of other countries. The second way was for the Soviets to launch a satellite first.

Eisenhower's supposed failures were enveloped in ironies. For example, during the prolonged furor in this country over the missile and space "gaps," the president, manacled by imperatives of secrecy, could not use vital facts to defend his record. Ike knew with substantial certainty that the Soviets were moving at a slow pace in building an intercontinental ballistic missile force. This knowledge came from top-secret pictures taken over the previous two years by a remarkable U-2 spy plane the United States had developed to make unimpeded flights in the stratosphere over the Soviet Union. But Eisenhower's hands were tied, and he could not reveal that U.S. technologists had won this vital reconnaissance race.

Aided by America's self-inflicted inferiority complex, the Russians easily convinced the world that their Sputnik signified they had leapfrogged ahead of the United States in military rocketry and space science. Eisenhower, silenced by the dictates of secrecy, viewed

Sputnik through a different lens. To him, this feat opened a door to open-sky surveillance that would in due course enable U.S. leaders to follow strategic developments behind the Iron Curtain on a day-to-day basis. Ike realized that this would represent a bonanza for American intelligence. He was also aware that in the long run, as the Soviets perfected their own spy satellites, mutual surveillance would aid the cause of peace by eliminating military surprises and helping the leaders of the superpowers understand each other's motives and behavior.

In his study of the missile-"gap" aspect of this larger contro-versy, Professor McDougall defends President Eisenhower's leader-ship and criticizes the political gamesmanship Senators Lyndon Johnson and John Kennedy used to alarm the electorate by painting a misleading picture of a "space and missile mess." The political pot began boiling in the first days of the Sputnik crisis when the Alsop brothers sensationalized the missile issue by reporting in their na-tionally syndicated column that officers in the Pentagon were "shud-dering" at the prospect that the United States was about to lose its "almost unchallenged superiority in nuclear striking power." John-son, then the Senate majority leader, responded for the Democrats by leading a high-profile investigation in 1958 that extracted guesses by military and intelligence experts that the Russians were preparing to deploy up to 1,000 ICBMs by the end of 1961.

The dire conclusions drawn by the Democrats about the Soviet challenge—and the urgency of winning the missile race—became both a theme of their 1960 presidential campaign and a goad that galvanized U.S. production of nuclear weapons to levels which gen-erated the enormous overkill capacity that became a fixture of the Cold War arms race. Thereafter, missile-gap fears exerted a powerful influence on American policy makers. History offers abundant evi-dence that the 1960 victory of the Kennedy-Johnson ticket provided a thrust that brought the U.S. stockpile to an all-time, overflow peak of 32,500 nuclear weapons in 1967.

Knowing that newly elected presidents were especially vulnera-ble to their arguments at the conclusion of national elections, the military-industrial-congressional complex was invariably ready with multibillion-dollar plans for new weapons systems. In 1969, for exam-ple, a scare argument that the Russians had achieved an edge in antiballistic missiles prompted the Nixon administration to waste $5.7 billion on a useless Safeguard antiballistic-missile system. In the 1970s, the indefatigable weapons lobby panted over gaps in chemical and biological weapons and stressed a need for crash programs to "harden" missile silos and underground command centers. Then, at the outset of the Reagan administration, veterans of the gap brigade staged a last, lavish hurrah when a self-styled Committee on the Present Danger demanded, and got, an extravagant military buildup by convincing President Reagan that a "window of vulnerability" was tempting the Russians to launch a first strike and eliminate the land-based missile system maintained by that sector of the triad known as the U.S. Army.

Over the years, crafty strategists of the military-industrial complex conjured up a succession of horror stories about imminent threats to America's survival. One obsession that kindled their fears in the last two decades of the Cold War was the fixed idea that the United States had to have the capacity to destroy the seventy-five underground "command posts" that had been built to protect Soviet military and civilian leaders in a nuclear war. This delusion was based on the fanciful supposition that after a nation-destroying nuclear exchange, it would be vital for the United States to have the capacity to "root out" all surviving enemy commanders, even though they would have no one to whom they could issue commands. Once this obsession acquired a policy status, it resulted in a huge expansion of the army's Minuteman program and, in the 1980s, the actual production of the air force's $1 billion-per-copy Stealth bomber.

History's judgments are sometimes expressed in statistics, and the disparity between the fear figures bandied about by the weapons-gap brigade and the actual outcome of the arms race between the superpowers constitutes a shocking verdict. The missile gap, from its beginnings in the fall of 1957 to its end in 1961, was a mirage. By 1962, the U.S. had deployed 180 ICBMs and had at least a 10-to-1 advantage in this crucial category of offensive weapons. Once he studied the data gathered by our spy satellites, Robert McNamara, President Kennedy's secretary of defense, conceded there was no missile gap. The official estimate of the Soviet force was 75 ICBMs, but in the mid-seventies Daniel O. Graham, a former chief of the Defense Intelligence Agency, revealed that the actual 1961 figure was 4.

Data published in 1989 by the *Bulletin of the Atomic Scientists* in the aftermath of the Cold War reveal additional monumental disparities between the contrasting nuclear forces of the superpowers. All during the 1950s, U.S. forces had an advantage in warheads—and in combat-ready, long-range bombers—so enormous an advantage that the scare stories about perilous gaps were outlandish. In 1950, for example, the United States had a 350-to-5 advantage in available atomic weapons; and a decade later, with the triad awash in nuclear weapons from the Eisenhower production pipeline, the most reliable estimates put this bulge at 18,700 to 1,700.

These incongruous figures explain why Dwight Eisenhower, in his famous farewell address at the end of his presidency, saw fit to warn the American people that a "military-industrial complex" was wasting billions by exerting "unwarranted influence" over the nation's arms policies and policy makers with a potential to waste hundreds of billions. This message originated in the mind of a military hero president who for years had almost single-handedly resisted unnecessary defense spending. It was the counsel of a leader who had failed in his last year in office to achieve what he wanted most—an arms-control treaty that would ban nuclear tests and pave the way for agreements to place controls on the ever-escalating nuclear arms race.

As he left office, Ike was worried by the prospect that military officers, arms-industry lobbyists, and some members of Congress were promoting buildups of overlapping, unnecessary armaments. Eisenhower's warning was dismissed by his contemporaries as the complaint of a tired old soldier, but as ordinary citizens gained access to facts that enabled them to evaluate the excesses of the Cold War, Eisenhower's farewell address became a bible for those who saw arms control and gradual disarmament as the only salvation for humankind.

The overpowering truth about the race for nuclear superiority is that in nearly all areas of competition the United States enjoyed a wide lead over its rival superpower. In *Race to Oblivion*, Herbert York, one of President Eisenhower's key advisors, described the pacesetter role the United States played in the postwar race for nuclear weapons:

Our unilateral decisions have set the rate and scale for most of the individual steps in the strategic-arms race. In many cases we started development before they did and we easily established a large and long-lasting lead in terms of deployed numbers and types. Examples include the A-bomb itself, intercontinental bombers, submarine-launched ballistic missiles, and MIRV. . . . In some cases, to be sure, they started development work ahead of us . . . but we usually reacted so strongly that our deployments and capabilities soon ran far ahead of theirs and we, in effect, even here, determined the final size of the operation.

Observing the same race from a different angle, in 1981 the historian-diplomat George Kennan reviewed what Victor Weisskopf had characterized as "the craziest arms race in history" and presented his assessment of our nation's moral responsibility for the leadership it displayed in setting the stage for an atomic Armageddon:

We must remember that it has been we Americans who, at almost every step of the road, have taken the lead in the development of this sort of weaponry. It was we who first produced and tested such a device; we who were the first to raise its destructiveness to a new level with the hydrogen bomb; we who introduced the multiple warhead . . . and we alone, so help us God, who have used the weapon in anger against others, and against tens of thousands of helpless noncombatants at that.

7

Pursuers of Peace
and Pursuers of "Victory"

The United States should always display a spirit of firmness without truculence, conciliation without appeasement, confidence without arrogance.

The world simply must not go on living in the fear of the terrible consequences of nuclear war.
—Dwight D. Eisenhower (1953)

Great lessons of history normally emerge only after distance provides a perspective for definitive judgments, but as the Cold War winds down and the prospect of an atomic Armageddon recedes, one truth of paramount importance is already visible. It derives from the realization that a third world war, which might have extinguished all life on this planet, was averted less through brilliant diplomacy than by prudent, personal decisions and initiatives made by leaders of the superpowers, who decided their "nuclear option" was irrational and exercised restraint. A memorable example of such an initiative came at the Cuban missile crisis, when Chairman Khrushchev, in his conciliatory letter to President Kennedy, concluded with the statement, "We are of sound mind."

Any effort to understand the events that produced a peaceful ending of the Cold War must begin with daunting questions that have long hovered over the rivalry between the United States and the USSR. How, we have wondered for four decades, could two nations in the grip of a frightening arms race—and whipsawed by ideological differences that appeared to be irreconcilable—avert a nuclear holocaust? How, in the years when communication between them was shockingly inadequate, were fateful miscalculations avoided? And how did the political leaders, who had the final say as the commanders of thousands of widely dispersed nuclear weapons, prevent a spiraling arms race from touching off a global conflagration?

Any search for answers to these questions must ultimately focus on military advantages the United States enjoyed until the mid-sixties and on decisions made since 1945 by the nine U.S. presidents and seven Soviet leaders who had the power to launch what Mikhail Gorbachev once described as "the nuclear tornado." With few exceptions leaders on both sides exercised caution, and their decisions against using nuclear weapons in any circumstances brought about a tacit condominium of coexistence, which ultimately prevented a nuclear holocaust.

U.S. PRESIDENTS AND THEIR CONDOMINIUM OF COEXISTENCE

As the 1980s ended, two comprehensive works were published, which chronicled the decisions made during this uneasy *modus vivendi*. The first was McGeorge Bundy's *Danger and Survival: Choices About the Bomb in the First Fifty Years*. The second, by John Newhouse, bore the title *War and Peace in the Nuclear Age*. Bundy and Newhouse trace the conflicts that could have produced a nuclear holocaust and examine the roles played by the leaders of the two enemy nations in resolving these conflicts.

Harry Truman established the post-Hiroshima pattern of prudence that would emerge as a constant feature of U.S. presidential leadership in the atomic age. Bundy describes the Truman of 1949 as a "different man" from the novice president who exulted over the holocaustal bombing of two Japanese cities. By his second term,

Harry Truman was the acknowledged leader of the "free world" and his latter-day policy making was guided by what he called his "strategy of peace."

President Truman's convictions were displayed in the restraint with which he responded to the military crises that arose on his watch in Berlin and on the Korean peninsula. Although the United States was the only nation to have an arsenal of deliverable nuclear weapons during his tenure, in neither instance did Truman contemplate preventive strikes against the Soviet Union or seriously consider using nuclear bombs as battlefield weapons. An impulsive handwritten note in his diary entry indicates that during one frustrating week in 1952, Harry Truman fantasized about the consequences of using the threat of nuclear destruction to force Stalin and Mao Tse-tung to end the Korean conflict. However, he never discussed this option with his war cabinet, and during the Korean conflict he fired the two war leaders—General Douglas MacArthur and Navy Secretary Francis Matthews—who publicly advocated using atomic weapons.

Prudence was Truman's polestar while he was the supreme commander of U.S. military forces. To him, bombs were presidential business, and he kept a tight grip on his nation's atomic weapons. Even in the darkest days of the Berlin blockade, he rejected the pleas of his secretary of defense that military officers be given physical custody of some atomic bombs. By the end of his presidency, no U.S. atomic weapons had been transported beyond the boundaries of the United States.

While only the United States had deliverable atomic weapons during his years in the White House, Harry Truman understood the mortal implications of nuclear war and set an example of restraint that influenced the course of the Cold War. Of his stewardship, McGeorge Bundy has written, "After Nagasaki he never came close to the use of even one [bomb] against an enemy." Harry Truman's final, official contribution to the ongoing dialogue about war and peace in the nuclear age came in a farewell radio broadcast. "Starting an atomic war," he told the world, "is totally unthinkable for rational men."

However, by approving the development of the hydrogen bomb, by endorsing the concept that U.S. armed forces should be equipped with thousands of battlefield weapons, and by supporting a huge expansion of America's bomb factories, Truman helped set the stage for an arms race that would, as the U.S. nuclear monopoly expired, escalate the risks facing the presidents who succeeded him. While the race for atomic weapons was acquiring momentum in the 1950s, the world needed a calm, confident leader who would continue Truman's policies of restraint and initiate a dialogue with Stalin's successors to reduce the fears and suspicions that were exacerbating relations between the superpowers.

Such a leader emerged when Dwight D. Eisenhower, another commonsense farm boy from the American Midwest, was elected president in 1952. A professional soldier who evolved into a consummate diplomat in his role as the supreme commander in Europe during World War II, Eisenhower believed that a live-and-let-live relationship between the United States and the USSR was essential. Dwight Eisenhower fit the pivotal decade of his presidency. In the words of Emmett John Hughes, his friend and confidant, he had "a tireless will to conciliate, a speechless horror of war, and a restless hope for peace."

DWIGHT EISENHOWER'S CONTRIBUTION

Most Americans, myself included, were taken aback by the nonviolent end of the Cold War. I was finishing months of research on this essay when the final curtain fell in 1991, and President Dwight Eisenhower emerged at the top of my list of surprises. Eisenhower, my survey told me, was the only postwar president who was not a cold warrior. I also concluded that his personal diplomacy in the 1950s set a pattern of conduct for his successors that influenced the outcome of the Cold War conflict.

There were many historical facts that led me to these conclusions. There was the recognition that in his eight years in the White House Eisenhower studiously shunned the martial rhetoric of anti-Communism. There was the revelation that President Eisenhower operated from the conviction that, "There's just no point in talking about winning a nuclear war." There was the evidence that he steadfastly rejected the counsel of his party's hawkish leaders that he use U.S. military power to roll back Communism. And there was the undeniable proof that it was Dwight Eisenhower who broke new ground by treating the leader of the Soviet Union as an equal and by starting face-to-face exchanges that led to treaties, agreements, and understandings that made it possible for the Cold War to end peacefully.

Having served for six years in Congress during the Eisenhower years, I had insights about some events, but it was the fresh perspective I gained from rereadings of Emmett John Hughes's remarkably forthright 1963 book, *The Ordeal of Power,* that caused me to revise my opinion of President Eisenhower's contributions to the cause of peace.

Valuable insights into the mind and faith of Dwight David Eisenhower were provided by Emmett Hughes's account of the genesis of the speech the new president gave in April 1953, a month after the death of Joseph Stalin, to the American Society of Newspaper Editors. Hughes was alone with Ike in the Oval Office when the president began his first musings about the message he wanted to deliver to the world. Eisenhower expressed his desires and his passion for peace that afternoon with these words:

> Look, I am tired—and I think everyone is tired—of just plain indictments of the Soviet regime. I think it would be wrong—in fact, asinine—for me to get up before the world now to make another of these indictments. Instead, just one thing matters: what do we have to offer the world. . . . The past speaks for itself. I am interested in its future. Both their government and ours now have new men in them. The slate is clean. Now let us begin talking to each other. And let us say what we've got to say so that every person on earth can understand it. Here is what we propose. And if you—the Soviet Union—can improve on it we want to hear it.

The magnanimous address the president ultimately delivered to the newspaper editors was the very opposite of a Cold War speech. Here are some of the themes Eisenhower used in presenting his vision of a world that could rise above the arms race and the hostility it was fostering:

Every gun that is fired, every warship launched, every rocket fired signifies, in the final sense, a theft from those who hunger and are not fed, those who are cold and not clothed. . . .

This is not a way of life at all, in any true sense. Under the cloud of threatening war, it is humanity hanging from a cross of iron. . . .

A world that begins to witness the rebirth of trust among nations can find its way to a peace that is neither partial nor punitive. . . .

This government is ready to ask its people to join with all nations in devoting a substantial percentage of the savings achieved by disarmament to a fund for world aid and reconstruction.

President Eisenhower's appeal renewed his country's moral leadership in the world. Regrettably, however, it did not evoke a favorable response either from Stalin's successors in the Kremlin or from John Foster Dulles, Eisenhower's hawkish secretary of state, or from the congressional leaders of the president's party.

There is abundant evidence that the 1950s might have been the most dangerous decade of the Cold War if Dwight Eisenhower had shared the anti-Communist phobias and aims of Dulles and the Republican leaders who wanted to use military muscle to achieve victories over the Communists. Soon after Stalin's death, for example, Secretary Dulles informed Emmett Hughes that he opposed diplomacy that might produce an armistice in Korea "until we have shown—before all Asia—our clear superiority by giving the Chinese one hell of a licking." Hughes also recounts that William Knowland, the Senate majority leader, "never wearied of forcing upon the President hours of argument in advocacy of his own favored schemes for remaking the world [by military force] notably by a bold American blockade of the coast of Communist China."

Dwight Eisenhower listened to such counsels, but he invariably exercised restraint. There were no American military adventures while Ike was commander-in-chief. He recognized that nuclear weapons had swept the world into an era when normal concepts of military victory and defeat were meaningless. And, knowing more about the slippery slopes of wars than his critics, he was never swayed from his conviction that it was wise to avoid small wars that might ignite larger conflagrations.

In the spring of 1954, for example, Eisenhower refused to assent when a phalanx of advisors, which included Secretary Dulles, Vice-President Richard Nixon, and Admiral Radford, the chairman of the Joint Chiefs of Staff, urged air strikes to support a beleaguered French army in Indochina. He exercised similar restraint later when urged to conduct an operation to bolster Nationalist Chinese troops stationed on two insignificant offshore islands (a move Chiang Kai-shek and his supporters in Congress hoped would pitch the United States into a war on the mainland of China). And in the fall of 1956 Eisenhower shocked the leaders of Great Britain and France when he condemned their invasion of the Suez Canal zone and supported a United Nations resolution that forced them to withdraw.

Dwight Eisenhower exercised caution in forming his judgments about using America's military might. And once he decided not to use his nation's military option, in the words of General Andrew Goodpaster, his national security advisor, "He was an expert at finding reasons for not doing things."

Knowing the word "coexistence" symbolized Communist treachery to Senator Knowland and other hard-liners, President Eisenhower eliminated it from his vocabulary. Yet one of his most important contributions to peace emanated from his conviction that reason would ultimately prevail if military confrontations were avoided and the leaders of the superpowers met and discussed the live-and-let-live realities imposed by the nuclear stalemate they were creating.

At his first face-to-face encounter with the Soviet leaders at Geneva in 1955, Ike quickly established himself as an effective spokesman for peace. The dramatic climax of this first summit meeting since the 1945 Potsdam conference came when President Eisenhower's assertion that "the United States will never take part in an aggressive war" evoked the spontaneous response from then Premier Bulganin, "We believe that statement." Richard Rovere, a journalist who witnessed the impact of this personal diplomacy, subsequently wrote that Ike possessed an "absolutely unique ability to convince people that he has no talent for duplicity."

Looking back at the 1950s, it is now clear to me that along with most of my fellow Democrats I misjudged Dwight Eisenhower's accomplishments in the field of diplomacy. We belittled his capacity for leadership because we felt that he was a stand-patter on domestic issues and lacked the political convictions and skills of our heroes, Roosevelt and Truman. And we did not fully appreciate his statesmanship in foreign affairs because we mistakenly assumed that the rigid, moralistic anti-Communism espoused by John Foster Dulles reflected Ike's views about war and peace and accommodations with the Soviet Union.

I realize now that few of us understood the subtle but profound differences between Eisenhower's outlook and that of Foster Dulles. Nor did we appreciate the ideas that animated Ike and motivated his military decisions and his personal strategy for peacemaking. We also underestimated the significance of having a military hero in the White House at a time when the nation was roiled by fears of Communist aggression. Looking back at the chief executives he had observed for over three decades, William Fulbright, the former chairman of the Senate Foreign Relations Committee, rated Ike as the most effective foreign policy president. Fulbright told a *New York Times* reporter in 1983: "My respect for Eisenhower grows almost daily. There wasn't this machismo factor like Kennedy and Johnson and Reagan."

On the overarching issues of war and peace, I now see that Dwight David Eisenhower was ideally equipped to serve as president in the perilous years of the 1950s. He was a calm soldier-statesman whose nuclear judgments—and opinions about our nation's military preparedness—could not be questioned. His credentials put him on high ground where, without incurring the wrath of right-wingers, he could conduct a campaign to convince the men in the Kremlin that the United States was not scheming to encircle or destroy the USSR. Similarly, he could enter into private negotiations with Nikita Khrushchev about national security issues without risking charges that his perception of the Communist threat was "soft."

With a venturesomeness that startled the world's diplomats, soon after John Foster Dulles succumbed to cancer in May 1959, Dwight Eisenhower became his own secretary of state and set out to use his reputation and goodwill to promote the cause of peace. Earlier he had confided to Emmett Hughes that he was dissatisfied with all the "martial clichés of the struggle against Communism" and bored with the familiar "definitions of American strength in terms of military power or simple anti-Soviet truculence." It was time, Ike thought, to bear witness to one's "positive beliefs."

What followed was a spasm of personal diplomacy Secretary Dulles would have abhorred. Ike invited Chairman Khrushchev to travel around the United States and to join him for a private weekend at his mountain retreat in Maryland, where a general amity was translated into a "spirit of Camp David." Eisenhower then scheduled two hectic airborne peace caravans that, in his last winter as president, took him first to eleven countries in Europe and Asia, and, weeks later, to Brazil, Argentina, Chile, and Uruguay.

Khrushchev, meanwhile, had reciprocated by inviting Eisenhower to spend nearly two weeks in the Soviet Union. This midsummer transcontinental tour was planned to include visits to Moscow and Leningrad, a tour of the Stalingrad battlefield (in the company of Russian generals), a stop at the chairman's summer *dacha* on the Black Sea, and a final stopover at Lake Baikal in eastern Siberia, before the president landed in Tokyo for an official visit to Japan.

The most important element of Dwight Eisenhower's peace program for 1960 envisioned the convening of a summit meeting that would include Chairman Khrushchev, France's President de Gaulle and the prime minister of Great Britain, Harold Macmillan. Ike set the stage for this conference by traveling to Europe for a weekend session at which the West's leaders discussed proposals that might improve East-West relations. This winter meeting produced an agreement to invite Khrushchev to a series of summits, with the first convening in Paris in early May.

But bad luck—and an exhibition of incredible stupidity by the leaders of the air force and the CIA—sabotaged President Eisenhower's plans for conciliation and aborted the most promising meeting of East and West leaders since the end of the Second World War. On May 1, 1960, a high-altitude U.S. reconnaissance aircraft on a needless spy mission that should have been cancelled was shot down over the heartland of the Soviet Union. Inept handling of this crisis by the president and his associates exacerbated the situation and put Khrushchev in a political bind, as a result of which he stalked out of the Paris Summit Conference and cancelled his invitation to Ike to visit the Soviet Union.

The Paris humiliation hung over President Eisenhower's last

months in the White House. As a result of the overblown "Sputnik scare," leading Democrats were already unfairly attacking him for a nonexistent "missile gap" and accusing his administration of laxity in letting Khrushchev and the Russians get ahead of us in education, space exploration, and world prestige. Ike endured these gibes, for he knew the United States enjoyed nuclear superiority over the Russians, and he likewise realized that in the coming years the Soviet's Sputnik success would be an instrument for peace by encouraging both nations to use spy-satellite technology to gather invaluable intelligence in ways that would ease military tensions.

Dwight Eisenhower did not achieve his ultimate goals, but he was nevertheless a towering figure of the Cold War. He worked together with the post-Stalin leaders to rearrange the furniture of diplomacy to make peaceful accommodations possible. Moreover, in a time of great danger, he was a risk-taker who broke new ground for peace and set a pattern of restraint that influenced the behavior of later leaders of the superpowers. He, more than any other leader, gave vitality to the supremely important precedent—honored for three decades on both sides of the Iron Curtain—that nuclear bombs were not to be used as weapons of war. The verdict of Chalmers Roberts, the *Washington Post's* chief diplomatic correspondent, that President Eisenhower was the leader who "broke the mold of the Cold War" may be history's verdict as well.

NIKITA KHRUSHCHEV'S REVOLUTION OF COMMON SENSE

Nikita Khrushchev was the most protean—and the most misunderstood—leader who came to power during the Cold War. Americans of my generation saw him as a crude, reckless, hard-line Communist who devoted his main energies to plotting the downfall of the democracies. This was the Khrushchev who pounded a table with his shoe at the United Nations, who issued rocket-rattling threats that made Berlin an anxious cockpit of the Cold War from 1958 to 1962, who provoked a frightening confrontation in Cuba by stealthily moving missiles into that island, and who, we were told through a mistranslation, uttered a belligerent "We-will-bury-you" boast at an international conference.

But the same panache that encouraged Khrushchev to be a risk-taker abroad led him to push home-front reforms that challenged the assumptions of the old Bolsheviks and subtly altered the outlook and the aims of Soviet society. If Nikita Khrushchev emerges as an important historical figure of his century, it will be because he started a renovation of the cruel, oppressive social-political system erected by Joseph Stalin. The famous "secret speech" he delivered in 1956 to the leaders of the Communist world initiated a fitful campaign of de-Stalinization that helped pave the way for the *perestroika* of Mikhail Gorbachev.

Fresh insights provided by the nonviolent outcome of the Cold War have not only elevated Eisenhower's repute as a peacemaker, but have also prodded historians to reassess Khrushchev's contributions to this turning point of history. This reappraisal is already under way. Characterizing Chairman Khrushchev as a "very remarkable man" who "transcended the system that made him," Edward Crankshaw has accorded him status as a "world statesman." The historian Adam Ulam has described the chairman's reforms as a "revolution of common sense." And the leaders of the Gorbachev generation have acknowledged him as the forerunner who made it possible for them to contemplate the changes that are altering post-Soviet society today.

It is also clear that lines of personal communication established by Eisenhower and Khrushchev created a bridge of understanding that helped their countries avoid a nuclear war. The exchanges that enabled President Kennedy and Chairman Khrushchev to resolve the Cuban missile crisis were conducted on that bridge, as were the negotiations that later produced the Limited Test Ban Treaty in 1963, the arms-control agreements of the 1970s, and the general relaxation of tensions that, for nearly two decades, characterized the relationship between the Brezhnev regime and the administrations of four American presidents.

Bundy's 1988 appraisal of Khrushchev's performance as a crisis manager has further enhanced his reputation. In his study of nuclear diplomacy, Bundy asserts that "no one has made a larger contribution than Khrushchev to our understanding of what can and cannot be done with nuclear weapons."

KENNEDY, KHRUSHCHEV, AND THE TIME OF MAXIMUM DANGER

The two most dangerous confrontations of the Cold War came at Berlin and Cuba during the presidency of John F. Kennedy, and each arose out of gambles taken by Nikita Khrushchev to test the will of his inexperienced adversary. Kennedy, the quickest of the quick learners, lacked the prestige and military acumen of his predecessor, but he took an unflinching stance when he and his advisors concluded that Khrushchev was bluffing and did not want the Berlin dispute to escalate into either a conventional or a nuclear conflict.

The Cuban crisis, a much riskier Russian gamble that brought the superpowers nearer to the edge of the atomic abyss, was both a test of nerve and a test of the value of the understandings and accommodations Eisenhower and Khrushchev had developed during their interactions in the 1950s. The deft diplomacy that resolved the Cuban missile crisis will always fascinate historians, for it embodies a landmark of restraint in a century marred by abject failures of diplomacy that produced the most destructive wars in all of human history.

Kennedy and Khrushchev and their advisors were the architects of that achievement, but the many studies of this gripping standoff also reveal that the moderation exercised on each side was facilitated by very good U.S. photographic intelligence and by insights and assumptions that had evolved out of interactions which occurred prior to the Cuban confrontation. Those insights allowed each leader to form sophisticated judgments concerning what their opponent would probably do, or not do, if face-saving compromises were proposed.

It is plain, for example, that during this grim October game of nuclear chess the respective ambassadors played a crucial role in interpreting the motives, fears, and probable next moves of the two protagonists. As a result of Eisenhower's tension-easing initiatives, ambassadors Charles Bohlen and Llewellyn Thompson had had numerous intimate conversations with Nikita Khrushchev that enabled them to form solid opinions about the character, convictions, and attitudes of the Soviet leader. Ambassador Anatoly Dobrynin was, similarly, a keen student of the American scene, and it is a good bet that his interpretations of the messages conveyed by Robert Kennedy during their private conversations influenced the ultimate decisions made by Nikita Khrushchev.

Three additional ingredients that evolved out of the *modus vivendi* devised by Eisenhower and Khrushchev made it possible for Kennedy and Khrushchev to work out a compromise under intense time pressures. The first involved the acceptance of the principle that satellite and aircraft intelligence was indispensable if both sides were to be able to verify the facts that surrounded their dispute. The second encompassed the vital ledge of trust built in the 1950s. And the third ingredient involved a common candor that would vouchsafe explicit, honest communications between the two beleaguered leaders.

In his recent work, McGeorge Bundy has traced the influence of these and other factors in his account of the Cuban crisis. His picture of Kennedy's cautious search for a compromise that would remove the missiles without humiliating Khrushchev is a story of statecraft that represents the apex of John Kennedy's presidency. He should also have added that John Kennedy took a leaf from Dwight Eisenhower's book when he rejected the advice of belligerent cold warriors in his circle of advisors who wanted to "solve" the Cuban impasse by bombings. By all accounts, it was the rational, conciliatory words Khrushchev used in the long letter he dispatched to the president at the moment of maximum danger that produced the turning point of the Cuban crisis. Every world leader who might gain control of nuclear weapons should be required to memorize the contents of this simple, eloquent document. It is a letter written, literally, on the rim of a precipice, and Bundy accords it "a high place in the annals of crisis communication."

Khrushchev went to the heart of the overarching issues and hastened to mollify Kennedy's concerns by offering assurances that he had no intention of firing the missiles newly emplaced on Cuban soil. "You may regard us with distrust," he stated forthrightly, "but you can at any rate rest assured that we are of sound mind and

tand perfectly well that if we launch an offensive against you,
ill respond in kind." The Soviet leader then explained his
reaction to the American blockade and outlined his anxieties about
the fate of his Cuban ally.

Khrushchev concluded his message with a solemn, forthright
appeal to Kennedy not to allow events to escalate into a nuclear war.
After three decades, the words he used to open a door to the compromise that quickly followed still have resonance:

> If you have not lost command of yourself and clearly realize what this
> could lead to, then, Mr. President, you and I should not now pull on the
> ends of a rope in which you have tied a knot of war, because the harder
> you and I pull, the tighter this knot will become. And a time may come
> when this knot is tied so tight that the person who tied it is no longer
> capable of untying it, and then the knot will have to be cut. What that
> would mean I need not explain to you because you yourself understand
> perfectly well what dread forces our two countries possess.

Events since 1962 signify that the resolution of the Cuban crisis
was a milestone that decisively altered modes of thought on both
sides of the Iron Curtain and fostered the nuclear peace that followed. Cuba, we now see, was a watershed event which tells us that
earth's inhabitants owe a debt to John Kennedy and Nikita Khrushchev for the example they set during the black days of that October
when they controlled themselves and the "dread forces" that could
have wiped out Western civilization. The lessons of Cuba enhanced
the authentic national security of both nations and advanced the
cause of world peace, because the choices made by Kennedy and
Khrushchev were imprinted in the minds of the leaders who followed
them and set an example that compromises can be worked out even
in dire emergencies. Indeed, historian Robert Divine believes the
Cuban confrontation "had a sobering effect on JFK and that if he had
lived he would have done far more than LBJ ever did to try to resolve
Cold War tensions."

THE PEACEFUL COEXISTENCE OF THE SUPERPOWERS

The peace that prevailed between the superpowers from October 1962 until the end of the Cold War in the fall of 1989 was influenced by axioms of prudence that grew out of the confrontation in Cuba. Each side recognized that there would be an atomic holocaust if either used nuclear bombs as war-fighting weapons. Similarly, each tacitly acknowledged that if either nation attempted to achieve political or diplomatic objectives by nuclear blackmail (as Khrushchev had done at Berlin), such a maneuver could trigger an accidental nuclear war. And each knew, despite the insistent arguments of some nuclear strategists, that it was dangerous to presume that any limited use of nuclear weapons would not rapidly escalate into a general conflagration.

The chilling lessons imparted by the Cuban confrontation injected a somber realism into diplomatic relations that opened new vistas for the leaders of the superpowers. This change generated a joint quest for peace-promoting compromises, which, in sequence, produced:

- the disappearance of Berlin as a military bone of contention that had to be resolved;

- the Limited Test Ban Treaty of 1963;

- the tacit understandings not to allow the miniwars in Vietnam and Afghanistan to disrupt ongoing negotiations about arms control and other sensitive diplomatic issues;

- the 1972 SALT agreements, signed in Moscow by President Nixon and Premier Brezhnev, which constrained the buildup of offensive weapons and encompassed the ABM Treaty by which the United States and the USSR agreed to severe limitations on defenses against ballistic missiles;

- the SALT II agreement negotiated by Presidents Ford and Carter; and

- the 1987 INF Treaty which broke new ground by dismantling and destroying an entire class of nuclear weapons.

Yet as significant as these efforts at accommodation were, the fears that fired the boilers of the Cold War were so powerful that worst-case assumptions were always in the forefront, encouraging each superpower to expand and improve its stockpile of nuclear weaponry. This schizoid aspect of the competition between the two nations—this schism between the peace ideas of leaders and the operating war plans they supported—is a paradox of the Cold War epoch that will fascinate students of history for many decades.

In the United States, the incessant struggle between the hard-liners (who supported every new weapon proposed and opposed any arms agreements with the Communists) and the advocates of arms control created a political minefield for presidents. With one exception, all of the presidents after Eisenhower recognized that the pursuit of peace entailed sustained efforts to achieve accommodations that would ease tensions between the superpowers. Their rhetoric varied, but Kennedy, Johnson, Nixon, Ford, and Carter all sought to avoid direct military challenges and to broaden the base of arms control agreements that, each hoped, would reduce the danger of future confrontations.

It was the world's good fortune that Ronald Reagan, the one postwar president who viewed this consensus with disdain, was a latter-day leader who came to power as the antagonisms of the Cold War were waning. Unlike his predecessors, Reagan scoffed at the concept of coexistence and believed the United States should strive for nuclear superiority. His haphazard campaign to reverse the course of the Cold War failed, but the dogmas and machinations of the Reaganites merit close scrutiny because they illuminate the ideological mind-set that could have pitched earth's inhabitants into the abyss of an all-out nuclear war.

RONALD REAGAN AND THE POWER TRIP OF HIS NUCLEAR STRATEGISTS

What, in the name of God, is strategic superiority? What is it politically, militarily, operationally, at these levels of [nuclear weapons] numbers? What do you do with it?

—HENRY KISSINGER,
1974 Press Conference

... "worst-case analysis," [is] a method of analysis that makes it utterly impossible for both superpowers simultaneously to recognize any given strategic situation as being safe for each of them.

—HERBERT YORK (1970)
Race to Oblivion

When it came to nuclear-policy making, Ronald Reagan was the odd man out among postwar presidents. A politician whose outlook was dominated by simplistic images of good and evil, Reagan exhibited little concern about the frightful risks that haunted Dwight Eisenhower and his successors when they contemplated the arms race between the United States and the USSR. Among his eccentricities was a near total lack of interest in the precautions taken by the leaders of superpowers to prevent miscalculations that might provoke nuclear confrontations. Indeed, Reagan made it clear at the outset that his goal was to reverse the "bad" policies of his predecessors.

Using the oversimplifications and misinformation that became a trademark of his presidency, Ronald Reagan encapsulated his foreign policy goals in slogans. Convinced the best way to promote peace was through a massive buildup of military strength, he belittled the concept (implicit in the treaties negotiated by his predecessors) that the cause of peace would be furthered "through pieces of paper." As part of Reagan's overt campaign to "roll back" Communism, he opposed any concessions that would restrict the ability of the United States to achieve nuclear superiority over the Soviet Union. And he believed technological breakthroughs would soon give American leaders power to settle the Cold War on their own terms.

Efforts of Reaganite hard-liners to intensify the Cold War aroused anxieties in many quarters here and abroad. The "evil empire" rhetoric he used to announce his new goals revived memories of the Stalinist era and chilled the hopes of those who believed the arms control agreements negotiated by the Nixon, Ford, and Carter administrations had established a foundation for stable relations with the Soviet Union. An additional complication arose from the hortatory concept of presidential leadership Ronald Reagan brought with him to the Oval Office. As the casting director of his administration,

Reagan assigned himself the role of persuading the public to support the broad goals he had enunciated. To him, his presidency began and ended with his speeches. He ratified decisions hammered out by his subordinates, but he did not like to run meetings, to referee disputes between his advisors, or to take an active part in devising plans to implement the goals he had outlined in his addresses to the American people.

This disengaged, hands-off style of leadership caused Ronald Reagan's administration to veer away from the path beaten by its predecessors and to pursue a different, more perilous, course. Reagan's cold warriors were driven by phobias which told them that U.S. security had been compromised by the policies of restraint previous presidents had followed. It was their conviction that the United States could win the Cold War by amassing overwhelming military power. Moreover, Reagan personally viewed the arms control compromises hammered out with the Russians by Presidents Nixon, Ford, and Carter as a sellout of American security.

During his first years in the White House, President Reagan's outlook was grounded in an assumption that the United States was in terrible danger and was headed for a military confrontation with the Soviet Union. That fear led him to push through the most costly program of peacetime rearmament in history, and encouraged him to impulsively endorse Edward Teller's trillion-dollar Star Wars scheme without consulting either his NATO allies, his secretaries of state and defense, or the U.S. scientific establishment. He moved on another front by allowing his CIA director, William Casey, to turn the armed struggles in Afghanistan, Nicaragua, and Angola into proxy wars to roll back the rising menace of Communism. A supreme irony enveloped all of these activities, for even as Reagan's vast campaign of rearmament got under way, the Soviet economic system was showing strains that would lead to its collapse before the decade of the '80s ran its course.

The changes he supported reflected both Ronald Reagan's visceral anti-Communism and the strategies devised by a clique of right-wing advisors who had won his confidence during his long campaign for the presidency. The presumption that animated the outlook of Reagan's advisors was that "soft" U.S. policies had allowed the Soviet Union to gain the upper hand in the nuclear arms race. By appointing members of this clique to policy-making positions in the State and Defense Departments and the CIA, Ronald Reagan not only turned his back on the consensus of caution that had evolved since the Eisenhower administration, but pushed initiatives that threatened to destabilize the behavior of the superpowers.

Ronald Reagan's hand-picked analysts were products of the strategy laboratories that came to birth in the first years of the atomic age. The air force first conceived the idea that it would be prudent to have secluded groups of supposed experts analyze the impact on war of nuclear weapons. Some members of this new profession did their studies at universities, but most worked at isolated think tanks supported by the Pentagon. They were given the task of developing war scenarios to encompass the consequences of foreseeable nuclear conflicts, and their profession soon acquired, and cherished, the title "nuclear strategists." One cannot fully understand the tortuous history of the Cold War—and the obstacles postwar presidents encountered in pursuing accommodations with the Soviet Union—without first understanding the influence this elite group gradually acquired over U.S. policy making. In the beginning these defense intellectuals worked behind the scenes, but the war scenarios they developed, using game theories and projections of imagined thermonuclear "exchanges," soon dazzled their patrons and won them an audience in the circles where important military and diplomatic options were analyzed.

The individual who established himself at the outset as the grand guru of nuclear strategy was Paul Nitze, a professional diplomat who had succeeded George Kennan as the head of the State Department's planning staff during the final years of the Truman administration. During the Eisenhower years, Nitze refined his theories of strategic one-upmanship as a Johns Hopkins University professor. Other luminaries who emerged as superstars in this exotic new field of intellectual endeavor were Henry A. Kissinger, James Schlesinger, and Herman Kahn.

Kissinger, then director of Harvard's International Seminar, argued for a more imaginative use of atomic bombs in his 1957 book, *Nuclear Weapons and Foreign Policy*. He theorized that nuclear war did not need to be as destructive "as it appears when we think of it in terms of traditional warfare." Moreover, as one of the bold new breed of self-appointed armchair generals, he argued that with "proper tactics" nuclear weapons could be used in limited wars without crossing the firebreak separating little wars from a general holocaust.

Another author who covered some of the same ground was James R. Schlesinger, a professor of economics at the University of Virginia. Schlesinger, who also nurtured a conviction that small bombs could be used as war-fighting weapons, argued that Americans had to "mature emotionally" and adjust to the heavy costs of limited warfare "as a condition of life." A treatise Schlesinger wrote in 1960 won him friends in high places, and he was soon catapulted out of the dark corners of the dismal science in Charlottesville into a position as the director of strategic studies at the air force's RAND Corporation in California.

Prior to Dr. Schlesinger's arrival, the seer of the RAND group was Herman Kahn, a roly-poly physicist with a scintillating mind, who let it be known that his IQ was one of the highest ever measured. Kahn had the mental agility of a science fiction writer, and he concocted new war games faster than his colleagues could analyze his old ones. His jargon-gorged 1960 book, *On Thermonuclear War,* provided a tour of the horizon from World War I through World War VIII, and included a description of a Doomsday Machine that, he avowed, would ultimately decide the fate of the earth.

An optimist who convinced himself that nations could recuperate after full-scale nuclear wars, Herman Kahn was a leading advocate of civil defense measures to use topsoil as a shield against the ravages of thermonuclear weapons. One of his subterranean schemes (a plan to use mines as "personnel and industrial shelters") made him a model for Dr. Strangelove in Stanley Kubrick's 1962 movie of that name.

Although in the decade after the Cuban missile crisis their fears and war scenarios were pushed into the background by the accommodations negotiated by the superpowers, some of the strategists who had developed close ties with the military-industrial complex were distressed by the treaties and agreements concluded by Presidents Kennedy and Nixon. It was their perception that the Kremlin invariably outmaneuvered the United States in arms control negotiations. They were dismayed, too, by the détente friendship Richard

Nixon developed with Leonid Brezhnev, and by his feverish protestations in the last desperate days of his presidency that the accommodations he had worked out with the Russians had laid the foundations for "a generation of peace."

The phobias of many nuclear strategists were magnified when Vietnam was "lost" to Communism in the spring of 1975, and when the administration of Gerald Ford pushed for the ratification of the SALT II disarmament agreement with the Soviet Union. This "failure" incited one militant group to enter the political arena under the banner of an organization they called The Committee on the Present Danger (CPD). Led by Paul Nitze, this band of zealots launched a campaign to warn the American people about the delusion of détente and the misguided policies that had produced "phony" peace agreements with the Soviet Union. As an effort to reorient the focus of American policy making, Nitze's CPD had a major impact in the mid-seventies. It brought the military-industrial lobbies and the dogmas and doctrines of the defense intellectuals into the inner sanctum of U.S. decision making for the first time. It forced President Gerald Ford to disavow détente and to back away from the SALT II treaty he and Kissinger had negotiated with Premier Brezhnev. It deterred Ford's successor, Jimmy Carter, from building on the peace initiatives of previous presidents, and its arguments pressured Carter to approve the elephantine MX missile "racetrack" in Utah and Nevada (a weapons system that has the dubious distinction of being perhaps the most harebrained scheme ever proposed by the Pentagon).

More important, the CPD made a major impact on politics when Ronald Reagan adopted its hard-line concepts and made them the centerpiece of his 1976 and 1980 presidential campaigns.

The rationale Nitze and his clique used to outline the need for emergency action was the old missile-gap argument dressed up in garish new clothes. In 1976, they belabored the "soft" policies of recent presidents and predicted that a "catastrophic shift" of military power would soon give the USSR "strategic superiority" if the missile trends of the seventies continued. Two years later, as self-appointed monitors of their nation's military decline, the committee warned that the strategic "edge" of U.S. forces had "slipped away." And finally, using a form of telepathy they did not bother to explain,

CPD spokesmen avowed that the men in the Kremlin "would consider themselves duty bound by Soviet doctrine [of world conquest] to exploit" the missile advantages they were acquiring.

Deluded by their anti-Communist demonology and their misreadings of postwar history, Paul Nitze and his coterie of nuclear theologians made a series of spectacular misjudgments. Fears, not facts, dictated their predictions. They were dead wrong about the imminent missile gap: the overall strategic nuclear balance between the superpowers was roughly the same in 1986 as it had been a decade earlier. They were wrong in their judgments about Soviet power and Soviet intentions. By 1982, for example, even their erstwhile brother, Herman Kahn, viewed their dogmas about an impending threat of Russian aggression as illusory. In his book, *Thinking About the Unthinkable in the 1980's*, Kahn described the low-risk stance taken by the Kremlin leaders during the Brezhnev era: "The Soviets are and have been prudent, cautious, and nonadventurous in pursuing foreign policy objectives outside the Communist bloc."

The Nitzeites also made grievous misjudgments about the strength and vitality of the Soviet system. Even as they were outlining their ominous scenarios about a looming "window of vulnerability," young Russian leaders like Mikhail Gorbachev, shocked by the economic stagnation that had become rampant under Brezhnev's regime, were concluding that the only way to save their nation was to open up Soviet society and hammer out disarmament treaties with the West.

Future generations will surely wonder how such a purblind clique could acquire sufficient clout to frustrate the peace plans of presidents and vault into positions of authority and power under the last president of the Cold War epoch. One cannot attempt to answer these questions without scrutinizing Dwight Eisenhower's military-industrial complex and the nuclear-strategy subculture that emerged after Hiroshima with the power it acquired to influence the nation's weapons policies and the thrust of its diplomacy.

It was inevitable that a priesthood that labored so long in a vineyard shielded from public scrutiny would presume that their special knowledge endowed them with a wisdom others lacked. Daniel Ellsberg, a veteran RAND corporation analyst, described the intoxicating impact of this process in a letter he wrote to his friend

Henry Kissinger in 1968 after President-elect Richard M. Nixon appointed Kissinger to head his national security staff:

> I've known people who've acquired [security clearances] and I have a pretty good sense of what the effects of receiving the clearances are. . . .
>
> First you will feel like a fool for having studied, written and talked about these subjects . . . for years without having known of the existence of all of this inside information. . . . Then . . . you will forget there ever was a time you didn't have it, and you'll be aware only of the fact that you have it now and the others don't . . . and that all other people are fools.
>
> Over a longer period of time, it will become very hard for you to learn from anybody who doesn't have these clearances. . . . You'll become incapable of learning from most people in the world, no matter how much experience and knowledge they may have.

Kissinger, his outlook tempered by the burdens of the authority he bore, helped Richard Nixon open doors to Red China and produce the first treaty to control the proliferation of strategic weapons (SALT I). He also had a role in orchestrating the Nixon-Brezhnev détente relationship, which became a foreign policy hallmark of the Nixon years. Despite the hard-line rhetoric that was a fixture of his political campaigns, Nixon demonstrated, once he had power, that he could pursue Eisenhowerlike policies of arms control and détente while conducting aggressive Cold War brinkmanship.

Two events changed the national mood and brought hard-line anti-Communism back into the mainstream of American politics. As Richard Nixon's presidency disintegrated, his concept of détente was shredded by right-wing critics who had been dismayed by his cozy friendship with Leonid Brezhnev. And the outcome of the Vietnam War evoked an argument from the same quarters that the Soviets had stolen a march in the missile race while the United States was trying to stop the expansion of Communist power in Southeast Asia.

These developments not only inspired the creation of Paul Nitze's Committee on the Present Danger, but also provided campaign ammunition that helped propel Ronald Reagan into power and produced the first postwar government dominated by ideological anti-Communists. Reagan's world was a black-and-white world, and, for him, the dark-colored glasses furnished by the Committee on the

Present Danger were a perfect fit. He had deplored Richard Nixon's détente waltz with Leonid Brezhnev, and he shared the phobias of his own nuclear strategists.

Ronald Reagan's 1980 victory swept Paul Nitze and other luminaries of the Committee on the Present Danger into key policy-making positions in the new administration, and they settled into their seats of power bent on reversing the misguided policies of their predecessors. On their watch, they assured their friends, there would be no cozy arms agreements with agents of the "evil empire." Their mission was to rebuild American military strength and give their president power to cow the rulers in the Kremlin.

In addition to Nitze, among the old-line members of the nuclear brotherhood who were given responsibility to carry out Reagan's foreign policy revolution were Eugene Rostow, Fred Ikle, and a veteran military strategist, General Edward Rowny. But it was two brash, hyperaggressive newcomers, Richard Burt and Richard Perle—trained by Senator Henry Jackson, a Democrat who was the archetype of a congressional hard-liner—who dominated arms control negotiations and set out to scuttle the rules of restraint that had long governed relations between the superpowers. Although neither Burt, thirty-three, nor Perle, thirty-nine, had had a day's experience in the executive branch of government, each believed he knew more about the arms race than anyone in Washington and neither had qualms about repudiating the policies pursued for over three decades by seven presidents.

As a consequence of their president's lack of interest in the details of arms control, and the passive roles played by their superiors, Burt and Perle seized inordinate power over war and peace issues during the first term of the Reagan administration. The power trip of these third-level bureaucrats—and the stratagems they used to dominate policy making for a season—were so unprecedented that journalist Strobe Talbot published a book in 1984, *Deadly Gambits,* to document their machinations. Burt and Perle held the belief that the only "safe" arms agreement with the Russians would be one they had personally designed and approved. The power these junior officials exerted during their odyssey of arrogance was dramatized in 1983, when, with President Reagan's acquiescence, they joined forces to sabotage an arms control compromise negotiated by their erstwhile mentor, Paul Nitze, during his highly publicized 1983 "walk in the woods" in Geneva, Switzerland, with his Soviet counterpart.

As pursuers of a "victory" over the Communists, President Reagan and his advisors deserve an egregious footnote in the annals of the Cold War. The chart below contrasts the differences between the guiding principles evolved by seven presidents and the confrontational approach adopted by the Reaganites:

The Presidential Consensus	*The Reagan Policies*
Avoid the trap of measuring the nation's military security by a weapons "numbers game."	Win the arms race by building an second-to-none arsenal of weapons.
To promote stability, each side should adhere to a tacit policy of coexistence.	Coexistence with Communism is morally repugnant and politically unthinkable.
Open conflict in outer space is to be avoided at all costs.	The United States should seek a decisive military edge in outer space.
On war and peace issues, the United States should be responsive to the United Nations and to the opinions of our European friends.	As with the Star Wars plan, the United States has a right to act unilaterally.
Leaders should shun pronouncements that incite fear and mistrust between the superpowers.	A U.S. president is justified in publicly attributing malign motives to Soviet leaders.
Preserve the nation's economic vitality in peacetime by restraining the demands of the military-industrial complex.	Launch a lavish weapons spending spree, which increases the national debt by nearly $2 trillion.
Take risks for peace by developing relationships based on mutual trust.	Arms control agreements based on trust are contrary to American interests.

Ronald Reagan's effort to reverse the policies of his predecessors aroused widespread dismay in the first term of his presidency. In 1982, the historian Barbara Tuchman, appalled by the monkeywrench tactics of the Reaganites, observed that "the control of nuclear war is too serious a subject to be left any longer to governments." And McGeorge Bundy commented later that the "fearful official propaganda" of the 1980s and the Reagan administration's "record of internal confusion and public misinformation" was a national scandal.

There are times when history plays tricks on those who presume they can alter the course of events. In Ronald Reagan's case, his desire to disrupt the peace process begun by President Eisenhower was thwarted by his own frailties—and by the forces of history, decades in the making, which came to a climax with the collapse of the Soviet Union's economic system.

It was the historical breakdown of Communism as a viable economic system that overtook Reagan's effort to "win" the Cold War. The turning point that signaled that a new epoch of history was at hand was the appearance on the world scene in 1985 of a Soviet leader, Mikhail Gorbachev, who wanted to end the Cold War in order to save what could be salvaged of the Soviet system.

8

The Atomic Apparat

So greatly did [the atom] seem to transcend the ordinary
affairs of men that we shut it out of those affairs altogether;
or rather tried to create a separate world, the world of the
atom.

—David E. Lilienthal (1963)

Certain subjects are so holy that it becomes an act of virtue
to lie.

—V. S. Naipaul (1980)

When our nation's leaders created the Atomic Energy Commission
in 1946 to succeed the Manhattan Project, they had five goals in mind.
First, they wanted to replace General Groves's one-man military
machine with a governing board of civilians. At the same time they
wanted to maintain and tighten the security system that they mistakenly assumed had preserved the "secrets" discovered by the atomic
scientists. Next, they wanted the new commission to manufacture a
stockpile of atomic weapons that would give the United States global
military supremacy. In addition, the law that established the AEC
authorized aggressive programs of research and development that

would enable the United States to exploit peaceful uses of the atom; and it directed the AEC to develop safety programs that would protect the health of the public and the atomic workforce from the radiation hazards associated with nuclear activities.

The Atomic Energy Act of 1946 was a radical law for a country whose Constitution was based on a concept of open government safeguarded by checks and balances devised to prevent overreaching by any unit of that government. The enactment of a law creating a powerful clandestine agency authorized to function with little sur- veillance by the country's elected lawmakers constituted an unprece- dented act of abdication by the Congress of the United States. The full extent of this abdication—and the awe and ignorance that hov- ered over the atom in the aftermath of Hiroshima—was reflected by Michigan's Senator Arthur Vandenberg when he expressed the hope that the members of the newly created Joint Committee on Atomic Energy (JCAE) selected to oversee the work of the AEC would never "know the secrets."

The congressional leaders shared Vandenberg's outlook and adopted the attitude that it was better to maintain a veil between members of Congress and the secrets than to trust their colleagues to deal with the realities of the atomic age. This decision prevented the American people and their elected representatives from participating in atomic policy making. It also created an echelon of decision makers who were, in the main, accountable only to themselves and who, if they chose, were free, as superguardians of the national security, to flout the laws and rules of ethics that governed the lives of other Americans.

The detached "government" within the federal government that the 1946 law created did not serve the nation well. It gave Americans a flawed nuclear-weapons program that functioned in obsessive secrecy with a minimum of outside supervision; and it produced a nuclear-power program that stifled criticism and dissent and, as described by the science historian Luther Carter, "exuded double talk delivered in the language of science."

This experiment cut against the grain of American democracy, and in 1974 provoked angry, disgruntled members of Congress to dismantle the Atomic Energy Commission. The shortcomings that produced this rebellion were many and varied. The AEC blocked creative thinking by impeding exchanges among scientists. It restricted critical review by denying citizens access to nuclear information. It fostered what David Lilienthal described as "arrogant self-adulation by atomic experts." And the Big Brother attitude that dictated the AEC's radiation safety policies ultimately engendered a poisonous mistrust between the nuclear establishment and ordinary citizens.

During the Cold War, the United States gained short-term advantages by using secrecy to shield details about such technological breakthroughs as guided missiles, spy satellites, and radar. But the post-Hiroshima perception of Americans that their country enjoyed a technical supremacy that would be long-lived was a fallacy. Few scientists shared General Groves's assumption that it would take the Soviet Union two decades to produce an atomic bomb. Although the fundamental principles of physics were in the public domain, in 1945 most Americans were given the impression "the secret" was locked in a Washington safe. Yet the United States' real secrets were ephemeral, for they involved technologies our engineers had devised to manufacture fissionable materials and the configurations our bomb-makers had devised to detonate their "gadgets." The fantasies that had motivated Congress to drape a shroud of secrecy over the Atomic Energy Commission were shattered when the Russians exploded an atomic device four years after Hiroshima and it was subsequently revealed that Klaus Fuchs, a British scientist who had been at Los Alamos, had transmitted crucial technical data to the Soviets sometime in 1945.

The leaders of our atomic establishment grasped the full significance of these events. Lilienthal and Oppenheimer agreed "this was another case of trying to keep a secret when there was none." Enrico Fermi declared that "security had become a ridiculous fetish." Glenn Seaborg, who would later serve for over a decade as chairman of the AEC, privately told his colleagues that secrecy was futile and "hampered exchanges among U.S. scientists rather than impeding Russian progress." And Eugene Wigner advocated a return to realism by expressing the hope that "we will stop glorifying our past."

Had the Soviet Union's nuclear coup in September 1949 occurred at a less hectic time, it is possible that our nation's leaders might have paused to ponder the real-world facts about the atom and might have asserted greater leadership over atomic affairs. But (as the chronology below attests) 1950 proved to be the most turbulent year of the atomic era—a year in which fears generated by the Cold War, the race for the hydrogen bomb, and the invasion of South Korea sent signals that reinforced the earlier belief that secrecy and national security were Siamese twins, and that neither Congress nor the American people could be trusted to make decisions about atomic policies.

Events of 1950 served as a catalyst that froze mental attitudes and fixed the course of atomic affairs for a quarter of a century. This development solidified the autonomy of the atomic establishment

Some Milestones of the Atomic Age and the Cold War

1948 • Berlin blockade, Communist coup in Czechoslovakia
     • Bombs tested at Bikini and Eniwetok atolls in the Pacific
     • AEC geologists locate uranium on the Colorado plateau

1949 • Mainland China falls to the Communists
     • U.S. uranium mining begins under AEC auspices
     • USSR explodes atomic bomb in August
     • Scientists debate plan for crash effort to build H-Bomb

1950 • Alger Hiss is convicted; rise of McCarthyism
     • President Truman announces decision to build hydrogen bomb
     • U.S. knowledge of the arrest of British atomic spy Klaus Fuchs undermines illusions about the secrets
     • U.S. builds new plants in Idaho, Colorado, Ohio, and Georgia to expand production of nuclear weapons
     • Korean War begins in June
     • Chairman of JCAE calls for the creation of an atomic army, navy, and air force armed with thousands of A-bombs
     • Los Alamos scientists select site in Nevada for testing of atomic weapons

1951 • Julius and Ethel Rosenberg arrested for atomic espionage
     • First bomb tests in Nevada
     • AEC unveils civil defense plans to bolster its contention that atomic war will not destroy civilization

1952 • U.S. explodes 10.2 megaton thermonuclear device in the Pacific

1953 • Soviet Union explodes its first hydrogen bomb

and confirmed Americans' view that decisions about atomic issues were so complex that they had to be entrusted to experts who knew the secrets. Moreover, it dictated that decisions about the testing of nuclear weapons, about measures needed to protect the American people from radiation releases of nuclear power plants and bomb factories, and about threats posed to human beings and the earth's environment by bombs detonated aboveground would be decided in secret by men who would later see themselves as "high priests" of an atomic brotherhood.

Any secret organization within a government develops a structure and management techniques that enable it to exercise its power. Thus the mantle of secrecy draped over the Atomic Energy Commission put a distinctive political stamp on that agency. When Congress ordered the AEC to guard the secrets of America's military might—and then indicated it did not want to know the facts concerning nuclear weapons—it gave that agency autonomy to make all but the most important decisions about our nuclear arsenal.

Consequently, the outlook and actions of AEC leaders were shaped by an awareness that they had complete control over the information that was fed to, and withheld from, the outside world, and by a realization that they could take whatever steps they deemed necessary to protect the nation's "secrets." Most significant, they were assured that they were free to operate above the law.

This Cold War culture quickly forged a mind-set that encouraged its leaders to speak with something akin to papal authority. In its early years, the AEC presented a face of patriotic purity to the American people. The often-used phrase "the Atomic Energy Commission says" was a voice from a mountain of the future, and the avowals of its experts were treated as gospels of the atomic age.

But the subtle, fateful question of cancer and other radiation hazards also confronted the leaders of our atomic establishment, for substances produced by their new alchemies, such as plutonium and cesium, were found to be the most fiercely toxic, long-lived poisons ever released into the environment. Because radiation emissions have no color or odor or texture that would signal their entry into the air, water, and foods ingested by human beings, and as there was a medical consensus that radiation causes cancers, atomic-age policy makers initially faced what should have been excruciating moral questions. Should the commissioners instruct their subordinates to put the medical facts before the public and then wage an aggressive educational campaign to teach the American people how to live with the realities of the atomic age? Should they trust the good judgment of ordinary folks and move forward on the assumption that people could and would adjust their lives to minimize the impacts of these realities? Or should they decide that such trust was inadvisable, suppress controversies by using their scientific prestige to support false assurances, and draw a curtain of secrecy to conceal the medical truths that lay at the heart of their enterprise?

History discloses that AEC's oligarchs chose the latter course and took a winding road that led them and their apparatus on a thirty-year ride, dominated by campaigns of disinformation, to persuade the public that their activities were not a threat to the public health. This campaign was effective because the vital facts were classified, the AEC's medical technicians were the recognized authorities on the subject of radiation and cancer, and the atomic apparatus could readily marshal a phalanx of leading experts to assure the nation that its safety precautions were adequate. In the 1950s and 1960s it was easy for such experts to intimidate and demolish critics who asked questions about bomb fallout, radiation safety, the siting of nuclear power plants, or the disposal of nuclear wastes. And once the themes and guidelines of the AEC's secret safety programs had been adopted, it had an efficient apparatus to take whatever action was needed to defend the dikes. The AEC sailed on calm seas in its "great" years.

If AEC administrators learned, for example, that some uranium miners on the Colorado plateau were absorbing the highest radon exposures ever recorded, they looked away without hesitation. If some officials had to employ damage control teams to sooth alarmed downwind citizens and cover up excessive fallout exposures from their Nevada bomb tests, they performed their tasks with zealous efficiency. If lawyers and scientists concluded they had to scuttle a lawsuit by misleading a federal judge and thus obstructing justice (as in the case of the Utah sheep), they dutifully did so. And if the top brass of the AEC felt they had to mount public relations campaigns to mislead the American people about fallout risks, or to conceal health hazards caused by emissions from their bomb factories, they had no qualms about launching such efforts with the rationalization that alleged "national security considerations" took precedence over the lives and health of their fellow citizens.

The psychology that produced such behavior had its roots in the policy of secrecy that put officials behind a veil and made them accountable only to themselves. As a result their politics of secrecy was based on a brand of absolute loyalty that ultimately corrupts and unerringly invites excesses. Thus, it was foreseeable from the outset that officials of the AEC would be tempted to lie, to impede justice, and to disregard duties they owed to unknowing citizens. The functionaries who executed this policy were not evil men, but rather loyal men who wore blinders and fulfilled their missions with such dedication and zeal that these virtues, in excess, resulted in dishonorable deeds, not unlike the "good Germans" who valiantly, and without moral reflection, followed the orders of their Führer. This sad history displays, once again, how the imperatives that govern the conduct of members of any apparat will bloat and distort the meaning of words like "loyalty," "duty," and "honor."

It is a measure of the power of these imperatives that, with only two notable exceptions, the AEC functioned as a monolith of obedience and conformity for nearly three decades. The exceptions involved three stubborn, fearless scientists (Harold Knapp, John Gofman, and Arthur Tamplin) who, as we shall see, would not tailor their conclusions about bomb fallout or radiation safety to fit a public party line proclaimed by the leaders of the AEC. This remarkable record of conformity displays, with the advantages of hindsight, how a secret organization can distort behavior within a government otherwise dedicated to the processes of open, democratic decision making.

Among other things, this record tells us how the closed, company-town cocoon created at Los Alamos and Livermore by our atomic apparat fostered compliant attitudes and ever-present fears about careers. It also reveals how a policy of hiding flaws emerged in 1979, when, at a hearing conducted in Utah by Senators Orrin Hatch and Edward Kennedy, Congress forced the declassification of key documents and sent a searchlight into the dark recesses of the Atomic Energy Commission. This hearing was convened to inquire into the mistakes and subsequent cover-ups related to Nevada bomb testing in the 1950s. Dr. Harold Knapp, a scientist-witness who had sought to focus the AEC's attention on some of its misdeeds and misjudgments when he worked for that agency in the 1960s, offered this summation to the senators: "They were so secure behind their high wall of classified information, they acquired the belief that they were both infallible and above the law."

A decade later, when another congressional committee conducted a three-year investigation of the systematic safety breakdowns at the government's nuclear weapons plants, Congressman John D. Dingell drew a similar conclusion. The failures, he wrote, were rooted "in a perverse devotion to secrecy and poor management" and "the classified nature of the process of making nuclear weapons contributed to a mind-set of emphasizing production at the expense of health and safety."

III

ABOVE THE LAW:
RADIATION TRAGEDIES AT HOME

9

The Betrayal

of the Uranium

Miners

I had to officially take the position that we suspected that the uranium miners may have health problems. . . . But we knew what they would be.

—Dr. Victor Archer
USPHS Epidemiologist (1990)

THE VICTIMS

On a blustery day in the winter of 1979, Bill Mahoney and I drove from Phoenix to the Navajo Reservation to conduct our first interviews with the widows of Navajo uranium miners. As we approached the Red Valley Chapter House, located a few miles west of the landmark spire known as Shiprock, I was reminded of an earlier trip through this colorful valley. As a freshman congressman, in the mid-fifties, I borrowed a jeep from the Navajo Nation and my wife and I drove through this rugged, remote region to appraise the need for additional roads.

Now, twenty-four years later, I was back as a personal injury lawyer to delve into the impact of an industrial tragedy on the health of the Indians whose hogans dotted the landscape in this part of the

Chuska Mountains. With the help of interpreters, Bill and I learned more than we ever wanted to know about lung cancer and about the epidemic that had settled like a plague over the families who lived in the vicinity of Cove and Red Rock and Lukachukai. We were told that some of the first uranium mines on the Navajo Reservation were located nearby and that Kerr-McGee, a major oil company, had been the main employer of the pastoral, mostly illiterate Navajos who found themselves caught up in the U.S. industrial system as apprentice underground miners.

Our interviews also revealed that the miners' lung cancer came unexpectedly and that few survived for more than a few months after the onset of their illnesses. Very few were smokers, and their environment affirmed that they breathed some of the cleanest air in the United States. The impact on the miners' families was severe. Most of the victims died in their thirties or forties, leaving their widows with families of seven or eight children.

None of the widows knew about or had received workmen's compensation benefits for the deaths of their husbands. Our quest for facts that afternoon encountered cultural barriers, for the Navajo language has no words to explain subjects such as workmen's compensation, lung cancer, radiation, or uranium. Through Navajo translators, we gradually elicited information that indicated an interesting pattern. Nearly all of the widows and their deceased husbands had grown up in the 1920s and 1930s, when the federal government provided few educational opportunities for Indian children. This meant that they had a childlike understanding of modern American life.

Bill Mahoney and I had both grown up on the edge of the Navajo Reservation, and we were familiar with the lifestyle of these Indians. As we compared impressions on our drive back to Phoenix, we discussed the spartan culture of the Navajos and admired the strength of the women we had met. We marveled that these young widows had held their large families together in a subsistence economy where wood-gathering and the raising of sheep and goats were a vital part of survival.

Over the years, during our decade-long, losing fight in the federal courts to force the federal government to accept responsibility for its misdeeds, the plight of these Navajo families became a family crusade. Our sons, Tom, Denis, and James, and our daughter, Lori, served as investigators on the reservation, and Lee formed a nonprofit organization which raised funds to finance the legal battle that ensued.

As our lives became intertwined with those of the Navajo families, we formed some unforgettable friendships. I will always remember Betty Jo Yazzie, the widow who lost two husbands to uranium mining. Her first husband, Kee Yazzie, a deaf mute, exemplified the grit of Navajo manhood. Through some remarkable manifestation of personal courage he did not let his disability confine the reach of his life. A small, muscular man, Kee Yazzie married Betty Jo, fathered seven children, and became a breadwinner by going underground with Navajo friends and working for fifteen years as a mucker before his untimely death at age forty-five.

There were the many memorable matriarchs (such as Grace Tuni, Rose John, and Rose Benally) who held their families together and somehow managed to give most of their children a high school education. When lung cancer claimed Rose John's husband, Tom, at age thirty-three and left her with five children ranging from six months to ten years, she did not falter. I inquired how she coped with her loss—and even got two of her children into colleges. Rose's reply was simple: "Our family was strong. We always worked together and helped each other." When Rose qualified for a $100,000 payment in 1992 after Congress enacted a law to provide modest "compassionate payments" to living miners and the widows of deceased victims, it did not surprise me that, without a pause, she shared her payment equally with each of her five children.

The often tearful occasions when the Navajo families gathered at our Santa Fe home to pick up their "compassionate payment" checks allowed us to experience their interaction and witness the respect and affection the children accorded their mothers. We remember how Rose Benally, the mother of twelve children, hired a Navajo boy to tend her sheep and goats so she could drive with her daughters and several grandchildren from Cove Mountain to Santa Fe to close a sad chapter in the life of her family. And we prize the Christmas card Mae Black sent from her home in Shonto, Arizona, informing us that with some of the money from her settlement, her sons built her a new "octagon house," and bought 100 bales of hay so her animals would be well fed while she awaited the arrival of spring grass.

In the family of Robert and Bertha James we saw a microcosm of twentieth-century Navajo life. Born about 1910, the now-deceased parents lived in a pastoral setting at Mexican Water, Arizona, where their five children grew up. Robert had little knowledge of the white man's ways, but he was a natural leader and became a member of the Navajo Tribal Council. Schooling was not available when the two older children, Lena and Eileen, were growing up, so they absorbed traditional ways and, beginning when they were five years old, their mother began to teach them the art of weaving fine Navajo rugs.

Ellen and Damon James thrived in high school. Ellen is now a professional silversmith and she and her non-Indian husband have a successful Indian-arts business off the reservation in Farmington, New Mexico. Damon is a skilled worker at the electric power station nearby. Ellen's son, Robert, is carrying the banner for the third generation. He has finished premed studies and will soon enter medical school. When asked how they planned to finance Robert's education, Ellen announced with pride that Robert, too, is a gifted craftsman and would pay for part of his schooling by selling works of art he produced.

A few months after our trip to Navajo country, I traveled to the village of Marysvale, Utah, to interview a group of non-Indian widows. Here in the jagged mountains of central Utah was another valley of death of the atomic age, now largely inhabited by sturdy Mormon families struggling with tragedies inflicted by a cancer epidemic foisted on them by the Atomic Energy Commission.

As a lung cancer laboratory secretly sponsored by the government, Marysvale was a shocker. The uranium discovered in crevices of the Antelope Range north of town contained rich ores, which (as measured by AEC experts) emitted record-breaking quantities of radon gas. As a consequence, in the 1950s some of the Marysvale miners absorbed more radiation in one week than miners who later worked for twenty years in the well-ventilated mines of the 1970s. The upshot was that these highly contaminated mines generated more lung cancer deaths per capita than any other uranium mines in the United States.

As tallied by widows who counted the headstones in the ceme-
tery they had nicknamed "Cancer Hill" thirty-one out of fifty Marysvale miners had already died, and new names were being added to
the list every year. Rell Frederick, one of the living miners I interviewed, underscored the extent of the carnage when he told me that
the eight miners who worked with him in one stope were all lung
cancer victims.

THE EVIDENCE

In 1948 the Atomic Energy Commission created a uranium mining
industry from scratch, and that agency was the sole purchaser of its
output for nearly two decades. When the AEC came into existence
on January 1, 1947, the United States was importing all of its uranium
from the Belgian Congo and Canada. The law that established the
AEC as the successor of the wartime Manhattan Project contained a
provision that gave the commission ownership and exclusive control
over all U.S. deposits of this strategic mineral.

Had it been so inclined, the AEC could have ordered the
installation of low-cost ventilation systems to protect U.S. uranium
miners. AEC safety experts could have designed such a program in
a matter of weeks. As there were no "national security" shortages of
this raw material in 1948, the AEC's decision to put the flow of ore
ahead of human health was a reckless act that sacrificed the lives of
hundreds of miners.

The gruesome upshot of this policy was on display three years
later when a prominent AEC medical expert, Dr. William F. Bale,
came to Marysvale to take readings that would enable him to establish a new method of measuring airborne radiation in uranium mines.
His survey revealed concentrations of radon 4,400 times greater than
the exposure then allowed in the nation's radium-dial-painting industry. Fully aware of the AEC's aggressive production policy, Dr.
Bale included this blunt compliment in the report he filed with the
AEC's medical doctors: "They [USPHS] seem to have conducted
their work so far without unduly alarming the miners as to the
hidden hazards that may exist, or in any way impeding mining
operations."

A few weeks after Bale's visit to Marysvale, I attended a Senate hearing held by Senators Edward Kennedy and Orrin Hatch that significantly advanced my education concerning the events that set the stage for the tragedy of the uranium miners. Three former federal health officers provided startling revelations about the failures of leadership which had produced that industrial scandal. The first witness was Merril Eisenbud, a onetime AEC safety specialist who had been involved in the initial effort to avert this tragedy. Next was Duncan Holaday, a USPHS industrial hygienist who endured a decade of frustrated efforts to persuade AEC officials to act. And the third witness was a Public Health Service epidemiologist, Dr. Victor Archer, who had been given the grim, unenviable task of tracking the lung cancer plague that afflicted the lives of the same miners.

The response of these men to the tragedy they had witnessed or unwittingly participated in reflected both the chill of the Cold War and the intimidating power of AEC officials during that era. All three were men of conscience who were shocked that AEC officials would close their eyes to the transparent tragedy the agency had brought about. However, none had had the temerity to blow the whistle on a secretive agency that was regarded as the nation's front-line defense against our Communist enemies. When members of Congress belatedly revealed the truths about this scandal, I was able to establish friendships with these men, and all three subsequently volunteered to help the victims in their quest for a legal forum where the sacrifices of their fathers and brothers and sons would be recognized and, perchance, compensated.

When I first conferred with Merril Eisenbud soon after the congressional hearings, he was one of the nation's leading authorities in the field of environmental health. He had been picked by Mayor John Lindsay in the 1960s to establish New York City's first Office of Environmental Protection, and I found him to be an astute individual with a keen sense of fair play. Although it was evident that he had a lingering sense of loyalty to the AEC, thirty years after the event Merril was still outraged that some faceless AEC official had vetoed a safety plan he had devised to protect the health of the uranium miners.

I learned in the spring of 1948 that Eisenbud and his colleague Dr. Bertram Wolfe had quickly identified the severe health hazards of uranium mining when they traveled from the commission's new Health and Safety Laboratory (HASL) in New York City to study radiation risks at the uranium mines and mills that were commencing operations in western Colorado under AEC auspices.

Eisenbud had come to Colorado from an industrial health triumph in Ohio, where he had quickly fashioned a system of controls that virtually eliminated beryllium disease in the world. The AEC needed the metal beryllium as a reflector for high-flux reactors, but the beryllium industry in Ohio had allowed this highly toxic substance to pervade its factories and to escape into the surrounding communities, where its workers lived. HASL dispatched Eisenbud to investigate the ensuing epidemic of lung disease, and he quickly conducted a survey that identified the causes of this medical disaster.

Knowing lives were at stake, Merril Eisenbud developed a clean-up regimen and fixed exposure limits that would protect the workers and their families. He then persuaded AEC officials to incorporate his safety program into their procurement contracts with beryllium producers. Eisenbud secured immediate approval of his plan despite the fact that compliance would modestly increase the price the government would pay for the end product. The AEC was not the sole purchaser of this metal and had no legal obligation to regulate the production of beryllium by its contractors. Nevertheless, Merril's superiors responded favorably to his argument that the Atomic Energy Commission had a moral duty to conduct its activities in a manner that would minimize hazards to the lives and health of workers who were part of the AEC's new chain of production.

Eisenbud explained to me that experience prior to World War II had taught industrial hygienists in this country to use conservative criteria in setting safety standards for industries whose employees were exposed to hazardous materials in their workplaces. It was considered "good practice," he said, to make an initial judgment about "allowable" exposures, and then to apply a "safety factor" and fix a performance standard five or ten times below that level. (General Groves provided an example of this technique in his autobiography, when he noted with pride that all of the workers at Oak Ridge, Tennessee, Hanford, Washington, and the other war plants of the Manhattan Project were protected from radiation dangers by "a large factor of safety.")

Because Wolfe and Eisenbud had studied the deadly consequences of prewar uranium mining in Europe, the unventilated
mines they inspected on their Colorado trip filled them with fore-
boding. The report Eisenbud wrote a few weeks later proposed that
the allowable radon contamination in uranium mines be set at the
same standard fixed in 1941 by the newly organized National Commission on Radiation Protection (NCRP) for U.S. workers handling
radiation products. He also recommended that the AEC's ore-
procurement contracts with the mining companies contain an enforcement mechanism that would compel them to adhere to this
safety standard.

Two disturbing developments greeted HASL's initiatives. The
first was the National Bureau of Standards' analysis of the gas samples in radon flasks Eisenbud and Wolfe had gathered in mines
during their Colorado tour. Some of the samples revealed concentrations of radon 500 times higher than the exposures allowed in workplaces by the NCRP. The second shock came in the form of a furtive
call to Dr. Wolfe from an AEC official in Washington ordering HASL
to "keep away from" the uranium mining problem. (The deliberations that produced this decision remained a national security secret
until 1980, when an NBC reporter extracted an admission from Jesse
Johnson, the onetime head of the AEC's Raw Materials division, that
this oral order came from one of the five commissioners.)

A year after Wolfe and Eisenbud were ordered to ignore the
plight of the uranium miners, the chief of Colorado's public health
service urged PHS officials to dispatch one of their industrial hygienists to his state to help him evaluate the hazards associated with the
new mining industry. Duncan Holaday, a seasoned sanitary engineer
stationed in Salt Lake City, was sent to Colorado to carry out this
consulting work. Appalled by the hazards he identified, Holaday took
on the burden of spearheading a desperate campaign to persuade the
AEC and the mining companies that a lung cancer epidemic would
occur unless emergency measures were taken to protect the lives of
the growing corps of uranium miners on the Colorado plateau.

In the following years, during the course of two depositions, two
visits to his home in upstate New York, and the trial of the case of
the Navajo widows in Phoenix, Duncan and I formed a friendship
that helped me understand the unique role he had played in the

uranium miner tragedy. Duncan was a lean, gangly man who appeared older than his seventy years, but his mind was clear and he easily recalled events surrounding his crusade to save the uranium miners. His wry sense of humor enlivened our many discussions. Once when I asked him to interpret a mendacious statement by a high-echelon AEC official, his mischievous response was, "Well, Stewart, we shouldn't expect these important patriots to tell the truth every time."

Holaday had excelled as a field man, and facts he uncovered in his first foray into the back country of the Four Corners area confirmed Merril Eisenbud's earlier findings. The initial radon readings he took in mines on the Navajo Reservation in December 1949 were so far off the chart that he felt those mines were death traps, and fired off reports recommending they be closed until "control measures" could be instituted.

When he obtained similar radiation readings at other mines in Utah and Colorado, Duncan Holaday's anxiety accelerated. He was unaware then that the AEC had made a secret decision to "stay away" from the problem and leave it in the lap of the states. However, as weeks went by and his cries for action were ignored, he sensed his opposition was a juggernaut that was gaining momentum day by day. He realized, too, that since the Public Health Service had no enforcement power, when he made recommendations to his superiors, he was "spitting in the wind."

Tenacity was another facet of Duncan Holaday's character, and he won approval to travel to Washington so he could convey his fears to some of the "higher-ups" and try to win support for his pleas to ventilate the mines. Duncan told me that he was crushed by the outcome of his one-man Washington crusade. All of the officials he conferred with—including physicians in high places in the AEC's Division of Biology and Medicine—expressed "concern," but no one was willing to translate their concern into an effort to force the leaders of the AEC to recognize that emergency action was needed to protect the lives of the uranium miners.

While he made his rounds during this trip, Duncan Holaday gained chilling insights that explained both the hard-line stance of the AEC and the reluctance of officials in his own agency to challenge the leaders of this powerful, secretive agency. Especially informative was a conversation with Dr. W. H. Hueper, an Austrian émigré with international credentials who had just been hired by the National Cancer Institute (NCI) to establish a new Center of Environmental Health.

Duncan contacted Dr. Hueper because he was a leading authority on the tragic "European experience"—a classic cancer epidemic that afflicted miners employed in mines in the Erz Mountains of Saxony where radioactive ores were recovered. He had also authored a definitive 1942 book, *Occupational Tumors and Allied Diseases*. Hueper assessed the exposure data Holaday had assembled and confirmed his worst fears. A physician noted for his blunt opinions, Hueper advised Holaday that 75 to 80 percent of miners who worked in some of the mines he had surveyed would succumb to lung cancer.

Hueper advised Holaday that he was naive if he thought the AEC hierarchy would help him bring the deadly dangers surrounding uranium mining to the public's attention. To prove his point, he recited the story of his encounter a year earlier with Dr. Shields Warren, the head of AEC's newly created Division of Biology and Medicine. Being fully cognizant of the radon risks in underground mines, Dr. Hueper had developed a plan for a systematic study by the NCI of remedies that could prevent a repetition of the European experience in this country.

When Shields Warren, the most esteemed radiologist of his day, learned about Hueper's proposed study, he concluded it would receive extensive media coverage that would alarm the miners, and so he used his power to kill it. In the tussle that followed, he apparently put Hueper under surveillance as a potential whistle blower.

A second clash soon occurred when the Austrian agreed to present a paper at a medical conference in Denver describing the European experience. Shields Warren intervened this time in ruthless fashion. He first had Hueper's speech censored, and then cowed his NCI superiors and forced them to issue an order forbidding their new bureau chief to travel west of the Mississippi River. Leaving no stone unturned, Warren subsequently made an effort to persuade the director of the NCI to fire Hueper. (I questioned Dr. Warren about this episode in July 1979 when I interviewed him in Boston at the radiation hospital that bore his name, and he did not dispute the accuracy of Hueper's story.)

Warren's actions were a preview of the autocratic tactics the AEC used to intimidate the health professionals in other federal agencies. There is evidence that the zeal Duncan Holaday displayed in Washington put him on the AEC's surveillance list. In subsequent years, any important uranium mining press release or report he prepared had to be cleared and edited by AEC censors. Such stage-managing assured that for two full decades the tragedy of this country's uranium miners would be acted out in a darkened theater from a script based on lies, illusions, and half-truths.

Despite his failure to find allies in Washington, Duncan returned to Utah determined to make a last-ditch effort to get life-saving controls installed in some of the mines. Working with a sympathetic associate, he began preparing a "report with the bark off," bluntly summarizing mine hazards and outlining low-cost steps the mining companies could take to reduce radiation to tolerable levels.

Holaday reasoned that if the prestige of the USPHS were thrown behind his Interim Report, he might have a chance to convince mine operators and the safety officers of the uranium states that vigorous emergency action was required. But all of his conferences and missionary work in the summer of 1952 produced meager results. His lonely campaign was doomed from the start because AEC officials watered down his report and insisted that it be discussed only in private meetings. His efforts accomplished little, he told me, because (as the AEC's experts well knew) the states were utterly unprepared to deal with radiation issues, and he had no authority to force the mining companies to act.

The AEC's abdication and the failure of Duncan Holaday's campaign combined to lock federal officials into a pattern of conduct that evoked a medical charade that constitutes a dark chapter in the annals of American medicine. In the fall of 1952, the knowledge key Washington officials had concerning the plight of the miners confronted them with life-and-death policy decisions. The lethal amounts of radiation in the mines had been certified by experts, and it was common knowledge that growing numbers of miners were daily entering the portals of those contaminated mines.

Holaday had followed a standard procedure of industrial health investigators in 1949 and 1950 when he entered uranium mines on the

Colorado plateau and took radiation readings to determine their hazards. It was also standard procedure (as Merril Eisenbud demonstrated at the beryllium factories) to take immediate corrective action once severe hazards were identified. The miners' safety was sacrificed and the rules of medical ethics were violated when federal officials who knew the facts and had the power to order remedial action ducked their responsibilities and ordered the PHS investigation to continue to ascertain whether a "problem" existed in the uranium mines.

As the main organizer of the initial investigation, in the spring of 1950 Duncan Holaday had helped his PHS colleagues assemble a team of physicians and industrial health technicians. This team meandered across the Colorado plateau that summer to gather data about health issues associated with uranium mining. Miners were given physical exams, work histories were obtained, and technicians took radiation readings in the mines they surveyed. Assigned the task of enlisting the cooperation of the mining companies, Holaday was taken aback when the operators insisted that they would participate only if the doctors agreed not to say anything that might alarm their miners. Though this ran counter to good practice in industrial hygiene, Duncan felt he had to assent or the investigation would be aborted.

With a clarity that cried out for action, the data gathered in 1950 by the PHS caravan dramatized the deadly health hazards in U.S. uranium mines. The study also provided the baseline facts Holaday used in his efforts to persuade Washington officials that emergency action was needed. Despite these findings, two years later high officials in Washington were pretending that the PHS study had to be continued to determine whether a "problem" existed.

Aware that any further investigation would be superfluous, Duncan Holaday was shocked when "the AEC crowd" began using the uranium miner study as a shield to fend off criticism of its inaction. He was especially outraged when the radiologists who led the AEC's Division of Biology and Medicine promulgated the story that there was "no evidence" that the health of American uranium miners was at risk. When he told me about this episode twenty-five years later in 1979, it was obvious that the cover-up of these prestigious physicians still stirred Duncan's ire. "I was stunned," he said, "that they would use this excuse to turn their backs on the miners, when all of us knew that the latency period for lung cancer was at least ten years and that once that period had elapsed, the bodies of dead miners would provide all the proof anyone could ask for."

(By the time the lung cancer epidemic arrived on schedule in the early sixties, the AEC was ready with a new pretext to justify its inaction. Its updated line was that there was not enough available data to enable the experts to set "reasonable" safety standards. Duncan regarded this excuse as "a gruesome joke." Standards for safe occupational exposure to radon had been fixed for U.S. industries before World War II, and Holaday was certain he and his colleagues had sufficient information in 1950 to design a program that would have protected the health of the uranium miners.)

The epidemiological study of several thousand U.S. uranium miners undertaken after 1952 was the Atomic Energy Commission's bastard child. The scope of that endeavor ranks it as the world's largest prospective study where avoidable deaths would measure the hazards to which workers were exposed.

Most epidemiological studies are retrospective and seek to identify the origin of epidemics. In some prospective studies, individuals or small groups of volunteers are informed about the risks involved and consent in writing to participate as test animals in a particular experiment. Conscientious physicians can readily carry out such experiments without violating codes of medical ethics. Noteworthy among such precepts is the "Nuremberg Code," drawn up by American lawyers in the notorious "Nazi Doctors Case," which was tried in Nuremberg, Germany, soon after World War II. (Though the code was written by Americans, to this day the United States has not adopted it.) The code is violated when people are exposed to health hazards without their consent or knowledge and become the unwitting subjects of medical experiments whose outcome may produce deaths and life-shortening disabilities. A cardinal tenet of this international code is, "No experiment should be conducted where there is an a priori reason to believe that death or disabling injury will occur."

The uranium miner study was of the latter kind. Its ultimate subjects were over 4,000 miners who were given periodic physical examinations and whose lives and deaths and work patterns were diligently tracked by a team of epidemiologists. The uranium mining industry had been created by the leaders of the U.S. government to provide the key ingredient of atomic bombs, and the AEC's world-class radiation experts were fully cognizant of the grave health risks. Worse yet, the miners were not informed of the radiation hazards in their workplaces and were never given an opportunity to choose whether they wanted to risk their lives and health. This deception deprived the miners of opportunities to take preventive action that could have reduced some of the radiation hazards in the mines where they worked.

As preparations were being made for the next medical caravan in 1954, a proposal for a separate "pilot study" of the miners was approved by Dr. Charles Dunham, chief of the AEC's Division of Biology and Medicine. The sanctioning of this study laid bare the crude hypocrisies that animated the AEC's medical hierarchy. The concept for the pilot study was developed by Dunham's assistant, Dr. Bernard Nebel. Although the AEC's official pose was that there was no evidence that any miner had been harmed, Nebel removed that mask by a bald statement averring that the pilot project rested on an assumption that the uranium miners had absorbed greater amounts of radiation than their European counterparts and that their body tissues offered "a unique opportunity" for medical researchers to study "the effect of radioactive materials on human beings."

Under the Dunham-Nebel pilot plan, the research would begin in morgues on the Colorado plateau where "participating patholo-gists" would "collect tissue specimens" from the ribs, kidneys, lungs, livers, and vertebrae of deceased uranium miners. These specimens, after appropriate slicing, would be distributed to selected laborato-ries, where other physicians would assess the damage done to the irradiated organs. The protocol studiously ignored all issues of medi-cal ethics. There was no requirement to tell the miners' widows that their husbands had been unwitting participants in a medical experi-ment; and the plan contained no instructions that researchers had to obtain the consent of the widows before their husband's bodies were autopsied and "sectioned."

This episode dramatized the degree to which the high-level AEC officials considered themselves to be not only above the law, but also above fundamental norms of morality. In any event, U.S. medical ethics was spared further embarrassment when the Dunham-Nebel study was aborted during its pilot-study phase. Although Nebel had reported that some of his colleagues were "highly enthusiastic" about the project's potential, apparently some of the participating pathologists he was counting on had queasy reactions. One skeptical physician wrote to an associate that he felt the scheme had "a Buchenwald touch."

As the larger epidemiological study moved forward, Duncan Holaday viewed the ensuing lung cancer epidemic as a foregone conclusion. He performed his assigned tasks with the resigned hope that once the miners began to succumb to lung cancer, the AEC would admit it had erred and adopt the preventive measures he had recommended to save the lives of the younger miners. As a troubleshooter, a gadfly, and an instructor in radiation safety, Duncan spent much of his time in the next decade espousing the canons of radiation safety.

Knowing that every well-ventilated mine would save lives, Duncan worked on several fronts: he prodded forward-looking mining executives to install ventilation systems; he set up sessions with safety officials of the uranium mining states to educate them concerning steps they could take to cleanse their mines; and when he crossed paths with AEC executives he needled them about their failures and about what might be accomplished if they changed their outlook. Although Duncan Holaday's predicament required him to resign himself to the sad outcome of an avoidable tragedy, his ironic approach to life helped him to deal with the industrial tragedy that dominated his career. "Well," he said to me once, "at least the AEC gave me a ringside seat at a unique parade of hypocrisy."

In 1956, Holaday found a soulmate who shared many of his anxieties and frustrations, when Victor Archer, the newly appointed director of the uranium miner study, arrived in Salt Lake City. A career PHS physician, Dr. Archer had been on the job twenty-two years when I first met him in his file-crammed office on the top floor of the federal building in the fall of 1978. He supplied me with key documents that I had requested, and I was immediately impressed with his willingness to concede that the Atomic Energy Commission had "largely ignored" worker safety in the first two decades of its existence.

Unlike Duncan Holaday, Archer was loath to criticize other U.S. officials, and his judge-not-lest-ye-be-judged temperament made it difficult for lawyers to elicit conclusions needed to clinch a case. But as Victor and I became friends, I learned that his sense of fair play guided his judgments as he recorded the details of the miners' unfolding tragedy. Victor Archer had had an earthbound upbringing on a ranch in the plains east of Lewiston, Montana, where he had rubbed shoulders with simple, rough-hewn men, and I surmised that his work experiences as a young man provided insights that helped him understand the grit and the gullibility of the men whose lives and deaths became the subject of his work.

I didn't fully appreciate Dr. Archer's character until I understood the history of his one-man campaign that made it possible for hundreds of the widows and miners abandoned by their national government to qualify for workmen's compensation benefits. In the early 1960s when his data revealed that the epidemic he feared had arrived, Victor knew it would be impossible for the widows to prove that their husbands' lung cancers had been caused by radiation exposures unless he testified on their behalf.

As the expert who was the custodian of the miners' work histories and who, alone, was in a position to proffer statistical proof concerning the probable medical cause of the deaths of individual miners, Dr. Archer recognized that he had an ethical duty to perform; our system of justice could not function unless he presented the deadly truths emerging from the uranium miner study. When Victor requested permission to appear before administrative courts, his supervisors ruled that he could not offer testimony on behalf of the miners' widows. However, he faced them down and subsequently spent substantial amounts of his work time preparing reports that were given authoritative weight by federal judges and other judicial tribunals in the uranium states.

The federal government's conduct was so relentlessly insensitive that there were times when I wondered why neither Holaday nor Archer went to the media and blew the whistle on the Washington officials responsible for this industrial tragedy. But on reflection, I understood the why of it. Whistle blowing was regarded as an unpatriotic activity during the bleak decades of the Cold War, and in its heyday the Atomic Energy Commission relished wielding its power to intimidate outsiders who dared criticize its decisions and pronouncements. I realized, too, that both men were PHS pros who enjoyed the challenges implicit in their work. I also sensed that Victor was not the whistle-blowing type, and that Holaday saw taking on the AEC behemoth as an exercise in futility. Duncan's answer one day when I broached the subject was, "Stewart, I never thought a little Utah tweet from me would have been heard in Washington."

IN THE COURTS

When we finished our investigation in 1979 and filed the *Begay* v. *U.S.* case in federal court in Phoenix, our legal research told us that the lawyers representing the government would rely, first and last, on its "sovereign immunity" ("the-king-can-do-no-wrong") argument to persuade the judge to bar the doors of his court to the claims of our clients. This contention—and the tendency of most federal judges to abstain if officials in the executive branch waved the wand of "national security"—loomed as the big hurdles we would have to surmount. But since the government provided the Navajos' health care and owed "trust responsibilities" recognized by the U.S. Supreme Court to Indian people, we were emboldened by the belief we could present a rationale that would force thoughtful federal judges to see the justice of our cause and override the antiquated concept of sovereign immunity.

By the time the *Begay* case, involving ten "representative plaintiffs," came on for trial in August 1983, Lee and other members of our family had sold enough lithographs donated by Navajo artist R. C. Gorman to defray the expenses of the trial. Dr. Archer, Eisenbud, Holaday, and other concerned witnesses who wanted to see justice done traveled to Phoenix to testify without being paid the witness fees they normally would have commanded.

As required by law in such cases, a federal judge (a friend from my days as an Arizona congressman) sat as a one-man jury. The case we presented during the following two weeks began with Eisenbud's testimony and outlined the whole sad story of the government's egregious negligence in sacrificing the lives of the Navajo miners.

The United States, all of us thought, presented a weak, shabby defense.

The government's attorneys conceded nothing, and endeavored to prove that the statute of limitations had run out by depicting the illiterate Navajo widows as individuals who were aware of the invisible radiation dangers in the uranium mines. Government lawyer Laura Rockwood spent a whole morning, through an interpreter, badgering the elderly widows with a series of accusatory questions whose thrust was, "You knew, didn't you, that your husband's lung cancer was related to his work in mines?" The shock was greater when the government sought to rebut the testimony of our medical experts by presenting testimony by Dr. Oscar Auerbach, a nationally known physician who brazenly opined that the lung cancers of the dead miners had been caused by cigarette smoking or by "sandy soils around their homes." In point of fact, the only evidence before the court was that none of the Navajo miners were smokers.

Our hopes were crushed after the last witness testified, when the judge volunteered his "thoughts" about the evidence. His ruminations revealed that there were no facts or witnesses or arguments that could have persuaded him to render a verdict against the U.S. government. Indeed, in his subsequent written decision he took pains to build a legal and factual firewall to protect the government from any liability. He first dismissed the Nuremberg Code as having no application in U.S. courts and then made an explicit finding of fact that those who carried out the uranium miner study were not "experimenting on human beings" but rather were "gathering data" so they could establish safety standards in the uranium mines.

Although there was no evidence whatsoever that any federal official at a policy-making level had made a decision that the nation's security would be endangered if the miners were warned about the radiation hazards, the judge nevertheless concluded that some anonymous federal official whom he did not (and indeed, could not) identify had actually made such a decision "based on considerations of political and national security feasibility factors." In his 1991 treatise, "Mengele's Birthmark: The Nuremberg Code in the United States Courts," Dr. George Annas found this finding "astonishing," and made the further observation that this Arizona jurist had "adopted one of the Nazi defenses as legitimate: in times of national emergency, research rules must take a back seat to national security."

Astute judges who want to make it extremely difficult for a losing litigant to overturn their decision on appeal append formidable findings of fact and conclusions of law to their opinions. We were crestfallen when this federal judge put such "locks" in his written decision. With our appeal options thus constricted, we decided that our best bet was to stress the Indian law aspects of our case in the brief we filed with the U.S. Court of Appeals in San Francisco. In essence, our appeal was based on the hope we might prick the conscience of the court and persuade its members to lift the Navajos' case out of the "national security" matrix created by the district judge's opinion.

There was a sudden flame of optimism on our side when William Canby, an Arizona judge who had taught Indian law at Arizona State University, was assigned to our three-man panel. Canby, the brother-in-law of Walter Mondale, was known to have a liberal outlook on social and ethical issues, so my oral argument was crafted to appeal to his sensibilities. Our son Tom (now New Mexico's attorney general), and Albert Hale (a young Navajo lawyer who had participated in the Phoenix trial) went to San Francisco to participate in the oral argument.

The highlight of the hearing came as the government's solicitor was arguing that the uranium miner study was necessary so the federal experts could obtain the data they needed to fix safety standards in the mines. We were startled when one of the judges, James M. Ideman (a district judge recently appointed to the bench by President Ronald Reagan) curtly interrupted with the comment, "I wouldn't dwell on that, counsel, you were using them as guinea pigs." In elation, Tom and Albert whispered, "We've won. Waive your closing argument."

Their hunch was dead wrong. This timid panel exhibited no inclination to challenge the hoary verities of sovereign immunity law. The unanimous opinion it subsequently published was a stale carbon copy of the lower court's decision.

With all the sweat and tears that everyone had invested in this cause, we had to file a petition beseeching the U.S. Supreme Court to review the Navajos' case. The odds against us, as we well knew, were better than 500 to 1. However, we had to put on a brave front for the Navajos and complete a final lap around the track Bill Mahoney and I had entered ten years before when we went to Red Valley to interview some Navajo widows.

I was devastated when the insipid decision of the Court of Appeals came down. But by the time the letter of the Clerk of the Supreme Court arrived with its curt "Petition Denied" message, my emotions were spent and the news came as an anticlimax. (As I was well acquainted with five justices, I had nurtured a faint hope that our petition might garner two or three votes, but I knew down deep that this was a frivolous fancy.)

The final task I faced was to write a letter to all of our Navajo clients explaining the result of our long quest for justice in the white man's courts of law. I tried, but I could not write that letter. And later when I was invited by the Red Valley Chapter to attend a meeting and explain the outcome of our lawsuit, I asked Albert Hale to represent me.

I did not go because I was humiliated and sick at heart.

I did not go because for so many years, and on so many occasions, I had urged the Navajos to be patient and to have faith in their country's system of justice.

I did not go because I was ashamed of the outcome of their lawsuit and could not think of a convincing way to explain to them such concepts as "national security" and "government immunity."

And I was ashamed to go because I didn't know how to explain to friends who had trusted me that the government in Washington that had betrayed them—and had needlessly sacrificed the lives of their husbands in the name of national security—could, under the law I had urged them to respect, avoid responsibility for the tragedies that had engulfed their lives.

10

Grotesque Lambs, Grotesque Justice

Jesus, it was bright! I put my hands up like that and you could doggone near see your bones. And then that cloud . . . mushroomed right over our camp and our herd. Pretty soon here comes some jeeps with Army personnel, and they said to us, "My golly, you fellas are in a hot spot." We didn't even know what they were talking about.

—Kern Bulloch
Sheepman

In the spring of 1953, the Atomic Energy Commission detonated eleven atomic explosions at its Nevada test site. AEC technicians then knew more about the effects of radioactive fallout than any experts in the world; thus they certainly realized it was highly improbable that sheep could safely graze on their customary pasture lands in the downwind zone less than fifty miles from ground zero. But the AEC's orientation was NOTHING MUST STOP THE TESTS, and no attempt was made to evacuate the area downwind from Yucca Flats. The test team was sure it could handle any public relations problems that might arise if something unexpected occurred.

This disregard for public health would, in later years, lead to hundreds of cancer deaths among the downwinders living in small hamlets in Arizona, Nevada, and Utah. The first "guinea pigs" to die as a consequence of this experiment would not be humans, but sheep.

As the AEC's test organization prepared the shots, about 12,000 sheep were grazing in an area 40 miles north to 160 miles east of the test site. This part of the Great Basin contains dozens of rugged mountain ranges, all trending north–south. (During the nineteenth century, when cartographers depicted mountains with hachures, the geologist Clarence Dutton once quipped that his Nevada map looked like "an army of caterpillars marching to Mexico.") Between these mountains are expansive treeless basins—50 or 60 miles across and up to 100 miles long. These sagebrush-clad valleys have a spacious grandeur that suffuses them with a world-apart aura. It's an aura few have experienced because this high desert is ranching country, where rugged men struggle to wrest a living from lean, arid land. In the spring of 1953, two brothers, McRae and Kern Bulloch, were tending a large herd of sheep near Coyote Pass, northeast of the test site.

Herding is one of the world's oldest professions. The job has a sun-up to sun-down rhythm that requires infinite patience. Depending on the season, the soil is frost-nipped or sun-baked; whatever the weather, the work is always tinged with loneliness. The herder is married to his flock and they are tied to the land in an incessant search for edible grass. Sheep, it has been said, "are born looking to die," and they must be safeguarded from coyote and eagle, blizzards, bad weather, and poisonous weeds. To these age-old hazards, the AEC was about to add an invisible new one.

A combination of factors would make the 1953 shots, code-named "Upshot Knothole," the dirtiest and most hazardous detonations ever conducted in the United States. Three of these explosions had a force over twice as powerful as the bomb that obliterated Hiroshima. Firing them on low, 300-foot platforms guaranteed that hundreds of tons of vaporized soil and steel would magnify the fallout over downwind areas in Nevada, Utah, and Arizona. Beginning on March 17, 1953, there was an average of one blast a week for almost three months. During that period, while the Bullochs slowly trailed their sheep east from the winter range at Coyote Pass to lambing yards at Cedar City, Utah, they and their animals were exposed to large quantities of radioactive fallout.

As the animals grazed, their wool sponged radiation particles from the air. But these external doses were just a tiny fraction of the total the animals received. Due in part to the way they feed and in part to their unusual stomach structure, sheep were highly vulnerable to incursions of radioactive poisons.

Unlike cattle, which tend to graze singly, sheep feed as a group. Heads down, sharp hooves tilling the ground, they nip and tear at the base of plants, mouths hovering on the surface of the earth. As they close-cropped the bunch-grasses, the Bullochs' animals were concentrating iodine-131 and other radioactive isotopes in their glands and organs.

Near the end of the 1953 tests, when the sheep reached the lambing yards near Cedar City, the Bullochs and other herdsmen immediately knew something out of the ordinary had happened. Wool sloughed off in clumps, most of the adult sheep had blisters and sores on their faces, and the new lambs were either stillborn with grotesque deformities or were so weak they were unable to nurse and died soon after birth. The mysterious malady claimed its victims with dispatch: within a few days nearly 5,000 lambing ewes and lambs were dead.

In testimony he presented in April 1979 to a joint congressional hearing in Salt Lake City, Utah, Kern Bulloch recalled the scene at the lambing pens:

> When they started to lamb . . . the lambs were born with little legs, kind of pot-bellied. As I remember, some of them didn't have any wool, kind of a skin instead of wool. . . . And we started losing so many lambs that my father . . . just about went crazy. He had never seen anything like it before. Neither had I; neither had anybody else.

There was a straightforward, scientific explanation for the disaster, but twenty-six years would elapse before the sheepmen understood what had happened. What they had witnessed was the killing power of concentrated doses of radioactive fallout; by the end of the congressional hearing they had a clear picture of the network of lies the Atomic Energy Commission had used to conceal this simple truth from the outside world.

The expert witness who helped the sheepmen understand the

AEC's masterpiece of mendacity was Dr. Harold Knapp. Knapp was a stubborn operations analyst who caused consternation in AEC circles in 1962, when he discovered that dairy cows in the downwind zone were ingesting fallout and concentrating it in their milk. Thus huge, hidden doses of radiation were delivered to milk-drinkers in downwind communities. Harold's findings concerning the dangers of internal doses were a bombshell. He was, in effect, accusing the AEC of covering up an acute hazard by pretending that the only fallout problem related to exposures inflicted by external doses of dust.

Harold Knapp told the congressmen that the crucial questions about the massive 1953 die-off of sheep should have been: "How much radiation did the sheep ingest?" and "How much fallout does it take to kill a sheep?" He began his testimony with the assumption that the big 1953 bomb tests were blanketing the sheep's feeding-ground with a fine, deadly dust composed of two hundred different radioactive isotopes of thirty-five elements. His second assumption was that grazing animals (which he described as "vacuum cleaners for fallout") were ingesting the fresh fission products deposited on their grass. He then proceeded to make estimates of the amounts of contaminated fodder an average sheep would consume on an average day.

Dr. Knapp's calculations constituted a shocking indictment of the AEC's disregard for the safety of the animals and humans in the fallout path generated by the tests. His calculus revealed that the lambing ewes' gastrointestinal tracts received horrendous exposures ranging from 1,000 to 3,000 rads of gross fission radioactivity, and that the ewes' thyroids received approximatley 20,000 rads of iodine-131 radiation. According to Knapp's extrapolations, the highly vulnerable fetal lambs probably absorbed doses one and one-half times greater than their mothers did. This presentation evoked from Congressman Bob Eckhart of Texas the wry comment: "It is obvious, Dr. Knapp, that both science and justice would have been better served if the original study team had listened to the sheepmen and given the AEC's Washington experts the task of herding their sheep."

Knapp's indictment was given credibility by the fact that the experts who came out from Washington knew in 1953 about the hazards associated with internal doses of radiation. When I interviewed Dr. Shields Warren, the head of the AEC's Division of Biology and Medicine from 1947 to 1952, he readily conceded such knowledge. Dr. Warren admitted that "from 1947 on" he and his colleagues knew "the basic facts" concerning the fission products released by atomic bomb tests. He further conceded that "food chain dangers" were on his mind "from the time of Hiroshima" and that his worries increased "when the 1946 Bikini tests revealed that seafood in the surrounding ocean environment was seriously contaminated." Dr. Warren's candor added extra insights into sheep experiments the AEC had conducted in 1951 at its Hanford, Washington, laboratory. The Hanford research demonstrated that lambing ewes and fetal lambs would be fatally poisoned if they ingested substantial doses of iodine-131.

When news of the sheep die-off reached Washington, the AEC sent a team of radiation experts, led by Dr. Paul Pearson, to Cedar City to conduct an investigation. The most significant members of Pearson's team were two veterinarians, R. E. Thompsett of Los Alamos and Marine Lieutenant Colonel Robert Veenstra, who had previously performed research for the commission involving animals exposed to radiation.

During the initial phase of the investigation, as the two doctors of veterinary medicine listened to the ranchers' stories and examined their dead and ailing animals with radiation detection devices, the ranchers sensed the visitors were convinced that the die-off was caused by fallout. This impression was underscored when they overheard one of the veterinarians describe the carcass of a dead animal as "hotter than a two-dollar pistol."

The sheepmen never saw the summaries Thompsett and Veenstra subsequently wrote, but the veterinarians' suppositions were correct, as their field reports concluded that radiation had been a contributing cause of the sheep die-off. Colonel Veenstra's opinion was influenced by the radiation he found in the spleen, kidneys, ribs, and liver of the dead animals he examined. Dr. Thompsett had studied the cattle and horses injured by fallout from the wartime 1945 Trinity explosion in southern New Mexico, and his opinion was based in part on a finding that the lesions on the Utah sheep were identical to the radiation burns he had observed eight years earlier on the Trinity animals.

Once Dr. Pearson and his superiors in Washington realized that the sheepmen thought they were entitled to be reimbursed for their losses, a systematic campaign was launched to crush their expectations. Steve Brower, a young county agricultural agent who was trying to help the ranchers understand the issues, watched with dismay as the campaign of deceit unfolded. His first inkling of the AEC's hard-line stance came when Dr. Thompsett, who had promised to send him a copy of his field report, informed him that this document was "picked up" by a superior who told him "to rewrite it and eliminate any references to speculation about radiation damage or effects."

Because Brower was perceived as a neutral party who had influence with the sheepmen, his office in Cedar City became a prime destination in the fall of 1953 for "a battery of people . . . constantly bombarding us with expert opinions . . . that the levels of radiation could not have caused the damage." A conversation still etched in Steve Brower's memory twenty-six years later involved a confidential appeal that there could be no payment to the ranchers because the AEC had an "official policy" that "under no circumstances could [it] allow the precedent to be established in court that the AEC was liable for radiation damages to either animals or humans."

After this revelation, the AEC's intense campaign to intimidate the sheepmen or to conceal the truth about the sheep slaughter did not surprise Steve Brower. He winced when in response to a question by County Commissioner Dough Clark, an itinerant AEC expert called Clark a "dumb sheepman" who "couldn't understand the answer [to his question] if it was given to him." Brower caught the underlying message when he heard Joe Saunders, a deputy manager of the test site, use this argument to quash Joe Pace's expectations: "Joe, the easiest thing we could do would be to pay for these sheep, but if we paid for them every woman who got pregnant, and every woman that didn't, would sue us." And knowing that the AEC was anxious to close out the sheep controversy so plans for the next round of tests could go forward, Brower was not surprised when, a few months later, the Atomic Energy Commission announced that its experts had concluded that fallout had not harmed the Utah sheep.

What caught my attention as I listened to Steve Brower's testimony at the hearing was the evidence he presented that the cover-up was dictated by an "official policy" which had been adopted by the AEC. I found this revelation fascinating because the AEC's pay-nothing-to-radiation-victims policy appeared to explain many things about the burgeoning atomic-age tragedies in the West. When I learned that the sheepmen would have quietly settled their claims for a total of the $220,000 value of their lost animals, as a personal injury lawyer I was flabbergasted to learn that the government had refused to enter into negotiations with the Utah ranchers. And this pay-nothing, admit-nothing policy appeared to explain why, over the years, AEC functionaries had spun webs of deceit to avoid responsibility for the radiation tragedies of the uranium miners and the citizens who lived downwind from the Nevada test site.

What, I wondered, was the source of this policy? Viewing it as a possible legal trump card for the radiation victims, we began a search for what we assumed was a highly classified AEC document. In response to our inquiries, the government's lawyers asserted that they were unable to locate such a policy document. Facts I gleaned later from Sterling Black and Clifford Honicker led me to conclude that this policy probably originated as an oral, wartime edict by General Leslie Groves that became so embedded in Los Alamos culture that it took on a life of its own after the war.

Sterling Black, the son of U.S. Supreme Court Justice Hugo Black, and I had formed a friendship in 1946 at the University of Arizona. Sterling had subsequently served for several years in the 1950s as the chief counsel at the Los Alamos lab. When we met again in Albuquerque in the 1980s, Sterling was dubious that the policy in question had ever appeared in writing, but he remembered a pervasive pattern of thinking at the laboratory that it was "extremely important for their enterprise" that "a little exposure to radiation was nothing worse than a bad cold." Black recalled, too, that Director Norris Bradbury and the administrators who called the shots at Los Alamos were "extremely rough" on employees who felt they had been injured by, or overexposed to, radiation in their workplaces.

Sterling also provided insights about the "cover-up culture" that existed at Los Alamos. Based on his experience, he thought that "the great corrupter of the organization and the people who ran it" was the absolute authority they had been given to classify information and then to limit access to these data to a need-to-know elite. Black saw this as a "gigantic tool for deception" that led decision makers to believe that their national security responsibilities put them beyond the laws that governed other Americans, and gave them the right to "deceive and manipulate the public whenever necessary."

Clifford Honicker is a Tennessee researcher who spent five years in the 1980s investigating the AEC's no-payments-to-victims policy. Honicker became interested in this subject when he stumbled onto a 270-page medical dossier in the University of Tennessee radiological archives concerning what happened to physicist Allan Kline after he survived a highly publicized plutonium-test accident in a remote Los Alamos laboratory in May 1946. Kline, an observer of Louis Slotin's "critical-test" experiment, was standing a bare three or four feet away from the plutonium cores when Slotin's finger slipped and a powerful flash delivered a 1,000-rad dose of radiation to Slotin's body. He died nine days later.

Allan Kline, whose body absorbed over 100 rad of neutron radiation, survived the medical ordeal that followed, but a few days after he was released from the Los Alamos hospital he was fired. The dusty dossier Clifford Honicker discovered thirty-eight years later contained the story of Kline's effort to discover the truth about his injuries—and the parallel story of the lies the AEC used to deny Kline access to his medical files. Fascinated by the evidence he had uncovered, Honiker became an atomic-age detective. He located Kline and other key witnesses and conducted an inquiry that took him to Los Alamos, to Washington, D.C., and into the presence of the same ghostly, unwritten "official policy."

In 1989 Cliff Honicker described his search and many of his findings about the AEC's "principles" and practices in a lengthy *New York Times Magazine* article describing a pattern of deceit worthy of the KGB. He saw that when either citizens or AEC employees claimed they had been injured by exposures to radiation, they would be advised "by those who knew" that "their ailments were unrelated to such exposures." Honicker uncovered a scheme to avoid at all costs "possible embarrassing medical legal suits." He concluded that the proprietors of our nuclear establishment had, from the outset, pursued a tacit policy that it was not "in the best interest of the AEC" to follow the facts to their logical conclusion.

.   .   .

In the 1950s when outsiders didn't know enough about radiation issues to ask probing questions, any official pronouncement by the Atomic Energy Commission was accepted as a truth vouchsafed by its stable of great scientists. Thus, when AEC press officers issued a final report in January 1954, affirming that secret "scientific studies" had absolved fallout as a cause of the sheep die-off, AEC leaders in Washington were certain that their findings would douse the embers of this dispute.

The AEC's final report was accepted in all parts of the country except in Cedar City, Utah, where a tiny band of livestock men, ignorant about radioactive fallout but knowledgeable about the behavior of sheep, were certain this announcement was not accurate. Kern Bulloch and his friends were not formally educated, but their rough-and-tumble lives had instilled in them a sense of fair play that made them stubborn adversaries when they felt they had been treated unjustly. In the weeks that followed they garnered the support of a tenacious young Cedar City lawyer, Dan Bushnell. Dan and his friends would travel together on a thirty-two-year legal odyssey during which they would watch in disbelief as officers of the government they once trusted corrupted the American system of justice.

THE SHEEPMEN'S QUEST FOR JUSTICE

When he filed *Bulloch* v. *U.S.* in federal court in Salt Lake City in 1955, Dan Bushnell knew he was a barehanded David challenging a government Goliath with unlimited resources, but as a staunch Mormon he was guided by a belief that the truth would eventually be known and fair play would prevail. Acutely aware that he could not win his case unless he could prove that fallout had been a cause of the sheep die-off, Dan operated on the assumption that the two veterinarians, Veenstra and Thompsett, were honest men who, under oath, would uphold their professional opinions and testify that fallout was implicated in the demise of the sheep. He also assumed that when government lawyers studied the facts they would do the honorable thing and agree to an out-of-court settlement covering the value of the lost sheep.

These assumptions were naive, as Bushnell belatedly recognized in 1979, when he read the trial documents declassified by the government. The settlement option was never discussed, and the need to suppress or alter the opinions of Veenstra and Thompsett was given a high priority soon after they finished their inspections at the Cedar City lambing pens. From the day the Bulloch case was filed, the single-minded goal of the government's team of trial lawyers, scientists, and physicians was to win the lawsuit by fair means or foul, and their concerted efforts in the months that followed deserve to be called "Operation Cover-up."

It was literally child's play for the trial team to run circles around a country lawyer who had neither the resources to conduct a wide-ranging investigation nor access to the government's secrets. Armed with the power to intimidate witnesses and to manufacture whatever evidence would serve its purposes, the federal team worked unceasingly on a five-point strategy to provide an airtight defense for the government and to destroy the foundation of the sheepmen's case.

The elements of this strategy, as revealed by declassified documents and Dr. Harold Knapp's analysis, include:

- a successful campaign to intimidate Veenstra and Thompsett to either disavow their initial opinions or to take a stance that they were not qualified to express professional opinions about radiation harm to grazing animals;
- the concealment of the results of the AEC's sheep experiments which would have given Bushnell the incontrovertible evidence he needed to link the death of the sheep to ingested radiation;
- the preparation of misleading fallout maps from the 1953 tests that eliminated "hot spots" and minimized the amounts of radiation on the grass;
- the filing of deceptive documents by the government's lawyers, which, by concealing crucial facts, misled the trial judge and desecrated the search for truth that is the essence of the American system of law; and
- the preparation and presentation of testimony, by a phalanx of twenty of what the trial team informed the court were the "best-informed experts" in the country, that, based on fallout "facts"

manufactured by the AEC's technicians, the radiation the sheep were exposed to could not have harmed them. At the trial, the identical, unswerving opinions of the witnesses "best in a position to know" impelled Judge Sherman A. Christensen to conclude that "the maximum amount of radioactive fallout in any area in which the sheep could have been, would have caused no damage."

Dan Bushnell told me that although he felt in 1955 that his adversaries were manipulating some facts, he was dumbfounded by the 1979 revelations of his courtroom adversaries' unethical conduct and the stratagems they had used to defeat his clients' claims. He was equally appalled that scientists would preside over cover-ups of scientific facts, that witnesses crucial to his case were silenced, and that a win-at-all-costs zeal had animated the government attorneys and influenced them to ignore the canons of ethics of their profession.

Dan Bushnell was crushed, but he realized that an appeal would be an exercise in futility. Thus, when Judge Christensen's *Bulloch* opinion was embalmed in a book of law in 1956 it had all of the adornments of finality. The odds were probably 100,000 to 1 that any future jurist would ever stir the ashes of this case.

But in the spring of 1979 these odds were changed and *Bulloch* v. *U.S.* became a Lazarus lawsuit when a public outcry brought two congressional committees to Salt Lake City. The furor had begun with allegations of dying soldiers who had earlier participated in atomic tests and it had gained momentum when civilians who had lived downwind from the Nevada test site began expressing their long-suppressed suspicions about cancer excesses in their communities. It acquired credibility in medical circles when a cautious Utah epidemiologist, Dr. Joseph Lyon, published a study in *The New England Journal of Medicine* which disclosed that five years after the inception of the Nevada tests, a leukemia epidemic was killing children in the downwind zone.

Testimony presented by witnesses who appeared before the congressional committees told Attorney Bushnell that the U.S. government had perpetrated a fraud on Judge Christensen's court during the trial of the Bulloch case. As I stood that morning in the back of the hearing room and conversed with Dan Bushnell and Kern Bulloch, I saw their amazement and anger as revelation after revelation dramatized the tactics the government had used to turn the Bulloch case into a travesty of American justice.

The most vivid evidence presented at the Salt Lake City hearing came from Steve Brower, now a professor at Brigham Young University's Graduate School of Management. Dr. Brower's cover-up accusations had special force because he had watched the deceptions of the AEC's damage-control team as a neutral observer. Here is his description of the tactics used by these officials: "When we finally did get this case into court, none of the technical data from [the government's] experts was allowed to be used and of course the Iron County sheepmen could not make a case that would stand up in court without this data. The original, preplanned strategy of the AEC worked because they had the indiscriminate power to intimidate, withhold, screen, change and classify any and all information, reports and data."

That abuse of power was underscored by follow-up testimony presented by top Carter administration officials. Director Donald Frederickson of the National Institutes of Health told the congressmen that he had reviewed the once-secret files and expressed the opinion that "it would have been extremely difficult, probably impossible, to conclude that radiation did not at least contribute to the cause of the death of the sheep." And the general counsel of the Department of Health, Education and Welfare testified that in 1953 the AEC officials had suppressed the dissenting opinions of Public Health Service doctors who had examined the irradiated sheep.

Dr. Knapp's penetrating analysis of the fallout realities and the findings and accusations in the report subsequently filed with the Congress by the House Subcommittee on Oversight and Investigations emboldened Dan Bushnell to initiate an effort to reopen the sheepmen's case. The subcommittee found that AEC officials had "knowingly disregarded and suppressed evidence," determined that Upshot-Knothole fallout was the most likely cause of the sheep die-off, and concluded that the government had "wrongly denied compensation to the sheep ranchers."

In 1982 when Dan Bushnell lodged a motion to reopen the Bulloch case and charged that officials of the United States had perpetrated a fraud on Judge Sherman Christensen's court, the distinctive facts surrounding this motion converted it into a landmark of American law. Bushnell's motion simultaneously charged that government lawyers had engaged in highly unethical conduct, that crucial evidence had been concealed from the court, and that federal officials had conspired to alter and/or suppress the testimony of crucial witnesses. In addition, what gave Bushnell's motion singular status was that twenty-six years had elapsed since the original trial—and the circumstance that Judge Christensen, now an esteemed senior federal judge, was available to preside over the reconsideration of his earlier decision.

This motion was followed by a four-day hearing at which Dan Bushnell spread the hidden documents on the record and had Dr. Knapp summarize his findings. A few months later Judge Christensen issued a fifty-six-page opinion that made judicial history. No other federal jurist this century has adjudged, twenty-six years after his initial decision, that high-level federal lawyers abetted by high-level federal employees defrauded his court by a campaign of deceit.

Sherman Christensen condemned Paul Pearson and other AEC officials who had concealed a contemporaneous Hanford experiment involving irradiated fetal lambs, which had produced "signs and conditions almost identical" with those exhibited by the Utah sheep. He found that Pearson, Dr. Bernard Trum, a veterinarian employed at the AEC's Oak Ridge laboratory, and some of the government's lawyers vitiated the process of justice through a sustained campaign of "deceitful conduct" that intimidated Veenstra and Thompsett, who then shifted their professional opinions about the poisoning of the ewes and lambs.

Judge Christensen likewise determined that Pearson, Dunning, and their aides misled him by "juggling" the radiation maps the AEC used at the trial to minimize the doses delivered to the sheep. He also found that the five lawyers who represented the AEC (Don Fowler, Charles Eason, John J. Finn, Llewellyn Thomas, and Chalmers King) breached ethical duties they owed to the court by concealing crucial facts and filing "highly deceptive" answers to pivotal interrogatories filed by the plaintiffs.

When Judge Christensen granted the sheepmen's motion for a new trial, Dan Bushnell assumed that, at long last, the settlement he had sought for a quarter of a century was at hand. The judicial precedents were clear that the government had only a remote chance of persuading an appellate court to overturn this verdict. It made sense, Bushnell reasoned, for the federal government in the 1980s to clear the slate by admitting that overzealous officials in the 1950s felt it was more important to shield the atomic establishment from criticism than to deal justly with citizens who were harmed by their activities. An appeal was promptly initiated, but Dan Bushnell was shocked when he realized that officials in the U.S. Department of Justice had decided to discredit Judge Christensen's exposé of the 1950s cover-up.

In what can only be described as a grotesque episode of American jurisprudence, the U.S. Court of Appeals for the Tenth Circuit, which sits in Denver, Colorado, rejected Judge Christensen's findings and cancelled the new trial he had ordered. The Tenth Circuit's *Bulloch* opinion looms as a prime candidate for any future Legal Hall of Irrational Opinions because it scorned one of the most honored precedents of American law—the rule that a court of appeals should sustain a trial judge's decision to grant a new trial if his or her decision is "permissible in light of the evidence."

Two facts underscore the solemnity of this rule of judicial restraint. During the twentieth century the United States Supreme Court has never reversed a trial judge who granted a new trial on the basis of newly discovered evidence; and in the Tenth Circuit's forty-year history prior to its 1986 *Bulloch* decision, that court had never overturned a new trial order issued by a federal judge in one of its lower courts.

In composing his *Bulloch* opinion (and publishing his inexplicable conclusion that "nothing new" was presented to Judge Sherman Christensen when he reopened the sheep case) Chief Judge Oliver Seth sought to close the door on this shabby chapter of American jurisprudence. Yet many scholars who have studied the rationale this jurist used consider the outcome of this appeal a gross miscarriage of justice.

11

*The Big Lies
of the Bomb Testers:
Death and Deceit Downwind*

The only victims of U.S. nuclear arms since World War II
have been our own people.

—HOUSE INVESTIGATIONS
SUBCOMMITTEE (1980)

The discipline of science, which supposedly involves a systematic search for truth, was poorly served. . . . The keepers
of the flame were a hooded priesthood.

—PHILIP L. FRADKIN
Fallout (1989)

At the end of World War II, when nearly all of the superstar scientists
made a quick exit from the Mesa, Robert Oppenheimer and General
Groves chose Dr. Norris E. Bradbury to be the new director of the
Los Alamos laboratory (LASL). Bradbury, a Stanford physicist who
had won a commission in the navy after Pearl Harbor and worked on
ordnance research during the war, had been assigned to Los Alamos
in 1944 and won his spurs in the explosives division as a deputy
serving under George B. Kistiakowsky. Commander Bradbury
proved to be a strong administrator, and when Congress later re-

placed General Groves with a five-man nonmilitary Atomic Energy Commission, Norris Bradbury became a powerful, pivotal figure in the atomic establishment.

Mammoth military expeditions were mounted to conduct the first postwar atomic bomb tests. The highly publicized explosions, detonated on atolls in the Marshall Islands 9,000 miles west of California, took months to assemble and coordinate. In 1946, for example, the preparation and execution of the "Crossroad" tests at Bikini required a task force of 200 ships, 150 aircraft, and 42,000 men. The Pacific sites had many drawbacks. Whimsical winds made it difficult to predict the paths fallout would follow, logistical problems were frustrating, and officials in the Pentagon complained incessantly about the exorbitant costs of the Pacific operations.

Bradbury and his bomb testers had begun agitating for a continental proving ground before the Soviet Union surprised the world by detonating its first nuclear weapon. As a response, in the summer of 1949, the AEC authorized a clandestine survey of possible sites. The North Carolina coast between Cape Hatteras and Cape Fear was initially considered a promising site, but studies were also made of Camp LeJeune, North Carolina, Texas's Padre Island, the Trinity site in New Mexico, the Dugway Proving Ground in western Utah, the Point Barrow area in Alaska—and of two air force bombing ranges in central Nevada.

The area that emerged as Norris Bradbury's first choice was the Las Vegas range, a secluded region that surely reminded him of the New Mexico desert where he had helped assemble components of "the Gadget" that became the world's first atomic bomb. The commander was exhilarated that such an ideal site was available. The enthusiasm he felt for this backyard test facility was still evident three decades later when, during a lawsuit brought by downwind civilians, he described its advantages to a federal judge. "The population problem," Bradbury effused, "was almost zero. . . . It was close to sources of technical supply. It was seventy-five miles from Las Vegas. Accessible by air. Accessible by road. And . . . one could have more effective diagnostic tests there than any place you could imagine, and do it safely."

In the surreptitious tradition of postwar nuclear-policy making, the Las Vegas site was selected—and ratified by President Truman—without any public discussion or consultations with governors or members of Congress. With a bland press release that might have passed for an announcement of the siting of a new air force base, on January 11, 1951, the AEC announced that it would begin exploding atomic bombs in Nevada in three weeks. The innocuous tenor of this press release (which had been massaged by uneasy, high-placed federal officials for weeks) conveyed three messages to the American people. It said the new bombing range was "readily accessible" to our secret bomb factory in New Mexico. It explained that this step would "speed up" the production of atomic weapons. And it offered the comforting news that radiological safety problems had been reviewed "by authorities in the fields involved" and that tests at the Nevada site could be conducted with "adequate assurance of safety."

The magisterial certainty that permeated this press release expressed the cavalier attitude toward public health concerns that subsequently dominated the outlook of Director Bradbury, his LASL associates, and the AEC apparatus in Washington. This announcement, with its implication that protecting civilians from radiation harm would be a paramount concern of the bomb testers, marked the beginning of a decades-long policy of public deception that later provoked George Kistiakowsky to denounce the atomic bureaucracy as "the most arrogant and contemptuous of the public interest" of all the nation's federal agencies.

Norris Bradbury had served his apprenticeship under General Groves and Robert Oppenheimer, but compared with his mentors he was not a complicated human being. One of his colleagues once described him as a second-rate scientist who was a first-rate manager. Bradbury had none of Oppenheimer's charisma, but Groves would have admired both his knack for delegating authority and the heavy hand he used to maintain secrecy and to preserve the company-town ambiance of Los Alamos. Bradbury, who enjoyed governing by edict, had such contempt for lawyers and the rule of law that he forced LASL's lawyers to live "outside" by denying them access to housing at his city.

Oppenheimer's brilliance was a hard act to follow, but with the departure of the prima donnas and the decompression that ensued at the end of the war, Norris Bradbury's low-key leadership was just what LASL needed. The new director's task, as he saw it, was to improve the "lousy bombs" (his words) of the Manhattan Project by designing more compact second-generation weapons that would use fissionable materials with greater efficiency.

Devoted to his work, Bradbury was so comfortable in the constricted atmosphere of Los Alamos that he remained there after his retirement. His career contrasted sharply with that of the man who became his rival bomb builder, Edward Teller. Bradbury was a cold warrior who did his job and never sought to make waves in Washington. Teller aggressively used the distinction he sought and won in the media as the "father of the H-bomb" as a springboard for personal power. He demanded a competing bomb factory of his own in California. And he sought off-the-record appointments with presidents and influential members of Congress at which, as a self-appointed geopolitician of the atomic age, he could peddle his ideas about what weapons and strategies the United States should adopt to defeat Communism and maintain America's nuclear supremacy.

Bradbury had no moral reservations about the terror bombing of the civilians who inhabited Hiroshima and Nagasaki. "My friends were getting killed," he explained. "I wanted to see the end of the war." Justifications based on military necessity also dominated the outlook of Bradbury and his bomb testers when civilians who lived downwind from the Nevada proving ground began complaining that they had been exposed to harmful amounts of radiation and that their children were dying of leukemia. In the 1950s, Norris Bradbury and his associates mounted an assiduous public relations campaign to counter such complaints and to reassure the American people that stringent safety precautions were being followed at the Nevada test site.

The cloak of secrecy that enveloped all facts put the AEC's publicists in a posture where they could literally wave verbal wands and demolish their critics. For example, a slogan fashioned by Los Angeles PR men—"The Atomic Energy Commission says there is no danger"—made all complaints and critics appear absurd. Scientists who paid no attention to the opinions of radiologists in their midst undoubtedly believed the no-danger gospel preached by the AEC. But as we shall see, there is unmistakable evidence that Norris Bradbury knew that those living downwind were being exposed to serious health hazards.

QUICK AND DIRTY TESTING

Bradbury's bomb testers were so excited by the prospect of having a backyard test site that their assessment of the health hazards was superficial. The Los Alamos committee of meteorologists and senior atomic scientists who performed this crucial study in the summer of 1950 readily concluded that the fallout they would "throw" on the ranches and small towns east and north of the test site would not cause serious harm. The quick and dirty guideline for permissible fallout they devised was based on an assumption that the health of the civilians would be adequately protected if they were not exposed to more than 3.9 rads of external radiation during each series of tests.

At least one scientist who participated in this exercise was uneasy about the outcome. Enrico Fermi insisted that the minutes of the meeting disclose that "our conclusions should stress the extreme uncertainty of the elements we had to go on and that we did our best with these." Worried by the uncertainties and the gung-ho attitude of the laboratory's leaders, Fermi also urged that the civilians down-wind should be warned to stay indoors and to take showers after the fallout drifted over their towns.

Underscoring the reckless haste of the bomb testers is the fact that they made their off-site safety decisions with a minimum of input from their colleagues in the Atomic Energy Commission's Division of Biology and Medicine (DBM). In 1950 the director of DBM, Dr. Shields Warren, was internationally recognized for studies he had performed concerning the impact of radiation on the human body. When I interviewed Dr. Warren at his Boston hospital in 1979, I learned that he was deliberately excluded from the conference that set the 3.9-rad exposure guideline for the off-site civilians. Warren ruefully admitted that the "expert" the Los Alamos scientists relied on to "bless" their safety guideline was Major General James P. Cooney, an army doctor who was spearheading the campaign to get the Nevada site approved.

Born into a Boston medical family at the turn of the century, Shields Warren was a pioneer in radiation research who, by hard work, rose to the pinnacle of his profession. As a Harvard Medical School professor, Warren became a standout in this new field of medicine by studying both the beneficial and the harmful impacts of radioactive substances. (During my interview, he informed me that when World War II began there were fewer than fifteen "real radiological experts" in the whole world.) In September 1945, Shields Warren headed a team of navy doctors that went to Hiroshima and Nagasaki and made the first systematic medical surveys of the deaths and injuries caused by the atom bombs.

To Warren, these devastated cities were medical laboratories where the effects of atomic explosions on human beings could be studied, and it was largely due to his leadership that a joint U.S.-Japan medical survey, named the Atomic Bomb Casualty Commission (ABCC), was created in 1947 to carry out what is today the largest ongoing epidemiological study in the world. It was, in part, the distinction Warren gained through this leadership that impelled the members of the new Atomic Energy Commission to persuade him to leave Harvard in 1948 and create its Division of Biology and Medicine in Washington.

During our July 1979 conversation at the Boston Radiation Laboratory that bore his name, Shields Warren admitted it was a serious mistake for the Los Alamos scientists to assume that the only risks to the civilians involved external exposures from irradiated dusts. He said he knew "from 1947 on" the basic facts about the toxic fission products (iodine, strontium, cesium, and plutonium) that would be released into the atmosphere when a nuclear bomb was exploded. Warren also said that "food chain dangers" were on his mind from the time of Hiroshima, and that his concerns on this score were heightened when his researchers discovered that fallout contaminated fish life during the 1946 Bikini tests in the Pacific.

Warren noted that the close-to-the-land lifestyle of the downwind families made them "especially vulnerable" to doses of radiation that would be inhaled in the out-of-doors or ingested through homegrown foods. In such a pastoral setting, he observed, it should have been taken into account that most of the residents ate fresh vegetables and fruit grown in their gardens and orchards. If people milked their own cows and consumed mutton and beef from animals that foraged in the region's pastures, he acknowledged, the risks of "radiation effects" would be elevated. As Shields Warren ruminated about one topic, I realized he was revealing a long-suppressed frustration concerning the "unprofessional" monitoring of the tests. He was told at the outset, he said, that there would be "relatively few" tests at the Nevada site. As a consequence, he envisioned the down-wind zone as another singular medical laboratory where the health impacts of the irradiated dusts on the downwind population could be studied objectively. Dr. Warren anticipated that DBM would receive funds to establish training schools where equipment and expertise could be developed to track the fallout scientifically and observe effects on the health of the human beings who lived in the downwind region.

Warren said that when the Atomic Energy Commission failed to support such a program, DBM never developed a cadre of profes-sionals who could have asserted control and carried out the kind of health-oriented monitoring that was needed. From a medical stand-point, he said, "things were pretty primitive" in the downwind areas in the 1950s. And it was clear he felt that the furor that later developed over fallout could have been avoided if his radiologists—instead of the pick-up teams of untrained personnel assembled for each series by the bomb testers—had been given authority to conduct systematic medical and biological studies of the environmental impacts of the dusts that fell from the mushroom clouds.

By 1951, the first phase of the atomic age was history, and Shields Warren and his colleagues at the Division of Biology and Medicine had developed wide-ranging insights about the health hazards as-sociated with exposures to radiation. They knew, for example, that U.S. physicians who endured repeated low-level exposures while administering X-ray treatments to patients had died of leukemia at a rate nine times in excess of that suffered by ordinary Americans. They knew from their research after the Trinity test in New Mexico that radiation released from atomic bombs would not descend evenly across the landscape, but that winds and precipitation and "terrain effects" would concentrate some of the fallout into high-risk "hot spots." They had learned, via the first medical findings of the Atomic Bomb Casualty Commission, that, after a latency period of three or four years, there was a marked increase in the incidence of leukemia among the Japanese survivors of the atom bombs. And the AEC's radiologists not only knew that infants and pregnant women were the individuals most at risk in the downwind zone, they were also acutely aware that the hazards would be reduced or avoided if the residents of exposed communities were either evacuated during the tests of big bombs or required to stay indoors when winds swept fallout clouds over their homes.

Once the new proving ground was in operation, this vital medical knowledge was shunted aside when the bomb testers decided to proceed on the assumption that the level of fallout they had deemed permissible wouldn't harm the off-site civilians. This attitude disturbed Dr. Warren, but his anxieties were partially assuaged by assurances that all of the big bombs would be tested in the Pacific and only a "relatively few" low-yield bombs would be detonated at the Nevada test site (NTS). A cautious course was followed in 1951 and in the spring of 1952 when the first sixteen NTS experiments were either airdrops (exploded several hundred feet above the earth to minimize local fallout) or small-yield surface shots that wafted only small amounts of radiation over the downwind zone.

This pattern was altered drastically in the spring of 1952, when four Hiroshima-size bombs, exploded on low towers, scooped up huge quantities of earth that precipitated large loads of fresh fallout onto ranches and small towns in Nevada and Utah. Shields Warren, then in the final days of his five-year stint as the founding director of the Division of Biology and Medicine, minced no words when he made a presentation to the members of the commission on May 14, one week after the 12-kiloton *Easy* shot was fired at the NTS. "I have concluded," he counseled his colleagues, that "we cannot risk any continental aboveground shots larger than" the *Easy* explosion.

THE BIG BOMBS AND THEIR VICTIMS

This was the crucial turning point for continental testing. When the commissioners elected to ignore Warren's warning and subsequently approved the detonation of monster tower bombs that had five times the power of the Hiroshima explosion, they set a course that sacrificed innocent civilians on the altar of fast-track bomb testing. That decision gave the testers a green light to take big risks, to pursue a "nothing-must-stop-the-tests" policy, and to push safety considerations into the background. It produced a series of tests the next year, code-named Upshot-Knothole (U-K), that were the dirtiest ever conducted in Nevada. And by rejecting the advice of the AEC's medical experts, and enrolling them in a campaign to cover up evidence of radiation harm to humans, that decision transformed the AEC's supposed scientific safety program into what Dr. John Gofman later described as a "scientific whorehouse."

The Upshot-Knothole tests were, by far, the most reckless ever conducted at the NTS. One Los Alamos safety officer observed that compared with the initial Ranger series in 1951, the U-K tests increased local fallout as much as 500 times. This series included five shots that vaporized tons of earth and exceeded the yield of the *Easy* explosion. The bombs were emplaced on 300-foot aluminum towers, and the most powerful, the 43-kiloton *Simon* detonation on April 25, 1953, threw so much debris into the jetstream that twelve hours later a spring thunderstorm precipitated 2 rads of radiation onto the environs of Troy, New York. Fallout in mid-May from the second largest, the 32-kiloton *Harry* shot, created a fearful moment for Norris Bradbury's test managers when the radioactive cloud it generated hovered amid rain clouds over St. George, Utah, the largest city in the "relatively uninhabited" downwind zone. Had a Troy-style "rainout" occurred that day, one fallout expert later calculated, it could have washed out 400-plus rads of radiation and "killed half or all of the people in town."

During the U-K series, LASL's monitors (who kept to the main roads and covered only an infinitesimal portion of the downwind zone) measured hot spots that clearly demonstrated that there were many serious violations of the 3.9-rad safety guideline. However, it was another, more ominous piece of evidence that verified that Shields Warren's worst fears were being realized: there were widespread reports to monitors that men, women, and children who were outdoors when fallout clouds deposited loads of radiation sustained burns on exposed parts of their bodies. The AEC's radiologists were aware that this meant the individuals harmed had, in a single incident, been exposed to somewhere between 10 and 50 rads of beta radiation.

Before the end of the seventy-nine days consumed by the Upshot-Knothole test, monitors had logged information from all sectors of the downwind zone. At the tiny mining town of Tempiute, Nevada, fifty miles from ground zero, postmistress Marjorie Perchet and two young girls, Theryl Stewart and Silva Ann Hines—all of whom subsequently succumbed to cancer—reported their injuries to a monitor. One hundred sixty miles northeast, on the lee slope of Nevada's second-highest mountain, 13,061-foot Mount Wheeler, four sheepmen (the brothers George, Dick, and Arlo Swallow, and Lee Whitlock) sustained facial burns that "extended up under their hats" and experienced "terrific headaches" in the two days after a discolored cloud passed by their camp. And the afternoon of the *Harry* shot, while prospecting at a mine fifty miles east of St. George, E. H. Ellett and Byron Davis and their wives experienced similar symptoms and were also afflicted by episodes of nausea and vomiting.

There were other beta-burn victims, many in remote areas, who at the time had no way to relate their injuries to the "safe" bomb testing under way in southern Nevada. Among them was Don Schmutz, a farmer who was working in his field near St. George as the *Harry* cloud hovered overhead; a St. George woman, Aileen Anderson, who tilled her garden and did her laundry in the outdoors the same morning; a young woman, Nevada Judd, who walked through a moist alfalfa field and sustained a burn on her leg that left a permanent scar; and Elmer Jackson, a Kanab, Utah, rancher who noticed a dark cloud as he herded cattle on the Arizona strip and arrived home with one side of his face severely burned. Most shocking of all, at a sheep camp in Hamlin Valley after the 15-kiloton *Grable* experiment (a historic first, involving the firing of an atomic shell from a 280-millimeter cannon) Elma Mackelprang watched tiny, whitish flakes swirl about and later developed a skin rash and nausea and vomiting, the classic symptoms of heavy contact with radiation.

Combined with the sudden deaths of over 5,000 sheep that were eating radiation-laden grasses in downwind pastures, the stories of the beta-burn victims should have compelled the AEC to heed the warning Shields Warren had made a year earlier. But Warren was gone, and none of his successors had the grit or the prestige to force the commission to put public health first and confine Nevada testing to small bombs and underground explosions. The sheep deaths caused a stir in Washington, but adroit suppression of bad news by test-site folks—a campaign of systematic suppression that marked the beginning of an intricate thirty-year cover-up—prevented evidence about the burned civilians from reaching the White House or the attention of the congressional overseers who were, on paper, the watchdogs of the nation's atomic establishment.

The unwritten rules that governed the cover-up meant that all burn victims received the same callous response from their government. A "there-is-no-danger" public relations effort involving films and safety lectures by atomic scientists was intensified by those in charge of test site operations. No physicians were sent to diagnose or treat the victims. And the investigators dispatched by the test manager to interview them conveyed the bland message, "Our experts say fallout can't cause this kind of harm." The investigators then prepared classified reports for their superiors belittling the victims' complaints and attributing their ailments, variously, to "sunburns," "a gastrointestinal disturbance," "hysteria," or "hypothyroidism."

The citizens of St. George received similar insensitive treatment the day of the *Harry* shot. The reckless misjudgments made by the test manager on that day of maximum danger in the downwind zone turned the performance of the monitors into a comedy of errors and produced tragedies for the families living in that region. In 1980 a secret "workshop" for some of the living monitors was convened to help the government prepare a defense to a lawsuit filed by fallout victims. William S. Johnson, the leader of the 1953 task force of monitors, recalled "there were no instructions, there were no procedures to follow with respect to what to do, and not to do." Johnson remembered, too, that "without warning" the test director, Alvin Graves, walked in, and "we had requirements laid on us to block highways, to monitor vehicles, and to wash and decontaminate . . . vehicles." He described a chaotic scene with "no permissible level" to guide the monitors who were sent to service stations to supervise these haphazard washing ceremonies. It was, as Johnson recalled nearly three decades later, "a shocking day."

Frank Butrico, the single monitor stationed in St. George on the day of the *Harry* explosion, had similar recollections. "I had the very distinct feeling," he recounted, "that if there was a plan, it sure wasn't made known to us monitors. . . . If something went wrong, what would we do? Just monitor." Butrico also had a vivid memory of the attitude of the "top-level people" when he returned to the test site headquarters. The paramount concern, he sensed, "was whether this was going to affect testing, and less of it as to what was really happening and what could be done about it." The "prime part of the discussion," he remembered, was "how much of this information are we going to disseminate . . . and let's consider the national security aspects."

The absence of any plan to protect the civilians produced a safety fiasco for the inhabitants of St. George. The appropriate time to warn people to take cover was *before* the fallout cloud arrived, but Butrico was not told the cloud was headed for St. George until it was over the city. The improvised warning (a radio announcement broadcast from Cedar City, sixty miles away) reached only those who were tuned in to that station—and as Butrico drove around the city he was appalled to discover elementary school children on their playground while the dark cloud still hovered overhead.

A moral dilemma also hovered over the St. George scene the day of the *Harry* shot. Having committed a blunder that imperiled the downwind civilians, common decency dictated that the bomb testers had a duty to inform the citizens of St. George about steps they could take to decontaminate themselves and reduce the health risks they had been subjected to. But Butrico's superiors, intoxicated by bloated conceptions of "national security" that imbued them with pitiless arrogance, never considered taking such action. When the dirty cloud had disappeared and irradiated dusts had settled, Frank Butrico was instructed to take a shower and throw away the clothes he was wearing. No such warning was ever given to the citizens of St. George.

The Upshot-Knothole tests were both a medical and a moral watershed for the Atomic Energy Commission and its bomb testers. The dead sheep, and overwhelming evidence that excessive amounts of radiation had been dumped on the downwinders, constituted proof that the safety assumptions devised to guide bomb testing in Nevada contained frightening flaws. Had an unbiased team of medical experts been invited to make an assessment of the fallout facts gathered in the spring of 1953, it is plain that constraints similar to those advocated earlier by Shields Warren would have been imposed on future tests at the Nevada site.

BIG LIES, BIG COVER-UPS

The classic cover-up the AEC launched that summer evolved into the most long-lived program of public deception in U.S. history. The flow of false information it produced created a cancerlike environment in which each lie generated additional misconduct and additional lies. And any search for evidence concerning the decisions that initiated the cover-up confronted a blank wall.

Cover-ups invariably engender illusions that warp the judgment of those who participate in them. The behavior of those in charge of developing nuclear weapons is a case in point. When AEC officials embraced the idea that their efforts would be discredited and disrupted if they admitted that radiation might cause cancers or that their activities were exposing innocent bystanders to excessive doses of radiation, they were entering a moral wasteland. All subsequent decision making was perverted by that twisted reasoning. It fostered a conviction that it was more important to protect the tests than to protect civilians. And it spawned a policy that the impact of radiation on human health and all "harmful" facts about radiation "accidents" had to be concealed from the American people.

Any cover-up must be implemented and enforced by designated agents, and one man emerged in 1953 as the quarterback of the AEC's damage-control effort. His name was Gordon Dunning. Although the personnel charts of the 1950s list him as a low-level "rad-safe" official in the Division of Biology and Medicine, documents demonstrate that he was clothed with authority to manage and suppress information about the radiation released by the testing of nuclear weapons. Dunning's name appears on all of the crucial cover-up reports in the AEC's secret files, and the doyens of his agency came to regard him as an aide who excelled at handling emergency situations and disarming potential critics of the bomb-testing program. Gordon Dunning's feats made him a legend—and on more than one occasion in the 1960s I saw commissioners smirk when his name was mentioned.

The son of a Presbyterian minister, Gordon Dunning grew up in Watertown, New York, graduated from State Teachers College at Cortland, where he majored in physical education and biology, and taught in upstate high schools before the onset of World War II. After the war, he won graduate degrees in science education from Syracuse University and was subsequently employed as an instructor for three years by St. Lawrence College before he turned up as a research analyst with the prestigious Atomic Energy Commission in 1951. Many of Dunning's Washington coworkers viewed him as something of a mystery man during his twenty years at the AEC. One facet of the mystery concerned his lack of qualifications to occupy the radiation safety position he filled at the agency. His credentials as a scientist were skimpy: he had never studied the subtle science of radiological medicine, and his experience as a classroom science instructor at a small college hardly equipped him to vault overnight into a domineering role as an expert on the environmental and health impacts of ionizing radiation.

Dunning's work history and the extensive paper trail he left demonstrate that he was not hired to do research, but was given a roving assignment to sequester and cover up evidence that the AEC's radiation releases were posing health hazards to humans. There is ample evidence, too, that he was highly effective. One detractor described him as a "superb technician" who misused his talents. Another colleague, who grudgingly admired the "almost fanatical" devotion he brought to his work, nurtured an image of Dunning as a "fireman" who appeared on cue whenever radiation "accidents" threatened to ignite flames of controversy. And the fact that he was quickly catapulted into the inner circle of the AEC hierarchy shows that the commissioners themselves were pleased with his achievements.

Gordon Dunning got his battlefield baptism during the muted but ticklish crisis that came after the Upshot-Knothole fallout. The stratagems he devised to smother evidence that innocent civilians had been exposed to dangerous doses of radiation told his superiors that he was a valuable addition to their staff. There was nothing sophisticated about the schemes of evasion he devised. For example, he covered up the information that monitors had gathered about the postmistress and the two girls who suffered skin burns at Tempiute by the crude expedient of dumping the information in a folder of "dead" documents. And he used a similar tactic to keep the AEC's physicians in the dark about the severity of the doses absorbed by the burned civilians.

But it was the deft, decisive way he handled the sheep emergency—a crisis that threatened the very future of the Nevada proving ground—that won kudos for Gordon Dunning in Los Alamos and Washington. At the outset, the bomb testers were confronted with overwhelming evidence that the ingestion of grass laced with potent, fresh fission products had killed over 5,000 sheep. Dunning had to deal with this reality, and he surely sensed that, if the AEC admitted that fallout had killed the sheep, a furor over the health risks being imposed on the downwind civilians would delay or restrict further testing in Nevada. This was an ominous situation for the bomb testers, for if state public health experts entered the picture they would inevitably conclude that the downwinders were also consumers of contaminated vegetation in the form of fruits and vegetables grown in their gardens.

In the aftermath of the Upshot-Knothole tests, these daunting facts created another proving ground that tested Gordon Dunning's ingenuity and personal ethics. He began by orchestrating a campaign to convince skeptical veterinarians, whom the AEC had called in for consultations, that "toxic weeds" or malnutrition had caused the die-off of the sheep. This endeavor culminated a few months later at Los Alamos when Dunning conducted an emergency exercise to complete a final report that would exculpate fallout as a cause of the sheep die-off. He now added a cunning twist to the cover-up craft he was perfecting. When Utah health officials and the veterinary experts he had assembled refused to concur in Dunning's written conclusion that "the lesions on the sheep were not produced by radioactive fallout," he first appealed to their patriotism by confiding that he needed a statement of some kind so "Commissioner Zuckert would open up the 'purse strings' for future continental tests." This ploy did not produce assent, so Dunning had the conferees sign a sheet of paper attesting their attendance at this meeting. A few days later in Washington he flourished those signatures as proof that the experts had reached a postmortem consensus that radiation was not implicated in the slaughter of the sheep.

The success of this sleazy exercise told Dunning he had a blank check from the commissioners to conceal any facts that might impede the continuation of testing in Nevada. Emboldened by tacit assurances that he was free to manipulate facts and people at will, Dunning turned next to a mass of evidence that indicated that the AEC's program to protect the downwind civilians was a shambles. The fallout facts gathered by the Upshot-Knothole monitors revealed widespread violations of the AEC's 3.9-rad safety standard. "Hot" spots had been identified in all sectors of the downwind zone, and reports of burns on the bodies of men, women, and children attested to the fact that large numbers of individuals had been exposed to hazardous amounts of radiation.

As he supervised work on official maps to depict where the fallout from each test was deposited, Gordon Dunning set out to prepare reports that would conceal truths about these hazards. The fact that all of the data he was collating was stamped "secret" further informed him that he was free to devise a technique that would cancel out evidence that wholesale violations of the AEC's safety criteria had occurred and large numbers of individuals had sustained overexposures. Dunning developed a simplistic formula to accomplish this aim. It consisted of "reduction factors" that could be applied mathematically to shrink the radiation dumped on the downwinders below the 3.9-rad threshold. These "Dunning factors" became a fixture in fallout calculations. They were not rooted in scientific or medical knowledge, but they enabled their author to wave a mathematical wand and expunge the hot spot islands identified by the monitors and to blot out the dangerous doses measured by the beta-burns.

In preparing the official maps that became an emblem of innocence for the bomb testers, Dunning used a refinement to further mask the excessive exposures sustained by many individuals. He did this by lumping the "reduced" dose measurements together into an "average" for each downwind community. These factored figures, as he intended, erased individual doses and transformed the victims into statistics. Thereafter, AEC officials pontificated that everyone who lived in a specific town had received the phony average dose shown on Gordon Dunning's maps.

The macabre mischief wreaked by the Dunning factors can best be illustrated by analyzing what happened in and around St. George after the infamous *Harry* shot. Monitors took over twenty actual measurements of the radioactive dusts that fell in the narrow valley of the Virgin River. The infinite dose measurements recorded in and around St. George ranged from 3 to 14.6 rads, and readings of 5.7 and 8 rads were taken at two of the Mormon villages (Hurricane and LaVerkin) in the valley. Since the *Annie* shot had already delivered a 5-rad dose to the environs of St. George in March, an honest count would have generated a conclusion that inhabitants who were living and working in the "hottest" parts of town could have been exposed to cumulative doses as high as 19.6 rads during the U-K tests.

To conceal such flagrant violations of the thirteen-week 3.9-rad exposure standard was a formidable challenge to Dunning and his rad-safe "experts," and the legerdemain they used to shrink the 1953 exposures was a masterpiece of obfuscation. When it came time to prepare maps and reports summarizing the doses inflicted on the citizens of St. George, the Dunning factors saved the day. An initial shrinkage of 50 percent, for example, was achieved by falsely assuming (via Dunning's "shielding" formula) that the inhabitants of St. George were in their homes while the *Harry* cloud was overhead. Then, by applying Dunning's "official body dose" factor, the remaining half was juggled and reduced a further 80 percent.

These mathematical convolutions were a godsend to the bomb testers. They made hot spot islands disappear, they dressed ugly facts in comely new clothes, and they provided a fictitious data base from which Gordon Dunning could prepare plausible fallout maps that attested that none of the cities and towns in the downwind zone had received cumulative doses of external gamma radiation that exceeded 2.5 rads.

One additional maneuver by Dunning ensured that nothing would disturb his authoritative pronouncements about off-site fallout. He knew external gamma doses were only part of the picture— and he also knew all about the additional pathways through which other deadly forms of radiation (isotopes such as cesium, plutonium, strontium, and radioiodine) could enter the body and deliver potent internal doses through inhalation or ingestion. The most obvious of these dangers was the prospect that the downwinder's cows were metabolizing massive amounts of radioiodine in their milk.

Dunning put a lid on the internal isotopes by the simple expedient of treating them as a nonproblem, but it was a slippery lid, and at intervals over the next two decades he became embroiled in controversies with critics who knew that his decision was medically monstrous. The first of these encounters came in the 1950s, when a perceptive Public Health Service monitor, Morgan Seal, showed Dunning a document he had prepared based on retrospective calculations that proved there must have been huge amounts of iodine-131 in St. George milk after the Upshot-Knothole tests. According to Seal, this "got Gordon excited" and "he got mad, red in the face, took it and threw it on the floor and stomped on it" with the admonition "Don't you do that."

Gordon Dunning encountered a more relentless adversary in 1962, when Harold Knapp, an MIT-trained mathematician who had been assigned by the AEC to study internal doses of fallout, wanted to publish the results of research that demonstrated that downwind milk drinkers had absorbed amounts of iodine-131 that were possibly 100 times higher than the official doses Dunning had bandied about for over a decade. When Dunning saw that Knapp was getting ready to expose some of his cover-ups, he sought to prevent the publication of Knapp's paper; but Knapp fought back with the truth teller's tenacity that gave him a place in history as the AEC's first whistle blower.

Harold Knapp, a self-styled "simple-minded New Hampshireman," was drummed out of the AEC's citadel a year later, but by the time he departed he had honed his skills as an operations analyst, and he knew the tricks and techniques Gordon Dunning had used to cover up massive releases of radiation into the environment. Knapp emerged sixteen years later as a Banquo's ghost of the troubled atomic establishment. At the 1979 congressional hearings, he was the star witness who described Dunning's medical frauds and threw a spotlight on the deceptions he and several associates used to corrupt justice and perpetrate a fraud on a federal court.

But in the fall of 1953, in the aftermath of the record-setting fallout generated by the Upshot-Knothole tests, radiation realities were largely defined by Gordon Dunning's "facts" and formulas. Indeed, conclusions Dunning fabricated provided the rationale—and the slogans—developed to reassure the downwinders that the next tests would be even safer than the U-K explosions. The AEC's public relations program consisted of a flurry of soothing speeches by atomic scientists to civic organizations and an all-is-well "safety film" that praised the downwinders for their patriotic contributions to the nation's military security. Downwind folk were also showered with thousands of copies of a pamphlet written in third-grade English that featured this caption under a drawing of a cowboy serenely riding his horse across a landscape framed by a mushroom cloud: "FALLOUT DOES NOT CONSTITUTE A SERIOUS HAZARD TO ANY LIVING THING OUTSIDE THE TEST SITE."

This pamphlet not only ignored the hot spots, the dead sheep, and the shocking hazards created by the *Harry* shot, it was the first salvo of a campaign to persuade the nation that fallout was harmless. AEC publicists wrote rave reviews about the "unusual safety record" the bomb testers had achieved. They belittled critics who argued that health perils were being overlooked. And they used this pronouncement from the Mount Olympus of the atomic age—"The Atomic Energy Commission says there is no danger"—to silence the lingering doubts of skeptics.

In 1955, as the next series of tests got under way in Nevada, Gordon Dunning was assigned the task of selling the AEC's safety gospel to the American people. In articles he wrote for national magazines, his presentations were couched in sophisticated language, but in reality he was reiterating the same simplistic messages delivered earlier to the downwind folks. The bomb testing in Nevada, he wrote, was being monitored by highly trained teams of scientists and physicians who had concluded that the health impacts of fallout from weapons testing were negligible. And to quiet the fears of scientists that radiation was contaminating the nation's milk, he affirmed that "The highest measured radiation exposure to the thyroid of human beings has been far below that needed to produce any detectable effects." Dunning, in keeping with the AEC's cover-up strategy, dealt with his subject without making any mention of cancer risks or of the long latency periods that would elapse before cancers manifested themselves.

The distortions and misrepresentations of this period fostered a bias at the AEC that made covering up unwanted evidence a way of life, and led the agency into a mode of operation that stifled internal debates about medical risks or better safety programs. This mind-set also made it impossible for the bomb testers to contemplate evacuating communities in the path of hazardous clouds, or to consider instructing the downwinders about practical steps they could take to minimize the impacts of radiation on their health and on the lives of their children.

The term "Big Lie" was coined in this century to describe a tissue of lies that are, by design and by constant and shameless repetition, transformed into a paramount "truth" that governs the thoughts and actions of an organization, a government, or a public. After the Upshot-Knothole tests, the AEC became the promoter—and the prisoner—of a Big Lie when a party line was established that the Nevada fallout was too meager to cause harm.

Big Lies exert a tyrannical influence over individuals and entities that embrace them, and the AEC soon geared itself to the dictates of the fallout "truths" it had peddled to the American people. This was easy to accomplish. Secrecy gave the AEC control over the facts it fed to the public, and its security system guaranteed that all employees would conform to whatever policy was promulgated. Thus, the test site operators' proclamation, "There is no evidence that radiation released by bomb testing has harmed anyone," became a catch phrase and a marching order for all employees of the Atomic Energy Commission.

This formulation of the Big Lie was a masterstroke for the AEC. It put the bomb testers on the offensive, and it shifted the burden of proof to ill-informed civilians who, AEC spokesmen could argue, knew little about radiation realities. The no-evidence formula also set the stage for a medical tragedy in Utah and Nevada, for it committed the AEC to a corollary policy of *not* searching for evidence that would undermine its thesis. That approach provided a shield for the AEC, but by foreclosing the kind of study-the-people medical research Shields Warren had advocated, it doomed the downwinders to become unwitting participants in a medical experiment in which their government would suppress data that revealed that their health and their very lives were being sacrificed on the altar of national security.

This bad-neighbor policy set the stage for the calamity that engulfed the lives of the downwinders. AEC radiologists were cognizant of the leukemia epidemic that had appeared among survivors of the atomic bombs five years after Hiroshima, and had the rigorous medical monitoring urged by Shields Warren been adopted, after a comparable interval of time they would have been watching for the possible appearance of excessive leukemia deaths among children living in the path of the fallout. But the Big Lie had not only ruled out such monitoring, it outfitted the AEC's radiologists with blinders that put the unfolding tragedy in the downwind zone beyond their range of vision.

Had radiologists in the Division of Biology and Medicine been allowed to request that state and local health officials notify them of new cases of leukemia in the counties nearest the test site, telltale evidence would have accumulated by the end of 1956 that the AEC's rad-safe planners had made mortal miscalculations. This ominous news would have appeared in the form of a clump of death certificates of children who had succumbed to this disease. The clue that would have linked those deaths to fallout was the fact that the time interval between the Nevada tests and the onset of the leukemias corresponded to the normal latency period for this disease.

However, as is so often the case with a Big Lie, those who were both the first persuaded and the most persuaded were the perpetrators themselves. Thus the AEC experts' self-imposed blinders prevented them from observing that the leukemia victims represented a revealing cross-section of the children living in the downwind zone. The victims' ages ran a gamut from three to fifteen, and the towns where their families lived suggested that all sectors of this zone were being impacted by fallout. Six-year-old Martin Bardoli, for example, lived on a Nevada ranch near Twin Springs, seventy miles north of the test site. Arlene Hafen, fifteen when her life was cut short, was a resident of St. George. Daryl Fox, stricken at age three, lived at Springdale, at the gateway to Zion National Park. Parowan, eighty miles north of St. George, was the home of nine-year-old Lucille Jones. And Van Mackelprang, dead at age five, lived 200 miles due east of the test site in Fredonia, Arizona.

This was only the beginning of a trail of tears for the downwind communities. In a five-year span between 1956 and 1961, fourteen children aged fifteen or under were victims of this dread disease. (Leukemia had a mortal impact in that era—every child afflicted died.) By immobilizing its experts and prohibiting research that would have produced discordant data, the see-no-evil discipline of the AEC's Big Lie produced an ironic, macabre outcome for atomic science and for modern medicine: the agency that carried the banner of a new age of science arbitrarily decided to restrict vital inquiries by its scientists; and, with the lives of innocent bystanders at stake, it adopted a "seek not, and ye shall not find" ukase that contradicted a cardinal premise of all scientific research.

The AEC adopted these policies to prevent the gathering of facts that would have undermined its credibility. This expedient, of course, mocked the scientific method by embracing the motto "My mind is made up, don't confuse me with facts," and thus sustained the charade that bomb testing was safe. As events unfolded, the atomic establishment was to pay a high price for this deceptive maneuver, but in the short run it extended the life-span of the Big Lie until 1979, when members of Congress secured the declassification of secret files that revealed the stratagems the AEC had used to conceal the truth from the American people.

POSTSCRIPT

Subsequent to Harold Knapp's abortive effort during the Kennedy years to lift the veil on what he called the AEC's "monstrous miscalculations" about the health effects of bomb testing in Nevada, there were only two instances prior to 1979 when there was a chance the Big Lie might be exposed. The first occurred in the 1960s when Utah medical officers sounded an alarm, and U.S. Public Health doctors were sent to several southern Utah communities to study the region's leukemia clusters and incidences of thyroid disease. When the publication of their findings threatened to arouse a medical furor, the ever-vigilant Gordon Dunning was called on to stem the crisis. After warning his superiors that publication of the PHS studies would "open a Pandora's box," Dunning raised so many questions about "flaws" in the techniques used by the researchers that timorous officials in the surgeon general's office shelved the reports and withheld them from the press.

The second, more serious, crisis originated within the AEC's family circle in 1969, when John Gofman, a distinguished physician who was in charge of radiation safety programs at the Livermore bomb factory, completed a pioneering study that demonstrated that the AEC's widely publicized "safe" doses of low-level radiation were, in truth, unsafe and were causing thousands of excess cancers. When AEC officials tried to intimidate him and suppress the results of his research, Gofman resisted and subsequently resigned in order to appeal his case to the public and to his peers in the American medical community.

John Gofman's study was not intended as a frontal attack on bomb testing: he had always believed the United States needed a nuclear arsenal—and besides, all Nevada tests had been conducted underground since President Kennedy signed the Limited Test Ban Treaty with the Soviet Union in 1963. What alarmed his superiors was his sweeping conclusion that the AEC had grossly underestimated the health hazards associated with all prior releases of radiation. His research generated evidence, for example, that the AEC had erred in assuming that there was a radiation exposure threshold, and that low-level doses of fallout could not cause cancers. Gofman and his colleague Arthur Tamplin also assembled evidence that radiation released into the environment could trigger so many forms of cancer that the risk of "excess deaths" was over ten times worse than the official estimates of the AEC's experts. Those findings sent tremors through the corridors of the AEC and informed its leaders that Gofman and Tamplin were challenging the core concepts of the Big Lie.

Yet Dr. Gofman had a constructive goal when he unveiled his conclusions. With nuclear power and other peaceful uses of nuclear energy in mind, he reasoned that it would be wise for the AEC to move forthwith to tighten its safety standards in order to minimize the doses of radiation that would be inflicted on atomic workers and the general public. Like Harold Knapp, John Gofman hewed to a conviction that the AEC should, in the spirit of good science, follow the facts wherever they led. He used these words to explain to a friend the creed that guided his medical research: "There is a cardinal and fundamental principle that nothing is accomplished by deviating one iota from the truth about the radiation effects and the doses."

Had they been open-minded, the leaders of the AEC would have responded to Dr. Gofman's challenge by revising their safety standards and safety programs. His work gave them an opportunity to announce that new knowledge of radiation risks had altered their outlook and that they intended to take prompt action to tighten all safety standards and safety practices. The other alternative was to hunker down, denigrate the work of Gofman and Tamplin, and use the AEC's prestige to reaffirm the "official truths" about radiation safety which they had espoused for two decades. With no apparent pause to evaluate these choices, they took the latter road.

The history of Big Lies tells us why these eminent scientists (Dr. Seaborg, then chairman of the AEC, was a Nobel laureate) and leaders of the atomic establishment elected to harass Gofman rather than consider altering its safety policies. Once a Big Lie gains sway over a nation or an organization, it strangles creative dissent and suggestions to alter important policies. Documents that trace the actions and reactions of top AEC officials indicate, for example, that they believed their credibility would be destroyed if they conceded that their statements about radiation safety were based on misjudgments. Dr. Charles Dunham of DBM expressed this unreasoning fear during the Knapp controversy when he told his associates, "If this is published, it will make us look like liars."

John Gofman's no-threshold findings evoked the same fear-ridden response, a reaction that caused the U.S. nuclear establishment to discard an opportunity to refurbish its image and renew its commitment to the spirit of science. Several years would elapse before independent radiologists confirmed Dr. Gofman's findings, but he and Arthur Tamplin provoked a national debate that put the AEC on the defensive and lent support to congressional criticisms that led to the dismantling of the agency in 1974.

As a result of smoke blown over this episode by AEC officials, the bomb testers' Big Lie emerged largely unscathed from the Gofman imbroglio. Commissioner James Ramey called Gofman and Tamplin "opera stars," and ridiculed their conclusions as a "hogwash syndrome." DBM's chief, Dr. John R. Totter, opined that his erstwhile colleague was "off on a wild tangent"; and a Dr. Sagan (not the famed astronomer) was whisked onto the "Today" show to make a resounding reaffirmation that "scientists were universally agreed that the levels to which the American public was exposed from fallout had been harmless."

Two changes in federal policies had to occur before John Gofman could be vindicated. The first came about when independent radiologists with no ties to the AEC were put in charge of determining the nation's radiation protection policies. The second flowed from congressional demands that vital documents in the archives of that agency be declassified.

In the summer of 1978, when Tucson attorney Dale Haralson and I began an investigation of the effects of fallout on downwind civilians, a spokesman for the Nevada test site greeted us with the same response that had been delivered in broken-record cadence to inquiring citizens, attorneys, and journalists for a quarter of a century: "There is no evidence that anyone has been harmed by fallout." The manager of the test site, General Mahlon Gates, chimed in later with the bland assertion, "I'd like to see statistics on how many people radiation has saved. . . . I don't think it has killed anyone."

However, we soon obtained startling new statistical data that encouraged us to persist. The source of this information was a University of Utah researcher, Dr. Joseph L. Lyon. Lyon, a cautious, Harvard-trained epidemiologist, who was the keeper of the Utah Cancer Registry, conducted a study of childhood leukemia deaths in southern Utah following the AEC's atmospheric tests in the 1950s. Using death certificate data, Dr. Lyon made the first nongovernmental analysis of the incidence of cancer in the affected areas. His clear-cut findings, later published in the prestigious *New England Journal of Medicine,* indicated that leukemia deaths among children were two and one-half times as great as the normal national death rate for this form of cancer.

In February 1979, Dr. Lyon's findings created a national sensation, which was magnified six weeks later when the near-meltdown of the Three Mile Island nuclear power plant in Pennsylvania unmasked the falsity of the atomic establishment's claims that nuclear power plants were "clean" and "safe." These shocks combined to produce the first relentless congressional investigation of radiation safety issues, which had been shielded from public scrutiny for two decades by the Big Lie and by the suave assurances of atomic scientists who had promoted nuclear-generated electricity and touted the supersafe technologies they had developed to "handle" radiation accidents.

These investigations marked the first time since World War II that Congress secured a wholesale declassification of documents relating to secrets long hidden from the press and the American people. As congressional aides prowled at will through once-sacrosanct archives of the AEC, documents they copied provided a road map into the minds of those who guided the bomb-testing program. Now open to scrutiny were the minutes of the Atomic Energy Commission's meetings, memos composed by those who managed the bomb tests, and documents that illuminated the outlook of those who executed the test site's safety programs.

Other than gritty details in the Dunning documents, among the thousands of pieces of paper released from the AEC's archives, the most revealing were those which disclosed what the leaders at the top thought and did. The prince of these leaders—the executive who served as Bradbury's top operations officer and presided over the creation of the Big Lie—was Dr. Alvin Graves. One Los Alamos associate who adjudged that Graves was a "third-rate scientist," described him as a "hard-driving, no-nonsense, militaristic type who never doubted the correctness of his decisions."

As a young physicist, Graves had won his atomic spurs as a member of the "fire brigade" that stood poised under the stadium at Stagg Field in Chicago to douse Enrico Fermi's famous chain reaction with cadmium if it ran wild. Graves was also a bit player the night of the Trinity test, when he was stationed in Carizozo, New Mexico, with vague orders to evacuate the citizens of that cow town if their community was showered with heavy fallout when the first atomic bomb was exploded on July 16, 1945.

Al Graves was chosen by Norris Bradbury to be the director of the dirtiest, most dangerous tests in the 1950s, and his bloodless experiences in the 1940s conditioned him to believe that radiation fears were exaggerated. This belief became a dogma when, in a Los Alamos laboratory in May 1946, Louis Slotin made a fatal mistake while attempting to position two halves of a beryllium sphere so close together that the encased plutonium was converted into a "critical state." The 1,000 rads of radiation Slotin's body absorbed killed him, and Graves, standing at Slotin's elbow, received a calculated dose of about 166 rads. However, he recovered after enduring three weeks of radiation sickness and resumed a normal life at the laboratory. The lesson Al Graves apparently derived from this experience was that non-lethal doses of radiation would not inflict permanent harm on human beings. A Los Alamos colleague who heard him express his opinions about radiation risks after the furor over fallout began in the mid-fifties, states that "Graves felt that strong men could overcome all but the most catastrophic exposures to radiation" and seemed to regard worries about harm from fallout as fears concocted in "the minds of weak malingerers."

It is clear that as the director of the Nevada tests, Alvin Graves was guided by a reckless, hairy-chested approach toward radiation safety. His convictions were set forth in a report he wrote in 1954 for colleagues who were reviewing the safety criteria that had supposedly governed testing during the three previous years. Al Graves was a blunt man who always stated his convictions uninhibitedly, and the words he penned in secret amounted to a confession that he had deliberately failed to follow safety guides he was responsible for enforcing at the Nevada test site:

Regarding the Upshot-Knothole tests, he not only conceded that "inhabitants of [nearby] communities were subject to exposures beyond the limit of 3.9r per quarter," but he stated foursquare that "numerous exposures of individuals beyond the limit have occurred in most operations";

Writing about his duties as test manager, he observed, "One must conclude that between the 'safe' laboratory standard of 3.9r/quarter and the 'militarily significant' dose of 50r there is a wide region in which one must operate if test operations are to be conducted";

After complaining that the safety criteria he had to function under were "meaningless," he crisply noted that it would be more honest to simply tell the public, "If one does not expose individuals beyond 3.9r/quarter you probably will not hurt them to any appreciable extent ... [and] if you expose individuals beyond 50r in a single dose you may make some individuals sick and reduce their efficiency for a few weeks or months."

As an expression of his belief that the 3.9-rad standard was absurd,

Graves enthusiastically endorsed a pending proposal that the bomb testers assuage the public's worries by making direct comparisons between fallout exposures and everyday industrial accidents. Under this plan, exposures of over 15 rads would be "reported as accidents" while lower exposures "would not be so reported." To Al Graves, such a commonsense change would both simplify the test director's decision making and "be extremely useful for public relations." His rad-safe people, he reasoned, "would have a guide which could interpret in terms of common experience" if they could explain to soldiers and civilians that a 15-rad exposure was "roughly equivalent to a case requiring a visit to a first aid station as, for example, a piece of carborundum in the eye or a cut finger."

And in the process of arguing that the AEC's safety program lacked balance, Graves complained that "whereas we let it be known that we avoid doses larger than 3 or 4r, we do not emphasize sufficiently that there is no evidence that doses as high as 20r have any demonstrable effect and no evidence that even larger doses have bad effects."

Alvin Graves saw himself as a general in charge of a military operation, and the disregard he exhibited for the safety standards he was supposed to enforce shaped the outlook of his organization. His view that low-level doses of radiation were harmless ignored the opinions of the AEC's medical experts, but no one had the temerity to challenge the reckless safety policies of a leader who "knew from personal experience" that the effect of a jolt of 100-plus rads of radiation would only disable a person for a couple of weeks.

Many of the lapses that unnecessarily imperiled the lives of the downwinders can be traced to Graves's cavalier attitude toward low doses of radiation: for example, the test organization's failure to evacuate the residents of threatened small towns; the order given to the rad-safe monitors stationed in downwind communities never to use the word "hot" to describe fallout; and the absence of any plan to warn citizens to remain indoors during the passage of dangerous clouds can be attributed to this pattern of thinking.

During the 1950s, Dr. Graves was the most effective spokesman for the AEC's there-is-no-danger gospel, and he redoubled his personal public relations efforts during the dirtiest tests. After the Upshot-Knothole fiasco, for example, he delivered a widely publicized address to the Utah legislature, met with 300 opinion leaders in

Salt Lake City, and gave speeches to physicians and University of Utah faculty members in which he outlined his cut-finger philosophy about radiation safety. Graves also appeared in Salt Lake City as the government's star witness at the first radiation lawsuit of the atomic age, where he persuaded a federal judge that fallout could not have killed the Utah sheep.

The militaristic mind-set that shaped Alvin Graves's outlook explains why he felt justified in taking chances with the lives of the downwind civilians—and why he made no distinction between the civilians and the soldiers who were ordered to take part in maneuvers in the environs of ground zero. This outlook also throws light on Graves's failure to mention the cancer risks associated with fallout—a strange omission which hovers over the cover-ups that mark this dark chapter of the atomic age. None of the declassified documents tell us why Alvin Graves flouted the opinions of the AEC's radiologists and ignored their insights into radiation health risks. Nor do they inform us whether Graves consulted radiological experts before concluding that a 15-rad exposure was the equivalent of a cut finger, or that the 3.9-rad/quarter safety standard was a meaningless sham.

By contrast, minutes of official meetings of the Atomic Energy Commission reveal that some commissioners entertained nagging doubts about the wisdom and the efficacy of the safety program they had approved for the NTS. In the winter of 1955, Senator Clinton P. Anderson of New Mexico, the new chairman of the normally acquiescent Joint Congressional Committee on Atomic Energy, traveled to Nevada to witness nuclear detonations. Los Alamos scientists were his constituents, and Anderson had never questioned their assurances that fallout posed no dangers to civilians. During a delay that lasted for several days, the senator began asking probing questions and was startled when a meteorologist told him that the probability of finding weather conditions that would meet all safety criteria was "about one day in twenty-five." This aroused Anderson's concerns about civilian safety, and on returning to Washington, he wrote a letter to AEC chairman Lewis Strauss requesting that the AEC evaluate the suitability of the NTS—under existing safety criteria—"for anything other than the test of very small yield devices."

Anderson's letter was a bombshell. It provoked personal outbursts which, like a flash of night lightning, revealed an organization locked into continental bomb testing it no longer believed in—and torn by doubts about a radiation safety program it had touted for a half-decade as risk-free. The AEC's role in fostering the illusions and deceptions that produced the Big Lie are revealed by these excerpts from the colloquy provoked by Senator Anderson's letter in late March 1955:

> Commissioner Willard Libby (physicist, Nobel laureate): I am pretty disturbed by this. I noted, Lewis, that you had cooled off about the Nevada site.

> Chairman Strauss (who possessed extra authority as President Eisenhower's science advisor): I had been cool long before. My coolness started in the spring of 1953, but I have never discussed this with Anderson. This is spontaneous.

> Commissioner Libby: I think this will set the weapons program back a lot to go to the Pacific.

> Chairman Strauss: I have gone along with the majority of the Commission that this is the thing to do.

> Commissioner Thomas Murray: You would not consider pulling back anything in the present series of tests?

> Chairman Strauss: If I were asked whether the two large shots should be made, and it were left to my sole decision, I would say load them on a ship and go out to Eniwetok and put them on a raft and set them off.

> Commissioner Murray: How long do you think that would take?

> Chairman Strauss: It could take you 60 or 90 days—and it may take you 60 or 90 days before you can get them off at this rate.

> Chairman Strauss: There is a Nevada legislator who has introduced a bill in the Nevada legislature . . . asking us to move out of the state. Both of the Las Vegas papers, which seldom agree on anything, published editorials agreeing that this was nonsense, that we brought a lot of prosperity to the state. This was a fine thing for national defense, and they rather laughed this fellow out of court.

> Commissioner Libby: That is a sensible view. People have to learn to live with the facts of life, and part of the facts of life are fallout.

Chairman Strauss: It is certainly all right, they say, if you don't live next door to it.

Mr. Nichols (general manager of the AEC): Or live under it.

Commissioner Murray: We must not let anything interfere with this series of tests—nothing.

Commissioner Libby: I think we ought to talk about this. I don't want radioactivity falling on people's necks, but it is an awfully serious thing.

Chairman Strauss: Another thing about it is that since the fallout patterns have been established pretty well . . . there are just about two optimum areas . . . the best route [was] north. Ten degrees east of that they get into more settled areas. There is another apparently optimum direction almost due south.

Mr. Nichols: Isn't it east?

Chairman Strauss: No. East they go over Pioche and over St. George, which they apparently always plaster.

Mr. Nichols: I thought it was just south of those two places.

Chairman Strauss: South of these two places is a very narrow corridor where if the wind shifts ten degrees in either direction then they are in trouble again. Of course, they really never paid much attention to that before.

Chairman Strauss: Al [Graves] and Herb York and Ken [Nichols] were talking, no decision made, about conducting future tests of anything except little ones in the Pacific. It is so easy to do things out there because you can do them one a day practically.

Chairman Strauss: I have always been frightened that something would happen which would set us back with the public for a long period of time.

Commissioner Murray: I am interested in the public all right, but . . . this Pacific idea you can talk all you want, Lewis, put them on a ship and get them out in 30 or 60 days, it will not be done.

Chairman Strauss: Fly them out.

As a footnote to the history of U.S. bomb testing, this colloquy is doubly fascinating. It provides action snapshots of three prominent leaders of the atomic age; and it is a sampler of the logic, rationalizations, and evasions that they and other "statesmen" used to justify decisions they made in the name of national security. The exchanges between the commissioners reveal how Dr. Libby, an eminent physicist, could refuse to pause and ponder safer alternatives and vote, with no apparent moral qualms, to imperil the lives and health of innocent civilians. (Two years later, Libby articulated the reasoning that guided his thought, when he told a congressional committee that a "very small" risk that a few hundred downwinders might be killed was worth taking when compared with "the risk of annihilation" by the Soviet Union.)

The commissioners' conversation also demonstrates how self-important cold warriors, operating in an environment of absolute secrecy, could become so obsessed by the race for marginal improvements in nuclear weapons that they readily ignored safety imperatives they were, by law, bound to uphold. And they inform us that Strauss, the leader of this enterprise, knew that excessive risks were being imposed on the downwinders—and sensed that the bomb-testing program he had inherited was acquiring the trappings of a Big Lie.

The circumstance that their operations were above the law—and that all of their deliberations were protected by a cloak of secrecy—not only insulated the bomb testers from the public and its prickly moral concerns, but also turned their decision making into an impersonal exercise. The framework of illusions they had created made it easy and convenient for them to conclude that no one had been harmed by fallout.

"The facts of life" concerning fallout presented one AEC official with an excruciating dilemma that forced him to analyze Nevada fallout with unflinching honesty and to decide whether his agency's no-danger dogma was an expression of a medical truth or a mask created to mislead the downwinders. In 1962, members of Norris Bradbury's family were "living under" fallout in a dangerous corridor of the downwind zone at Zion National Park, due east of St. George. His son, a park ranger, his pregnant daughter-in-law, and his first grandson, age two, resided in a canyon near the park.

Bradbury surely knew that small children—and especially embryonic children in utero—were exceptionally vulnerable to the impacts of low-level radiation. As a result, he made a special trip to Zion and took action to protect his grandchildren. He showered the parents with safety tips ("Keep them indoors on windy days . . . don't let them eat snow," etc.) and provided airline tickets to his daughter-in-law so she and her son could visit relatives during the month-long 1962 tests. Norris Bradbury behaved as a concerned grandparent should have—but the acts he performed in secret to protect his family attest that the bomb testers knew the downwinders faced dangers and thus knew that they were actors in a tragedy whose script was being dictated by a Big Lie.

12

The Strange Ride
of the Peaceful Atom

Where science fiction goes, can the atom be far behind? My
only fear is that I may be underestimating the possibilities.
—GLENN T. SEABORG
AEC Chairman (1971)

Launched by President Truman's proclamation that scientists had
"harnessed the basic power of the universe," and lofted into a stratosphere of wonderment by W. L. Laurence's awed description of the
"cosmic" powers acquired by his Mesa Men, an article of faith of the
nuclear age developed that life on earth would be transformed by
atomic science. In the decade after Hiroshima, three hypotheses were
advanced by the atomic scientists to describe the changes that would
supposedly occur as the benefits of the "peaceful atom" were bestowed upon the human race.

The first of these themes rested on the assumption that the
atomic scientists would soon remove the constraints of ignorance that
had hampered human activity since the dawn of scientific thought. A
related hypothesis held that the splitting of the atom would generate
a global superabundance of cheap and inexhaustible supplies of energy. And a third premise that flowed from these presumptions was

that free energy would liberate human beings from their dependence on the earth's resources by making it feasible to synthesize whatever food, minerals, or new fuels any society might need.

My generation eagerly accepted these assurances. There were no debates or serious discussions because we did not know enough to question their validity. Indeed, events had conditioned us to regard the scientists who built the bombs as supermen whose gaze reached beyond our limited horizons.

A nonscientist who initially helped kindle optimism about the potential of the friendly atom was David Lilienthal, the first chairman of the Atomic Energy Commission. Lilienthal was vague about specifics, but his predictions about the "incredible possibilities of atomic science" had portentous overtones. In a *Collier's* magazine article in 1949, he noted that it was a "great privilege to be alive . . . when a discovery akin to finding fire or electricity" came along; and in an interview with another magazine the same year, he envisioned that in the next decade atomic advances would prolong human life and produce more food for the world.

David Lilienthal subsequently had grave misgivings about the promises he made to the American people, but when word filtered down in the early 1950s that atomic scientists had perfected techniques to miniaturize nuclear "packages" to produce the atomic bazookas and artillery shells ordered by the Pentagon, forecasts of atom-powered automobiles, washing machines, and wristwatches seemed to be substantiated. Expectations were heightened further by stories that our nuclear engineers were involved in crash programs to develop atomic airplanes and submarines.

The year 1955 was my freshman year as a member of Congress, and I remember it as a red-letter time for the friendly atom. At the global level, it saw the convening of an international Atoms for Peace Conference in Geneva, at which, for the first time, scientists from the United States and the Soviet Union outlined competing plans to harness nuclear energy for peaceful purposes. And in the United States, 1955 saw the unveiling of plans and forecasts that gave nuclear projects the highest priority on our nation's agenda.

The hold of the peaceful atom on American thought was enlarged by the publication in 1955 of a book, *The Fabulous Future.* Assembled by the editors of *Fortune* magazine, it featured forecasts by eleven U.S. leaders of the changes in American life they anticipated in the next twenty-five years. Dr. John von Neumann set the framework for this symposium with a prediction that by 1980 all energy would be virtually without cost ". . . free like the unmetered air." A superstar mathematician, a veteran of the Manhattan Project, and at the time an AEC commissioner, von Neuman foresaw that the "main trend" of atomic research lay in the direction of the "transmutation of elements, or alchemy not chemistry." He also envisioned the "control" of the climates of specific regions, concluding his essay with this paean to the promise of atomic science: "What power over our environment, over all nature, is implied!"

Another exuberant *Fortune* forecaster was David Sarnoff, the influential chief executive of the Radio Corporation of America. Esteemed for his vision and pioneering work in electronics, Sarnoff prophesied that the world was "merely on the threshold of the technological age." Bullish about an atomic battery his company was developing, he asserted, "It can be taken for granted that before 1980 ships, aircraft, locomotives and even automobiles will be atomically fueled." Sarnoff also envisioned in the same time span a cure for cancer, and predicted that "small atomic generators, installed in homes and industrial plants, will provide power for years and ultimately for a lifetime without recharging."

Amid such waves of optimism, it was not surprising that the first road map for the approaching age of supertechnology was written by scientists in collaboration with business executives. *The Next Hundred Years*, prepared in 1957 by Harrison Brown (another alumnus of the Manhattan Project) and some of his colleagues at Caltech, evolved out of seminars with executives of thirty of the nation's largest corporations. These authors envisaged the emergence of a "technical-industrial civilization" anchored by "vast, integrated multipurpose chemical plants supplied by rock, air, and seawater, from which would flow a multiplicity of products ranging from fresh water to electric power, liquid fuels and metals." According to these savants, the main obstacle to the attainment of this resource utopia was a probable shortage of sufficient engineers to build and maintain the wonderworks needed by the world's poor nations.

A similar euphoria also permeated the Rockefeller Panel reports published in 1958–59. Prepared under the guidance of leaders such as Dean Rusk, Henry Kissinger, and Arthur Burns, those studies were treated by the press as unofficial white papers about the American future. In the process of endorsing the supertechnology hypothesis, the Rockefeller luminaries pronounced that, "Already the proven resources of uranium and thorium, in terms of energy equivalent, are at least 1,000 times the world's resources of coal, gas, and oil," and they added a prophecy that the world was "on the verge of a major revolution in available energy."

A dramatic announcement that a nuclear submarine had been developed and tested was the first technical achievement that seemed to validate these forecasts. The shakedown cruises of the USS *Nautilus* and its 1958 Jules Verne voyage under the North Pole provided a showpiece that seemed to demonstrate the feasibility of the Atomic Energy Commission's plans for a nuclear utopia.

But the *Nautilus* was not a harbinger of atom-powered airplanes or home reactors. Rather the naval reactor was a one-shot masterpiece produced for use in a radiation-forgiving environment by a gifted naval engineer, Captain Hyman G. Rickover. The *Nautilus* was a triumph of industrial engineers, not of nuclear scientists. It worked because Rickover was a ruthless perfectionist who overcame obstacles by demanding exquisite technical results from the engineers he hired, trained, and, not infrequently, fired.

However, those who assumed that Rickover's invention was a forerunner of other atomic machines ignored the fact that all naval activities are conducted in the one earthly environment that can accommodate huge, gross releases of radiation. The *Nautilus* and its sister ship, the *Triton* (which encircled the globe in 1960 without completely surfacing), were a success because these submarines had a size and configuration that enabled technicians to design small reactors that could operate within their hulls. In addition, the envelope of water in which these ships functioned resolved the radiation shielding and safety problems that would confound the efforts of land-oriented nuclear engineers to develop workable reactors for other purposes.

But in the 1950s these distinctions were overlooked by the zealous promoters of the "marvels" of the new age. Rickover's submarines, and the small nuclear generating station his engineers erected on the Ohio River for the AEC at Shippingport, Pennsylvania, thus became symbols of the atomic tomorrow. His boats were held up as evidence that engineering advances would soon transform industrial societies, and his accomplishments offered assurances that nuclear engineers would soon devise technical solutions to any problems that might impede the advance of the peaceful atom.

More than any other development in the 1950s, the myths whipped up by Rickover's successes created a bandwagon mentality for the atom and fostered a surge of optimism about our technological prowess that permeated American thought from the 1950s until the mishap at Three Mile Island in 1979. (With their characteristic facility for euphemism, the atomic establishment referred to this near-catastrophe as an "excursion" and an "event.") The odyssey of the *Nautilus* opened the doors of the U.S. Treasury to all kinds of ill-considered schemes. It galvanized the AEC's expensive effort to develop an atomic-powered airplane and nuclear rockets, and it pumped money into a project to design a starship for interplanetary travel propelled by tiny atomic bombs.

This optimism made 1957 a watershed year for the atomic establishment and for what might, with hindsight, be called "science by cesarean section." With the intention of bringing the atomic revolution to birth on a fast schedule, the Atomic Energy Commission took action on several fronts. It pushed a plan through Congress for enormous subsidies to induce electric power companies to build nuclear generating stations. It adopted Edward Teller's "Plowshare Project" to use bombs as nuclear dynamite to accomplish "geographical engineering." And it accelerated developmental research on its two "ultimate" sources of energy for the planet: the breeder reactor and fusion power.

SCIENCE BY CESAREAN SECTION

One of the AEC's most wasteful programs was a crash effort to build a nuclear airplane. This project excited the imaginations of congressmen on the Joint Committee on Atomic Energy (JCAE) and was nurtured for a decade by scare stories, invented by the Pentagon and the aerospace industry, that Soviet engineers had stolen a march and were leading a "race" to bring this technology to fruition. A triumph of atomic optimism over common sense, several of the influences that produced the strange ride of the peaceful atom converged in this bizarre undertaking.

From the very beginning aeronautical engineers identified insurmountable obstacles: the reactors were projected to weigh over 250 tons; there were no materials available that would stand up to high-intensity radiation in the interior of the reactor; and the added weight of shielding adequate to protect the crew and passengers from radiation made flight infeasible. But it was customary to brush aside such negative findings during the first phase of the atomic age. In those days, if atomic scientists said something was theoretically achievable, the public assumed that sooner or later engineers would overcome any technical obstacles.

In a latter day, when the promises of public officials are subjected to intense scrutiny, it is difficult to imagine the deference accorded to the seers of the atomic establishment when they outlined plans for atomic airplanes and helicopters and nuclear rockets. The nuclear aircraft project survived for a decade because it provided employment for hundreds of engineers and 14,000 people in seven states, but also because the premises of its promoters were never challenged. No critics spoke up, for example, when Dr. Seaborg touted the AEC's nuclear rocket program by declaring: "What we are attempting to make is a flyable compact reactor, not much bigger than my office desk, that will produce the power of Hoover Dam, from a cold start, in a matter of minutes."

It was a time of profligate faith in the captains of the atomic age. By the time President Kennedy cancelled the atomic aircraft project in 1961, it had squandered the energies of some of the nation's best engineers and had cost U.S. taxpayers the 1991 equivalent of $5 billion.

PLOWSHARE

Edward Teller's pet program, the Plowshare Project, was a seventeen-year research effort that provides additional insights into the Godlike power exercised by the high priests of the atomic establishment. The euphoria that surrounded Plowshare listed the benefits that would accrue to the human race as nuclear scientists widened their conquest of the natural world. Among the blessings of the peaceful explosions Teller envisioned were earthmoving on a planetary scale, the construction of harbors, canals, and highways, the geologic stimulation of the extraction of oil and natural gas, the creation of subterranean cavities, and the facilitation of steam-power generation. The objectives of weather and earthquake control were later added to this list by Dr. Seaborg, the program's stepfather. Teller subsequently assured members of Congress that the colonization of the moon would be facilitated by applying technologies developed by Plowshare.

Plowshare must surely rank as the preeminent "black hole" research project conducted by the Atomic Energy Commission. Cavities and craters strewn across the American landscape are monuments to the "planetary" ambitions and fantasies of its promoters. This grandiose scheme achieved none of its goals. Every Plowshare project was a failure; and every hole it dug in the earth led, with undiminished dedication, only to plans for the next excavation. Trevor Findlay, the author of a definitive 1990 book, *Nuclear Dynamite*, has summarized the outcome with his assessment that peaceful nuclear explosives "proved to be uneconomic, environmentally hazardous, [and] an impediment to disarmament and arms control efforts."

From the outset, the judgment of Teller, Seaborg, and their associates was blurred by their failure to acknowledge that the radiation released by their experiments would imperil human health. These leaders learned nothing from the outcry aroused by their first planetary engineering project, a scheme to excavate a harbor near one of the most fragile environments in the United States: the Eskimo village of Point Hope, Alaska. In 1961 they seemed equally oblivious to public concerns about radiation dangers when they conducted their first actual field test, a 5-kiloton explosion in a desert near Carlsbad, New Mexico, designed to produce steam to power electric generators. This misfire released radioactivity at the shaft which measured an astronomical 10,000 roentgens per hour.

Teller, who enjoyed provoking public disputes, was convinced his bombs were destined to alter the earth in beneficent ways. In 1958, for example, he proposed that the Strait of Gibraltar be closed with a nuclear detonation to convert the Mediterranean Sea into a lake so the Sahara could become an irrigated oasis. However, the megaproject at the top of his Plowshare wish list was the excavation of a sea-level waterway to replace the Panama Canal.

Edward Teller was alarmed on two counts when President Kennedy and Chairman Khrushchev approved their history-making Limited Test Ban Treaty (LTBT) in 1963, prohibiting bomb tests that emitted radiation into the atmosphere. He was apprehensive that any limit on bomb testing would endanger our national security, and he also sensed that such a curb might impede his plan for a new Panama Canal. Those concerns emboldened Teller to lead an unsuccessful fight to persuade the Senate not to ratify the LTBT.

Teller's fear that this ban would prohibit "planetary" engineering in both the United States and the USSR proved to be well founded. There was no way to carry out large-scale cratering without contaminating the atmosphere and showering surrounding areas with irradiated debris. But the final nail in the Panama Canal coffin was driven by scientists who studied the environmental side effects of Teller's plan. Their ecological findings infuriated Teller and his allies, when the viability of their plan was undermined by estimates that from 100 to 400 bombs would have to be detonated (in a tropical setting where over 25,000 people lived) to accomplish the necessary excavations. A Cornell University ecologist, Lamont Cole, provided this epitaph for Teller's scheme: "[It is] the most irresponsible suggestion I can remember since Admiral Byrd's senile proposal to blow the ice caps off Antarctica."

Undaunted by his unbroken string of dry holes, and openly contemptuous of the environmentalists and politicians who had begun raising questions about his plans, Edward Teller wound up the Plowshare caper of his Livermore laboratory with two inherently absurd experiments. In 1971, seemingly oblivious to the engineering realities, he revived the Carlsbad idea of using big bombs in deep cavities (later called a "pacer technology") to create high-pressure steam to generate electricity. This idea was smothered in its cradle when analysts at the Los Alamos laboratory pointed out that it would require at least two 50-kiloton nuclear explosions per day to maintain the pressures needed to make such a scheme work.

This rejection meant that Teller's last attempt to change the world with peaceful explosions revolved around a plan to "stimulate" natural gas production in New Mexico and Colorado by creating caverns in the petroleum provinces of those states. As the 1970s began, these zany field tests produced a national debate that, for the first time, put the economics, and the environmental side effects, of a Plowshare project into a down-to-earth focus where ordinary citizens could ask penetrating questions about the assumptions of the atomic scientists.

Although, in true cheerleader fashion, Chairman Seaborg pronounced the first two tests "highly successful," the public was not fooled, and he and Teller, shorn of their Olympian robes, were plunged into ground-level arguments with ordinary folks who felt that the economics of gas stimulation was a joke and who sensed that their environmental concerns were justified. And while some presidents and public men had always treated him with a reverence akin to awe, now Edward Teller found himself embattled by ranchers and conservative Western politicians who were asking pointed questions about the contamination of their air, their rivers, and their underground aquifers.

Always feisty, and always loath to admit he might have erred, Teller responded by describing Wyoming's Senator Gale McGee as feeble-minded and a "nincompoop." The leaders of the Western states, who were to be the recipients of Teller's dubious gifts, might well have suggested that these epithets be pointed in the opposite direction had they known that the full implementation of the AEC's plan to exploit the gas fields in these states would have involved the detonation of between 10,000 and 15,000 nuclear bombs.

NUCLEAR POWER ALTERNATIVES

Recognizing that the invention and development of electric power was one of the seminal technological achievements of modern times, the atomic scientists concentrated their effort to harness the friendly atom on techniques to generate electricity by atom splitting. Over the years, the development of fission power (in essence, an effort to replace the burning of fossil fuels with nuclear power) was given the highest priority by the atomic establishment.

However, intoxicated by the belief that it was possible to develop machines to generate endless, inexhaustible sources of electricity or direct energy, research was undertaken in the years after Hiroshima to (a) develop a fission "breeder reactor" that would produce more plutonium fuel than it consumed, and (b) search for a technique to harness the force (fusion) that makes the sun shine.

FUSION

For over three decades, the goal of fusion research has been to build a machine to harness the violent process that powers the stars and ignites hydrogen bombs. The daunting challenge confronting scientists and engineers working on this project has been to design a reactor that would provide inexhaustible energy by enabling operators to manipulate thermonuclear reactions in temperatures exceeding 100 million degrees Celsius.

Fusion research was an outgrowth of the postwar conviction that scientists and engineers, given adequate support, could accomplish whatever they undertook. It is clear now that had the initial decisions been made, not on theories fashioned by physicists, but rather on the basis of assessments conducted by careful economists and engineers, the United States would not have supported an aggressive, expensive quest for fusion power. The concept that a vessel might be built to contain and control the titanic heat of the sun was preposterous in 1950, and it remains preposterous today.

Until recent years, the same secrecy and awe that shielded Edward Teller from serious criticism for so long prevented citizens from forming their own judgments about fusion. But this program, too, has finally been overtaken by history. After characterizing the saga of fusion research as a "black comedy," Bob Davis, a science writer for the *Wall Street Journal*, recently wrote this epitaph for the program: "Nuclear-fusion researchers promised endless energy by the year 2000; they delivered boundless laughs instead."

Fusion occupies two special niches in the annals of the atomic age. Never has so much talent and money been deployed to accomplish so little. The $2–billion plus spent so far on this venture recalls the myth of Icarus, who, in attempting to fly to the sun, fell back to earth to his doom. Fusion research was characterized by its capacity to be kept afloat by an endless stream of frothy, self-serving announcements about dramatic "breakthroughs" in nuclear engineering. From its first days, hype has been the mother's milk of fusion research.

THE BREEDER REACTOR

During the Manhattan Project years, Leo Szilard, Louis Turner, Enrico Fermi, Eugene Wigner, Walter Zinn, Hans Bethe, and other physicists developed theories that a nuclear reactor might be built that would "breed" more fuel (plutonium) than it consumed while simultaneously generating electricity. The idea of endless energy from "peaceful" atoms excited the atomic scientists, and at the conclusion of the war the designing and building of a prototype of this dream machine was given a high priority by the newly formed Atomic Energy Commission.

The search for this holy grail evoked a national commitment across four decades that expended over $10 billion, consumed the creative talents of some of the nation's best scientists and engineers, and became the most costly energy research project in U.S. history. The first phase of the campaign culminated on a lonely plateau in 1953 near Arco, Idaho, when chemists separated minuscule quantities of plutonium from the uranium fuel in a small reactor and the chairman of the AEC made a dramatic announcement that breeding had been accomplished.

The second phase involved a pioneering project financed by a consortium of twenty-five private electric power companies. This venture matured in 1963, when the Fermi-1 power plant "went critical" at a site on the outskirts of Detroit. The effort to demonstrate the commercial potential of the friendly atom was led by officials of the Detroit Edison Company, who craved the distinction of operating the world's first breeder to feed electricity into a consumer grid. However, the ill-starred $140-million plant functioned at full power for less than one hundred days—and it merits mention in the *Guinness Book of Records* as the producer of the most expensive energy ever generated by an electric utility.

But Fermi-1's appalling balance sheet was only one aspect of a larger debacle. America's first two breeders were also environmental and engineering disasters. There were partial core meltdowns at Arco in 1955 and at the Detroit plant in 1966. Precursors of the larger meltdowns at Three Mile Island and Chernobyl, the warnings implicit in the design and operating mistakes surrounding these "excursions" were either ignored or covered up by the promoters of these projects. Until its credibility was shredded in the 1970s, the AEC and its allies in the private sector were invariably successful in glossing over their failures and fiascos.

In addition to the go-slow warnings presented by the Arco meltdown, as the 1960s began there were already formidable arguments against making plutonium-oriented energy the centerpiece of U.S. research. Dr. Wigner was convinced it was too risky to accumulate thousands of pounds of "fundamentally explosive" plutonium "at one place." And, with one eye on its "fiendishly toxic properties" and the other on human safety, a prominent AEC official, Robert E. Wilson, held the view that "If there ever was an element that deserved a name associated with hell, it is plutonium."

But such negative thinking was brushed aside when Dr. Glenn Seaborg, a scientist who had won a Nobel Prize for discovering plutonium, was appointed chairman of the AEC by President John F. Kennedy. Convinced his agency needed a new mission, Seaborg promptly sent a recommendation to the president that with its potential to be a perpetual source of energy, the breeder would best exemplify U.S. "technological leadership" in the 1960s.

A gentle, mild-mannered man, Glenn Seaborg nurtured a vision that once the planet's fossil fuels were exhausted, plutonium would be the ultimate source of energy for earth's inhabitants. After perusing speeches in which Seaborg outlined his plan for a world propelled by a "plutonium economy," Richard Hewlett, the official historian of the AEC, characterized Seaborg's outlook this way:

> . . . it was always extremely important to him that he discovered a new element that would be the salvation of mankind. . . . It's all sort of naive in a way, but he believed it. Plutonium to him was very sacred. . . . He saw the whole world revolving around this technology, and here he was at the center of it all.

Many leaders of the nuclear community shared Dr. Seaborg's vision of an energy-hungry world rescued by the output of plutonium reactors. The director of the AEC's Oak Ridge Laboratory, Dr. Alvin Weinberg, identified by one observer as one of that community's "preeminent visionaries" was dubious about fusion, but he believed that the development of breeder machines was, simply, "the most important technological enterprise man has ever undertaken." Enraptured by the potential of breeders, U.S. presidents from John Kennedy to Jimmy Carter supported the stream of appropriations that moved Seaborg's dream of plutonium plenty on a strange, twisting ride to a rendezvous with oblivion in 1984 at the Clinch River in Tennessee.

In one aspect, the story of the Clinch River breeder reactor is a study of what happens when gifted scientists are so engrossed by a fixed idea that they become semimystics. It is a study, too, of the technological optimism that has dominated postwar thinking in this country and has, at times, encouraged individuals pursuing illusory goals to make irrational decisions. Victor Gilinsky, a nuclear regulator who observed the Clinch River drama from a front row seat, once used this language to explain the obsessive behavior of the promoters of breeder reactors: "It promises endless energy, and once you're on to that, you see your way through to infinity."

That Glenn Seaborg's breeder program survived for twenty-four years despite the warnings implicit in the partial meltdowns in Idaho and Michigan offers mute testimony concerning both the appeal of a machine that might produce endless energy and the political power atomic scientists could exert when they appeared as wise men bearing gifts for humankind. The project's survival was a triumph of utopian fantasies over common sense. From its inception, the proponents of the Clinch River scheme wore blinders that allowed them to ignore the apparently insurmountable obstacles that lined the path they wanted to travel.

The deadly negatives attached to plutonium were, and will always be, implacable. Its 24,000-year half-life and its "fiendishly toxic" radioactivity would burden future generations with unmanageable environmental problems. There are also reactor safety problems, which engineers may never be able to resolve with required certainty. And if, as Seaborg envisioned, hundreds of tons of plutonium extruded from friendly reactors were in commercial circulation and thus became the world's fuel of the future, resourceful terrorists would have little difficulty obtaining sufficient quantities to make bombs.

DR. WEINBERG'S FAUSTIAN BARGAIN

Alvin Weinberg, however, saw things differently. In a remarkable and oft-cited 1972 paper, "Social Institutions and Nuclear Energy," published in the prestigious journal, *Science*, Weinberg asked: "Is mankind prepared to exert the eternal vigilance needed to ensure proper and safe operation" of a system of breeder reactors? His reply was both positive and euphoric:

> This admittedly is a significant commitment that we ask of society. What we offer in return, an all but infinite source of relatively cheap and clean energy, seems to me to be well worth the price.

Dr. Weinberg did not quantify the "price" to be paid, and the "significant commitment" that society would have to make in his "Faustian bargain" for cheap and abundant energy. The price, he said with remarkable simplicity, would be nothing less than "the absolute necessity . . . of keeping the wastes under some kind of surveillance in perpetuity" by what Weinberg called a "priesthood" of nuclear guardians. This in turn, he wrote, would entail "a vigilance and a longevity of our social institutions that we are quite unaccustomed to."

In his enthusiastic endorsement of the breeder reactor, Weinberg apparently failed to consider the full human implications of his proposed "bargain." The "price" might be the surrender of the open society. Jefferson once observed that "eternal vigilance is the price of liberty." (And as the Russians today are discovering, disorder is another "price of liberty.") The "vigilance" that Jefferson had in mind was that of the people, in whose hands he placed the inalienable "right of rebellion" against an arrogant state "priesthood," determined to protect the "longevity" of its regime.

Accordingly, in the minds of many critics, Weinberg's ethically and politically insensitive attempt to defend the breeder reactor has turned out to be a conclusive *reductio ad absurdum* argument against it. By suggesting that we might have to forgo, "in perpetuity," the "disorder" of an open and democratic society, along with the right of rebellion against "stable" but despotic political institutions, Weinberg may have forgotten, as one observer put it, that Faust got the worst of the bargain.

A final argument which should have sidetracked the breeder in the 1960s involved the prospect that, even if the government invested $10 billion in up-front research, the price of the electricity it generated would be uneconomical. Edward Teller, always ready to deliver obituaries for nuclear programs he had not fathered, announced at the end of the breeder fiasco that *cost* was the Achilles' heel of this technology. And, reveling in his new role as an economist, he once deflated a haggler who sought to use the "success" of France's Superphoenix breeder as a counterargument with the ironic response, "[Yes] the Superphoenix will be a big success—just as big as the Concorde."

THE FISSION POWER FIASCO

Both fission and fusion energy involved forty-year campaigns, and if the breeder was a program that never got off the ground, fission power can best be described as a rash technological effort that achieved a premature takeoff followed soon by a crash landing.

Beginning with the international Atoms for Peace Conference in Geneva in 1955, and motivated in part by its obsessive "race" for scientific prestige with the Communists, the United States was the leader in nuclear energy development around the world. Under the aegis of the Atomic Energy Commission, a feverish effort was mounted to jump-start a fission-based commercial nuclear power industry in this country which would serve as a model for the world's engineers and deliver the benefits of the peaceful atom to humankind. This endeavor grew into the most expensive, high-risk industrial venture undertaken by the federal government in the twentieth century.

From its inception in the 1950s, the fission-electricity program moved forward on a fast track, propelled by the most sumptuous subsidies ever offered to private entrepreneurs. Not only was the technology developed at great cost in federal plants and laboratories transferred by the AEC free of charge to utility companies, but whenever roadblocks appeared, officials of that agency raced to remove them.

As the designated grand marshal of the new age that was coming to birth, the AEC became at once a huckster for nuclear power and an avid promoter bent on doing everything possible to facilitate the advent of the peaceful atom. For example, if no insurance consortium could see its way clear to write contracts to protect utilities from the incalculable damages caused by catastrophic accidents, the AEC and its eager allies in Congress swiftly secured the enactment of a law to put this risk on the backs of American taxpayers.

That law, known as the Price-Anderson Act, reveals, to the critical observer, the authentic doubts of the nuclear promoters hidden behind the promotional fog of public relations experts. For in facing the prospect of tort liability from reactor failure, the promoters' own investments were on the line.

The essential provision of the Price-Anderson Act was simple and straightforward: the commercial nuclear power industry was to be allowed a $560 million limit on liability on all claims due to catastrophic reactor accidents.

The testimony of industry advocates to Congress in support of the act (and its extensions in 1975 and 1987) revealed that such a liability limit was a necessary condition to the development of commercial nuclear power. Thus the industry admitted, in effect, that it was unwilling to accept full responsibility for the privately acknowledged risks of nuclear accidents, and preferred to persuade the federal government to transfer the risks of nuclear power generation from the investors and the industry, on to the U.S. Treasury and the potential victims of such an accident.

The implications of the legislation are stark, if we consider the most likely scenario: had the Three Mile Island incident assumed Chernobyl-like proportions, with full meltdown, rupture of the containment vessel, and winds prevailing toward the New York–Boston corridor—and if the resulting fallout had been the same as that suffered by the inhabitants of Ukraine and Byelorussia in 1986—the fatalities would probably have been counted in six figures, and the injuries (and shortened lives) in the millions. In that case, under the provisions of Price-Anderson, a distribution to all casualties and survivors of the $560 million limited by the act would have amounted to payments to each claimant (or survivor) of perhaps a few hundred dollars.

Price-Anderson was by no means the only largesse given the nuclear industry by the federal government. When the cost of enriched uranium adversely impacted the economics of atomic power, the AEC sweetened the pot by selling this fuel at cut-rate prices. And when it was obvious that expensive engineering add-ons to generating stations were needed to protect the public from radiation "excursions," an obliging AEC relaxed its regulations so its industrial partners could forgo safety measures in order to cut costs. With equal alacrity, all during the bandwagon days of nuclear power the AEC's leaders minimized or covered up the horrendous expenses and risks that would attend the transportation and disposal of the long-lived radiation wastes emitted by these plants.

With the runway thus paved by the AEC, the takeoff of fission power was meteoric—and reckless. In one big surge between 1964 and 1968, the dates that mark the licensing of Jersey Central's large, 600-megawatt Oyster Creek unit and the time it started operating four years later, the AEC licensed thirty-eight larger plants, some up-sized to over 1,000 megawatts. This lunge reflected not only the euphoria that emanated from the inner sanctum of the Atomic Energy Commission, but the intoxicating optimism about technology that permeated industrial circles in the 1960s.

This exercise of mindless rubber-stamping by the AEC (all thirty-eight were licensed as "research" reactors) was precipitate on two counts: the scale-up in size exacerbated the engineering risks, and the utilities that obtained these expedited permits were plunging ahead in the absence of reliable economic data and before they had had any experience building or operating the complex new machines.

Soon after this great leap got under way, warning signs began appearing. The cost of constructing the new plants began escalating at rates that, before most units were completed, would raise the installed price to levels six to eight times above the original projections touted to consumers. Anxious citizens began appearing at the AEC's licensing hearings to raise questions about the safety and siting of proposed new stations. And the price shocks delivered in 1973 by the Arab oil embargo fostered energy thrift, which altered the economics of the utility industry by drastically reducing the demand for electricity.

These developments made 1974 a watershed year and dictated a cascade of cancellations that prompted *Business Week* magazine to feature a cover story at the end of 1978 that observed: "The lights are going out for nuclear power in America." Nineteen hundred and seventy-four, not 1979, the year of the Three Mile Island scare, was the year this impetuous young industry stalled in midair. Two startling facts tell the story: no power stations ordered after 1974 were built; and of the seventy-five plants on the order books that year (including twenty-eight already in various phases of construction), all were cancelled outright.

THE AFTERMATH

During the decline and fall of the nuclear power industry, some proponents of nuclear power sought to place the blame for this plunge on the "obstructive tactics" of environmentalists. Others identified the newly created Nuclear Regulatory Commission and the delays and costs of its "excessive safety requirements," subsequent to the accident at Three Mile Island, as the culprit that made atomic power uneconomical. But in a 1985 assessment printed under the heading "Nuclear Follies," *Forbes* magazine put the blame on the managers of the electric utilities. Terming the collapse "a defeat for the U.S. consumer, for the competitiveness of U.S. industry [and] for the utilities that undertook the program," Forbes asserted, "The failure of the U.S. nuclear power program ranks as the largest managerial disaster" in industrial history.

In truth, however, the masterminds who stage-managed this disaster were not the unwary utility executives who hastily clambered aboard the nuclear bandwagon, but icons of the atomic age like Seaborg and Teller and Alvin Weinberg who pushed for a crash program because they wanted to bring the bounties of the friendly

atom into existence in their lifetimes. After wrestling with the consequences of their self-deceptions, Commissioner Gilinsky felt the
ever-present, heavy hand of these redoubtable captains on the throttle.
"The whole nuclear business," Gilinsky says, "has been top-heavy
with deep thinkers and true believers." He attributes the monumental
misjudgments of the atomic epoch to "a cast of mind that is sure it sees
the inevitable future and is burning to get on with it."

Once they committed their companies to nuclear pioneering,
many electric power executives, without even recognizing the magnitude of the risks they were taking, made spectacular misjudgments.
This does not mean, however, that it would be just to make them the
sole scapegoats of the nuclear power debacle. Rather, they were
swept along onto an uncharted path by the glowing assurances of
scientists who were certain their atomic utopias were achievable.

Since the initial impetus provided by the inventions of Thomas
A. Edison and George Westinghouse, the U.S. electric power industry had achieved technical advances by incremental engineering; that
is, there were no startling technological leaps in this highly regulated
public service enterprise, and its overall performance was so steady
that the constant dollar price it charged its consumers varied little
between 1930 and 1970. Whether it related to increases in the size of
central stations, in the voltages carried by transmission grids, or in
improvements in the efficiency of delivery systems, prior to the
advent of nuclear power the hallmark of electrical engineering was
cautious step-by-step growth.

Influenced by this history, electric power executives were not
the moving force behind the foolhardy push for nuclear energy. The
dynamism that sustained this drive flowed from the cocksure mind-
set of atomic scientists and engineers who presumed that if the
execution of their theories pressed technicians against limits they had
never encountered before, engineers would promptly "remove" such
limits. Never shy about using his Nobel laureate prestige to influence
public opinion, Chairman Seaborg sought out opportunities to assure
the American people that he was "absolutely certain" his nuclear
scenarios were achievable in the near term. In one of his miniprofiles
of the chairman, historian Hewlett described the source of Dr. Seaborg's supreme self-confidence. To Hewlett, "Seaborg tended to
have an elitist attitude ... he believed that a Nobel prize winner knew

more than a good physicist, that a good physicist knows more than the man in the street."

In addition to basic economic miscalculations, the collapse of the fission power program was attributable to an unbridgeable gap between the command decisions of elitist scientists and the insuperable assignments thrust upon hapless engineers by these decisions. After the crash, some sought to scapegoat the nuclear engineers, but the construction nightmares that delayed and hobbled the fission power program were inevitable once the AEC adopted an unrealistic, forced-march action plan. Richard Hewlett described the outcome: "It was not in the Olympian realms of the nuclear scientist that the obstacles were found but rather in the frustrating work-a-day world of the mechanic, the electrician and the plumber."

Impelled by Olympian hubris, the AEC's headlong fission power program was marked for failure from its inception. Indeed, C. P. Snow, the British physicist-cum-novelist, may have had this very enterprise in mind when he penned his memorable axiom: "Technology . . . is a queer thing. It brings you great gifts with one hand, and it stabs you in the back with the other."

THE ATOM DISTORTS THE PURPOSE OF U.S. SCIENCE

The United States paid a heavy price for the all-out support it gave for three decades to the grandiose projects proposed by the promoters of atomic panaceas. The priority accorded to these schemes, combined with the appropriations lavished on the pet projects of the military-industrial complex, distorted the performance of American science and starved the civilian sectors of the economy.

Virtually alone among the early promoters of atomic energy, the first chairman of the Atomic Energy Commission, David Lilienthal, eventually came to appreciate its limitations and its capacity, combined with the growing power of the military-industrial complex, to warp the national purpose. In his 1963 indictment of the atomic establishment, Lilienthal rejected the premise that the future of the human enterprise was bound up with the future of atomic science. To make his case that an imbalance in our overall scientific enterprise was giving an adverse tilt to the economy, Lilienthal pointed out that "two-thirds of the trained minds available for exploring our scientific and technical frontiers are absorbed by the atomic energy and space and defense activities of this country."

Lilienthal paid a heavy price for his candor. I recall the scathing comments AEC Commissioner James Ramey and Congressman Chet Holifield (a domineering member of the joint congressional committee) made in my presence about Dave Lilienthal, and I also recall the smears they used in their campaign to demolish the arguments he presented in his 1963 book, *Change, Hope and the Bomb*. In the immediate postwar period, Lilienthal was an esteemed and exemplary public servant, and I found his analysis of the misconceptions that had distorted the performance of his old agency both prescient and profound.

Lilienthal's central thesis was that it was a mistake to try to create a "separate world of the atom" that would function under a cloak of Big Brother–knows–best secrecy. Wary of the "grand solution" panaceas of the atomic establishment, he asserted in 1963, when atomic optimism was at its apex, that the truly important public policy issues were "human issues, rather than atomic issues" decided by an elite group of experts. When it came to these "human issues," he reflected, "all of us," including the scientists, "are laymen."

Lilienthal also concluded that the Cold War had harmed the democratic process by freezing assumptions about nuclear matters and stifling creative dissent. He questioned the prevailing dogma that more and bigger nuclear weapons increased our nation's security. And he underscored the importance of skepticism and urged his fellow citizens to distrust "one-track minds and one-track solutions."

More in sorrow than in anger, Lilienthal observed that the atomic establishment had failed to deliver on the "fantastic promises" it had made to the American people. The indictment he outlined in his book was sharp and severe. It read:

The reality is that the Atom had not justified the separate and unique status which Congress understandably assigned it in 1946.

The Atom has not been the single necessary weapon.

The Atom has not revolutionized industrial society.

The Atom has not produced revolutionary advances in medicine or industry.

The peaceful Atom has not ushered in a "New World" but has rather become a part, quite a minor part, of the old one.

And yet the official sponsor and trustee of the Atom in this country, the Atomic Energy Commission, has hardly changed at all.

David Lilienthal, a voice in the wilderness in the sixties, was for me a liberating voice of sanity in the 1970s. He was a friend, and with new eyes, I saw him as a statesman who dared to puncture myths he had helped to create in the awe-filled first years of the Atomic Energy Commission.

One personal lesson I absorbed in the 1970s was that when a person's outlook has been shaped by illusions, disenchantment is a gradual process. In the first phase of the antinuclear crusade, I was disturbed by the severity of the charges made by critics who were casting doubts on the stewardship of Dr. Seaborg and other icons of the atomic establishment. The tone of this criticism was unsettling. Since Hiroshima, my generation had viewed the atomic scientists as seers who were working overtime to bring the benefits of the atom to fruition for humankind.

To our sorrow, we have discovered that our atomic obsessions, combined with our misconceptions about the prowess of the Soviet Union, have exerted a profound, ironic, and, in the balance, negative impact on the history of the second half of the twentieth century. It was, in the final analysis, the warped priorities and obsessive Cold War agendas of the two superpowers that offered Japan and Germany opportunities to concentrate their energies on their civilian sectors and to swiftly emerge as economic and industrial rivals of the nations that had leveled their industrial foundation three decades earlier.

David Lilienthal was a true prophet. A decline in the technological leadership and economic strength of the United States of America occurred during the era when it concentrated its best brains on its NASA circuses, on its Big Science megaprojects, and on the new superweapons it was developing to win its race with the Soviet Union for nuclear supremacy.

IV

REFLECTIONS ON THE COLD WAR AND
THE ETHICS OF THE NUCLEAR ERA

13

Nuremberg:

The American Apostasy

Justice is the first virtue of social institutions. . . . Each person possesses an inviolability founded on justice that even the welfare of society as a whole cannot override. For this reason, justice . . . does not allow that the sacrifices imposed on a few are outweighed by the larger sum of advantages enjoyed by many.

—JOHN RAWLS (1971)

The war crimes trials in Nuremberg and Tokyo at the end of the Second World War marked a landmark effort to establish a body of law that would deter aggression and reduce future atrocities by rapacious nations. President Roosevelt raised the flag of American morality by leading a campaign to create international tribunals to preside over the trials of Axis war leaders, and his successor, Harry S Truman, underscored its importance by asking Justice Robert H. Jackson of the U.S. Supreme Court to serve as the chief prosecutor.

The Nuremberg courts sought to develop a body of legal precedents that would evolve into a code governing the conduct of civilized nations. Three categories of offenses were defined during the trials that followed: Rulers who violated international treaties or initiated wars of aggression against their neighbors were brought to the bar of justice for "crimes against peace." War leaders who committed conventional violations of the laws or customs of war, including "wanton destruction of cities . . . or devastation not justified by military necessity," were prosecuted. And inhumane acts authorized by generals or political leaders against civilians either before or during a war were deemed prosecutable as "crimes against humanity."

After the trials of Hitler's henchmen, separate subsidiary proceedings in Europe were conducted by military tribunals of the victorious nations in their respective zones of occupation. In its zone at Nuremberg, the United States took the lead in prosecuting Nazi physicians who performed experiments on inmates of "inferior races" in Hitler's concentration camps.

Evidence adduced during the Nazi doctors case encouraged a group of American military judges to promulgate principles of law that became known as the Nuremberg Code. The goal of these legal pioneers was to establish a code of conduct that, through rulings by judges, would subsequently be transformed into an international common law that would enable physicians and the public at large to understand the conditions under which experiments on human beings might be both permissible and humane.

The Nuremberg jurists enunciated ten rules to govern future medical experiments. Three tenets dominate this code:

- [In experiments with human subjects] the voluntary consent of the human subject is absolutely essential . . . there should be made known to him the nature, duration and purpose of the experiment; the method and means by which it is to be conducted; all inconveniences and hazards reasonably to be expected; and the effects upon his health or person which may possibly come from his participation in the experiment. The duty and responsibility for ascertaining the quality of the consent rests upon each individual who initiates, directs or engages in the experiment. . . .

- No experiment should be conducted where there is an a priori reason to believe that death or disabling injury will occur. . . .

- During the course of the experiment the scientist in charge must be prepared to terminate the experiment at any stage, if he has probable cause to believe . . . that a continuation of the experiment is likely to result in injury, disability, or death to the experimental subject.

Because it was a powerful expression of American ethical norms, many lawyers and physicians anticipated that this medical code would be promptly adopted by U.S. courts and set a standard of care for human experimentation in this country. Justice Jackson apparently believed that new legal foundations had been laid at Nuremberg. In his report to President Truman, he observed: "One of the chief obstacles to this trial was the lack of a beaten path. A judgment such as has been rendered shifts the power of precedent to the support of these rules of law."

Even though this legal framework was fashioned by U.S. judges, it has not been followed by courts in this country. This outcome is a reflection on the impact of the Cold War on American thinking. One of the legacies of our obsession with "national security" is that some elements of our society put a seal of approval on conduct U.S. judges condemned at Nuremberg.

THE CODE AND THE CIA

In 1953, only five years after the Nuremberg Code was promulgated, the director of the CIA, Allen Dulles, authorized a wide-ranging program of medical tests designed to ascertain whether human beings could be "brainwashed" if they were secretly fed mind-altering drugs. Under the same cloak of protecting the nation's security, the army followed suit, and over the next several years unsuspecting soldiers, CIA employees, and civilians were surreptitiously and involuntarily "enrolled" as test subjects.

The health effects of these experiments have never been fully assessed, but it is known that at least two subjects died and the physical and mental health of others was impaired. In 1953 Frank R. Olson, a civilian biochemist who worked for the army at Fort Detrick, Maryland, jumped from a high building after CIA agents laced his drink with LSD. Over two decades elapsed before members of his family learned that he was a victim of a CIA experiment.

In the 1950s, army physicians supervised similar experiments to determine the efficacy of LSD as a "truth serum" for use in questioning suspected spies. According to army documents, this drug induced an "extreme paranoiac reaction" in Private James R. Thornwell, a black soldier. Those who conducted this experiment subjected Thornwell to "extreme mental and physical abuse" and threatened to continue his stupor "indefinitely, even to a permanent condition of insanity."

When evidence about these experiments came to light in the 1970s, lawyers representing Thornwell and Olson's widow forced federal officials to admit that government zealots had violated the Nuremberg Code. In supporting special legislation to indemnify Thornwell, Secretary of the Army Clifford Alexander described his treatment as "unconscionable." And President Gerald Ford, shocked by news stories about the Olson tragedy, gave an order to his attorney general to abandon the government's time-worn "national security" defense and compensate the widow of this victim.

THE CODE AND THE URANIUM MINERS

The Atomic Energy Commission was the architect of an egregious U.S. violation of the Nuremberg Code. As we have seen, this violation evolved out of the AEC's crash effort, beginning in 1948, to develop domestic supplies of uranium on the Colorado plateau.

The AEC was responsible for the uranium miner tragedy because its leaders created the problem and ignored a straightforward solution that would have averted the resulting epidemic of lung cancer. It was the AEC's radiation-safety experts who, when the uranium mining industry was in its infancy, identified the hazards in unventilated mines and stood ready to devise a plan to eliminate or minimize health risks associated with underground mining. As the AEC's Merril Eisenbud told Congress in 1979, aggressive action would have prevented this tragedy. However, those who had the power to transform death traps into clean workplaces elected to turn their backs on the problem they had created.

This decision became a landmark of duplicity and produced the most gruesome masquerade of the atomic age. For over two decades, executives who knew everything there was to know about radiation hazards played the role of unctuous undertakers of a lung cancer epidemic foreseen by their experts. The we-are-waiting-for-facts pose the commissioners and their functionaries adopted in the 1950s was specious, for they knew it would take at least ten years for the first lung cancers to appear. And in 1961 their evasive attitudes took on a new dimension when USPHS statisticians affirmed that the epidemic had arrived on schedule, and AEC officials then adopted the stance that they were waiting for "appropriate" federal officials to set "reasonable" safety standards for the uranium mining industry.

THE CODE AND THE DOWNWINDERS

The testing of nuclear weapons in Nevada also occupies a special niche in the annals of Nuremberg Code violations. Once President Truman approved a continental test site in 1951, AEC officials had to decide how to handle the radiation contamination issue. In this instance, the exposed group would not be miners working in remote mines, but over 25,000 country people who would be showered with fallout and become unwitting participants in exciting experiments that the whole nation would follow with avid interest.

One alternative was to tell these ranch families and small-town folks the truth about the risks and then implement a plan to give them maximum protection from the radioactive debris resulting from the Nevada tests. Such an approach would have had important advantages. Humanitarian concerns would have been satisfied. And the American ideal of open government would, once again, have been fulfilled.

Instead, the AEC elected to follow a different policy. Knowing that it would take years for bomb-caused cancers to appear, these officials decided to adopt a pose that made the downwinders unsuspecting participants in a medical experiment.

No effort was ever made to explain to the downwinders the "method and means" of the bomb tests or "the hazards reasonably to be expected" from these explosions. Instead, the Atomic Energy Commission appealed to the downwinders' pride, assuring them that the fallout was not hazardous to their health. The upshot was a campaign of deception built around the theme "The Atomic Energy Commission says there is no danger." For a full decade, on the radio and in print, this broken-record nonwarning was the AEC's Nevada theme song.

This campaign ranks as a serious violation of the Nuremberg Code. Despite their evasions and self-deceptions, every knowledgeable AEC expert who gave serious thought to the issue was aware that the men, women, and children living in the downwind zone were being used as guinea pigs.

THE AEC'S HUMAN EXPERIMENTS

The most odious medical tragedy of the atomic age involved a series of secret radiation experiments sponsored and financed by the Atomic Energy Commission, using unsuspecting U.S. citizens as laboratory animals. Most of these tests were performed in the 1940s and 50s and some of the 1,000-plus members of this clandestine cohort were surreptitiously monitored for over four decades.

Most of the individuals whose bodies were burdened with assorted isotopes of radiation were defenseless members of our society. The roster of "participants" included sick men and women who became unwitting guinea pigs when hyperactive physicians concluded (erroneously in many cases) that they were terminally ill and injected doses of plutonium into their veins. Another group was composed of retarded teenagers in a Waltham, Massachusetts, state school, who were fed radioactive iron and calcium in some of their food by scientists from Harvard University and M.I.T. after the teenagers were informed that they had been ushered into a "science club."

Other innocent participants included 751 pregnant women in Tennessee who were given injections of irradiated iron to determine its effect on fetal development. A followup study of the children birthed by these women found a higher-than-normal cancer rate. In another experiment, nearly 200 patients with leukemia and other cancers were exposed by Oak Ridge National Laboratory medical personnel to high levels of radiation And in Oregon, the testicles of sixty-seven prisoners were irradiated to ascertain the effects of radiation on sperm production.

Details concerning these experiments were guarded as important national secrets by our government until late 1993 when Hazel O'Leary, President Clinton's Secretary of Energy, began to tell the American people the truth about these abuses of medical ethics. During the ensuing furor, some physicians who defended the decisions of the atomic establishment sought to justify these experiments by contending that little was known about the health risks associated with the various exposures. Others tried to put a positive face on tests conducted without obtaining informed consent by maintaining that these experiments nevertheless produced advances in medical knowledge.

Dr. Glenn Seaborg, the long-time chairman of the AEC, admitted writing a memo in 1944 in which he urged that "a program to trace the course of plutonium in the body be initiated as soon as possible." In 1993 Dr. Seaborg insisted that he knew nothing about the plutonium injection experiments. "Oh God, no," he told a reporter, as he explained that what he had in mind was experiments with animals. Some old-guard medical men defended the experiments by arguing that the conduct of the AEC's doctors should be condoned because they were merely following "the prevailing ethics" of the postwar period.

This argument cannot withstand close scrutiny. It ignores the legal framework surrounding postwar testing, and it disregards the existing canons of medical ethics. When the Nuremberg Code was presented to the world by U.S. officials in 1947, it encompassed one of the important moral lessons of the Second World War and constituted an authoritative summation of the law of informed consent. And in the period before this code was proclaimed, gruesome news stories about the Nazi doctors' experiments had heightened the moral awareness of the American medical community.

IN CONCLUSION

The radiation tragedies were a product of the broad authority given to the CIA, the Atomic Energy Commission, and the other security agencies created by Congress and given charters to operate in a shadowy world of secrecy. The hidden "governments" created by these charters were led by administrators who came to believe that they were charged with responsibility to do whatever they deemed necessary to combat the inroads of Communism here and abroad. Moreover, once these officials realized that they were free to ignore the Constitution and the laws that governed the conduct of other citizens, it became inevitable that the concepts of American morality explicated in the Nuremberg Code would be regarded as impractical and idealistic.

The fact that U.S. judges almost uniformly refused to recognize the worth and validity of the Nuremberg rules in the postwar era measures the influence of the hysteria generated by the Cold War. I believe this abdication—this demonstration that the sense of justice of our judges was warped by a deference to "national security considerations"—marks a moral failure of American jurisprudence.

It also explains why it took forty years for Nuremberg issues to reach the U.S. Supreme Court, and why that august body was also cowed by "military necessity" arguments. When our highest court finally accepted a case involving James Stanley, an army serviceman who was secretly administered doses of LSD, it failed, by one vote, to apply the humane strictures of the Nuremberg Code. But there is a belated prospect that the law clothed in morality will ultimately prevail. One dissenter, Justice Brennan, quoted the express words of the Nuremberg Code to affirm the primacy of "moral, ethical and legal concepts." Characterizing the conduct of the army's brainwash researchers as "beyond the bounds of human decency," Justice Sandra Day O'Connor refused to follow the logic of the court's majority that the experiment arose "out of or in the course of an activity incident to [military] service" and declared that "no judicially crafted rule should insulate from liability the involuntary and unknown human experimentation alleged to have occurred in this case."

14

Sakharov and Teller:
A Study of Cold War
Morality

Sakharov's love of truth and strong belief in the inviolability
of the human being, his fight against violence and brutality,
his courageous defense of the freedom of the spirit, his un-
selfishness and strong humanitarian convictions have turned
him into the spokesman for the conscience of mankind,
which the world so sorely needs today.

—NOBEL PEACE PRIZE CITATION (1975)

He is a danger to all that is important. . . . I do really feel it
would have been a better world without Teller.

—I. I. RABI (1968)

Americans who had lived through the anxious decades of the Cold
War were astounded in the fall of 1989 when the Soviet Union
allowed the nations of eastern Europe to achieve political independence through nonviolent protests. And we watched mesmerized in
the summer and fall of 1991 as the Communist conglomerate known
as the Union of Soviet Socialist Republics (USSR) disintegrated
before our eyes and was replaced by freestanding states, imitating
democratic procedures to create new governments.

This seemed almost miraculous to the men and women of a generation that had participated in the most destructive global war in history and had witnessed the creation of weapons of mass destruction that at times made a nuclear war seem inevitable. Indeed, before Mikhail Gorbachev transformed the dialogue of the Cold War, we were dubious that the ideological gulf that separated the superpowers could be bridged in our lifetimes.

There have been few interludes of genuine peace in a century dominated by blundering diplomacy and hyperaggressive nationalism. As a consequence, the end of the Cold War offers a rare opportunity to study the fears, obsessions, and miscalculations that impelled the world's most powerful nations to lock themselves into the most perilous and costly arms race in history.

I believe the most logical place to commence such a study is to ask questions about the emotions and misconceptions that guided the national security thinking of the superpowers and brought them to the brink of nuclear war:

- What, for example, led leaders on both sides to conclude that they were making decisions that advanced their nation's security when, in fact, day by day, they were pursuing policies that put the lives of their citizens in greater peril?

- Why did each nation, particularly the United States, studiously exaggerate and misjudge the economic power and military prowess of its adversary?

- Why, for so long, were these leaders so loath to recognize that each would gain economic strength and security if they negotiated genuine arms control agreements?

- Knowing that a modicum of trust was essential if there were to be meaningful agreements to ease tensions, why did the same leaders frequently use rhetoric that exacerbated and perpetuated mistrust? And why did they routinely neglect opportunities to establish and enhance trust?

- Since the paramount goal of each nation was the preservation of its own society, why did leaders on both sides assume, without question or challenge, that its adversary was an aggressor country whose aim was world domination?

284

- Despite ample evidence that they were not dealing with madmen, why did leaders from Acheson to Reagan and from Stalin to Brezhnev invariably justify their policies by mouthing the classic Cold War cliché: *"The only thing they understand is force"*?

- And after it was clear that Mikhail Gorbachev represented a transforming force in his country's history, why did U.S. leaders continue to base their outlook on old, outdated assumptions about the implacable nature of Soviet society?

In the coming decades, historians will comb the archives in Washington and Moscow for definitive answers to these and other, related questions. But since immediate insights are needed, it would be useful to examine the lives of the two creators of the new weapons of annihilation, and their subsequent confrontation with the moral consequences of their scientific work. Both the Soviet scientist, Andrei Sakharov, and his American counterpart, Edward Teller, significantly influenced the course of the Cold War, and the startling contrasts in the contributions of each to the equation of war and peace loom as one of the incomparable human dramas of this epoch.

As designers of their nation's thermonuclear bombs, Sakharov and Teller were accurately described as Siamese twins of military science during the first grim decade of the East-West conflict. In secret laboratories, each helped his nation diversify and expand its arsenal of apocalyptic weapons. And as the arms race escalated in the 1950s, each used his talents to invent more lethal bombs for his country.

However, the paths trod by these physicists diverged in the 1960s to produce one of the extraordinary paradoxes of the Cold War epoch. Sakharov, a patriot who lived and worked under the ceaseless surveillance of the KGB, developed, in the private depths of his great soul and intellect, humanistic concerns that convinced him that the arms race of the superpowers was inherently irrational. In due course his convictions led him to compose a manifesto calling for a peaceful convergence of the socialist and capitalist systems—an act of conscience that won him the Nobel Peace Prize.

Edward Teller, by contrast, assumed a militaristic role in the Cold War drama. Using the enormous influence he acquired as the putative father of his country's H-bomb, and later as the gray eminence of the Livermore nuclear weapons laboratory, he became the preeminent promoter of new weapons and strategies that he believed would put the United States in a position where it could win a nuclear war. Had there been a prize for the individual who did the most each year to quicken the pace of military competition, Teller would surely have been a perenniai candidate for that honor.

ANDREI DIMITRIEVICH SAKHAROV

Andrei Sakharov was unknown in the West when, in 1968, he released a peace manifesto which resonated around the globe. The issuance of such a declaration from the bowels of the Soviet war machine by a scientist soon identified as a father of his nation's H-bomb was a watershed event of the Cold War. Had Sakharov not completed his memoirs before his death in 1989, we would have difficulty understanding the influences that shaped his character and emboldened him to flout the rules of his totalitarian government by becoming a peacemaker. Our perception of this man and his place in history is aided, above all, by what his widow, Yelena Bonner, has described as the absolute honesty that characterized his life and thought.

Although he was born in 1921, as Lenin and his Communist comrades were energetically laying the foundations of their new proletarian society, the influences that shaped young Andrei's character emanated from the Russian culture of the tsars. All of Sakharov's forebears were members of the Russian gentry, and one finds many of the virtues and values that guided their lives in the novels of Leo Tolstoy.

Sakharov's maternal grandfather was a soldier whose valor during the Russo-Turkish War won him advancement to the nobility and to ultimate status in Russia's officer class as a major general. Sakharov's father's father, Ivan, a descendant of a long line of priests, broke the family mold when he enrolled at the university in Nizhny Novgorod (during the Communist regime, named Gorky) and became a turn-of-the-century Moscow lawyer whose circle of friends was composed of Russian intellectuals, including the influential writer Vladimir Korolenko.

Nurtured by this environment, Sakharov's father, Dmitri Ivano-vitch, developed diverse cultural interests. A friend of the Russian composer Scriabin, he studied at a famous Moscow conservatory and apparently had the talent to become a composer or concert pianist. However, science seemingly had a stronger grip on his mind, and he won recognition as a teacher and as the author of textbooks and popular works about physics. Although he never acquired a graduate degree, his son informs us that Dimitri Sakharov taught physics in college-level classrooms during the first four decades of Communist rule and won a certain degree of independence and some fame among educators.

Andrei Sakharov acquired many of his insights about life from great works of Western literature, which he found in private libraries kept by members of his family. He memorized Pushkin's poetry and his reading ranged from works of Shakespeare, Goethe, Hugo, Dickens, Gogol, Jules Verne, and H. G. Wells to American authors such as Mark Twain and Jack London. He also informs us that his paternal grandmother had a strong influence on his outlook toward life's challenges. He remembers reading and discussing with her almost every page of Leo Tolstoy's books *Childhood*, *Boyhood*, *Youth*, and *War and Peace*—and he recounts that Tolstoy's narratives allowed the two of them to enter the lives of a whole world of people "we knew better than our own friends and neighbors."

In the early 1900s, members of Sakharov's family were drawn into Count Tolstoy's orbit. Following the 1905 revolution, Sakharov's grandfather supervised the publication of a collection of essays advocating the abolition of capital punishment that featured Tolstoy's celebrated declaration "I Cannot Keep Silent." And the uncle who became Sakharov's godfather, the well-known pianist A. V. Goldenveiser, was a follower of the great novelist and subsequently wrote a book, *Talks with Tolstoy*. Many of the ethical themes that Andrei Sakharov espoused during the humanitarian campaigns of his later years were rooted in Tolstoy's moral concepts.

THE PATH TO BOMBMAKING

At the astonishingly young age of twenty-eight Andrei Sakharov emerged as the primary designer of the first Soviet H-bomb. This accomplishment parallels that of such near-contemporary theoretical physicists as Wolfgang Pauli, Richard Feynman, and Murray Gell-Mann.

By Western standards, Sakharov's education was both abbreviated and unconventional. He developed his initial craving for science at age thirteen, for example, when his father withdrew him from school and gave him a crash course in physics and mathematics at home. Later, in 1938, his performance as a high school honor student won him admission to the Moscow University physics department, but when Hitler's invading armies overran vital war plants, the Soviet Union desperately needed trained engineers. Thus, in 1942, Sakharov was awarded a degree in defense metallurgy. Now twenty-one, he was to spend the war working first in a cartridge factory and later in a munitions laboratory.

Early in 1945, with the German armies in retreat, young Andrei was allowed to resume his education, whereupon he enrolled at the Physics Institute in Moscow. Eager to work on the cutting edge of theoretical physics, Sakharov began work on a master's degree when his father's friend Igor Tamm accepted him as a graduate student at the Physics Institute of the Academy of Sciences (FIAN). Tamm, a gifted teacher who subsequently won the Nobel Prize for Physics, established a special relationship with Sakharov and became a mentor whose every word seemed a revelation to his student.

By the summer of 1947, under Tamm's tutelage, young Andrei had become infatuated with theoretical physics and felt that his work was on the highest levels of scientific inquiry. Suddenly, a year later, his career was thrust onto a different track when his teacher informed him that he had been selected to be part of a top-secret research group at FIAN that would investigate the possibility of building a hydrogen bomb. Created by Stalin's Council of Ministers, this team was called the Tamm Group, and in short order Sakharov found himself in a theoretician's paradise working with fierce intensity on the physics problems surrounding nuclear explosions.

The first task of Tamm's team was to evaluate the preliminary studies prepared by Yakov Zeldovich and his colleagues who, at a secret laboratory, were completing work on the Soviet Union's first atomic bomb. Andrei Sakharov's meteoric rise as a weapons scientist began in the fall of 1947, when he proposed a radically different design for a thermonuclear charge. With Igor Tamm's approval, Sakharov's concept soon became the foundation of the Tamm Group's bomb research. (General Leslie Groves, who was convinced it would take the backward Russians twenty years to catch up with his scientists, would have been dumbfounded by this development. It was incomprehensible to Groves that a twenty-six-year-old Soviet physicist might, in a few months, generate ideas that would enable the Soviets to move abreast of the thermonuclear theorizing performed at Los Alamos over a period of three years by Edward Teller, Stanislaw Ulam, and their associates.)

Lavrenty Beria's KGB machine oversaw all work on nuclear weapons, and early in 1949 Beria personally "requested" that Tamm and Sakharov move to the Russian "Los Alamos" (known as "the Installation") south of Gorky in eastern Siberia, and head the H-bomb project. On August 12, 1953, their work culminated in the successful test of the USSR's first thermonuclear device.

That explosion was a milestone in what Sakharov later called the "Heroic Age" of Soviet military science. It was a signal that Soviet atomic scientists were functioning at the same level as their U.S. counterparts, and it also served as a starter's gun for the race to develop nuclear weapons that was to become the centerpiece of the superpower rivalry. On a personal level, the test on the steppes of Kazakhstan elevated Andrei Sakharov to a pedestal of high prestige, when, in recognition of his work as the principal designer of the Soviet Union's hydrogen bomb, the leaders in the Kremlin awarded him their highest honors: the Stalin Prize and the Hero of Socialist Labor medal.

Encouraged by this breakthrough, in the final days of 1953 the new leaders in the Kremlin made two far-reaching decisions regarding the nuclear arms race. On the basis of a report presented to the Presidium by Sakharov, a decision was made to order the Installation to develop and test by 1955 a lightweight thermonuclear bomb that could be delivered to distant targets by an intercontinental ballistic missile. The second order instructed an impressive team of missile scientists, headed by Sergei Korolev, to design a rocket-propelled missile powerful enough to carry the second-generation H-bomb described by Sakharov.

After the 1953 test, Tamm returned to his research in Moscow and Andrei Sakharov replaced him as the chief of the Installation's Theoretical Division. Sakharov faced an immediate crisis when he realized that the report he had presented in haste to the Presidium was based on mistaken assumptions about the feasibility of adapting the bulky H-bomb design just tested to the missiles being built by Korolev and his engineers. Sakharov resolved his dilemma by ignoring the command decision made in the Kremlin and thus developing a different bomb configuration that would fit the constraints placed upon the missile makers. Feverish studies generated an original concept that Sakharov described as "the Third Idea." With the support of Igor Kurchatov, the scientist who led the effort to produce the Soviet Union's first atomic bomb in 1949, this plan was quietly substituted for the "classical" device tested in 1953. This act of insubordination put Sakharov in a precarious position. He responded by taking full responsibility for the design of the new device and the procurement of the needed "new material." In his memoir, he relates that he propelled the project onto its new track "relying on intuition, and without waiting for the resolution of all theoretical questions or final calculations."

The high point of Andrei Sakharov's weapons work came in November 1955, at the same Siberian proving ground, when his new weapon was detonated from a high altitude in accordance with the plan of its anxious inventor. The successful test of this prototype, Sakharov says, "essentially solved the problem of creating high-performance thermonuclear weapons" and made it possible for Soviet bombmakers to develop a wide array of H-bombs. Ordinary Russians and the outside world knew nothing about Sakharov in 1955, but at home there were additional medals and prizes, and a prominent general articulated the esteem of the Communist elite when he described Sakharov as "our secret gold reserve."

While breakthroughs had been achieved that enabled the Soviet Union to challenge U.S. hegemony in nuclear weaponry, Sakharov was to continue his work at the Installation for another thirteen years. Like his American counterparts, in the aftermath of the 1955 test, he and his colleagues designed devices to fit an array of military weapons, and Sakharov admits that there were times when he poured extra energy into efforts to ensure the success of these special projects. He was caught up, for example, in the mindless excesses that resulted in the production and testing of the 58-megaton Big Bomb exploded over Novaya Zemlya in the fall of 1961. There was no rational military application for a holocaustal device several thousand times more destructive than the bomb exploded over Hiroshima, but Sakharov confesses that he "dreamed up" one possible use for this monstrous bomb.

(In an effort to justify the zeal that gripped the weapons scientists, Sakharov asserts that "the physics of atomic and thermonuclear explosions is a theoretician's paradise," and cites the rationalization Enrico Fermi once used at Los Alamos: "After all, it's superb physics." Sakharov and his colleagues, he explains, regarded themselves as "soldiers" in a scientific war, and he adopted the knee-jerk rationale of bombmakers on both sides of the Iron Curtain: endless, hideous advances in weapons technology, they claimed, were vital in order to "preserve the parity necessary for mutual deterrence.")

As bomb science fell into conventional patterns, Sakharov's work at the Installation became more diversified. There was exotic research relating to possible "breeder explosions" and there were studies of the feasibility of nuclear propulsion systems to support space flight. Also, Sakharov and his associates (like their counterparts in the United States) carried out experimental research into possible peaceful uses of nuclear explosions, in addition to intensive work analyzing the pros and cons of antiballistic missile (ABM) systems.

Beginning in 1963, Andrei Sakharov set aside time to have a fling at "grand science." Working sometimes in collaboration with Yakov Zeldovich, he pursued hypotheses about cosmology and astrophysics and wrote scholarly papers that appeared in Soviet science journals. This partial withdrawal from bombmaking apparently gave Sakharov the detachment he needed to crystallize the ideas about war and peace that had been on his mind for several years. Increasingly obsessed in the 1960s by the "utter insanity of thermonuclear warfare," Andrei Sakharov began in solitude to compose the lofty plea for international amity that would lead to his break with the Soviet establishment—and to his Nobel Peace Prize.

THE PATH TO PEACEMAKING

Some observers have concluded that Sakharov's crusades flowed from an "inner transformation" that changed the course of his life in the 1960s. Yet a study of his life reveals that there was no road-to-Damascus conversion: there was always a moral beacon in his mind. His memoirs disclose that those years were marked by intellectual growth that widened his outlook and deepened his concerns about the survival of the civilization that, in large measure, had flowered through the endeavors of scientists like himself.

Sakharov's striving becomes even more inspiring when we consider that the world he inhabited was extremely constricted. He traveled abroad only once, and he had few opportunities to converse with his peers and interact with the international scientific community of which he was a part. Sakharov's *Memoirs* indicate that, despite the constraints that otherwise could have stunted his growth, he grew into one of his century's commanding figures because he had, in Igor Tamm, a teacher and best friend who was himself a giant of his time.

Sakharov says straightaway that he loved Igor Tamm. Not long before his death, he wrote: "Perhaps the great fortune of my early years was to have had my character molded by the Sakharov family ... and then to have come under the influence of Igor Tamm." Tamm was not a one-dimensional figure whose life was dominated by science. His independent spirit and his passionate, wide-ranging interest in social and cultural issues made him a perfect mentor for a student whose horizons needed expansion. Tamm's optimism, his belief that science should leave a positive legacy for humankind, his "absolute integrity and courage, and [his] willingness to reexamine his ideas for the sake of truth" left a permanent imprint upon Sakharov's mind.

In their three years together in the close world of the Installation, these two were constant companions. Amid their intense work on the H-bomb, their conversations ranged over such hypersensitive areas of Soviet society as "the repressions, the camps, anti-Semitism, collectivization, [and] the ideal and real faces of communism." An idealist who retained his youthful convictions about the vitality of socialism, Tamm had been a revolutionary who knew Lenin and had faced execution more than once. Here was "education" on an Olympian scale, as Sakharov later acknowledged when he wrote: "Tamm's every word seemed a revelation to me."

Tamm's teachings reinforced many of Sakharov's basic convictions and gave him the confidence and courage to take a stand for principles he considered vital. After the 1953 H-bomb test, Sakharov first began to worry about the "human and moral dimensions" of his work. His anxieties deepened in the exhilarating aftermath of the 1955 test, when the stark "military implications" were obvious, and he was gripped by a fear that this "newly released force could slip out of control and lead to unimaginable disasters."

Andrei Sakharov first articulated his uneasiness about his invention at a post-explosion banquet hosted by Marshal Mitrofan Nedelin, the military director of the test and Deputy Minister of Defense. In his moment of triumph, Nedelin invited Sakharov, now the superstar of the Soviet Union's bomb squad, to present the first toast. Sakharov rose and intoned something like: "May all our devices explode as successfully as today's, but always over test sites and never over cities." In his *Memoirs,* he describes the upshot:

> The table fell silent, as if I had said something indecent. Nedelin grinned a bit crookedly. Then he rose . . . and said: "Let me tell a parable. An old man wearing only a shirt was praying before an icon [saying] Guide me, harden me. Guide me, harden me. His wife . . . [responded] Just pray to be hard old man, I can guide it myself." Let's drink to getting hard.

Andrei Sakharov was humiliated by this crude rebuke ("as if . . . lashed by a whip"). Although he was already fully aware that the Kremlin leaders would make all war-use decisions ("I wasn't *that* naive"), Marshal Nedelin's warning was unmistakable: "We, the inventors, scientists, engineers and craftsmen, had created . . . the most terrible weapon in human history, but its use would lie entirely outside our control."

Uncowed by Nedelin's hazing, Sakharov soon shifted his focus for action to the loss of human life because of fallout from nuclear weapons exploded in the atmosphere. This, he felt, was an issue concerning which he might have an impact on policy making. His first initiative on this front came in 1956, when he read the medical-scientific literature concerning the random casualties caused by radioactive fallout from atmospheric tests. He concluded that the lives of hundreds of thousands of unsuspecting human beings could be saved if such tests were reduced or conducted underground. Convinced that such a step would also help contain the nuclear arms race, Sakharov engaged in an insistent campaign to persuade his country's leaders that they would gain favor throughout the world if they publicly advocated the elimination of further atmospheric tests.

Sakharov's message was not heard outside the Soviet Union. Also unnoticed by world opinion was an argument which he presented a year later in a USSR scientific journal debunking the claim of Edward Teller and other American bombmakers that the U.S. had developed a "clean" H-bomb that would not emit radioactive fallout. These farsighted initiatives nevertheless stamp him as a prophet whose ethical concerns presage the furor over fallout that came to a climax in 1957 when 9,235 scientists throughout the world presented a petition to the secretary-general of the United Nations demanding a global test ban agreement.

To understand the risks Andrei Sakharov took, one must first understand the primacy he gave to the moral duties that devolved on him when he acquired authority and fame as the creator of the Soviet thermonuclear bomb. His credo was that the moral capital one acquired should be spent, not sequestered—and to him, imperatives confronting humanity took precedence over the supposed national security needs of any nation. Despite the constant KGB surveillance under which he lived and worked, Sakharov says, he was "baffled" by the don't-get-involved attitude of colleagues who had Hero medals to prove their loyalty, yet refused to deal with the ethical dilemmas their labors had thrust upon them and the entire human race.

Andrei Sakharov was not attuned to the Marxist doctrine that important social changes would invariably be galvanized by a faceless, impersonal "locomotive of history." With an instinct that Leo Tolstoy would have admired, he believed each individual should seize any opportunity to sow seeds of change. Moreover, once the leaders of his country elevated him to a pinnacle of prestige, Sakharov felt duty-bound to use his prestige to support ideas and causes that would improve the prospects for peaceful coexistence between nations.

In 1958, when this self-appointed pleader attempted to influence

Soviet policy making, he had one failure and one success. In an effort to reduce radioactive fallout, Sakharov developed a new set of testing guidelines that would have limited the number of Soviet atmospheric explosions. He then persuaded the ailing Igor Kurchatov, the scientist esteemed as the driving force behind the USSR's first atomic bomb, to personally present this plan to Chairman Khrushchev at his vacation retreat in the Crimea. An annoyed Nikita Khrushchev rejected Sakharov's proposals out of hand. Sakharov's success came the same year, when he first met the up-and-coming Leonid Brezhnev and, in the company of Installation Director Yuli Khariton, presented him with a protest against a planned reallocation of resources for scientific and military research.

When Sakharov next expressed a strong opinion in the Kremlin, he was met with a tongue-lashing from Nikita Khrushchev himself. At a summit meeting of sixty atomic scientists and Party leaders, Khrushchev announced, without discussion, what Sakharov regarded as a "politically motivated" decision to resume nuclear testing in the fall of 1961, thus breaking the two-year moratorium agreed to with President Eisenhower. Sakharov scribbled a note and passed it down the aisle to the chairman. The message ended with a blunt question, "Don't you think that new tests will seriously jeopardize the test ban negotiations, the cause of disarmament, and world peace?" Khrushchev read the note, glared at Sakharov, but held his response until the state banquet later that evening.

Before the dinner guests were seated, Chairman Khrushchev gave a rambling speech during which he angrily denounced "Academician Sakharov" for moving "beyond science into politics" and "poking his nose where it doesn't belong." The guests' faces were frozen as Khrushchev castigated his star bomb designer for daring to question his decision to initiate a new round of bomb tests. At the conclusion of his tirade, Khrushchev uttered the cliché that Cold War insiders on both sides of the Iron Curtain had been using for a decade to squelch their critics: "We understand the politics of this struggle, and you do not. We must conduct our policies from a position of military strength. We cannot win this contest if we show weakness, or if our enemies feel we are not as strong as they are."

Looking directly at his critic, the Soviet ruler wound up his diatribe with this scathing remark: "Sakharov, don't try to tell us what to do or how to behave. We understand politics. I'd be a jellyfish and not chairman of the Council of Ministers if I listened to people like Sakharov!"

A test of Andrei Sakharov's moral stamina came a month later, when he and Khariton met with the chairman to obtain approval for the final plan for the new round of atmospheric tests. While Khariton had the floor, Khrushchev interrupted with the question "Does Sakharov realize that he was wrong?" Without flinching, Sakharov responded, "My opinion hasn't changed, but I do my work and carry out orders."

The storm produced by these confrontations blew over when the tests in the fall of 1961—including the test of the gargantuan 100-megaton Big Bomb, which Sakharov had designed—were executed without a hitch. In the winter of 1962, there was another pompous ceremony in the Kremlin, at which Chairman Khrushchev presented a new round of toasts, awards, and prizes to his bomb squad, including a third Hero of Socialist Labor medal to Andrei Sakharov, putting him in a special pantheon of Soviet patriots.

By 1962 Sakharov's character had hardened into stern stuff, and neither official laurels nor threats by high officials altered his basic conviction that testing in the atmosphere was "a crime against humanity, no different from secretly pouring disease-producing microbes into a city's water supply." A year of feverish testing by both superpowers—1962—was another turbulent time for Andrei Sakharov. At the Installation, he was supervising the design of a miniaturized bomb that would fit on the tip of a missile and would thus be a key element of the USSR's strategic armory. However, a complication soon arose that rekindled his one-man crusade against unnecessary tests. Bomb designers at the rival Second Installation had developed and were demanding a test of a competing bomb, which differed "only slightly in its tactical and technical features." The prospect of duplicate tests and unnecessary fallout angered Sakharov, and in the summer of 1962 he mounted an intensive campaign on several fronts to cancel one of these explosions. After he failed to persuade Efrim Slavsky (the powerful minister in charge of military technology), Sakharov had a face-to-face confrontation with the head of the rival laboratory, Evgeny Zababahkin. The fruitless argument that ensued became emotional, with Sakharov screaming at his adversary, "Zhenya, what are you doing? This is tantamount to murder!" In desperation, with the scheduled detonation only hours away, Sakharov used the KGB's high-frequency phone to make a direct appeal to Chairman Khrushchev to postpone the impending test. Khrushchev listened but refused to get involved.

Overcome by his impotence to prevent a "terrible crime," Sakharov reports, "I put my face down on my desk and wept."

While this episode was a crushing defeat, in the fall of 1962 the events of history were setting the stage for a victory for Sakharov's principles the following year. The flurry of tests by both superpowers produced a variety of warheads that, for an interval, assuaged anxieties on both sides about who was "ahead" in the weapons race. And the holocaustal scare evoked by the first nuclear confrontation of the Cold War, the Cuban missile crisis, sent a message to decision makers in Moscow and in Washington that the time had come to consider agreements that would inculcate restraint and improve the prospects for some kind of coexistence.

As part of his overall effort to reduce or eliminate fallout (and just prior to the fight over the duplicate tests), Sakharov made a special appointment to see Efrim Slavsky to present the case for a partial test ban. He was aware that three years earlier President Eisenhower had proposed a treaty to eliminate all nuclear tests except those conducted underground. He knew, too, that protracted negotiations with the Americans on a possible Limited Test Ban Treaty (LTBT), had made no progress, because Igor Tamm and the other Soviet negotiators were under instructions to oppose the Eisenhower option.

Without mentioning Eisenhower's idea, Sakharov outlined what the Soviet Union would gain in world opinion if it provided leadership that led to a partial test ban. Such an initiative, he pointed out, would be "timely from a political standpoint" and would probably be welcomed by the Kennedy government. Seemingly sympathetic, Slavsky observed that, "Of course, the boss himself [Khrushchev] will have to decide," and promised to pass Sakharov's idea on to his superiors.

Several months later, in the aftermath of the Cuban crisis, Slavsky told Sakharov that there was lively interest in his concept "at the top" and that it was likely that the Soviet Union would soon assume leadership on this issue. On July 2, 1963, Nikita Khrushchev proposed a partial test ban in a speech he delivered in East Berlin. As Sakharov had foreseen, President Kennedy responded warmly and, with a swiftness that astonished the world's diplomats, a Limited Test Ban Treaty with global ramifications was negotiated in Moscow and signed in the short span of thirty-four days.

Modest as always, Andrei Sakharov did not seek recognition as a "father" of the LTBT. Rather, he privately savored the prospect that this agreement might reduce the risk of thermonuclear war and save the lives of "hundreds of thousands, possibly millions" of innocent people.

THE MANIFESTO

There were important changes in Andrei Sakharov's life at the Installation in the mid-sixties. Most of the exciting questions surrounding the physics of nuclear explosions had been resolved by the time the 1962 tests were complete, and Sakharov found fewer challenges as bombmaking became routine. Like their U.S. counterparts, he and his colleagues at the Installation devoted large amounts of creative time studying the feasibility of peaceful nuclear explosions, and subsequently concentrated on "operations research" concerning antiballistic missile (ABM) systems and possible ways to counter them. With a yen to do original work in science, Sakharov spent most of his time pondering and writing about the "grand" mysteries of cosmology.

At heart Andrei Sakharov was a reformer, and knowing that he could influence the Kremlin leaders' decision making from time to time, he intervened on behalf of causes he considered important. In 1964, for example, he wrote a blunt letter to Khrushchev, urging him to "open his eyes" to the harm being done to Soviet science by the genetic fakery peddled by the powerful Party hack T. D. Lysenko. He put his nose into public affairs again when Communist Party reactionaries mounted an effort to rehabilitate Stalin soon after Khrushchev was ousted. This protest took the form of a collective letter to Leonid Brezhnev, signed by twenty-five Soviet "celebrities," urging him to resist such an action.

During this period Sakharov called the head of the KGB, Yuri

Andropov, on behalf of the imprisoned dissident Yuli Daniel; and after he became involved in the work of an *ad hoc* Committee to Save Lake Baikal, he telephoned Brezhnev to express his personal views about a pending plan to develop polluting industries along the shoreline of this pristine natural wonder. Although such interventions violated the norms of the Communist system, as long as Sakharov expressed his opinions in the Soviet tent and confined his protests to domestic matters, his moral idiosyncrasies were tolerated. Moreover, the immense contributions he had made as a master builder of nuclear weapons influenced leaders who were angered or upset by his intrusions either to chastise him in public forums or to overlook what they regarded as errant behavior. Apparently even Nikita Khrushchev had a furtive admiration for his ethical stands, for the former chairman included this laurel in the memoir he wrote after he was deposed: "[Sakharov] was . . . a crystal of morality among our scientists."

In January 1968, when he began composing the long essay he later entitled "Reflections on Progress, Peaceful Coexistence, and Intellectual Freedom," Sakharov knew that if he allowed it to be published in the outside world, he would cross a line that would make him a "renegade" in the eyes of Soviet leaders. It was, he informs us, the conferences on nuclear war strategies at secret military facilities that finally persuaded him he had to act. For Sakharov, these war games dramatized the apocalyptic changes in warmaking brought about by the weapons he had designed. Now he understood and was haunted by "the horror, the real anger, and the utter insanity of thermonuclear warfare," and the threat that such a war posed to all of the earth's inhabitants.

As he examined specific plans for thermonuclear strikes to obliterate specific enemy targets, the sheer magnitude of the contemplated destruction "transformed the unthinkable and monstrous" into "a fact of life." Sakharov realized that if civilization was to survive, "the technical, military, and economic problems were secondary" and the fundamental issues were "political and ethical."

As he began composing the ten-thousand-word essay that would become the crowning achievement of his life, Andrei Sakharov surely wondered whether it was possible for anyone, least of all a physicist cooped up in a bomb factory, to frame an appeal that might alter the course of an ideological conflict driven by a dogma that the "security" of the superpowers would be served by the expansion of thermonuclear bomb arsenals. Indeed, from the beginning, Sakharov's endeavor was engulfed by limitations that made it appear to be a quixotic enterprise.

As the director at the Installation, he functioned in an environment as hermetically sealed from the outside world as the KGB could make it. Like his friend Tamm, he purchased a shortwave radio and followed Cold War trends by listening sporadically to BBC or Voice of America broadcasts, but in 1968 there was no Igor Tamm at his laboratory with whom he could discuss the ideas woven into his text. And, worse yet, writing was not a skill Sakharov had mastered, so he was forced to teach himself the art of expressing his cogent arguments in the process of constantly rephrasing of his drafts. Moreover, knowing little about modern mass communications, Sakharov was unsure whether he could find a way to transmit his message to the global audience he wanted to reach.

With the honesty that was the hallmark of his character, Sakharov made no effort to conceal the ideas he was incorporating into his text. His drafts were typed by his secretary at the laboratory, and there are good reasons to believe that Yuri Andropov, the relatively liberal head of the KGB, followed the progress of his writing, while presumably hoping it would, in the end, be a stillborn exercise in semantics. To the end of his life, Andrei Sakharov considered himself a Russian patriot. The paramount aim of his entreaty was to help his country avoid the abyss of nuclear war, and before his manifesto was "thrown over the transom" to the West by a Moscow friend, he mailed a copy to Chairman Brezhnev.

The publication of the complete text of Sakharov's plea in the *New York Times* on July 22, 1968—and an accompanying story that identified the author as the designer of the USSR's H-bomb—created a sensation that sped his message around the globe. And the wing-borne words, which enabled his appeal to soar above the stale dogmas of the Cold War, made the Soviet physicist a symbol of hope for peace-loving people in all parts of the world.

Sakharov set the stage for his argument by enunciating two primary themes:

- He described adverse developments in the last half of the twentieth century (thermonuclear war, hunger, the "narcotic of mass culture," the spreading of mass myths by "treacherous demagogues," and environmental degradation) that were clouding the prospect for human advancement.

- He identified intellectual freedom as the indispensable ingredient of a "scientific democratic approach" to progress by observing that "freedom to obtain and distribute information, freedom for open-minded and unfearing debate, and freedom from pressure by officialdom and prejudices" were indispensable if the human advance was to continue, and he summarized his plea for sanity with this portentous warning: "In the face of these perils, any action increasing the division of mankind, any preaching of the incompatibility of world ideologies and nations, is madness and a crime."

Because its tenor was so evenhanded and was so plainly animated by a profound love of humanity, Sakharov's manifesto attracted a worldwide audience. Western readers, initially startled that its author was a bomb scientist, were impressed that a Soviet citizen would attempt to ease the Cold War crisis by presenting an appeal that would transcend the festering quarrels of the superpowers and call for a global dialogue free of national pride and militaristic slogans.

What added grit and grist to Sakharov's manifesto was his ambitious blueprint for a peaceful convergence of the Communist and capitalist systems before the end of the twentieth century. In 1968 this concept seemed utopian, but Sakharov based his plan on optimism that such an outcome was politically feasible. Indeed, one of his primary aims was to foster pragmatic thinking on both sides of the Iron Curtain in order to melt the ideological animosities that had long fueled the engines of the nuclear arms race.

Before Hiroshima, the great Danish physicist Niels Bohr warned that the only way to avert a nuclear arms race was to create an "open world" where scientists of all nations would search for new insights into nature's secrets, and all knowledge about the behavior of atoms would be shared. Faced with the secretive, self-contained society ruled by Joseph Stalin's iron hand, Roosevelt and Churchill ignored Bohr's counsel. But Niels Bohr's great truth hovered in the background until, in one of the supreme ironies of the Cold War, it was reinserted into the international dialogue by a physicist who labored in the ultrasecret world of a bomb factory created by Stalin. When he breathed new life into Bohr's idea in 1968, Andrei Sakharov fulfilled two objectives. He refurbished Bohr's thesis that the integrity and freedom of science had to be safeguarded if science was to be in the vanguard of civilization and achieve its full potential. And he simultaneously enunciated the *glasnost* concept that, two decades later, would become the centerpiece of Mikhail Gorbachev's plan for the restructuring of Soviet society. The publication of Andrei Sakharov's "Reflections" evoked amazement in the West. Herbert York, who was working in the White House in 1968, recalled his personal astonishment with these words: "I [had] never heard a single suggestion that there might be people in the Soviet nuclear establishment who were pressing for moderation. . . . The picture of the Soviet Union as being, in effect, a vast prison camp simply did not allow room for such an idea."

The revelation that the author was the designer of the Soviet H-bomb was breathtaking, but it was the manifesto's humanistic formula for international cooperation and the cogency of Sakharov's argument for coexistence that gave his appeal such power and poignancy. One measure of the scope of that appeal is that in a matter of months over eighteen million copies of "Reflections" were published in all parts of the world, a dissemination that galvanized a wave of fresh thinking about peace strategies, which subsequently eased the tensions of superpower competition.

Despite a suppression campaign by the KGB, Western radio broadcasts informed the Russian intelligentsia of the reception Sakharov's words received abroad, and through the self-publishing typewritten press known as *samizdat,* "Reflections" enjoyed a wide circulation among the Soviet elite. The future would reveal the impact that this essay would have on the minds of restive young Communists, but the old men in the Kremlin viewed Sakharov's manifesto as a threat to their hegemony and took steps to isolate the author and to demean his motives.

Despite the fact that he was a recipient of his nation's highest honors for peacetime service, Andrei Sakharov became an instant outcast when he refused to disavow his statement of conscience.

Here, too, the situation was enveloped in ironies. A patriot who had no hidden agenda, Sakharov did not seek a "struggle" with the rulers in the Kremlin. In fact he still considered himself a "part of the establishment." His aim was to reform, not overthrow, the Soviet system, and he confessed that "deep down I still felt that the government I criticized was my government."

The method Soviet leaders used to deal with Sakharov underscores the ideological rigidity that held sway in the Kremlin in 1968. The decision did not take into account the fact that, by then, Andrei Sakharov had probably done more than any other Soviet scientist to enable his country to attain parity in its weapons race with the United States. Nor was any effort made to plumb Sakharov's motives, or to contemplate whether the USSR might benefit from using his manifesto as an ornament that would favorably influence world attitudes toward Communism by revealing that even its bombmakers were anxiously exploring avenues to peace.

But the old men of the Brezhnev era were incapable of contemplating such subtleties. With many of Stalin's heirs still in power, Sakharov's heresies simply could not be tolerated. Abrupt, peremptory disciplinary measures were taken: Sakharov was stripped of his clearances and was never allowed to reenter the laboratory where he had achieved so much for his country as its preeminent armorer of the nuclear age.

A MODERN MOSES

In his memoir *The Joy of Insight,* the eminent American physicist Victor Weisskopf describes his friend Sakharov as a "Moses who led his people to a better world and died before they arrived." Sakharov, like Moses, had to endure a long period of wilderness wandering before elements of the world he envisioned began to emerge with the advent of Mikhail Gorbachev.

The hostile environment in which Sakharov lived as a castoff was created by omnipresent agents of the KGB who sought to repress the dissemination of his ideas by isolating and belittling him. Had the unbending ideologues in official circles tried to understand Andrei Sakharov's personality and motives, they might have taken a different approach to the "problem" he presented. Their bomb scientist was, in reality, a shy intellectual—the very opposite of a revolutionary. Sakharov valued order and felt that social and political changes should come about through nonviolence. As he had repeatedly demonstrated in his notes and phone calls to the men who made the big decisions in the Kremlin, his aim was not to oust his country's leaders. Rather, he wanted to reorient their outlook so they would favor reforms and new approaches to world affairs that would lead toward paths of peaceful coexistence.

Although at times his moral fervor impelled him to do bold things, Andrei Sakharov was at heart an uncombative, private person who shunned personal publicity. During long visits at Sakharov's apartment in the mid-seventies, Hedrick Smith of the *New York Times* was surprised by Sakharov's modest, unpretentious manner. To Smith, Sakharov was "an inward man, a Russian *intelligent,* an intellectual through and through." Having witnessed his friend's "instinct to avoid the limelight" and his lack of sophistication concerning public relations, Smith subsequently concluded that the KGB's persistent slander campaigns ultimately radicalized Sakharov and turned him into a biting critic who granted interviews to Western journalists and condemned the failures of the Soviet system.

Because he was not encouraged to pursue an active life in science, Andrei Sakharov devoted large amounts of time in the 1970s to lonely protests at trials of Soviet citizens who had attempted to assert basic freedoms in public forums. This activity caused some latter-day observers to catalogue Sakharov as a "dissenter" and to conclude that these protests constituted his paramount contribution to the revolution brought about by Mikhail Gorbachev. Such a judgment misreads Sakharov's personal history: to identify Andrei Dimitrievich as a dissenter is to diminish the seminal role he played in world history as a *glasnost* pioneer.

Preeminently an idealist and philosopher, Andrei Sakharov deserves stature as one of the giants of the Cold War epoch, for the ideas he enunciated in "Reflections"—and in essays he subsequently wrote to update his concepts—influenced the course of events in his own country and in the world at large. In 1980 (soon after Sakharov had been bundled off to the closed city of Gorky) Pyotr Kapitsa, an elder statesman of Russian physics, dispatched a plea for clemency to KGB Chief Yuri Andropov. Kapitsa, who understood Sakharov's high-mindedness, used these words to defend the supposedly subversive role his friend had been playing in Soviet life:

> Ever since the time of Socrates, active hostility to heretics has been commonplace in the history of culture.... The source of human creativity is dissatisfaction with the existing state of affairs.... Since only rare individuals command the talent required to express dissatisfaction in a creative way, we ought to cherish and take good care of those few who do.

But in the winter of 1980, the moribund men in Leonid Brezhnev's geriatric circle were in no mood to cherish A. D. Sakharov. To the contrary, exasperated by statements he had made to American journalists condemning the invasion of Afghanistan and advocating a boycott of the upcoming Olympic Games in Moscow, they were ready to invoke the ancient penalty imposed by the czars to silence their prominent critics: banishment. The Presidium's decree stripped Sakharov of his medals and honors and deported him to Gorky, a city off-limits to foreigners.

Leonid Brezhnev and his backward-looking entourage failed to realize that it was too late for damage control, too late to stop Sakharov's truths from "corrupting" the minds of younger men who would soon gravitate to positions of power in the Soviet Union. The crude techniques of thought control used by Stalin had become a sieve in an age when messages borne by radio, television, and tape cassette pierced national boundaries and inspired independent thinking. Moreover, if the USSR was to provide dynamic leadership in the future, it was vital for its next-generation leaders to have access to the global marketplace of ideas.

It is patent that Sakharov's manifesto had a special appeal to the rising Party officials and intellectuals who had gained glimpses of a different, more modern society during the thaw promoted by Nikita Khrushchev. We know, for example, that some of the most forward-looking leaders waiting in the wings—men with names like Mikhail Gorbachev, Boris Yeltsin, and Eduard Shevardnadze—were appalled by the sluggishness of Brezhnev's regime and dismayed by the absence of any effort to revitalize Soviet society.

In due course, historians will identify the varied forces that paved the way for the restructuring program Mikhail Gorbachev unveiled to the world in the fall of 1987. It is already clear, however, that Gorbachev deserves recognition as the preeminent peacemaker of the twentieth century. In seven tumultuous years, he transformed his country's political and economic system and took initiatives that ended the nuclear arms race and brought the Cold War to a nonviolent conclusion.

There is abundant evidence in Mikhail Gorbachev's writings and statements that the concepts Andrei Sakharov presented in "Reflections" percolated in his mind and had a pervasive influence on his thinking. There are marked similarities between the theses Andrei Sakharov outlined in his 1968 manifesto and the core ideas Gorbachev set forth in his 1987 book, *Perestroika*. Both men addressed radical appeals to a world audience, and although Sakharov enunciated his heresies nineteen years prior to *Perestroika*, the overlap of the themes adduced in the two documents is both stark and startling:

- Sakharov called for a new dialogue that would rise above the deadly dogmas of the Cold War; the subtitle of Gorbachev's book is *New Thinking for Our Country and the World.*

- Each was a patriot who recognized the shortcomings that were strangling progress in their country, and each believed the Soviet system had to be renovated if it was to survive and prosper.

- Both men felt new forms of international cooperation were urgent if a global disaster was to be averted.

- Sakharov had argued that "freedom for open-minded and unfearing debate" was the *sine qua non* for human progress; Gorbachev echoed this idea in the *glasnost* (openness) concept, which was the centerpiece of his plan for *perestroika* (restructuring).

- Sakharov's assessment that "the division of mankind threatens it with destruction" resonated in Mikhail Gorbachev's plea for a dialogue that would lead to coexistence and shifts in political power without violence.

- A vital evolutionary change advocated by each involved a gradual convergence of socialism and capitalism.

- Each also envisioned an end to the nuclear arms race and a concomitant enlargement of peacemaking efforts by the United Nations and other international institutions.

Mikhail Gorbachev, who spent his first two years as general secretary consolidating his base of political power, waited until 1987 to present the full details of his revolutionary *perestroika* campaign to the world. But before this campaign got under way he sent a signal to the world about the seriousness of his new thinking by cancelling Andrei Sakharov's exile in Gorky and by a notable personal phone call in which he invited the scientist (whom he had never met) to return to Moscow and "go back to your patriotic work."

What ensued is history. Sakharov, now a personal symbol of Gorbachev's *glasnost* policy, became a leading advocate of reforms, won office in the first popularly elected Soviet parliament, and became both a stern critic and a sometime ally of Gorbachev and his government. Before he died three years after his exile ended, Sakharov witnessed, in an extraordinary sequence of events, the fulfillment of many of his hopes and prophecies. He played a role in helping the human freedoms and democratic reforms he had advocated take root in the life of his country. He applauded as the United States and the USSR agreed to eliminate a dangerous category of nuclear missiles from European soil. He looked on as some of the nuclear weapons he had helped design were scheduled for dismantling. And, in the last weeks of his life, Andrei Dimitrievich surely felt waves of gratification when Gorbachev exercised restraint and the Soviet satellite countries in eastern Europe won their independence through nonviolent protests and political reforms.

Of all of the impossible dreams Sakharov outlined in his "Reflections," he must have been most astonished and gratified to find the climate of world opinion improved, and the course of international affairs set upon a promising new pathway to peace, in large measure through Russian initiatives. He must have been heartened, too, by the prospect that the world might no longer be divided into the opposing camps that had long generated poisonous suspicions and hatreds and had placed the entire planet in nuclear peril.

A model of modesty, Andrei Sakharov had no need to seek

vindication or personal glory for the contributions he made as a global peacemaker. Sakharov relates in his *Memoirs* that three weeks after Stalin's death a far-reaching amnesty was proclaimed and the paranoid conspiracy charges lodged against the Kremlin physicians who treated Stalin in his last illness were dropped. Igor Tamm, he informs us, heard the news on his shortwave radio and ran into Sakharov's office shouting, "They've freed the doctors," and then exclaimed ecstatically, "Have we really lived to see it? Have we really lived to see this moment?"

One wonders whether A. D. Sakharov did not experience a comparable delight in his last days.

Whatever the case, it is possible that students of history may someday decide that the life story of Andrei Dimitrievich Sakharov, a man characterized by Hedrick Smith as a "meek-mannered soul," encompasses a singular saga in which an individual who personified meekness did, for an uncertain interval, enable his kind to "inherit the earth."

EDWARD TELLER

Edward Teller was born in Budapest in 1908 into one of the assimilated Jewish families that had risen to prominence in Hungarian society. His father, Max, a prosperous lawyer, was part of the professional elite that influenced the commercial and cultural life of his nation. Max Teller's success in the world of business provided both security for his family and the means to give his only son access to the best educational institutions.

In the last half of the nineteenth century, Budapest was a haven for the talented children of Jewish families who had earlier ventured out of the ghettos of eastern Europe. Before the turbulent events of World War I undermined the rickety foundations of the Austro-Hungarian empire, the self-proclaimed Queen City of the Danube was renowned for its tolerance and general enlightenment. In 1863, a Hungarian monarch began conferring noble titles on nonpracticing Jews who made contributions that uplifted his society, and by 1914 nearly 350 Hungarian families of Jewish extraction had been ennobled.

The general glow of enlightenment encouraged Budapest's elite to place a premium on their children's education. Although Hungary's institutions of higher education did not measure up to those in some western European nations, Budapest fostered a high level of instruction in secondary education that produced a crop of scholars which has long been viewed with amazement by science historians. In all, seven Hungarians who began studying science in Budapest's secondary schools of that era (von Karman, de Hevesy, Polanyi, Szilard, Wigner, von Neumann, and Edward Teller) subsequently achieved international eminence as natural scientists. Edward Teller was the youngest of these savants.

Teller has revealed surprisingly few facts about the influences that shaped his personality and character. He has revealed little about his formative years, and has not identified any teacher, friend, or mentor who helped frame his world view or his outlook on life. His boyhood imagination was excited by Jules Verne, like his counterpart Andrei Sakharov's, but he does not identify his heroes or the friends who left a mark on his character. He informs us that the two professors who contributed the most insights to his career as a scientist were Germany's Werner Heisenberg and Denmark's Niels Bohr, but there is no mention of writers or thinkers who opened his eyes to the human predicament, or to the realities of war and peace.

However, we do know a great deal about Teller's days as a student and professor in the years before the onset of World War II. Although he had exhibited signs of mathematical genius in high school, Max and Iona Teller decided that he should become a chemical engineer and carve out a future for himself in the world of commerce. This decision led to his enrollment at the Institute of Technology in Karlsruhe, Germany. Sponsored by the I. G. Farben combine, the institute was probably the best school in Europe for a student who wanted to train in this specialty. Edward's parents escorted him to Karlsruhe to ensure that his living arrangements were satisfactory.

Edward Teller informed his biographers that during his two years at the institute he pursued his chemistry curriculum "under duress" and was a drudge-type student who "studied virtually all the time." A turning point in his academic career came when a versatile young professor enlivened a chemistry class by weaving the new science of quantum mechanics into his course of instruction. Here was an intellectual challenge that lifted Edward's mind into a new realm, and his enthusiasm for physics became so intense that his father finally agreed to let him study this daunting, "impractical subject."

The year 1928 was an auspicious one for any student to begin the study of physics. Under the tutelage of giants like Niels Bohr and Ernest Rutherford, the period that would later be called the "golden age" of physics was already under way: each year new discoveries enlarged the foundations of a new branch of the discipline soon to be called "nuclear physics." With an ease that bespoke genius, at age twenty Edward Teller gained access to some of the best universities and finest teachers in Europe and became a fast-learning scholar in this exciting field of science.

Teller's first break came when the University of Leipzig accepted his application for admission. Here learning pivoted around the seminars of Werner Heisenberg, a youthful physicist who had been a pioneer in the field of quantum mechanics. A creative rapport between the German and his Hungarian student culminated after two years when Heisenberg presented Edward Teller with a Ph.D. in theoretical physics. As a Heisenberg protégé, Teller, at twenty-two, had one of the keys to the larger kingdom, and in the decade that followed, his career moved on a track that put him in the inner circle of nuclear physics.

Upon graduation Dr. Teller secured an assistantship at the University of Göttingen, where he encountered eminent practitioners of his profession and wrote collaborative papers with several of his peers. When Hitler came to power in 1933, Teller lost no time in joining the exodus of Jewish scientists. As a refugee, Teller became what Albert Einstein once called a "bird of passage." He first secured a lectureship at the University of London, and soon afterward won a Rockefeller fellowship that enabled him to study for nearly a year at Niels Bohr's prestigious Institute of Theoretical Physics in Copenhagen.

One of the rewarding friendships Edward Teller made in Denmark was with George Gamow, a physicist who grew up in Odessa in the Soviet Union and whose imagination was as mercurial and fertile as Teller's. Having won international recognition by describing the behavior of alpha radiation decay, Gamow defected to the United States after participating in a high-level 1933 conference in Brussels. Several months after their minds meshed in Copenhagen, he would become one of Edward's important friends.

In 1935 Gamow, the newly appointed dean of the physics department at George Washington University, became Teller's benefactor when he offered his friend a full professorship if he would emigrate to the United States. By accepting this timely invitation, Dr. Teller became part of what the British science historian C. P. Snow would later refer to in his book *The Physicists* as "the greatest emigration of intellectuals since the collapse of Byzantium." During the ensuing years, Gamow and Teller staged a series of international seminars in the capital city of their new country that significantly enlarged the horizons of nuclear physics. Networks he developed in cooperation with other physicists served to put Edward Teller on a path that led unerringly to Los Alamos and, ultimately, to his obsession with the feasibility of superexplosions involving the fusion of atoms.

The possibility that atomic bombs might be designed and manufactured first came into sharp focus in the United States in January 1939, at the fifth annual Washington Conference on Theoretical Physics, arranged by Gamow and Teller. Niels Bohr himself brought news from Europe that uranium had been split by neutrons, a report that sent scientists scurrying to their laboratories to determine whether the resulting fission might produce a chain reaction. By the summer of 1939 this phenomenon had been verified by physicists on both continents, and their experiments signaled the advent of the atomic age.

The story of the making of the first atomic bombs, related with admirable terseness by C. P. Snow and, in more recent times, with definitive elegance by Richard Rhodes, needs no retelling here. The details about the wartime approval of the bomb project by a president, the working party of elite scientists assembled in secrecy on a mesa in New Mexico, the mistaken surmise that a fateful race with Hitler's bomb builders was under way, and the wonder evoked by the test explosion in the desert on July 16, 1945, are now (along with the barnacles of myths that inevitably encrust such events) etched in the common memory.

By his own admission, Edward Teller was a malcontent at Los

Alamos. At a reunion four decades later, his onetime friend Victor Weisskopf undoubtedly spoke for those assembled when he described the days of their camaraderie and joint endeavors as "the most exciting years of our lives." Dr. Teller's experience was very different: to him, the "finesse" with which Robert Oppenheimer managed people was "deeply repulsive." As a theorist who had a distaste for details, Teller came to view the project as a "bomb assembly problem," and when his best friend, Hans Bethe, was picked to supervise his work, Teller "went on a strike," was labeled a "problem child," and was kept busy thereafter performing "odd jobs" assigned by Oppenheimer.

The real source of Teller's rebellion, however, was related to his aversion to working under others and to a resentment that his pet idea—the design of a superbomb that would use the heat of an A-bomb to trigger the fusion of atoms in hydrogen—had been put on the back burner. Even though that decision was dictated by the timetables and imperatives of the war with Hitler, Teller elected to blame Robert Oppenheimer for his frustration. This episode, and the egocentric role he subsequently played to the hilt as the "father" of the H-bomb, highlights the mind-set that guided Edward Teller's conduct over the years. Teller could not bring himself to be a team player at Los Alamos, because he envisioned himself as a captain who had special insights about what had to be done to make his new country supreme and safe.

At the war's end, all of the eminent scientists at Los Alamos, save one, scrambled to return to their classrooms and laboratories. The exception was Teller, who stayed on for several months in the hope that he could win support for a crash effort, under his aegis, to test the feasibility of his H-bomb concept. After Oppenheimer and his successor, Norris Bradbury, refused to make such a commitment, Edward Teller filed his resentments in the back of his mind and departed for the University of Chicago.

THE PATH TO POWER AND GLORY

In the summer of 1949, Edward Teller took a one-year leave of absence to return to New Mexico to help design better nuclear weapons. He asserts that he took this step to "work on the laboratory's regular weapons program" and "had no intention of working on" the superbomb when he arrived at Los Alamos. However, the nation's preparedness outlook was drastically altered when Igor Kurchatov and his team of scientists and engineers detonated the Soviet Union's first atomic bomb on August 29, 1949. President Truman's announcement of Stalin's bomb (dubbed "Joe One" by U.S. officials) sent shock waves through Washington and jarred those in the atomic establishment who had underestimated the versatility and the verve of Soviet scientists and technologists.

The tremor Joe One sent through the nation's capital sparked a reappraisal of U.S. military and diplomatic policies. President Truman first gave a green light to a crash program to expand the nation's nuclear weapons factories, and after conferring with his secretaries of state and defense—and with David Lilienthal, the chairman of the Atomic Energy Commission—he made a follow-up decision in January 1950 to accelerate research on the feasibility of developing a hydrogen bomb.

Edward Teller's life has been embossed by myths: myths concocted by Teller himself, and myths fashioned by his admirers and detractors. One of the most durable of these myths revolves around a contention that Robert Oppenheimer conspired to delay U.S. H-bomb research and that Teller led a fight that forced President Truman to act. This contention not only distorts the events surrounding that episode, but flies in the face of the realities of Cold War politics, which dominated policy making during Harry Truman's presidency.

Joe One was a rude signal that the enormous security advantages the United States enjoyed as a result of its nuclear weapons monopoly would soon end. As the arm of government in charge of the development and production of atomic bombs, the AEC's recommended response to this new threat was a critical element in the decision-making process. As a consequence, the commission promptly requested that its General Advisory Committee (GAC) of scientists, chaired by Robert Oppenheimer, evaluate possible military responses to the Soviet breakthrough. The GAC was not empowered to make policies. By law, its statutory role was to provide technical advice to the Atomic Energy Commission.

Among the Manhattan Project veterans serving under Robert Oppenheimer's chairmanship on the GAC in 1949 were Enrico Fermi, I. I. Rabi, and Harvard president James Conant. After deliberations that ultimately focused on the moral issues presented by such a weapon, the GAC recommended that the United States not mount an all-out research effort to determine whether it was technically feasible to develop hydrogen bombs that could be delivered to military targets. In framing their unanimous recommendation, the members of the GAC knew they were dealing with a political issue that would be resolved by the president of the United States. They knew, too, that generals in the Pentagon and some of their colleagues would regard their ethical arguments as idealistic or misguided.

It was the thousand-fold escalation of destruction envisioned by this proposed new weapon that forced the GAC advisors to ponder its impact upon the human future. To some, Hiroshima had been defensible in military terms, but now they recoiled at the prospect that three or four H-bombs could turn the infrastructure of industrial civilizations into rubble and kill most of the inhabitants of nations the size of England or France or Italy.

As members of a technical committee which had no power to make political decisions, the GAC might have been content to provide the government with an analysis of the scientific and technological problems surrounding further thermonuclear research. But, driven by qualms that it might "become a weapon of genocide," they decided to wrestle with the transcendent moral issues presented by the creation of such an apocalyptic weapon. Enrico Fermi articulated their apprehensions when he argued that an effort should be made to negotiate an international agreement "to outlaw the thing before it was born."

Three years earlier such a commonsense argument might have garnered widespread support, but by the time Igor Kurchatov's team of scientists detonated their first atomic bomb, the rising tensions of the Cold War had divided the world into two hostile camps. Once Stalin made his belligerent moves in Czechoslovakia and Berlin in 1948, there was little traffic on the bridges of diplomacy between the United States and the USSR until after the Soviet dictator's death in 1953. Joe One not only delivered a sharp jolt to smug assumptions about the supremacy of U.S. science, it created a feverish race for nuclear weapons that dominated the superpower's military rivalry for the next four decades. In this atmosphere of mistrust, President Truman had no choice but to approve a vigorous program to explore the feasibility of a thermonuclear bomb.

To his admirers, Edward Teller is the dauntless patriot who preserved our nation's nuclear superiority. The legend they have woven around his life begins with a thesis that he was the "prime mover" who led a campaign that "captured Washington" and forced President Truman to approve Teller's plan to develop the H-bomb. The historical record does not support this contention. The most reliable account of the events that led up to President Truman's decision appears in the detailed journal kept by one of his principal advisors, Chairman David Lilienthal of the Atomic Energy Commission. Lilienthal's chronicle is authoritative because his desk was the nerve center of this controversy, and he had the ear of the president and spoke frequently with Truman's most trusted advisor, Secretary of State Dean Acheson.

The important events that preceded President Truman's decision are recorded in Dave Lilienthal's journal. He provides incisive descriptions of the individuals inside and outside the government who were trying to influence Truman's thinking. He recounts, for example, the aggressive pro-bomb role played by his associate, Commissioner Lewis Strauss, and he identifies E. O. Lawrence and Harold Urey as the atomic scientists who were the most forceful proponents of an emergency effort to develop a thermonuclear weapon. Lilienthal also records the impact of the arguments advanced by Pentagon officials and the doomsday warnings presented to the president by the chairman of the Joint Committee on Atomic Energy, Senator Brien McMahon.

The reader of Lilienthal's journal is made aware of the hysteria Joe One generated in some quarters, and his entries make it clear that at the end of January, when the H-bomb issue arrived at the president's desk, the drums of the Cold War were rattling Washington's windows and creating irrepressible political pressures for decisive action.

Facts in Chairman Lilienthal's daybook puncture the fantasy created by Teller and his friends that Truman's H-bomb decision grew out of a "titanic struggle" in which Edward Teller triumphed over Robert Oppenheimer and his allies on the GAC. Contrary to Teller's version, Lilienthal's eyewitness account describes a different arena with diplomats and military men in the central roles. In the four months after Joe One there were many evaluations of the president's options, but the conclusive analysis was made by a cabinet-level group consisting of Secretary of State Acheson, Secretary of Defense Louis Johnson, and AEC chairman Lilienthal. There is no evidence that Teller exerted any influence on Truman's decision; indeed, his name is not even mentioned in the sixty-five pages of entries David Lilienthal made in his journal as this Cold War episode unfolded.

Teller and his coworkers spent four years experimenting with different designs and theories before they tested a thermonuclear device that could be converted into a military weapon. For the faceless team of bomb builders, this was a remarkable achievement. But for Dr. Teller, the solitary recognizable face that emerged from this effort, the 15-megaton Bravo test at Bikini in March 1954 was an event that transformed his life. Thereafter, the mythomania that swirled around the creation of this weapon focused on Teller alone. Soon heralded as the "father of the hydrogen bomb," Teller acquired a stature that enabled him to tower above the other scientists of the Los Alamos generation.

While this father-myth did wonderful things for Teller's career, it also generated mischief by creating the impression that the H-bomb represented a stroke of genius by a single scientist. Although modesty apparently influenced him to belittle his own role, the concept of a hydrogen bomb actually originated in Enrico Fermi's mind. In 1941 Fermi advanced the theory that a fission bomb (still a figment in the mind of physicists) might be used to "kindle" a thermonuclear explosion. A first-things-first scientist, Fermi kept his theory to himself during the war, but Edward Teller, his disciple, became obsessed with this idea, and his H-bomb-now crusade made him the odd man out at Los Alamos.

Ultimately, usable hydrogen bombs emerged as the end product of a decade of trial-and-error science where both American and Soviet bomb builders were concerned. Sakharov and Teller were in charge of conceptualizing the projects, but the talents of many engineers, mathematicians, and physicists were needed to perfect gadgets that could fit into airplanes or be mounted on the tips of missiles. The "classical Super" design that Teller nurtured at Los Alamos was based on miscalculations that led to a dead end. However, Teller stubbornly insisted that his Super be the centerpiece of research and development until a colleague, the mathematician Stanislaw Ulam, demonstrated (with the aid of the most advanced computer then available) that Teller's bomb would fizzle.

The ultimate, successful design evolved in the winter of 1951 out of creative interaction between Ulam's insights into the technology of thermonuclear explosions and Teller's willingness to explore a different kindling configuration. Once a test proved that this design functioned as planned, Edward Teller belittled Ulam's contribution and pushed him off center stage. This unprofessional conduct rankled most AEC insiders and initiated a dispute over scientific ethics that continues to this day.

THE SCIENTIST WHO PLAYED GOD

In the spring of 1951, Los Alamos engineers and physicists began work on devices that would test the feasibility of thermonuclear explosions. A field test, the bulky Mike shot in November 1952, demonstrated that the Ulam-Teller configuration worked, and the bombmakers then concentrated on modifications that would enable them to design small-package H-bombs that could be delivered to targets by U.S. bombers.

As his new career would reveal, by temperament Teller preferred to operate outside the controls and channels imposed by government organizations, and once his leadership role was established at Los Alamos he took steps to establish a personal base of power. One Los Alamos colleague who witnessed his angry outbursts observed, "What Teller would consider a favorable atmosphere for work would be one where everybody revolved around him."

Teller resolved this problem by persuading his ardent new air force friends to finance a competing bomb laboratory at Livermore,

California, under his personal aegis. As he was preparing to open his new laboratory in the spring of 1952, Teller, emboldened by his triumphs, decided to consolidate his power by destroying the reputation of Robert Oppenheimer. This daring thrust came in the form of secret accusations to FBI agents that Oppenheimer had conspired to delay American development of the hydrogen bomb.

In due course, Teller's allegations—which were made against the backdrop of Senator Joseph McCarthy's cascade of charges that Communist spies had infiltrated the federal government—became the centerpiece of legal charges brought against Oppenheimer by the AEC. With Edward Teller as the decisive witness at a sensational loyalty trial in the summer of 1954, Oppenheimer's reputation was besmirched when the AEC voted to sever his access to classified information and to terminate his work as a science advisor to the government.

This outcome, which was tantamount to a finding that Robert Oppenheimer was a security risk who might have transmitted secrets to the Communists, achieved the aim Edward Teller apparently had in mind when he first lodged his accusations with the FBI. Oppenheimer, the elegant prince of the atomic age, was removed as a rival, and Teller, the patriot who had produced the awesome new weapon Oppenheimer had supposedly tried to smother, had suddenly vaulted into the saddle as the authority figure of the nuclear establishment.

This turnabout combined with other events to add drama to Teller's emergence as the father of the hydrogen bomb. Many truths lay hidden from view, but a flood of articles and books made Teller a household name and depicted him as a wizard who had preserved America's lead in nuclear weaponry. Moreover, his warnings about Soviet treachery and his willingness to "unmask" Robert Oppenheimer won him the permanent admiration of right-wing conservatives and made him a favorite of this country's hard-line anti-Communists.

In a memoir he wrote near the end of his long service at Los Alamos, Stan Ulam surely had Teller in mind when he observed that in the process of acquiring power, some scientists "underwent a personality change." The physicists who laid the foundations for the nuclear age—Einstein, Rutherford, Bohr, and Fermi—were reflective men, who considered themselves part of an international community of scholars. The discipline that governed their scientific work influenced the way they approached other subjects and guided the decisions they made in their daily lives. As members of a community of scholars, they shared common moral values and often pondered the impact their work might have on humanity as a whole. As individuals, they instilled in their students an intellectual detachment that made them loath to ally themselves with political crusades concerning issues that lay beyond their area of expertise.

No scientist of the Los Alamos generation underwent a more drastic personality change than Edward Teller. Those who knew and liked him in the 1940s remembered his openness, his desire for friendship, his playful mind, and his curiosity about all aspects of U.S. culture. Yet the Hungarian physicist who came into view as the "mystery man" behind the H-bomb assumed a very different persona.

One trait of the new Teller was on display in the tactics he used to diminish the reputations of his friends Ulam and Oppenheimer. A power-seeking trait was manifest as Teller began writing articles and books that portrayed him as an authority on the life-and-death problems of the atomic age. Indeed, by the end of the 1950s he appeared to many Americans as a messiah who foresaw how future wars would be fought and was blessed with insights their political leaders lacked. He alone, it often appeared, was working day and night to thwart Communist treachery and aggression.

Edward Teller made his debut as a geopolitician during the international controversy over the radioactive poisons being broadcast into the environment of the northern hemisphere by the bomb tests of the two superpowers. The health hazards imposed by this fallout became a humanitarian cause in the spring of 1957 when leaders and public figures such as Einstein, Jawaharlal Nehru, Albert Schweitzer, Bertrand Russell, Linus Pauling, and Pope Pius XII created a worldwide furor by demanding a moratorium on testing.

President Eisenhower, who felt a curb on tests would help contain the arms race, was preparing to agree to an interim test ban with Khrushchev when, at a secret meeting in the White House,

Teller and two associates from the Livermore laboratory persuaded him not to act. Teller prevailed by promising the president that if he allowed testing to continue, Livermore scientists would soon perfect a "clean bomb" that would "solve" the fallout problem and make nuclear warfare "civilized."

The dispute over fallout escalated a few months later in 1957 when a stop-testing-now petition bearing the names of 9,235 scientists from forty-eight countries was presented to Secretary-General Dag Hammarskjold of the United Nations. Those petitioners were motivated by a common conviction that radiation emitted by bomb tests was inexorably increasing the incidence of cancer and other diseases in people in all parts of the world. The moral issues raised by this impressive group of physicians, biologists, and geneticists left the United States and the USSR in a posture where, for the first time, they had to weigh the consequences of their acts and consider alternatives to aboveground testing.

Edward Teller tendered what was essentially the response of the U.S. government. Donning the mantle of a medical expert, he presented a rebuttal in *Life* magazine under the banner headline, "Dr. Teller Refutes 9,000 Scientists." This conspicuous reply marked the beginning of Edward Teller's career as a freewheeling nuclear guru for the nation at large. Since the inception of the Manhattan Project, scientists had served as behind-the-scenes advisors to presidents and other important officials. But animated by a cavalier conviction that his scientific knowledge armed him with insights the nation's leaders lacked, Teller wanted to be a policy maker himself and sought out opportunities to sell his panaceas to the American people.

Dr. Teller's handling of the medical and biological issues raised by the 9,000 scientists displayed the authoritative manner he would use in the future to demolish and discredit his critics. He said, "Global fallout from testing is not dangerous, but the fallout scare is." Teller offered reassurance that "radiation from test fallout is very small . . . [and] its effect on human beings is so little that if it exists at all it cannot be measured." And he opined that "radioactive fallout from [hundreds of 'peaceful' Plowshare explosions] would be negligible."

His fallout arguments identified Edward Teller as a disputant who gave no quarter to his opponents. With unconcealed disdain he treated the 9,000 scientists as an ill-informed group out of touch with the realities of radiation biology. He saw no need to cite medical evidence to substantiate his assertions, but simply assumed that a pronouncement propounded by the father of the hydrogen bomb could not be challenged.

A similar self-assurance guided Teller's response to the moral issues raised by the 9,000 scientists. Invoking bomb secrets his critics could not question, he averred that further tests were crucial for "humanitarian" reasons: his scientists, he explained, were "well on the way" toward the creation of "clean" bombs that would save the lives of millions of noncombatants in future nuclear wars. Teller's "humanitarian hydrogen bomb" appeal foreshadowed a tactic he would use in the future to win policy disputes by finessing ethical arguments offered by critics of the nuclear arms race. In the perspective of history, Teller's clean bombs proved to be a hocus pocus he invented to win an argument. To this date, thirty-five years later, no such device has ever come forth from his Livermore laboratories—or anywhere else. However, his avowal that a breakthrough was at hand swayed public opinion and sidetracked President Eisenhower's effort to stop aboveground testing.

In 1958 the difference between Andrei Sakharov's ethical outlook and that of Edward Teller was stark. After conferring with Soviet medical experts and reading the scientific literature on the subject, Sakharov concluded that the radiation being released into the environment was jeopardizing the lives of hundreds of thousands of human beings. He presented his case in a magazine article, "The Radioactive Danger of Nuclear Tests," which was distributed abroad by Soviet embassies. Citing the "serious moral dilemma" confronting the superpowers, Sakharov made this appeal for mutual restraint:

... each and every test does damage. And this crime is committed with complete impunity, since it is impossible to prove that a particular death was caused by radiation. Furthermore, posterity has no way to defend itself from our actions. Halting the tests will directly save the lives of hundreds of thousands of people, and it also promises even greater indirect benefits, reducing international tension and the risk of nuclear war, the fundamental danger of our time.

The contrast between the outlooks of these two physicists to the fallout threat is paradoxical, because the morally callous view was presented by a representative of a free society, and the humanitarian plea was voiced by a Communist scientist. Sakharov underscored reducing international tensions, while Teller's paramount concern was that of winning the arms race. Sakharov's holistic view of the problem led him to give top priority to a step that might reduce the risk of nuclear war, while Teller saw a test ban as a trap that would prevent his country from attaining nuclear superiority over its adversary.

Sakharov was then unknown in the West, but had Edward Teller known the author of this article was his Soviet counterpart, his pervasive cynicism about Soviet intentions would in all likelihood have led him to regard Sakharov's statements as enemy propaganda. Teller's view of Soviet society was invariably rigid and unbending. He believed that the rulers of the USSR were duplicitous and that the arms control treaties negotiated by John F. Kennedy and subsequent presidents were betrayals of American interests. At every juncture, he operated on the supposition that Soviet scientists and engineers were stealing marches in the weapons race. In 1962 he summarized his dark view of the contest with Communism by stating, "Appeasement on our side and confident expansion on the side of the Communists have been the dominant themes of the postwar years."

THE SUPERSTRATEGIST

Edward Teller crossed a bridge when he left his laboratory in the summer of 1960 to write a book, *The Legacy of Hiroshima*, in which he sharply criticized America's postwar leadership and presented a strategy to win the conflict with the Communists. *Legacy* marked the transformation of the bomb designer into a politician who wanted to shape history and play a major role in the world of diplomacy and politics. This new Teller wanted to stiffen the backbone of his adopted country and speak to the people over the heads of their elected leaders.

Egotistical in tone, *Legacy* was a sermon by a scientist who felt that he alone understood the imperatives of the Cold War. Teller began his testament with warnings that the Russians had seized the lead in education, science, and nuclear technology. The United States, he announced, had followed a disastrous course since Hiroshima and was "on the road to the loss of freedom."

With an indictment that established him as a hero in the eyes of right-wingers, Dr. Teller pinned the blame for the decline of American power on everyone except military men and the designers of hydrogen bombs. He asserted that President Eisenhower's moratorium on nuclear testing was "idiotic and dangerous," and he characterized Ike's efforts to improve relations with the Soviet Union as "a drift toward appeasement."

There was ample blame, too, for his fellow citizens. In the Teller view, the temper of America had been altered by the advent of cataclysmic weapons. To him, *fear* (as exemplified by the "hysteria" over fallout) had displaced the buoyant spirit of the war years, and he felt the resulting anxiety had sapped the nation's will to prepare for, and to win, the looming military showdown with world Communism.

Although he never visited the USSR, Teller maintained a fixed, frightening view of Russian prowess. Besides spreading alarms about weapons "gaps," he was convinced that war planners in Moscow were working from a constantly. updated plan to win an all-out nuclear war, while the United States did not have such a plan. Moreover, he held the opinion that Soviet Communism was an adversary, "more powerful, more patient, and incomparably more dangerous than German Nazism."

Over the years, when Edward Teller looked eastward he saw an "increasing tide of Communist power." One Nobel laureate who served with him on many committees, described the mind-set produced by Teller's paranoia: "To Edward, the Russians were always nine feet tall with a three-foot yellow streak down their backs." Even after the thaw that came with Nikita Khrushchev, Teller saw no possibility of peaceful change. In the 1960s, Ralph Lapp, a physicist-journalist who wrote books about the race for nuclear weapons, described him as "more militant than the most hard-bitten General." To Edward Teller, the only path to peace was a path lined by superior military weapons.

In presenting his three-point military-oriented strategy for survival, Dr. Teller posed as a seer who had the capacity to envision both the scenario of a probable thermonuclear war and a plan that would enable the United States to survive, and to win, such a conflict. In 1962 he stated categorically that "an all out [nuclear] war would be dreadful for all participants. But there would be a winner and a loser." Thus, the centerpiece of his preparedness plan was a massive construction project by which the nation's schools, hospitals, museums, libraries, auditoriums, supermarkets, and nuclear power plants would be converted into underground community shelters, equipped with survival stocks of food and water. "To survive [a nuclear attack]," Teller counseled his countrymen as late as 1982, "is a duty, it means there is a future for us and for those who want to win."

The ghoulish aspects of Teller's scheme for a subterranean America caused him to be viewed by some critics as an incarnation of the protagonist in the 1964 film *Dr. Strangelove*. In *Legacy* Teller did not dwell on the molelike existence of H-bomb survivors with no housing, water, electricity, or medical services. Instead, he strove to make this "victory" thinkable by offering cheerful predictions about the ultimate outcome. He assured his readers that "even an all-out nuclear attack would be no worse than some of the terrible events of past wars," and described a chins-up scenario in which those who survived would energetically rebuild America's industrial plant to "its pre-attack capacity within five years."

The other parts of Dr. Teller's early strategy to deter Communist aggression were relatively simple. He favored a second-strike retaliatory force that would not be vulnerable to a first-strike attack. (This force, already adopted as a policy under President Eisenhower, was coming into existence in the form of nuclear submarines armed with ICBMs.)

A highly controversial military concept Edward Teller envisioned as essential for U.S. security was the development of forces that could engage in "localized, limited nuclear wars" to forestall Russian aggression against our allies. Assuming the garb of a general, Teller favored the creation of "new theories of battle tactics, new varieties of nuclear weapons, [and] new kinds of fighting men." Once his plan was implemented, he saw "hit-and-run guerrilla fighters" armed with nuclear weapons spreading over the countryside with a capacity to "destroy any military target—including a marching army of enemy soldiers." Seemingly unconcerned about the response of enemies who were also armed with nuclear weapons, Teller did not bother to explain how his "limited" nuclear wars would remain limited.

Legacy contained two pages that foreshadowed the passion that would obsess Edward Teller in his later years: the creation of antimissile missiles that would intercept and destroy incoming enemy rockets in outer space. This crusade became a revolving technology caper—known successively as Safeguard, Palisades of Fire, Star Wars, and Brilliant Pebbles—that cost tens of billions and ultimately won distinction as the biggest fiscal black-hole project of the Cold War. Teller relentlessly pursued this scheme for three decades, muttering every step of the way that a Soviet conquest of the world was inevitable if his team of scientists were not given the support they needed to perfect his superweapon.

When the U.S. Senate overwhelmingly ratified the Limited Test Ban treaty (LTBT) in September 1963, President Kennedy and Chairman Khrushchev regarded it as a potential turning point in the Cold War. In the aftermath of the Cuban missile confrontation, John Kennedy saw it as an effort to ease tensions and emphasize live-and-let-live diplomacy. Andrei Sakharov, who had urged Soviet leaders to take the initiative that led to the consummation of the treaty, considered it a development of "historic significance . . . a step toward reducing the risk of thermonuclear war."

Edward Teller, however, viewed the LTBT in a different light. He regarded the treaty as just another instance of appeasement, and subsequently led the fight against the LTBT. Using doomsday phrases, he denounced the treaty in a stormy appearance before a Senate committee. After asserting that Soviet scientists were "far ahead" in developing antimissile arms, Teller warned that a test ban treaty would "weaken" efforts by the United States to defend itself and was in reality "an inevitable step toward war." To him, the most appalling aspect of the LTBT was that it would put shackles on U.S. technologists while leaving their Soviet counterparts free to cheat by conducting clandestine tests in caverns.

Dr. Teller was not deterred by his defeat. Always cocksure, he retreated to his laboratory where, with undiminished energy, he pursued his self-appointed mission to build a missile "shield" that, he believed, would enable the United States to escape the constraints imposed by the weapons standoff that governed the rivalries of the superpowers. Although most scientists were dubious that an effective antimissile system was feasible, Teller was normally contemptuous of peers who did not share his perception of the Soviet threat or his vision about the military benefits of superweapons in outer space.

Teller's campaign encountered serious obstacles in the 1970s. The shadow cast over policy making by the Vietnam trauma induced caution in the White House, and two treaties sponsored by President Nixon during the interval of détente with the Russians banned the further testing of some ABM missiles and put restrictions on the deployment of experimental interceptor rockets. But Edward Teller, who never allowed adverse developments to daunt his belief in a concept he had nurtured, kept the best and the brightest talent at Livermore working on his revolutionary project and waited for the political tide to turn.

This turn came in 1980 with the election of Ronald Reagan, a longtime friend who viewed Teller as the great, heroic figure of the atomic age. Elated, Teller began a personal, back-door lobbying effort at the White House for the testing and deployment of X-ray lasers that, he assured the new president, would deliver the United States from the grip of the nuclear balance of terror and give the nation military dominance over the Soviet Union. This campaign came to fruition two years later in March 1983, when, in a television address, President Reagan endorsed Teller's plan (soon to be dubbed "Star Wars") and launched a program that became the most costly military research effort in U.S. history. Star Wars bore the hallmarks of Edward Teller's career as a designer of ultimate weapons. It was a scheme he alone concocted, and it was developed in the secret confines of a self-contained "government" he ruled on the fringe of the nation's national security apparatus.

The heralded rise and ignominious fall of this technological extravaganza, announced with great fanfare by the president, throws a lurid light on the life of a scientist who, though on the government payroll, was unconstrained by normal rules of procedure. It likewise illuminates the influence Edward Teller acquired as a grand architect of the Cold War. And it reveals the character flaws that made him a dangerous leader in an age of apocalyptic dangers.

The Strategic Defense Initiative (SDI), as Ronald Reagan called it, was a manifestation of Edward Teller's political power and his guile. SDI was initially based on Teller's concept that an "X-ray laser" device could be configured and deployed into outer space which would channel the blast of an exploding nuclear weapon into beams of concentrated X-rays that would destroy incoming enemy missiles.

This was to be the crowning glory of Edward Teller's scientific career and it exemplified the influence he exerted at the summit of the U.S. government in the 1980s:

- The X-ray laser "miracle" came to life through a process of self-deception that was one part science and two parts fantasy.
- This inchoate "weapon" was privately peddled to the highest officials in Washington by one man, and did not undergo scrutiny by dispassionate experts before it was initiated.
- SDI was launched on an air bubble of inflated promises.
- It was administered by its author with an autocratic fervor that subverted the periodic reviews that would have revealed its misconceptions and flaws.
- It was driven by the whims and hopes of its inventor, rather than by the constraints and critical review that normally govern scientific-technological research and comparable military research and development.

A trenchant critique of the SDI fiasco has been written by William Broad, a science writer for the *New York Times* who covered the story from start to finish. Broad's two books, *Star Warriors* (1985) and *Teller's War: The Top Secret Story Behind the Star Wars Deception* (1992), are both brilliant exposés of this extravagant fantasy. The latter book, in particular, is both an incisive personal profile of Edward Teller, and a critical examination of his career as the doyen of this country's military-industrial complex.

In assessing Edward Teller's Star Wars performance, Broad penned these conclusions and questions:

Over the protests of colleagues, Teller misled the highest officials of the U.S. government on a critical issue of national security, paving the way for a multibillion-dollar deception in which the dream of peace concealed the most dangerous military program of all time.

The SDI episode was full of riddles. How could Teller . . . a man dedicated to discovering the truth and eminently successful in that regard, end up betraying the central principle of his profession? How could close colleagues fail to save Teller from himself? And how could the federal government, with its ranks of experts and advisers, allow itself to be so completely deceived?

I believe the answers to these questions can be found in deep-seated defects in Teller's character. The methods Teller used to achieve his ends were rooted in a penchant for self-deception that often dictated his thinking and his actions. His inclination to mislead others stemmed from a conviction that he had a wise man's license to override general rules and to say and do whatever might be necessary in order to protect what he perceived to be "the national security." And his distorted perception of the Communist threat colored his ethical outlook and caused him to espouse a consistently militant anti-Communist crusade.

TELLER'S CONVOLUTED MORALITY

Dr. Teller's jingoism lay at the heart of the contrast between his attitude toward the Cold War conflict and that of Andrei Sakharov. In the 1968 manifesto Sakharov addressed to his countrymen and to the world, he invoked the highest moral principles and called for global dialogue free of national chauvinism and militaristic slogans. Confronting the frightening prospect facing humankind, Sakharov made this plea: "Any action increasing the division of mankind, any preaching of the incompatibility of world ideologies and nations, is madness and a crime."

As the first notable appeal of its kind from behind the Iron Curtain, this plea for peace struck a chord that resonated in world opinion. But had Edward Teller read Sakharov's manifesto, he would undoubtedly have regarded it as Communist propaganda designed to trick the West into lowering its nuclear guard. As a leader, Teller was the antithesis of his Russian counterpart. His agenda was animated by national chauvinism and militaristic slogans, and he justified his endless search for a superweapon by preaching the incompatibility of ideologies and nations. One reason Teller belittled efforts by U.S. presidents to ease tensions between the superpowers was his perception that progress toward peace would derail his plan to achieve military dominance over the Soviet Union.

The contrast between the ethical outlooks of the two bomb designers was extreme. The Russian studied the predicament of earth's inhabitants and sought to put the survival of the human race first. In contradistinction, the Hungarian-American surveyed the same scene and concluded it was urgent to devise a shield to provide absolute security for the citizens of one country, his own, at the price of nuclear terror for the other.

Edward Teller took pride in being the preeminent anti-Communist hard-liner, and the rigid framework that guided his thought made him the chief critic of statesmen, church leaders, and scientists who sought to inject universal moral values into the on-going effort to develop alternatives to the arms race. In 1962, when the Russians had an ample arsenal of hydrogen bombs, Teller conceded that it would be immoral for the United States to initiate a nuclear war. Otherwise, it was his unrelenting view that those who used moral arguments to support various peace proposals were "soft-headed" dupes or "unrealistic" fools who didn't understand the irrepressible nature of the Communist threat.

A prime source of Edward Teller's influence in political and military circles was the reputation he cultivated as a person who knew Communism firsthand, and who could thus foretell the intrigues and technological tricks that the Communists would use to gain an advantage in the arms race. Teller exploited the cachet he acquired as an expert on Communism, both to intimidate his critics and to enhance his stature as a giant of the nuclear age. In a 1991 interview, Teller's longtime Livermore colleague, Dr. Ray Kidder, described to reporter William Broad how Teller used the cloak of authority he acquired to demolish arguments advanced by his opponents:

Teller was possessed with the threat of Soviet world domination. It consumed him entirely for the second half of his life. He knew he was right, and anybody who failed to understand the enormity and primacy of this threat was simply a fool unworthy of serious consideration.

Writers with contrasting outlooks who have sought to analyze Edward Teller's motives and behavior have agreed that his outlook was warped by delusions about the Communist threat. Stanley Blumberg, his admiring biographer, concedes that his "childhood experiences had made him paranoid about the Russians." And Richard Rhodes, one of Teller's critics, recently identified two "character defects" that, in Rhodes's view, drove Teller "to extremes." These were "a terror of Russia that is irrational enough to be termed clinical" and a "grandiosity that makes him believe that anything is possible and nothing is unethical in the pursuit of an ever more elusive security."

These character traits may help explain the myths Teller fostered which made him a leading Cold War ideologist and gave him status with hard-liners as the "arch anti-Communist" of the postwar era. For four decades, Edward Teller was a pursuer of nuclear panaceas and his world revolved around these myths, half-truths, and fantasies:

- that the Soviets were on the verge of gaining strategic superiority;
- that his defensive nuclear weapons could provide total security for the United States;
- that any limits on the design and development of new weapons was dangerous; and
- that talk of coexistence was a snare because the Soviet cheating would turn any arms control agreement into a sham.

Paranoia imperils the public weal when it is linked with zeal and with access to the levers of power. Thus it was the coming together of these ingredients, and the skills he mastered as a political operator, that made Edward Teller a force to reckon with and transformed him into a leader who became a driving force behind an ever-escalating arms race.

Edward Teller had trouble veiling the contempt he felt for the presidents he supposedly served under and for the various efforts they made to work out accommodations with Soviet leaders. He made a barbed comment to John F. Kennedy after JFK asked some penetrating questions about Teller's scheme to use nuclear explosions to excavate a new Panama Canal. When Kennedy inquired how long it would take to prepare such a plan, Teller indicated it would take less time for him to get ready than for the White House to approve such a project.

Near the end of the Reagan administration, when a reporter asked Dr. Teller which of the presidents he had dealt with had the best grasp of technological issues, his reply was acerbic: "No competition . . . Ronald Reagan." Reagan's superiority, Teller opined, lay in his willingness to act on the advice proffered by his science advisors. He then volunteered his disdain for "the people who would not listen . . . Ford, Kennedy, Eisenhower and, above all, Jimmy Carter." (As a result of his education at the U.S. Naval Academy, Carter, a nuclear engineer, may have been the most technically sophisticated individual ever to preside in the Oval Office.)

THE MELANCHOLY ENCOUNTER

In mid-November 1988, Andrei Sakharov and Edward Teller had what might have been a felicitous opportunity to strike a joint blow for peace when they crossed paths during Sakharov's one visit to the United States. Knowing he was in Washington to participate in a meeting of a peace organization, President Reagan invited the Soviet scientist, then an unofficial emissary for Mikhail Gorbachev, to confer with him—and the hosts of a long-planned dinner to honor Teller contacted Sakharov and urged him to drop by and to participate in the tribute to his onetime rival.

Had Teller and his hard-line admirers been less obsessed with their quest for military superiority, this encounter could have been a memorable occasion. It might, perhaps, have been transformed into a celebration of the notable step toward disarmament taken by the leaders of the superpowers in the preceding year. Or, had Dr. Teller been inclined to be magnanimous, this coming together might have produced a dramatic joint affirmation that the time had come to move toward the "open world" envisioned in the aftermath of Hiroshima by Niels Bohr, where scientists would be "a brotherhood working in the service of common human ideals."

But it cut against Teller's grain to be magnanimous to any representative of Soviet Communism, and the grizzled cold warriors who had arranged the agenda had not gathered in their black ties to hear what they regarded as "soft" appeals for peace. To the contrary, they had packed one of the capital's largest ballrooms to honor Edward Teller for his Star Wars scheme and to present him with an award for his "integrity and courage in public life."

Andrei Sakharov, in faltering health, but with an honesty and courage tempered by long years of persecution, spoke in character that evening. He had presented a plea for restraint to Ronald Reagan earlier that day, but felt that the president "somehow managed to ignore" his arguments. Now, after graciously expressing his "deepest respect" for Edward Teller, he pulled no punches in reiterating the arguments Reagan had disregarded. Speaking as a world citizen, rather than as a spokesman for his nation, Sakharov warned that it would be a tragedy for peace and a "great error" if the United States insisted on developing Teller's Strategic Defense Initiative (SDI). If Star Wars weapons were deployed in outer space, he warned, they would "destabilize the world situation" and "There would be a temptation to destroy them, and this in itself could trigger a nuclear war."

Sakharov had to depart immediately after his speech, so he was not present to witness the response to his remarks. The initial rejoinder after his departure came from the master of ceremonies, William F. Buckley, Jr. Buckley generated sustained applause when he said: "We honor Dr. Sakharov and wish him everything in the world, but we don't wish to give him, as a souvenir from America to take back to Moscow, a lapsed resolution to proceed with our SDI." Next, President Reagan, in a taped message on a giant screen, saluted Teller for his SDI work and cited him as a "sterling example of what scientific knowledge, enlightened by moral sense and a dedication to the principles of freedom and justice, can do to help all mankind."

With one of the verbal thrusts he had used often over the years to undermine the arguments advanced by critics, Edward Teller went out of his way in his brief acceptance speech to disparage Sakharov's credibility. He told his audience that since Sakharov's security clearance had been revoked two decades earlier, it was obvious that Sakharov was ill-informed about the latest Soviet advances in antimissile research. "It is not surprising," Teller explained, "that our points of view should differ."

In the year of his life that remained, Andrei Sakharov, now an elected member of the fledgling Soviet parliament, sacrificed his health by serving as a rallying point for the forces of democracy in the Soviet Union. His death, in December 1989, evoked encomiums in his own country and around the world. Observing that he was haunted by the weapons he had helped to create, Elie Wiesel, another winner of the Nobel Peace Prize, recalled Sakharov's "total fearlessness, his all-consuming passion for peace and justice." And the *New York Times,* noting that "in an earlier age he might have been a Socrates or a Bacon challenging the established order in search of scientific truth," lauded him as "one of those rare figures who appear at turning points of history."

The paradox that a morally oppressive Communist system would produce a Sakharov—and that the world's leading democracy would elevate a Teller to a position of great power—was a phenomenon of the Cold War epoch that will long fascinate historians and students of ethics. The contrast between the lives of Sakharov and Teller remained vivid until the very end. In the final months of Andrei Sakharov's life, as the Communist empire was visibly collapsing, Edward Teller's mind was seemingly closed to the changing world around him. He refused to give up his bombs and his fascination with their unending military perturbations. Indeed, his paramount priority in 1989 involved a campaign to persuade the newly elected president George Bush to adopt his latest missile-shield concept—a crackpot idea to which he gave the glitzy code name "Brilliant Pebbles."

"Brilliant Pebbles" would serve as an appropriate epitaph for Edward Teller. "Man of Peace" might suffice for Sakharov.

15

The Subversion
of American Democracy

The fight against Communism diminished us. . . . It left us in
a state of false and corrosive orthodoxy. It licensed our excesses and we didn't like ourselves the better for them. It
dulled our love of dissent and our sense of life's adventure.
—JOHN LE CARRÉ (1993)

Born after World War I, schooled by the Great Depression, propelled into the thick of a global war that set new standards for
carnage and spawned a weapon that could wipe out whole civilizations, reflective men and women of my generation should have
valuable insights to offer their descendants. The end of the Cold War
offers a rare opportunity to ponder the mistakes and miscalculations
that have made this century a fear-filled period of history. This is
surely an auspicious time for a dialogue that might alter attitudes and
institutions so that future conflicts can be moderated and controlled.

As the twentieth century began, the leading nations of western
Europe were immersed in war planning that, from 1914 to 1918, produced the most disastrous war up to that moment in history. A key
tenet of the culture of force fabricated by these war planners was that
the military conflicts they envisioned would be short, glorious, and

334

sweet. When that illusion was punctured by a standoff on the Marne River at the end of the first month of World War I, national pride and martial attitudes were so entrenched that negotiations that might have produced a sensible truce were impossible. The outcome was a mindless four-year slaughter described later by historian Barbara Tuchman as "murderous insanity."

The blunders that prolonged the First World War fostered the economic chaos and political upheavals that, in the aftermath of the war, generated the conflicts and instabilities that defined and dominated the world environment during the remainder of the twentieth century. In effect, the 1918 armistice cast a curse over the postwar era by afflicting Europe with political upheavals that acquired the names of fascism, Hitlerism, and Stalinism. The upshot, within two short decades, was a second war that far surpassed the first in death and destruction.

At the conclusion of World War II, my generation believed that a long era of real peace was at hand. Germany and Japan, their war machines crushed and their largest cities and industries devastated, stood amid ashes symbolizing the awful price of aggression in an era of total war. And the success of a global conclave in San Francisco to organize a United Nations offered assurance that new institutions were being created that would enable statesmen to develop patterns of international consultation and cooperation to resolve disputes without resorting to war.

Our peace hopes were also buoyed by the prospect that the Allied nations would devote their resources to the work of reconstruction. The magnitude of the death and destruction inflicted by Hitler's armies on the Soviet Union underscored this expectation. The Nazi forces had killed as many as 20 million Russian civilians and soldiers, more casualties than suffered by all other Allied nations combined. Thus, it seemed logical to assume that Stalin would be preoccupied for years, repairing his nation's shattered economy and providing housing and consumer goods for the survivors whose sacrifices had made the Soviet Union's victory possible.

Several developments reinforced our feeling that an enduring peace had been won. There was, for example, the speed with which our country demobilized its soldiers and dismantled its huge military machine, and the haste with which 10 million employees in our war industries were thrown out of work and onto the peacetime job market in a matter of months. The United States had no perceived enemies in the fall of 1945, and the prevailing euphoria is indicated by the circumstance that our leaders felt no need for military alliances or for the maintenance of a large standing army.

The capstone of this self-confidence, of course, lay in the realization that our nation enjoyed special military security because it had, in the atomic bomb, a master weapon that no other country possessed. In the aftermath of Hiroshima, the very existence of this scientific monstrosity evoked compelling new arguments for peace.

The most influential book published in the United States during the first months after the war's end was a seventy-nine-page pamphlet entitled *One World or None.* A compilation of eighteen essays written by Albert Einstein, Niels Bohr, and many of the scientists who had helped create the atomic bomb, *One World* was a vivid appeal for the elimination of war. It featured warnings that there would be a global catastrophe if powerful nations allowed their disputes to escalate into conflicts involving atomic weapons. *One World* reached a wide audience, and its message quickened interest in the concept of world government and created a groundswell of support for international control of the atom by the United Nations.

One World, and the facts that supported its arguments, had a restraining influence on U.S. policy makers. Not only were American leaders loath to brandish the atomic bomb, but when David Lilienthal assumed office as the chairman of the Atomic Energy Commission, the nonmilitary agency created by Congress to guide the nation's nuclear future, he was startled to learn that he could count his country's operational atomic bombs on the fingers of one hand.

Try to imagine the euphoria of individuals who emerged as survivors of a prolonged, brutal war. The World War II generation had both practical and idealistic reasons to believe that its victories had laid the foundation for a sustainable period of peace. The winners of that war, for example, faced an immediate humanitarian challenge of housing and feeding millions of displaced persons. It seemed evident, too, that the bulk of the resources of the Soviet Union and the other nations of western Europe would have to be dedicated for many years to the work of restoration and reconstruction. The priority given to nation-building, it appeared, would foster a political climate that would reduce the frictions that produce wars.

It was my generation's misfortune that a political riptide would transform our optimism into an illusion. This turnaround was a shock, for when Germany surrendered we had no way of knowing that the imperatives of what would come to be called the Cold War were already agitating Joseph Stalin's mind. Nor did we realize that in two short years international disputes would sunder the grand alliance into two hostile camps.

The abruptness of this change shocked most Americans. During the war, we had admired the bravery of Soviet soldiers and the great battles they had won over Hitler's supposedly superior armies. And even though he remained a shadowy figure in our minds, the "Uncle Joe" Stalin of the war years who held successful strategy meetings with Roosevelt and Churchill came across as a shrewd bargainer who probably wanted and needed a long peace. Stalin's ruthless prewar purges of his political opponents had horrified us, but we remembered, too, that there had been no serious disputes or military confrontations between the United States and the USSR in the 1930s.

The main reason we were surprised by the turn of events that marked the beginning of the Cold War was that our knowledge of Stalin and of the contorted history of his country was so meager. Perhaps we would have sensed that our friendly wartime alliance with the Soviet Union was ephemeral, and that the peace we had cherished would be short-lived, if we had understood the world view of Joseph Stalin and the power he had to fix the course of postwar history and consequently to transform our nation, almost overnight, into the Soviet Union's chief enemy.

THE COLD WAR AND THE CLOSED WORLD
OF JOSEPH STALIN

To gain insights into the mind of Joseph Stalin one must delve into his personal history and into the failures that isolated his country from the waves of change that altered social and political life in Europe in the nineteenth century. Stalin was the product of the one large European nation that shunned the liberalizing changes fostered by the American and French revolutions and that still maintained feudal institutions at the turn of the century.

In many aspects, the Russia of Stalin's formative years was an anachronism—a relic of eighteenth-century Europe. The czarist governments he fought as a young revolutionary refused to experiment with democratic reforms and had no tradition of respect for human rights. As a result, Joseph Stalin acquired his ideas about government and political power in a largely illiterate, stratified society where

- free elections and decision making by elected officials were unknown;
- the control exercised by all-powerful czars was enforced by an omnipresent secret police;
- dissent was a passport to gulag prison camps; and
- the main benefits of progress accrued to an elite.

This history helps explain both Joseph Stalin's mind-set and the techniques of terror he used in the 1930s to eliminate his rivals and assume dictatorial sway over his nation's affairs. In his rise to power, the cardinal concept that Stalin embraced was iron-clad dominion over whatever domain he ruled. We know now that this impulse, rather than Communist dogma concerning world conquest, was the driving force that guided his actions when the shooting stopped in 1945 and he surveyed an empire that comprised one-sixth of the globe.

Stalin's style of governance, the complete opposite of an open society, would have been envied by the most oppressive czar. Decisions were promulgated through personal ukases rather than laws. The most important organ of government was an omnipresent secret police, which kept dossiers on all citizens and used electronic eavesdropping as its prime tool of surveillance. Travel abroad was tightly controlled. It was a serious offense for any Russian to engage in friendly conversation with a foreigner. And individuals who dared to criticize Stalin or his policies were either shot or exiled to concentration camps without any opportunity to defend themselves.

The best window we have into the mind of the Soviet ruler in the last years of his life was provided by Yugoslavia's Communist heretic, Milovan Djilas, in his 1962 book, *Conversations with Stalin.* Djilas, who worshiped Stalin when he first met him in the spring of 1944, provides insights that help explain the origins of the Cold War. According to Djilas, "Thanks to both ideology and methods, personal experience and historical heritage, he [Stalin] regarded as sure only what he held in his fist, and everyone beyond the control of his police was a potential enemy."

A year later, when doubts about Stalin's leadership were already stirring his conscience, Djilas participated in further exchanges when he accompanied Marshal Tito on his first visit to Moscow. Three months earlier at Yalta, Stalin had promised Roosevelt and Churchill that there would be free elections in the central European countries his troops had conquered. However, the Soviet dictator made it clear to his guests that he had no intention of keeping this commitment. In the course of this monologue, he outlined for Tito the basic premise of the policy he was preparing to pursue: "This war is not as in the past," Stalin confided. "Whoever occupies a territory also imposes on it his own social system. Everyone imposes his own system as far as his army can reach. It cannot be otherwise."

Some students of history have called Joseph Stalin an enigma, but a close analysis of his personal history reveals the sharp edges of his character. He had a mind that understood the importance of modern technology, but his world outlook was not dissimilar to that of a warlord of an earlier era who believed that military power was the be-all and end-all of life. He rejected the peace plans of his former allies and started the confrontations that led to the Cold War because he viewed talk about a lasting peace as a scheme of the "capitalist imperialists" to gain advantages in the ongoing struggle for power.

That reaction was not just another expression of Joseph Stalin's cynicism. His life experiences told him that guns and armies were the inexorable arbiters of history, and he instinctively regarded all peace proposals as either plans advanced by fools or a trick by potential enemies to get him to lower his guard. Djilas, a soldier who had experienced the gore of guerrilla warfare, found "something terrible" in a drunken prediction Stalin made as his soldiers were completing their bloody march through Hitler's heartland: "The war shall soon be over. We shall recover in fifteen or twenty years, and then we'll have another go at it."

That mind-set explains Stalin's distorted postwar priorities and why he decided to put military preparedness first and to deny his people the higher standard of living they would have enjoyed if there had been a prolonged period of peace. It also caused him to take a wary view of his former allies' efforts to get him involved in activities that might produce new patterns of international cooperation. His grudging acceptance of a perfunctory role in the United Nations, his lack of interest in international control of the atom, and his refusal to participate in the newly created World Bank and International Monetary Fund were all dictated by a conviction that he might somehow lose control and see his military plans disrupted if the Soviet Union participated in programs to promote common goals of prosperity and amity.

THE SAD, SHORT PEACE

After the Potsdam summit conference in July 1945, Premier Stalin withdrew into his Moscow shell, and between that time and his death in 1953, he exhibited no interest in participating in high-level meetings to resolve the disputes that were shattering the wartime grand alliance. Rather, he spent his days devising strategies to effectively impose his own system on the territory his armies had occupied. The scenario for the opening phase of the Cold War was written in the Kremlin. The moves Stalin made and the reactions they evoked by his former allies can be traced year by year:

1946

- Anxiety arises in the West as signs indicate that Stalin shows no intention of allowing free elections and is busy establishing Communist puppet governments in the countries of central Europe.
- In a speech at Fulton, Missouri, Winston Churchill accuses Stalin of breaking his wartime pledges and building an "Iron Curtain" around the territory his armies control.

- The United Nations is unable to develop a plan to bring the atom under international control.

1947

- Stalin revives the Comintern (disbanded during the war) putting the USSR in a position where it can direct the "struggle" of the world's Communist parties.
- Worried that economic chaos might open the door to Communist takeovers in such western European nations as France and Italy, the United States establishes a European Recovery Program (the Marshall Plan) and begins providing billions in nonmilitary aid for economic reconstruction.

1948

- In February, a Communist coup crushes Czechoslovakia's nascent democratic government.
- In June, Stalin creates a dangerous flash point by having his military commanders abrogate the Potsdam agreement governing the status of Berlin and by imposing a land blockade on access to Berlin.
- The United States responds with a dramatic, yearlong airlift that provides the necessities for the beleaguered Germans who reside and work in West Berlin.

1949

- In April, the United States and eleven nations in western Europe form a new military alliance (NATO) as a counterforce to the Soviet Union's huge standing armies in central Europe.
- In August, U.S. officials are startled when they discover, four short years after Hiroshima, that Stalin's scientists have detonated an atomic bomb—an event that serves as the trigger for a race for nuclear weapons and prompts alarmed congressmen to urge the production of thousands of atomic bombs.
- The fear that a tide of Communism is rising in the world is heightened when Mao Tse-Tung's armies seize control of continental China.

1950

- Without knowing that Andrei Sakharov and a team of Soviet scientists were nearing a breakthrough in the same field, President Truman in January approves a crash program to design and test an American hydrogen bomb.

- An additional strain of virulent anti-Communism is injected into the bloodstream of American politics when Senator Joseph McCarthy captures headlines by alleging that Communist spies have been allowed to infiltrate sensitive federal agencies.

- In June, the Cold War is suddenly transformed into a shooting war for young Americans as North Korean armies, with Soviet approval, invade South Korea; thus, only five years after Hiroshima, U.S. soldiers, under United Nations command, are engaged in a brutal war on the Asian mainland that will last for four years and result in nearly five million military and civilian casualties.

By the time of his death in 1953, Joseph Stalin's policies had produced a bipolar world and hostile attitudes that would cast his shadow over the remaining years of the twentieth century. The drift toward disaster was, of course, accentuated by the advent of nuclear weapons and by the joint failure of the United States and the USSR to agree on international controls that might have avoided the arms race that followed, once each nation possessed the know-how to manufacture H-bombs. By the time Stalin died, the two rivals were already locked into a monstrous race for weapons of mass destruction that would ultimately confront humanity with a survival dilemma subsequently described by Notre Dame's Theodore Hesburgh as "the greatest moral problem of all time."

Richer and more powerful than its adversary, the United States was the overall pace-setter in this grim contest. Herbert York, one of President Eisenhower's science advisors, has advanced a convincing argument that over the years our scientists and engineers generated "more ideas and inventions of all kinds, including ever more powerful and exotic means of mass destruction" not out of malice but motivated by "a sort of technological exuberance." In any event, the competition between the two Cold War rivals spawned military-industrial complexes on both sides that developed and deployed weapons capable of destroying cities and industries in a matter of hours.

On our side, arguments were advanced by politicians and self-appointed strategic experts that "gaps" had emerged and that the United States was falling behind in crucial areas of armament. These arguments helped propel the arms race into an ever-ascending spiral of overkill. For many years, policies of secrecy made it impossible for laymen to grasp that such arguments were fallacious, but as the Cold War was ending, Father Theodore Hesburgh provided a forthright description of the path this competition followed:

> In all honesty it should be said, as it often is not, that we introduced most of these new systems first, with the Soviets quickly following suit. For example, we had the atom bomb in 1945, they in 1949; we had the intercontinental bomber in 1948, they in 1955; we the jet bomber in 1951, they in 1955; we the H-bomb in 1952, they in 1953; they beat us by one year to the intercontinental ballistic missile in 1957. We introduced photo-reconnaissance from satellites in 1960, they in 1962. We initiated submarine launched missiles in 1960, they in 1964. We launched the solid fuel ICBM in 1962, they in 1966. They beat us to the anti-ballistic missile, albeit a crude one, in 1966, ours came in 1974. We were the first to initiate multiple re-entry vehicles in 1970, they did likewise in 1975.

THE DEGRADATION OF DEMOCRACY

The Cold War and the nuclear arms race it fostered had profound, adverse impacts on basic American institutions. The changes they induced altered the fundamental functioning of our democracy, warped our sense of ethics, and sapped our economic strength by influencing leaders to squander the nation's wealth.

This country's Constitution envisioned an open society where all of the facts were in full view and "error of opinion," in Jefferson's imperishable phrase, would be "tolerated where reason is left free to combat it." Secret power, secretly exercised, was anathema to the framers of our Constitution. Indeed, power was directly divided among three separate branches of government for the express purpose of preventing presidents with imperious impulses from usurping kingly prerogatives, except when the nation was caught up in actual war emergencies.

Yet in the aftermath of World War II, two developments undermined open government and subverted the separation of powers embedded in the Constitution. The first involved the mantle of secrecy that surrounded the invention of the atomic bomb.

Although the Cuban missile crisis was handled with admirable restraint, the decision-making process used by President Kennedy exemplified a pattern of overreaching by the executive branch that produced a pervasive constitutional crisis in our government. During the first secret week of this emergency, the president took two actions that set bad precedents. He excluded from his fourteen-man group of advisors a leader—the Speaker of the House—who was the constitutional officer second in line to assume presidential powers if events took a tragic turn. And although he brought outside individuals deemed "wise men" (Acheson, Lovett, and McCloy) into his inner circle, he did not seek Dwight Eisenhower's opinions and failed to invite the bipartisan leaders of the House and Senate (Mansfield, Dirksen, McCormack, and Halleck) to participate in deliberations that involved the fate of the republic. These decisions foreshadowed similar actions by future presidents who, under the guise of defending freedom, created a closed world of governance in which, all too often, the constitutional functioning of our democratic institutions was constricted.

The second development related to the fears of Communist aggression generated by Stalin's Cold War policies. These developments combined to create a war environment in Washington, to turn the White House into a command post in an undeclared war against Communist expansion, and to circumscribe congressional participation in decision making about policies affecting the nation's security.

During President Truman's administration, obsessions about national security altered the relationship of the American people to their government by constricting the openness that had been a hallmark of American democracy.

Through steps unprecedented in peacetime:

• A "loyalty program" was instituted to remove potential subversives from federal employment.

- A peacetime espionage agency, the CIA, was created and given global surveillance responsibilities, which included tracking the activities of U.S. citizens who traveled abroad.

- The FBI developed secret dossiers on citizens whom Director J. Edgar Hoover deemed persons of dubious loyalty.

- A new, elite group of advisors—nuclear physicists, assorted technologists, and "security experts"—soon emerged as a clandestine government of policy makers who donned robes as unelected legislators with inordinate power to influence policy making in Washington.

By betraying the essential openness of our society, these developments undermined democratic practices and traditions and produced fundamental changes in our basic institutions. The commander-in-chief function of the president, for example, was magnified in ways that encouraged most occupants of the White House to spend most of their time micro-managing national security affairs. The Congress was converted into a docile body that had no access to the basic facts surrounding these same issues and consequently failed to perform crucial oversight functions assigned to it by the Constitution.

The adoption of pervasive "security clearance" procedures intensified the erosion of our nation's democracy by mocking the idea of open government and altering the pattern of decision making in Washington. This change not only circumscribed congressional participation in vital national defense decisions, but it also created a new class of scientific and technological advisors who, operating under the umbrella of awe created by the atomic scientists, shaped the options later presented to the nation's leaders. In his 1970 book, *Race to Oblivion,* Dr. Herbert York, a prominent insider during the Eisenhower administration, noted that such experts were able to gain unwarranted power because they had acquired "the reputation of being magicians who were privy to some special source of information and wisdom out of the reach of the rest of mankind."

Similar abuses occurred in other sensitive areas of government where officials armed with "clearances" made life-and-death decisions under the guise of protecting the nation's security. The nation's spymasters and the managers of its atomic weapons programs were a case in point. Working under a blanket of secrecy by means of which they could ignore the laws that governed ordinary citizens, these policy makers habitually covered up their mistakes and misjudgments by lying to Congress and the American people.

It is one of the Cold War's fascinating ironies that the only president who enunciated profound doubts about the hazards this conflict posed to our constitutional institutions was Dwight Eisenhower, the only general to serve as president of the United States in the twentieth century. Eisenhower, in his much-quoted farewell address, warned the American people about the pitfalls surrounding national security decisions and the lurking danger that "public policy" would be "captured by a scientific-technological elite." Dr. York, his aide, informs us that Ike was worried that his successors might be swayed by "wild ideas [and] phony intelligence" and find themselves in situations involving "the transfer of control over our destinies from ourselves and the statesmen and politicians we select into the eager hands of strategic analysts, technologists, and other experts."

President Eisenhower was prescient, but our society was so obsessed with something called national security that his warnings were largely ignored by his successors.

THE WITHERING OF POLITICAL MORALITY

It was inevitable that a culture of deceit would evolve out of the constricted environment that enveloped decision making in Washington. Honesty would be devalued. The unending search for truth, a touchstone of the American system since Jefferson's day, would be circumscribed. Vigorous debate would be stifled. And the openness and candor that had long characterized the relationship between presidents and their constituents would be sacrificed on the altar of national security.

These changes cut against the grain of a creed of public stewardship that, for nearly two centuries, had provided a framework of fixed truths and moral principles for U.S. policy makers. Until the advent of the Cold War, American leaders usually took pride in setting an example for the world by adhering to high standards of justice and morality in their dealings with other nations. But this tradition was abandoned as the ideological disputes with Communism intensified and important decisions were increasingly made under a cloak of secrecy. Indeed, the sway of the new cult of secrecy enshrined a national security credo that transformed deceit into dutiful exhibitions of patriotism.

By severing the link between power and morality, these steps produced profound changes in American life. They introduced the toxins of ideological anti-Communism into our national dialogue. They produced a we-are-at-war mentality that exalted military power and diminished the role of U.S. diplomacy. And they fostered a crusading Leader-of-the-Free-World zeal that warped the outlook of our leaders.

Indeed, the new morality and its imperatives altered both our national dialogue and the behavior of our elected leaders. Its manifestations were evident in the strident anti-Communism Richard Nixon used during his public career to cast doubt on the loyalty of his political opponents. Its commands were visible in the overblown commitment John F. Kennedy made in his inaugural address when he declared, "Let every nation know . . . that we shall pay any price, bear any burden, meet any hardship, support any friend, oppose any foe, in order to assure the survival and the success of liberty."

The dictates of this Cold War morality also lay at the heart of the mortal miscalculations that encouraged three presidents to wage a ten-year war in Vietnam, that wasted the lives of young men in a "fight against Communism" that was, in truth, an indigenous struggle by the Vietnamese people to throw off the yoke of domination by outside nations. Another manifestation of this amoral mind-set evoked Ronald Reagan's disastrous misjudgments in the last decade of the Cold War when he launched the most costly peacetime military buildup in U.S. history. President Reagan's bellicose decisions were outlandish, for he initiated his campaign to roll back the Communist threat at the very time Mikhail Gorbachev and a new generation of Soviet leaders were emerging who wanted to end the nuclear arms race and promote a dialogue that would lead to authentic peaceful coexistence.

Our country paid a high price for the rigid attitudes generated by the Cold War ethic. The unbending hostility of the hard-liners, for example, made it extremely difficult for U.S. leaders to ease tensions and build bridges of trust. This failure was highlighted by the circumstance that the public appeals that did the most in the 1970s to soften the mood of the Cold War and initiate a politics of reconciliation emanated from Andrei Sakharov and Germany's Willy Brandt, the chancellor of a wounded nation rising out of the ashes of defeat.

THE ECONOMIC BLUNDERS OF THE SUPERPOWERS

In his farewell address, President Eisenhower urged the American people to be on guard against "the acquisition of unwarranted influence by the military-industrial complex." This warning came from a cautious, farsighted, professional soldier who, in the final years of his presidency, had become skeptical of technologists and their congressional allies who were peddling scare stories about imminent threats to our national security and advocating extravagant expenditures for sophisticated new weapons systems to close supposed gaps in our defenses. Dwight Eisenhower, in his later years, took a long view of what it would take for his country to prevail in its contest with the Soviet Union. On both military and moral grounds, he rejected arguments that the United States should seriously consider a first-strike attack or might somehow survive and win a nuclear conflict. President Eisenhower was intuitively distrustful of crash military programs that made excessive demands on the nation's intellectual and financial resources. He favored a program of preparedness that would husband the nation's economic strength for the long haul; and until Ronald Reagan came to power, Ike's example had a subtle, restraining influence on his successors.

It was the West's good fortune that, lacking Eisenhower's prescience, Joseph Stalin bound his nation to strategic priorities that ultimately led to the collapse of the Soviet system. Had Stalin committed his nation's rich resources to peaceful pursuits—and to the development of a dynamic economy that would have shared its largesse with his neighbors in central Europe—his young government might have played a profoundly different role in the second half of the twentieth century. But such a course of action never entered the mind of the Russian dictator. Stalin's definition of national security began and ended with the math of military force. He had two paramount goals at the conclusion of World War II. The first was to maintain a huge standing army in order to subjugate the territory his troops had won during that conflict. His second martial aim involved an all-out effort to develop atomic weapons.

Stalin's authority had such an imperious sweep that the plans and policies he adopted became a sacred writ that pledged his nation's resources to the voracious demands of its military-industrial complex. With an overall economy much smaller than that of his newly anointed enemies, Stalin's actions sacrificed the basic needs of Soviet consumers for a plan to make the USSR a military superpower. Stalinist priorities locked Soviet consumers into a low standard of living, and created pressures that forced Soviet planners to suck the lifeblood out of the economies of their "friendly" satellites.

In the final analysis, the gravedigger of Soviet Communism was Joseph Stalin. The Soviet system collapsed because Stalin's grand strategy was based on rigid concepts that stifled innovation and misallocated his nation's resources.

Through a strange twist of history, the fall of the USSR as a military superpower coincided in the decade of the 1980s with a fiscal hemorrhage that heralded the end of U.S. hegemony as the world's economic superpower. In some ways, the doctrinaire approach Ronald Reagan used in sponsoring the most costly peacetime military buildup in American history was as flawed and simplistic as Stalin's. A fervid anti-Communist whose animosities apparently blurred his view of the dry rot that was undermining Soviet strength, Reagan was the only postwar president who disregarded President Eisenhower's precept of avoiding excessive arms expenditures that would mortgage the nation's economic future.

President Reagan's military extravaganza was a mistake on two counts. It served no concrete national security interest; and it came to fruition just as a charismatic new Soviet leader was launching initiatives that would bring the Cold War to a peaceful conclusion. Ronald Reagan's unilateral arms race produced a historic shift in the arena of global economics. While the United States was using its resources to enhance its status as a military superpower, Japan and Germany, unfettered by "defense" expenditures, altered the equation of economic power by leapfrogging into world leadership in crucial areas of technology and productivity.

With his inimitable penchant for sloganeering, Ronald Reagan called his military program "Peace-through-Strength." In reality, Reagan's priorities reduced U.S. strength by distorting the nation's economic performance and setting the stage for a period of fiscal stagnation. A more accurate appellation for Mr. Reagan's military caper might be "National Weakness through Superfluous Arms."

As the Cold War fades into history, it is not surprising that a consensus is emerging among historians that many of America's leaders made spectacular misjudgments and greatly exaggerated the threat of Communism. A new generation of historians, such as H. W. Brands, Barton Bernstein, Walter LaFeber, Melvin P. Leffler, and Lloyd Gardner, is forcing us to recognize that these leaders were wearing blinders that caused them to misinterpret Soviet motives. These leaders failed to see that the Russian system was decrepit and would collapse if the West exercised patience. It is increasingly clear, too, that the American people were badly served by politicians and intellectuals who beat the drums of the Cold War and by the barons of our military-industrial-congressional complex who served up incessant scares.

16

Lessons

of the

Cold War

We have wasted our substance now for 30 years and more fighting some phantom Russian. We've neglected America in favor of Russia. It's time that we thought about America. I say get our own house in order: To thine own self be true.

—I. I. Rabi (1987)

The swift, nonviolent end of the Cold War has the potential of being a seminal turning point for humankind. It provides a vista to contemplate the mistakes and misperceptions that brought Americans of my generation to the brink of a planetary holocaust. And it offers valuable insights about the human condition and about possible new pathways to peace.

The economic and political environment now emerging provides a once-in-a-century opportunity to build a better world by putting common goals above the selfish ambitions of nation-states. In the 1990s, this is no utopian dream. The evolution of the European Economic Community (EEC) is dramatizing the possibility that nations can prosper and promote peace by working together to achieve common economic objectives. The EEC can make a powerful statement as it builds a superstructure that rises above the ashes of the hatreds and rivalries that produced two hideous world wars in the first half of this century.

The lessons of the Cold War have both global and local implications. Some of them are explored below.

ON THE PROMISE OF INTERDEPENDENCE

I believe the best hope for a lasting peace lies in the growth of regional and global institutions that make interdependence attractive by encouraging nations to work together to achieve common goals. The expansion of the United Nations peacekeeping function is a sign that this process is already under way. A new era of international peacekeeping may be at hand if the world's leaders recognize that aggressive behavior by outlaw nations will not be tolerated.

On a different stage, the most hopeful long-term trend for peace is the strengthening of ties between nations as a result of the rapid growth of world trade. The mutual trust and patterns of economic interdependence that are evolving out of new commercial relationships are laying a sturdy foundation for peace. It is already clear that common gains generated by world trade are softening the sharp edges of nationalistic quarrels, which have been the root cause of past wars.

The full import of this trend came to me one day as I read a *Wall Street Journal* story about the billions of dollars Japanese entrepreneurs were spending to buy real estate and important industries in Hawaii and California. Although dismayed by the evidence that our trade deficit with Japan was widening, I saw a silver lining in these economic clouds. Each increment of Japanese ownership, I consoled myself, is diminishing the possibility there could ever be another Pearl Harbor.

In many parts of the world, trade is already creating powerful bonds between nations engaged in mutually productive commerce. As onetime enemies reap benefits from common economic endeavors, nations may redefine national security—and military expenditures may be seen as obstacles to progress.

Ecology is another overarching cause that has the potential to be a powerful force for peace. Since it concerns the survival of the human species, the environmental issue evokes an ecumenical spirit that has an ever-widening resonance. Its importance was certified when the 1992 United Nations Brazil conference went on record as the largest, best-attended global conclave in history. From that gathering came a call for worldwide action, based on an awareness that human activities may alter the global climate, and a recognition that a full-scale nuclear war could block earth's access to the solar energy that renews and sustains life on this planet.

As the poet Archibald MacLeish once observed, the appropriate metaphor for modern life is that we are "riders on the earth" together. What is making environmental protection a crusade for peace is that the inchoate pact with nature, which is gaining new adherents every year, requires new relationships among peoples and nations based on the most intrinsic values of all—sharing, caring, and cooperation. The fateful challenge facing earth's inhabitants involves a need to serve the cause of life by mounting coordinated programs of action that reach across the artificial barriers erected by nation-states, languages, and cultures to sustain a life-giving habitat for humanity.

It is a symbol of hope that, throughout the world, the better-educated generation now ascending to power seems attuned to these truths. Unlike their elders, they have a feeling of belonging to a community that is larger than any nation and more spacious than any culture.

ON DISARMAMENT AND ARMS CONTROL

With the end of the nuclear arms race, Dr. Hans Bethe has suggested that during the transition that lies ahead, less than 100 atomic weapons mounted on nuclear submarines will be a fully adequate deterrent to preserve the peace. Working through the United Nations, the United States should take the lead in a campaign to ultimately reduce the bombs in the world's nuclear arsenals to zero—and to prevent further proliferation of those weapons. The United States should begin with a unilateral declaration that our bomb testing has ended and we have no plans to develop additional nuclear weapons.

ON THE CLEANSING OF OUR CULTURE

The Cold War, with its myths and distortions, was an aberration that harmed the American people and damaged our culture. Today, the body politic of the United States can be compared to an ocean liner that has gone for decades without removing its barnacles. To reclaim the freedoms and the openness that should be distinctive features of our society, we must dismantle the national security state we created to combat Communism and return to the constitutional principles and ethical values that animated our democracy's evolution.

Wide-ranging action must be taken by our nation's leaders if our national life is to be refurbished. The restoration of constitutional government and open, democratic decision making will not be easy. We should begin by:

- drastically reducing the classification of information in order to end the secrecy that has encouraged mendacity in high places and has restricted the participation of Congress and the American people in their government's decision making;
- ending the clandestine influence of nuclear "high priests," strategy elites, and assorted "wise men";
- diminishing the baleful influence of the military-industrial complex;
- reclaiming basic freedoms by curbing the authority of the nation's "security" organizations (the FBI, the CIA, and their acolyte agencies) to monitor the lives and "political activities" of U.S. citizens whose only "crime" involves the exercise of free speech and free thought;
- eliminating protections that have placed agencies and officials responsible for national security beyond the rule of law that governs the lives of ordinary citizens; and by
- playing a major role in widening cultural tolerance and understanding, so ethnic, religious, and ideological conflicts will not endanger the world's peace.

THE LESSON OF PATIENCE

One of the vital lessons humanity can learn from the nonviolent end of the Cold War is that even seemingly intractable conflicts can be resolved peacefully if adversaries are patient and exercise restraint. As a blend of prudence and moral courage, patience—by allowing time for events to reset the stage of history—can be a supreme expression of wisdom. In the end, it was not military force that ended the ideological quarrel between the United States and the USSR, but, rather, gradual changes that permitted Soviet society to evolve and empower a generation of leaders with new goals and values.

This intriguing outcome offers several lessons for historians and statesmen. It says, for example, that our own hard-liners (who for decades mouthed the dogmas that Soviet leaders would respond only to force, and that no ground "lost to Communism" could ever be reclaimed) misled the American people by allowing prejudices to distort their interpretations of the dangerous drama in which they were participating. It was also a rebuke to the ideologists and war planners, such as Edward Teller, who at one time or another favored preemptive attacks or limited-war confrontations that would have risked the destruction of civilization. And it cast a cold light on the civil defense enthusiasts who tried over the years to convince their fellow citizens that the United States could emerge as a "winner" out of the irradiated rubble of a nuclear war.

And on the other side of the ledger, peace bought by patience was a vindication of the views of farsighted, magnanimous Americans, such as George Kennan, Robert Frost, Victor Weisskopf, and Theodore Hesburgh, who believed that peaceful evolution was possible and offered a hand of friendship to the Soviet leaders who crossed their paths.

ON ECONOMICS AND WORLD LEADERSHIP

In his groundbreaking 1988 work, *The Rise and Fall of the Great Powers: Economic Change and Military Conflict from 1500 to 2000*, Yale's Paul Kennedy identified some of the profound misjudgments that leaders of great powers have made over the past five centuries in failing to match their economic resources to their military aims. Kennedy's central conclusion that "nations rising to supremacy by winning wars tend to get overextended in ways that undermine the source of their wealth" was to some economists a timely warning about the disparities of the 1980s between the extravagant military apparatus we had deployed around the globe and the fiscal resources of our limping domestic economy.

The object lessons underscored in Professor Kennedy's best-selling book should have been a wake-up call for American leaders. Even as he wrote, trends portending an ominous long-term erosion of U.S. economic power were being recorded in business journals. Under President Reagan's aegis, for example, the United States had mortgaged its future by accumulating a burden of internal debt financed, in large part, by loans extended by Japanese investors. Moreover, the dynamics of global growth was producing a realignment of power, as Japan and Germany, required by the "victorious Allies" to refrain from military research, development, and production, were marching on a path toward economic parity with the United States. And, more ominous yet, there were indications that our nation's once-vaunted leadership in technological innovation and commercial productivity was undergoing a process of erosion, as over half of its scientific and engineering talents were devoted to military research and development.

An element of improvidence was added to this scene when U.S. leaders elected to ignore the urgent need to develop a coherent strategy that would gear military programs to actual economic resources. This tendency was dramatized by President Bush's penchant for boasting, after Communism's collapse, that the United States was now the world's only military superpower. But Bush's braggadocio had a hollow ring, for even as he spoke, the economic activity that supported our bloated military machine was exhibiting signs of stagnation.

Like the shortsighted leaders of imperial Spain and Victorian Great Britain, some of our politicians have been so obsessed by a need for increases in military prowess that they have disregarded the decline of their country's economic power. When, in the first decade after the end of the Second World War, the United States controlled roughly 40 percent of the world's wealth and power, it could logically assume the burden of maintaining a military umbrella over the community of non-Communist nations. But this logic was shattered in the 1980s as the U.S. share shrank toward 20 percent and a new generation of leaders in the Kremlin began sending conciliatory signals that they wanted to end the Cold War and work together to build a relationship which would lead to an era of peaceful coexistence.

ON THE DANGERS OF DOGMAS AND
DOGMATISTS—AND THE REMEDIES

Myths and misconceptions generated by the Cold War contest have warped our national ethos and sacrificed vital freedoms. If our society is to regain the resilience and openness that once made our democracy a model for other countries, we must reaffirm our cherished political ideals and institutions, namely:

- that *secrecy* is a poison to the body politic of our society;
- that free access to and public dissemination of information is essential to the maintenance of free political institutions;
- that mechanisms of oversight investigation and "checks and balances" must be kept intact and operative;
- that the Constitution embodies an abiding distrust of unchecked government and "the insolence of office";
- that the rule of law must never be compromised, so that public officials will never entertain the thought that they are not answerable for their actions to the public that they presumably serve.

In addition, if we have learned anything of lasting value from our misadventures in the Cold War, we will:

- be on guard against individuals whose outlook has been distorted by ethnic or ideological biases;
- break the shackles of secrecy so that truth can compete on a level playing field with myths and falsehoods;

- recognize that pathways to lasting peace will never be paved with stones of hate;

- resist the temptation to exploit the advantages won by the collapse of Communism by subjecting our former adversaries to "economic colonization" and culturally insensitive and unsolicited "advice"; and

- be skeptical of presidential doctrines that can be readily transformed into emotional arguments for the use of military force: "If you want war, nourish a doctrine," wrote William Graham Sumner in the aftermath of the jingoism of the Spanish-American War. "Doctrines are the most frightful tyrants to which men are ever subject, because doctrines get inside a man's own reason and betray him against himself."

Finally, through our media and educational institutions, we must be constantly reminded of who we are as a people, and what we stand for—that when we are called upon to sacrifice for "national defense," what we are defending are moral and philosophical traditions that proclaim the dignity of human beings and the inviolability of their rights.

In short, during the sad history of the atomic age and the Cold War, our political institutions have not failed us; our leaders have betrayed those institutions, and thus the American people. The remedy lies, not in a replacement of those political institutions or a reconstruction of our laws, but rather in a reaffirmation of those institutions and a determination to enforce and extend the rule of law.

And so, paramount among the tenets of this report to future generations, is this: We give to you, in our Constitution, the Bill of Rights, and other founding documents of our Republic, and in the institutions and law which embody them, the supreme expression of political wisdom and morality of our civilization. And in the failures of our own generation, we offer you a lesson and extend a warning: this priceless political legacy is forever vulnerable to subversion by special interests, by inflated fear, by self-serving rhetoric, and by public ignorance and indifference. Jefferson's maxim is timelessly true: "Eternal vigilance is the price of liberty."

A TIME FOR MORAL POWER

The best hope for peace in the next decades rests on a widening moral consciousness that will elevate regional and global goals above the narrower concerns of particular nations. In this country, the Cold War's end is giving fresh choices to the generation now assuming power. The new generation can cling to outdated concepts of national security and operate on the assumption that the United States must maintain its status as the world's military superpower. Or it can ease out of its costly role of world policeman and help transform the United Nations and regional groups into entities that can settle disputes that threaten order and curb aggression and enforce collective security.

From the inception of the American Revolution, the United States of America exerted inordinate influence on world affairs by both precept and example. The United States produced the solitary moral giant among the national leaders during the nineteenth century—and his name was Abraham Lincoln. Measured by an ethical yardstick, the supposed great statesmen of that era—Metternich, Bismarck, and Gladstone—appear as pygmies when compared with President Lincoln.

Abe Lincoln's acts and utterances as the president of a young country caught in the "fiery trial" of a bitter civil war made him a moral lighthouse on the headland of the nineteenth century. The ethical purpose of human existence was always on Lincoln's mind: he was a leader who wanted his country to have a "just influence" on human progress, and, as messages to humankind, his words have never lost the incandescent glow they acquired in the aftermath of his assassination.

As Alfred Kazin and Garry Wills have reminded us, President Lincoln's greatest statements reflected a magnanimity unknown in Europe. He informed his enemies that if they surrendered, it was his goal to preside over the ensuing peace "with malice toward none, and charity for all." He was convinced that his nation's experiment in self-government was "the last, best hope of earth," and at Gettysburg he renewed and enlarged his nation's commitment to democracy by reaffirming the proposition that "all men are created equal."

The most egregious lapse in American moral leadership came

about when the doctrine of manifest destiny generated the hemispheric imperialism that marred U.S. policy making during and after the Spanish-American War. In 1912, President Taft evoked the messianic spirit that animated American statecraft during that era when he spoke these vainglorious words: "The day is not too far distant when three stars and stripes at three equidistant points will mark our territory: one at the North Pole, another at the Panama Canal, and a third at the South Pole. The whole hemisphere will be ours in fact, as by superiority of race, it already is ours morally."

Yet, despite the imperialistic impulses generated by U.S. conquests during the war with Spain, American presidents exerted a conspicuous moral influence on world affairs in the first half of this century. President Theodore Roosevelt won the Nobel Peace Prize by mediating the end of the Russo-Japanese War in 1905. Woodrow Wilson won respect for American idealism by his ethical crusade at the conclusion of the First World War for a just peace enforced by a League of Nations. And through the war aims he enunciated in his Four Freedoms declaration and by leadership that made the creation of the United Nations a reality in 1945, Franklin Roosevelt added luster to the American tradition of giving morality primacy over power politics.

Is it possible, one wonders in the aftermath of the Cold War, to turn the American mind-set back in the direction of Abraham Lincoln's legacy? Is it unrealistic to hope that the oncoming generations will want a country capable of playing a role as a moral superpower in the twenty-first century? They might very well desire this if they reflect that, through example and reason, rather than force, this country's founding fathers and founding documents have been defining exemplars and statements of political morality for over two hundred years. True, it will take a major effort to achieve such a reorientation. With its premise that a balance of terror meant security, and that security was tied to the number of nuclear weapons available for use at a given moment, the weapons culture stifled discussion about the profound ethical dilemmas that hovered over the atomic age from the time of the Hiroshima holocaust.

Such a shift toward Lincolnian magnanimity might well begin with two steps. The first would involve taking back the splendid burdens of democratic government by eliminating secret decisions by a "national security" apparatus. As Garry Wills has reminded us, "Democracy is wounded at its very center when only a 'cleared' elite can discuss policy, not the body of the people at large." The second step would entail purging our minds of the Cold War myths and illusions that have blurred the vision of the American people for the past four decades. Honesty must be the hallmark of any nation that wants to build new pathways to a better world.

Part of such a reorientation would also involve the enunciation of principles that might guide a fresh quest for world peace. Our nation might begin by seeking to unite the world community behind concepts that would lead to a renunciation of nuclear war. One proposal might involve a universal commitment that the initiation of a nuclear conflict cannot be justified on moral grounds in any conceivable circumstance. A related international declaration would make it a crime against humanity for any nation to use a nuclear weapon.

This brand of leadership would renew Abraham Lincoln's belief that the United States had an obligation to "light the way" for other nations. Lincoln was a war president who never boasted of his country's military prowess. To him the future of humanity was more important than the future of any nation or cause.

This visionary hope was expressed not long ago by a distinguished atomic scientist and a great poet. At a Los Alamos reunion in 1983, Victor Weisskopf issued this challenge to his former colleagues, "Our century ought to be remembered as the age in which humankind acquired its deepest insights into the universe and learned to control its martial impulses."

And the Nobel laureate in literature, Czeslaw Milosz, issued a related challenge when he wrote:

Goethe had an intuition that something was going wrong, that science should not be separated from poetry and imagination. . . . Maybe we are going to return to a very rich era when poetry and imagination are once again alongside science.

Appendix A

June 27, 1945

MEMORANDUM TO SECRETARY OF WAR HENRY L. STIMSON

MEMORANDUM ON THE USE OF S-1

Ever since I have been in touch with this program I have had a feeling that before the bomb is actually used against Japan that Japan should have some preliminary warning for say two or three days in advance of use. The position of the United States as a great humanitarian nation and the fair play attitude of our people generally is responsible in the main for this feeling.

During recent weeks I have also had the feeling very definitely that the Japanese government may be searching for some opportunity which they could use as a medium for surrender. Following the three-power conference [at Potsdam] emissaries from this country could contact representatives from Japan somewhere on the China coast and make representations with regard to Russia's position and at the same time give them some information regarding the proposed use of atomic power, together with whatever assurances the President might care to make with regard to the Emperor of Japan and the treatment of the Japanese nation following unconditional surrender. It seems quite possible to me that this presents the opportunity which the Japanese are looking for.

I don't see that we have anything in particular to lose in following such a program. The stakes are so tremendous that it is my opinion very real consideration should be given to some plan of this kind. *I do not believe under present circumstances existing that there is anyone in this country whose evaluation of the chances of success of such a program is worth a great deal. The only way to find out is to try it out.*

—Navy Undersecretary Ralph Bard

source: Harrison-Bundy Files, Records of the Office of the Chief of Army Engineers, folder 77, microfile reel 6.

Appendix B

September 12, 1962

MEMORANDUM TO THE PRESIDENT

Repeatedly during my Soviet Union trip I found myself asking this question:

WHAT CAN THE UNITED STATES DO TO ENCOURAGE AND ACCELERATE THOSE CHANGES IN THE SOVIET SYSTEM FAVORABLE TO OUR OWN LONG-TERM OBJECTIVES?

Some observers undoubtedly tend to overstate the liberalization that is occurring, but nevertheless there is a consensus that significant changes have taken place in the post-Stalin period. (Perhaps the best recent summary is the Edward Crankshaw article which appeared in the London *Observer* September 9.)

Some of my own tentative conclusions after eleven days in the Soviet Union were these:

1. There is an unmistakable and deep-seated respect for American power and American prowess. This means that at all levels the Soviet people are inordinately curious about the American way of getting things done. This is a very healthy condition.
2. A pattern of economic incentives and awards is developing in the Soviet Union which, in the long run, might also significantly alter the Soviet system. Some of the more interesting things which we observed (although caveats apply to each) were:

   a. double-pay wages for the dam builders on the Siberian frontier;
   b. ten-year loans for private homes at Bratsk;
   c. the growing attachment of the managers and the elite to what one might call dacha living.

3. There is evidence of a growing awareness by the Soviets that their ability to compete is inhibited by the secrecy and suspicion which dominate their thinking. The experience of the Soviets with their exchange programs—and the activities of the vital State Committee

for the Coordination of Scientific Research Work—has apparently convinced them that a limited "open-window" policy is beneficial to their own system. It is predictable that this window will be opened wider as time passes.

4. The Communist Party apparatus will, of course, remain dominant, but much important decision-making power is gravitating towards the scientists, engineers and managers who are the doers who make their system go and also have strong Party ties. For the most part, these are pragmatic men who are far more interested in building their country than in pursuing Marxian theories of revolution. A form of agnosticism, one might say, is showing up.

Therefore, it is my feeling that we have an opportunity to influence this process of liberalization, and I strongly recommend that a fresh study be made of this whole problem to determine what new courses of action might be pursued with profit.

As a starter, it seems to me we are missing a bet in not arranging more high-level exchanges. Visits to the Soviet Union by the Vice President, the Attorney General and selected members of the Cabinet would be very worthwhile. Return visits by men in high places—Kozlov, for example—would be equally effective.

Secretary of the Interior

Notes

Knowing this work will provoke disputes and discussion, in the notes that follow I have highlighted books and articles that might help readers form independent judgments about the events and issues that are the central focus of this book.

Chapter 1: Notes on a Journey

10 The Kefauver-Libby exchange: hearing conducted in April 1955 by the Senate Subcommittee on Civil Defense.

12 The full text of my report to President Kennedy appears in Appendix B.

13 Robert Frost's conversation with Nikita Khrushchev was reconstructed by his interpreter, F. D. Reeve, in *Robert Frost in Russia* (Boston: Little, Brown, 1963).

14 Under the title "Robert Frost's Last Adventure," I belatedly published this essay in the June 11, 1972, issue of the *New York Times Magazine.*

16 My brother's Tucson speech is filed with his papers in the University of Arizona Library.

18 The story of the beginning of the antinuclear campaigns is recounted in Robert Lewis's *The Nuclear Power Rebellion: Citizens Versus the Atomic Industrial Establishment* (New York: Viking, 1972).

20 *"The Forgotten Guinea Pigs,"* the 1980 report by the House Subcommittee on Oversight and Investigations, can be obtained from the U.S. Government Printing Office.

Chapter 2: The Myths of August

25 W. L. Laurence's paeans to the atom appear in *Dawn Over Zero* (New York: Knopf, 1946); *The Hell Bomb* (New York: Knopf, 1950); *Men and Atoms* (New York: Simon & Schuster, 1959). The text of Laurence's historic eyewitness report was released by the Pentagon in September 1945.

27 The 1945 Smyth Report, *Atomic Energy for Military Purposes,* was issued by the U.S. Government Printing Office.

30 Those who feel that I may have exaggerated Laurence's influence on initial perceptions of the atomic age should refer to the coverage provided by *Life, Time,* and the *New York Times* in the weeks after Hiroshima.

30 Hutchins: from Ralph Lapp's *The New Force* (New York: Harper & Brothers, 1953), p. 137.

30 Spencer Weart's *Nuclear Fear* (Cambridge, MA: Harvard University Press, 1988) examines the origins of atomic myths and identifies many of the myth-makers who inflated the atomic age's nuclear balloons.

33 Paul Boyer's book, *By the Bomb's Early Light,* contains many insights about the impact of the atomic bombs on American thought and culture (New York: Pantheon, 1985).

Chapter 3: The Manhattan Project Plain

36 Thomas Power's conclusion is controversial, but he deserves credit for a thorough analysis of the German situation in *Heisenberg's War: The Secret of the German Bomb* (New York: Knopf, 1993). See also chap. 1 of McGeorge Bundy's *Danger and Survival* (New York: Random House, 1988).

36 British intelligence: *Heisenberg's War,* pp. 284–85.

37 SIS knowledge: see Power, *Heisenberg's War,* chap. 26.

37 Peierls, *Bird of Passage* (Princeton, N.J.: Princeton University Press, 1985), pp. 166–69.

38 General Groves's glowing recital of his endeavors appears in *Now It Can Be Told* (New York: Harper, 1962).

38 Nichols: Rhodes, *The Making of the Atomic Bomb* (New York: Simon & Schuster, 1986), p. 426.

40 Nichols, in Peter Goodchild, *J. Robert Oppenheimer: Shatterer of Worlds* (Boston: Houghton Mifflin, 1980), p. 56.

41 The official story of the Alsos caper appeared in S. A. Goudsmit's book, *Alsos* (New York: H. Schuman, 1947). In *Now It Can Be Told,* General Groves depicts his spies as war heroes.

41 British intelligence: *Heisenberg's War,* pp. 285–85.

43 The only extensive book devoted to the feats of the maestros of technology, *Manhattan Project: The Untold Story of the Making of the Atomic Bomb,* was written by a French journalist, Stephane Groueff (Boston: Little, Brown, 1967).

44 C. P. Snow, *The Physicists* (Boston: Little, Brown, 1981), pp. 102–15.

45 Millikan, in D. Keveles, *The Physicists* (New York: Vintage, 1979), p. 307.

46 Two engineers who were important leaders at Oak Ridge later wrote collegial memoirs about their work. See Arthur M. Squires, *The Tender Ship* (Boston: Birkhauser, 1986), and Dobie Keith's self-effacing 1946 article, "The Role of the Process Engineer in the Atom Project," in *Chemical Engineering,* vol. 53, p. 112.

48 The text of Dr. Weisskopf's lament is in the August 1983 *Bulletin of the Atomic Scientists.*

Chapter 4: Hiroshima: The American Tragedy

General texts concerning World War II bombing and its barbaric ending:

Professor Malham M. Wakin's anthology, *War, Morality and the Military Profession* (Boulder, Colo.: Westview Press, 1979), provides insight into the agonizing issues associated with modern warfare.

The most critical studies of the U.S. bombing campaign that culminated at Hiroshima and Nagasaki have been presented in two volumes that appeared in the 1980s: Ronald Schaffer's *Wings of Judgment: American Bombing in World War II* (New York: Oxford University Press, 1985) and Michael Sherry's *The Rise of American Airpower: The Creation of Armageddon* (New Haven: Yale University Press, 1987). I have drawn extensively on the work of these two historians.

In his new book, *Ethics and Airpower in World War II: The British Bombing of German Cities* (New York: St. Martin's, 1993), Stephen A. Garrett presents a measured moral indictment of the war strategy pursued by Winston Churchill.

For those who want to study the Dresden holocaust, I recommend David Irving's *The Destruction of Dresden* (New York: Holt, Rinehart and Winston, 1967). See also the article in the March 1985 issue of *Harvard Magazine* written by Dieter Georgi, a survivor who later became a prominent theologian. Dr. Georgi accuses the Allies of practicing "the worst of what Hitler had taught them."

50 Hemingway's words are excerpted from a piece he wrote for *Pravda* in July 1938. Long afterward, this article was discovered in the Kennedy Library and was first published in the United States in 1982 in the *Washington Post*.

53 Leahy's epigraph can be found on p. 442 of *I Was There* (New York: McGraw-Hill, 1949).

53 Shirer, *The Rise and Fall of the Third Reich,* 30th ed. (New York: Fawcett, 1990), p. 111.

55 "block by city block": Max Hastings, *Bomber Command: The Myth and Reality of the Strategic Bombing Offensive* (New York: Dial Press, 1979), p. 139.

56 "crowning achievement": vol. 3, p. 109, of U.K. official *History of the Air Offensive against Germany,* by Webster and Frankland (London, 1961).

59 General Curtis LeMay told his story in *Mission with LeMay* (Garden City: Doubleday, 1965). As a result of prolonged research, Michael Sherry has provided the big picture in chaps. 9 and 10 of *The Rise of American Airpower*.

62 The best biography of Franklin D. Roosevelt to date is James McGregor Burns's *Roosevelt: The Soldier of Freedom* (New York: Harcourt Brace, 1970). Dr. Burns skirts the paramount moral issues by conveying the impression that FDR was unaware of the terror bombings of Japan's cities. His "it is doubtful Roosevelt understood" reference appears on p. 596 of this work.

64 Schaffer's Stimson questions in *Wings of Judgment,* p. 180. Sherry also puts a sharp focus on Stimson's deviousness in *American Airpower,* pp. 292-97.

68 Among the prominent members of the COA team were John Marshall Harlan, Thomas Lamont, Guido Perera, Elihu Root Jr., Fowler Hamilton,

and R. L. Stearns, the president of the University of Colorado. The firebombing strategies developed by this best-and-brightest cohort, and the absence of ethical qualms about the mass cremations their plans encompassed, are documented in Sherry, *American Airpower,* pp. 194–204 and 227–36.

69 Sherry presented his "no moment of choice" thesis in the July 1987 issue of *The Bulletin of the Atomic Scientists,* pp. 12–15. Schaffer outlined his similar theory in *Journal of American History,* Sept. 1980, pp. 318–34.

71 With the help of 6,000 soldiers who gathered facts and collated them in an advanced computer system, the "whiz kids" provided a daily flow of data into the offices of Arnold and Secretary Lovett. Their summaries embraced the tonnage of bombs dropped, estimates of the damage inflicted on specific enemy targets, etc. Interviews with Arjay Miller and Notre Dame professor David Lowell Hay.

72 Those who want to form their own judgments about Secretary Stimson's motives and mind-set should relate his diary entries to his preeminent position of power, and to the events that were swirling around him as he wrote. Microfilm of selected portions of his journal can be purchased from the Yale University Library, New Haven, Conn. 06520.

74 the OWI plan: Sept. 1991 interview with Dr. Taylor, and correspondence with his OWI associate, Dr. Alexander H. Leighton.

76 For Stimson's explanations and rationalizations see *On Active Service in Peace and War* (New York: Harper & Brothers, 1947), pp. 616–33.

Chapter 5: Hiroshima in Retrospect

84 "Magic Intercepts" went to Stimson and John McCloy: *New York Times,* Aug. 11, 1993.

85 Ambassador Grew outlined his efforts to initiate surrender talks in his autobiography, *Turbulent Era: A Diplomatic Record of Forty Years* (Boston: Houghton Mifflin, 1952). Dr. Leon V. Sigal has provided a good summary of Grew's campaign in *Fighting to the Finish* (Ithaca, N.Y.: Cornell University Press, 1988), pp. 112–17.

86 Hoover's statement and his larger views are at pp. 344–50 of Richard Norton Smith's biography, *An Uncommon Man: The Triumph of Herbert Hoover* (Wyoming: High Plains, 1990).

86 "give them the works": Hopkins's May 29 and May 30 cables to the president (in U.S. Department of Defense "Entry of the Soviet Union," pp. 72–74).

87 The growth of the sentiment for surrender in 1945 at the highest levels of the Japanese government is described by Dr. Sigal in chaps. 1 and 2 of *Fighting to the Finish.*

87 Walzer: *Just and Unjust Wars* (New York: Basic Books, 1977), p. 268.

88 Stimson's memo to Truman: Stimson's diary, July 2, 1945.

89 Sherry, *American Airpower,* presents a wide-ranging account of the work of

the Interim Committee (pp. 316–30), and his footnotes identify the primary sources.

93 John Dower's *War without Mercy: Race and Power in the Pacific War* (New York: Pantheon, 1986) is the definitive work on this subject. During one of our talks, Dr. Dower stated, "The more I do history, the more it is clear that myth usually overpowers fact." His first chapters contain numerous references to American "exterminationist" attitudes.

94 Elliott Roosevelt in *War without Mercy*, p. 55.

95 Groves to Marshall: Groves, *Now It Can Be Told*, p. 324.

95 Donovan's quote: in *Conflict and Crisis* (New York: W. W. Norton, 1977), p. 96.

95 Truman's description of the Japanese as "savages" is in his Potsdam diary (see vol. 4, no. 3 of *Diplomatic History* [1980], p. 324).

98 Truman's Jan. 12, 1953 letter to Cate is in vol. 5 of *The Army Air Forces in World War II* (Chicago: University of Chicago Press), p. 712.

98 In his splendid biography of President Truman (New York: Simon & Schuster, 1992), author David McCullough relies on the memoirs of Secretary Stimson and Mr. Truman as primary sources in reiterating the long-standing official U.S. explanation of the war use of the two atomic bombs. However, he provides one new piece of information that undermines Truman's contention that he made the decision to drop the atomic bombs. During an interview McCulloch conducted with George Elsey, a personal aide who was with the president at Potsdam, Elsey asserted: "He made no decision because there was no decision to make," p. 442.

98 For the full text of General Handy's order see Groves, *Now It Can Be Told*, p. 308.

99 The *Los Angeles Times* ran Barton Bernstein's debunking article, "The Myth of Lives Saved by A-Bombs" on July 28, 1985, sec. 4, p. 1. Concerning President Truman's obvious angst, Bernstein wrote: "Believing ultimately in the myth of 500,000 lives saved may have been a way of concealing ambivalence, even from himself."

99 MacArthur's prediction: See William Manchester's *American Caesar: Douglas MacArthur* (Boston: Little, Brown, 1978), p. 513.

100 Justice Pal's long-ignored dissent: *International Military Tribunal for the Far East* (Calcutta: Sanyal & Co., 1953), pp. 620–21.

100 Sherry's opinion of Truman: *American Airpower*, p. 297.

101 Hyde Park agreement: FRUS, the Quebec conference of 1944, pp. 492–93.

103 Henry L. Stimson was the first insider to present an account of the development and war use of the atomic bombs. It was he who implanted the myth in American minds that a prime function of the Interim Committee was to help decide how these bombs should be used. *On Active Service*, pp. 616–17.

That Henry L. Stimson made a strenuous, highly successful effort to transform his version of the decision to use the atomic bomb into *the* authentic history of that episode has been well-documented. In a probing essay, "Seizing the Contested Terrain of Nuclear History," (*Diplomatic History*, Winter 1993), Barton Bernstein reveals how Stimson worked in 1947 with his Boston friends, Karl T. Compton and James B. Conant, to present an account of the A-bomb decisions that would "affirm the rectitude of American leaders" and confirm for historians the wisdom that informed their judgments.

105 the Groves footnote, *Now It Can Be Told*, p. 327.

107 the June 27 memorandum Bard submitted to Secretary Stimson has never received the attention it deserves. To remedy this neglect, I have reproduced it in Appendix A. Fifteen years after Hiroshima, in the Aug. 15, 1960, issue of *U.S. News & World Report*, Ralph Bard elaborated on the circumstances that evoked his objections and prompted him to resign.

107 In his later years, after friends urged him to record his recollections, John McCloy wrote a memoir concerning his moral reservations about the decision to use the A-bombs to destroy Japanese cities. After his death his statement was delivered to James Reston and appears in the Appendix of Reston's *Deadline* (New York: Random House, 1991), p. 493.

109 In a reflective piece, "Our Worst Blunders in the War," in the *Atlantic* (Jan. 1950), pp. 30–38, the veteran *New York Times* military expert, Hanson W. Baldwin, lent strong support to the wartime arguments advanced by McCloy and Bard. It was Baldwin's thesis that U.S. leaders committed a series of major mistakes in the last months of the war:

- by failing to develop "peace aims";

- by not modifying FDR's unconditional-surrender formula;

- by not recognizing that Japan's military situation was hopeless;

- by not trying to negotiate a peace with Japan after Hitler was defeated; and

- by not giving the Japanese a clear warning about the destructive power of our atomic weapons.

110 In his bestselling memoir, *Crusade in Europe* (Garden City, N.Y.: Doubleday, 1948), Dwight Eisenhower set forth the doubts he expressed to Secretary Stimson at Potsdam concerning using the atomic bomb as a war weapon (p. 443). He restated his convictions in *Mandate for Change*, the book he composed after leaving the White House (Garden City, N.Y.: Doubleday, 1963), pp. 312–13.

110 MacArthur: Manchester, *American Caesar*, pp. 511–14.

111 Leahy: the admiral set forth his views in chap. 23 of his war memoir, *I Was There* (New York: Whittlesly House, 1950).

112 The English scientist who wrote the introduction to C. P. Snow's posthumous book, *The Physicists* (Boston: Little, Brown, 1981), was Dr. William Cooper. Cooper observed that Snow considered science "as an intrinsically

moral activity" and felt the human enterprise could succeed only through "men's magnanimity."

112 To study General Groves's pitiless attitude toward the Japanese enemy, scrutinize chaps. 19, 23, and 25 of his book.

117 The complete text of Andrei Sakharov's essay, "Reflections on Progress, Peaceful Coexistence, and Intellectual Freedom" was published in the July 22, 1968, issue of the *New York Times*.

121 See Cray's biography of General Marshall (New York: Norton, 1990), p. 538.

122 Emperor Hirohito's oral history: the text, transcribed by Hidenari Terasaki (a diplomat who often served as the emperor's interpreter), was published in Tokyo in Nov. 1990 by the magazine *Bungei Shunju*.

123 The "conventional conclusions" are summarized in Robert Butow's official history, *Japan's Decision to Surrender* (Palo Alto, Calif.: Stanford University Press, 1954).

125 Robert Guillain's cry of the heart is on p. 241 of his book, *I Saw Tokyo Burning* (Garden City, N.Y.: Doubleday, 1981).

Chapter 6: The Crazy Race for Nuclear Supremacy

129 Weisskopf: Los Alamos fortieth-anniversary speech, reprinted, pp. 24–26, *Bulletin of the Atomic Scientists* (Aug. 1983).

130 Senator McMahon's speech: *Journals of David Lilienthal*, vol. 2 (New York: Harper & Row, 1964), pp. 584–85.

131 Truman: Lilienthal, *Journals*, p. 594.

133 Kennan: Einstein Peace Prize speech, May 19, 1981.

134 York: *Race to Oblivion* (New York: Simon & Schuster, 1970), p. 12.

135 McMahon, U.S. Senate speech, Feb. 3, 1951.

136 NEPA: for a succinct account of this ill-conceived research effort, see "Take the A-Plane: The 1 Billion Nuclear Bird That Never Flew," in *Science*, 1982, pp. 46–55.

140 Dr. Mark's critique of the excesses of weapons production appears in the March 1983 *Bulletin of the Atomic Scientists*, pp. 45–51.

141 Professor McDougall's book (New York: Basic Books, 1985) should be a bible for students who want to understand the political excesses unleashed by Sputnik.

145 York, *Race to Oblivion*, pp. 230–31.

146 Kennan, Einstein speech, May 19, 1981.

Chapter 7: Pursuers of Peace and Pursuers of "Victory"

To me, the most insightful memoir by a high-level official who was a pursuer of peace is George Ball's *The Past Has Another Pattern* (New York: Norton, 1982). For a guide to the arms race and the risk-filled gyrations of the "nuclear intellectuals" see Ball's review of Strobe Talbot's *Deadly Gambits* in the *New York Review of Books* (Dec. 8, 1984). On this subject, I also recommend Charles R. Morris's *Iron Destinies, Lost Opportunities: The Arms Race Between the USA and the USSR, 1945-1987* (New York: Harper & Row, 1988).

149 Bundy re Truman's stewardship: *Danger and Survival* (New York: Random House, 1988), p. 231.

149 Truman's farewell: his Public Papers, p. 1197, Jan. 15, 1953.

150 Emmett John Hughes, *The Ordeal of Power* (New York: Atheneum, 1963), is invaluable because it ranks as the most candid, illuminating book written by an intimate about a postwar president. "Tireless will," p. 154; "no point in talking," p. 203.

151 "tired of just plain indictments," ibid., p. 103.

152 Quotes from ASNE address, ibid., p. 113.

152 Dulles, "one hell of a licking," ibid., p. 110.

152 Knowland's arguments, ibid., p. 123.

153 Rovere, ibid., p. 114.

154 Fulbright, *New York Times* interview, Oct. 11, 1983.

154 Ike and "martial clichés": Hughes, p. 276.

155 Michael Beschloss's book, *Mayday: Eisenhower, Khrushchev and the U-2 Affair* (New York: Harper & Row, 1986), is the most complete account to date of the mistakes that sabotaged Ike's final peace initiative.

157 In chap. 9 of *Danger and Survival*, Bundy has provided the most complete account yet written of the resolution of the Cuban missile crisis. His tribute to Khrushchev's statesmanship is at p. 441.

160 Khrushchev's message to JFK: *Department of State Bulletin* of Nov. 19, 1973, pp. 639 et seq.

160 From Robert Divine's April 15, 1991, letter to the author.

163 York, *Race to Oblivion*, p. 237.

167 The extraordinary story of how Paul Nitze and his CPD band of "defense intellectuals" influenced American politics—and vaulted into positions of power in the Reagan administration—was related by Anne H. Cahn and John Prados in the April 1993 *Bulletin of the Atomic Scientists*. Their article, "Team B: The Trillion-Dollar Experiment," describes a singular episode of the Cold War in which a tiny elite manufactured myths and scare stories and convinced a president that the country was in terrible danger and that trillions had to be spent to shore up the nation's security.

168 Ellsberg: *Rolling Stone*, 1973.

170 Talbot, *Deadly Gambits* (New York: Knopf, 1984).

171 Barbara Tuchman: article in Greenwich, Conn., *Times*, May 1982.

172 Bundy: *Danger and Survival*, p. 611.

Chapter 8: The Atomic Apparat

174 Carter's description of the inept, arrogant mismanagement of nuclear waste in the United States is in *Nuclear Imperatives and Public Trust: Dealing with Nuclear Waste* ("Resources for the Future," 1987.) The *New York Times's* Keith Schneider, whose five years of digging into the safety fiascos and cover-ups of the nuclear weapons complex made him an authority on that subject, composed a broader, harsher indictment in his foreword to Carole Gallagher's poignant book, *American Ground Zero: The Secret Nuclear War* (Cambridge, Mass.: MIT Press, 1993). Cold War secrecy inevitably inflicted great damage on what Thomas Jefferson once described as the "brotherly spirit of science." George Kistiakowsky apparently had this untoward development in mind when he made the wry observation: "In science as in art there are Picassos and then there are individuals who prepare Pentagon briefing charts."

Chapter 9: The Betrayal of the Uranium Miners

200 Dr. Annas is professor of health law and director of the Law, Medicine and Ethics Program at Boston University School of Medicine and Public Health. His essay, "Mengele's Birthmark: The Nuremberg Code in the United States Courts," in vol. 7 of the *Journal of Contemporary Health Law and Policy,* is adapted from the book *The Nuremberg Code: Human Rights in Human Experimentation* (New York and Oxford: Oxford University Press, 1991), which Annas coedited with M. Grodin.

202 Under the caption *Begay* v. *United States,* the lost cause of the Navajo uranium miners is recorded for posterity in these lawbooks:

- the trial judge's ruling: 591 F. Supp. 991;
- the opinion of 9th Circuit Court of Appeals: 768 F2d 1059.

The author has an extensive private archive of documents relating to the uranium miner tragedy.

Chapter 10: Grotesque Lambs, Grotesque Justice

205 In two October 1982 issues of *Science* magazine, vol. 218, science writer R. Jeffrey Smith wrote a mordant commentary, entitled "Atom Bomb Tests Leave Infamous Legacy," on the implications of Dr. Knapp's work. The late Harold Knapp deserves an admiring monograph or a biography. His wife, Barbara, and I have the data he gathered and the analyses he prepared, and we are willing to share these data with historians or authors.

210 Cliff Honicker's article, "The Hidden Files: America's Radiation Victims," is in the *New York Times Magazine,* Nov. 19, 1989.

211 The Utah sheepmen's quest for justice wended its way through the federal courts for a total of thirty-three years. The legal name it acquired in the law books was *Bulloch* v. *U.S.*:

- Judge Christensen's 1956 decision: 145 F. Supp. 824;
- Christensen's 50-page 1982 opinion, which found that U.S. officials had committed a fraud on his court: 95 Federal Rules Decisions, p. 123;
- the ineffable 1986 ruling of the Court of Appeals: 763 F2d 1115.

Chapter 11: The Big Lies of the Bomb Testers: Death and Deceit Downwind

My sources for this chapter—and for the preceding lawsuit chapters as well—derive from over a decade of work reviewing tens of thousands of documents and interviewing hundreds of victims and witnesses who were caught in the invisible undertow of the radiation released into the environment by their government.

Philip Fradkin's *Fallout* (Tucson: Arizona University Press, 1989) is the best book-length study of the downwinders and their encounter with the officials who misled them.

The 1984 landmark radiation-law opinion, *Allen* v. *U.S.*, written by Bruce Jenkins, the Utah federal judge who tried the fallout case, is in 588 F. Supp. 284.

246 The colloquy of the commissioners: see the official March 1955 minutes of the Atomic Energy Commission.

Chapter 12: The Strange Ride of the Friendly Atom

Richard Ford's book, *The Cult of the Atom* (New York: Simon & Schuster, 1982), contains an incisive analysis of the premature takeoff and crash landing of the U.S. commercial nuclear power program. Ford's first chapter, "High Priests," is essential reading for those who want to understand the visionary outlook that generated this venture. This essay (pp. 37–50) contrasts the misjudgments that doomed this program with the masterful engineering that enabled Admiral Hyman Rickover to create a fleet of nuclear-powered submarines.

252 *The Next Hundred Years: A Discussion Prepared for the Leaders of American Industry* (New York: Viking, 1957).

256 *Nuclear Dynamite* (New York: Pergamon Books, 1990).

261 Hewlett about Dr. Seaborg: Ford, *Cult of the Atom*, p. 23.

262 The plutonium-proliferation problem was explored in *Foreign Affairs* (Summer 1980) by Amory and Hunter Lovins and Leonard Ross in the article "Nuclear Power and Nuclear Bombs."

267 "Nuclear Follies": *Forbes*, Jan. 30, 1985.

268 Gilinsky, Speech to *Financial Times* Conference on World Electricity, London, England, Nov. 13, 1988.

268 "elitist": Ford, *Cult of the Atom*, p. 76.

270 Lilienthal's turnabout testament is in *Change, Hope and the Bomb* (Princeton, N.J.: Princeton University Press, 1963).

Chapter 13: Nuremberg: The American Apostasy

I have relied on the work of Professors Annas and Grodin, *The Nuremberg Code,* in shaping this chapter.

282 The U.S. Supreme Court's treatment of the Stanley case can be found in *U.S. v. Stanley,* 483 U.S. 669 (1987).

Chapter 14: Sakharov and Teller: A Study of Cold War Morality

Sakharov: For his life and work, I had to rely almost exclusively on his splendid autobiography, *Memoirs* (New York: Knopf, 1990).

For a refresher on the life and times of Count Tolstoy, I read A. N. Wilson's absorbing biography, *Tolstoy* (New York: Norton, 1988).

293 Marshal Nedelin: *Memoirs,* pp. 194–96.
295 Khrushchev's rebuke: ibid., 215–17.
302 York's citation is in *Bulletin of the Atomic Scientists,* May 1988, p. 28.
305 Kapitsa's defense: ibid., 302–4.

Teller: The extensive literature about Dr. Edward Teller can be divided into three categories:

1. There are the two admiring official biographies written by Stanley Blumberg and his coauthors, Gwinn Owens and Louis Panos: *Energy and Conflict: The Life and Times of Edward Teller* (New York: Putnam, 1976) and *Edward Teller: Giant of the Golden Age of Physics* (New York: Scribner's, 1990).

A passage from *Energy* that reflects the fawning approach of these authors follows: "Sakharov had advantages, other than exceptional intelligence, that Teller did not share. He was not burdened by having to fight political battles over the morality of his scientific endeavor. There appears to have been no Oppenheimer in his path. Sakharov had the full scientific resources of Mother Russia at his disposal. Even after Truman's famous H-bomb directive, Teller had to fight conflicting priorities."

2. The second category embraces volumes Teller wrote himself to sell his fellow Americans on his strategies about how to win the Cold War and to achieve the full potential of peaceful uses of nuclear energy. The most influential of these books were, *Our Nuclear Future* with Albert Latter (New York: Criterion, 1958) and *The Legacy of Hiroshima* with Allen Brown (Garden City, N.Y.: Doubleday, 1962).

3. Two critical works present very different, unheroic portraits of Dr. Teller. They are Norman Moss's *Men Who Play God: The Story of the H-Bomb and How We Came to Live with It* (New York: Harper & Row, 1968) and William Broad's *Teller's War: The Top-Secret Story Behind the Star Wars Deception* (New York: Simon & Schuster, 1992).

315 To get the full picture, consult vol. 2, David Lilienthal's *Journals* (New York: Harper & Row, 1964), pp. 583–633.

318 In my view the best study of the Oppenheimer treason trial is the late Philip Stern's *The Oppenheimer Case* (New York: Harper & Row, 1969).

321 Sakharov's appeal was part of Khrushchev's campaign to ban further bomb tests. His article appeared in a book distributed in 1958 by Soviet embassies which bore the title *Soviet Scientists on the Danger of Nuclear Tests.*

327 Broad, *Star Warriors* (New York: Simon & Schuster, 1985).

328 Teller's "penchant for self-deception" via mythmaking was explored by Princeton physicist Frank von Hippel in an article, "The Myths of Edward Teller," in the March 1983 *Bulletin of the Atomic Scientists.*

330 Kidder quote in Broad, *Teller's War,* pp. 281–82.

330 Rhodes, *New York Times Book Review,* Feb. 11, 1990, p. 33.

331 "No competition": ibid., pp. 259–60.

331 the "melancholy encounter": ibid., pp. 258–59.

Chapter 15: The Subversion of American Democracy

334 John le Carré: *New York Times,* Op-Ed page, May 4, 1993.

339 Djilas, *Conversations with Stalin* (New York: Harcourt Brace, 1962). The most revealing passages are on pp. 96–116.

342 York: *The Advisors* (San Francisco: Freeman & Co., 1970), pp. xiii, ix.

343 Hesburgh, p. 6, 1989 Morgenthau Memorial Lecture delivered to the Carnegie Council on Ethics and International Affairs in New York.

345 York, *Race to Oblivion,* pp. 11–13.

346 York, ibid., pp. 9–12.

350 For two good samples of the work of post Cold War historians, see H. W. Brands' *The Devil We Knew: Americans and the Cold War* (New York: Oxford University Press, 1993) and Barton Bernstein's essay *The Cuban Missile Crisis Reconsidered,* in vol. 14, no. 2, of *Diplomatic History* (Spring, 1990).

Chapter 16: Lessons of the Cold War

355 Kennedy, *The Rise and Fall of the Great Powers* (New York: Random House, 1988).

Index

Wills, Garry, 359, 361

Wilson, Robert E., 261

Wilson, Woodrow, 50, 113, 360

Wings of Judgment (Schaffer), 49, 64, 68–70

Wolfe, Bertram, 188–90

World Bank, 340

World War I, 50, 113, 308, 335, 360

World War II:

area bombing in, 54–57, 59–61, 63, 65, 67, 69

biological warfare in, 111

blitzkrieg in, 53

British bombing strategy in, 52, 54–57, 70

ending of, 335–37

firebombings in, 56–57, 59–61, 63, 64, 65, 68, 71, 74, 75, 78, 91, 92, 100

gas warfare in, 62

German bombing strategy in, 52, 53–54

German cities bombed in, 54–57, 93–94

Japanese cities bombed in, 57, 59–71, 94

military targets in, 55

"rules of war" in, 51–53, 69, 76

strategic vs. terror bombing in, 57, 58, 61, 63, 64–65, 66, 69–70, 74, 75–77, 93–94

"total war" concept in, 54, 56

U.S. bombing strategy in, 52–53, 62–71, 93–94

x-rays, 223, 326, 327

Yazzie, Betty Jo, 185

Yazzie, Kee, 185

Yeats, William Butler, 27–28

Yeltsin, Boris, 305

York, Herbert, 129, 134, 145, 163, 247, 302, 342, 345, 346

Zababahkin, Evgeny, 296–97

Zeldovich, Yakov, 288–89, 291

Zinn, Walter, 260

About the Author

STEWART L. UDALL was born in St. Johns, Arizona, in 1920 and received his entire education in the public schools of his native state. He was a gunner on B-24 bombers in the Second World War. Before being elected to three terms in Congress in the 1950s, he practiced law in Tucson. In 1960, John F. Kennedy appointed him as the 37th Secretary of the Interior and he served in that office for eight years under Presidents Kennedy and Johnson. Since returning to Arizona in 1979, Mr. Udall has divided his time between writing and representing citizens of his region who were suing the federal government for radiation injuries inflicted on them by the nation's nuclear weapons industries. He and his wife, Lee, have been married for forty-seven years and have four sons and two daughters. They now live in Santa Fe, New Mexico.